A Marxist Archaeology

A Marxist Archaeology

RANDALL H. McGUIRE
Binghamton University
State University of New York
Binghamton, New York

With a New Prologue by the Author

PERCHERON PRESS
A Division of Eliot Werner Publications, Inc.
Clinton Corners, New York

Library of Congress Control Number 2001098636

This Percheron Press paperback edition of *A Marxist Archaeology* is an unabridged republication of the edition published by Academic Press in 1992 supplemented with a new prologue by the author.

ISBN 0-9712427-4-7

Printed in the United States of America

For
Mike-Advisor, Friend, Colleague
Ian-Friend, Colleague, Compadre

I could not have written this book without the insights, knowledge, support, and intellectual stimulation that both of you have given me. It is not, however, the book that either of you taught me to write.

PROLOGUE TO THE PERCHERON PRESS EDITION

I wrote in the preface to *A Marxist Archaeology* that I was convinced I had completed the book at a moment that was both too late and too early—too late after the fall of the Soviet "Empire" and a decade of conservatism had blinded people to socialist ideals, and too early before the end of history was revealed to be a simmering mirage and the promises of capitalism the delight of few and the ruin of many. Ten years later the moment may be too late but it is no longer too early. As I write this prologue, the United States is still reeling from the destruction of the World Trade Center and the triumph of capitalism has not vanquished all of its foes. It is also clear that in China the promise of capitalism has been realized in a dictatorship every bit as oppressive as that of Chairman Mao but without the security of the socialist regime. In the lands of the former Soviet Union, the rich have gotten fewer and wealthier and the poor more numerous and poorer. In the United States predictions that the boom of the 1990s would never end have been refuted by the cyclical reality of capitalism that Marx described.

Ten years after the original publication of this book, archaeologists may still ask why we should seriously consider Marxism at this time. The two answers to that question remain the same as they did in 1992. The first answer addresses the place of Marx's thought at the dawn of the twenty-first century and the second addresses the value of Marxism for the study of archaeology. I will briefly comment on both answers in this prologue and I will use this prologue to react to some of the critics of the book and update some of its themes. The volume itself remains the lengthy answer to the second question

MARXISM AT THE DAWN OF THE TWENTY-FIRST CENTURY

Many scholars today claim we live in a postindustrial world that is fundamentally different from the capitalism that Marx described. I would argue that the modern world fits Marx's analysis of capitalism better than the world of the second half of the twentieth century or perhaps even Marx's own world.

The twenty-first century begins with a world more industrial than it has ever been in its history. Industrial production, however measured, exists at higher levels today than in the past. Whether we speak of the number of people employed in industry, or the number of goods produced, or the distribution of factories around the world, there are more. We may speak of specific cities or even nations as being postindustrial, that is, as having changed from economies based on industrial production to economies based on service, information, or whatever. Perhaps we should not be surprised that the scholars who view the world this way tend to come from these places, but in no real objective sense is the world postindustrial.

For much of the second half of the twentieth century, capitalism in the core states of the U.S. and Europe did not fit all of Marx's expectations. In the United States profits increased even as the real wages of the working class rose. Since the late 1970s, however, capitalism has come to look much more like the world of Marx. Workers' real wages peaked in 1973 and even with the boom of the 1990s they did not recover to these levels—but the level of profits did. The rich do get richer while the poor get poorer. The movement of industrial production out of the core states has not resulted in a postindustrial world, but instead in a world like Marx's with capitalist classes that derive their wealth from the sweat of an impoverished working class that cannot afford the fruits of its own labor. What has changed is the scale of these relations with the classes no longer living in different neighborhoods of London, but on different sides of the world.

One of the weaknesses of Marx's analysis was that he did not adequately consider imperialism and colonialism. He wrote in a world in which capitalism dominated, but it did so through wage labor in the core states and other forms of labor organization in the peripheries. Marx fixed his gaze on the capitalist labor relations of the core and gave little attention to other labor forms on the periphery, i.e., in the colonies. Today wage labor is the dominant form of labor relations in virtually the entire world.

Derek Sayer (1987:ix) commented, "Marx's thought lives in so far as it is interpreted anew by others in light of their changing needs." With this in mind we need to realize that not all of the ways that Marx's thought has been interpreted have been good or desirable. Indeed, some interpretations of Marx's thought have been loathsome, oppressive, pernicious, and despicable. As Klejn (1993) has noted, a Marxist praxis does not guarantee a desirable outcome and it can restrict creative scholarship when applied in a dogmatic way.

I agree with Sayer that we must remake Marx to fit our time, but I would add that we must also remake him to correct the errors and excesses of many of his past interpreters. My answer of how to do this lies in escaping a totalitarian notion of Marxism, by which I mean a notion that in capitalism class exploitation is the source of all exploitation and that a Marxist analysis of class thus accounts for all exploitation. I would argue instead that class exploitation is fundamental in capitalism and thus an essential component of any analysis of exploitation, but that there also exist other forms of exploitation based on such social factors as gender and race. These different forms of exploitation do not exist independently of each other and people do not experience one without the other. Thus a Marxist analysis of class is one entry point to the study of exploitation that can allow us to look at the dialectic between these different forms of exploitation, but it is not the only approach to such an analysis and it benefits from other approaches based on gender and race. It was this reserve and relativism on my part that disturbed the critics of the book.

CRITIQUES OF *A MARXIST ARCHAEOLOGY*

Predictably the critiques of the book came from two directions. Some reviewers rejected the book as not being a true Marxist work and processual critics expressed concern that the book was not scientific enough in its approach. It is perhaps paradoxical that both of these sets of reviewers had the same core problem with the book.

The most severe critics were themselves Marxists. Timothy Taylor (1993) bemoaned the pluralism of the book and argued that it is unclear if the work is in fact Marxist. In a Spanish review of the work, Antonio Gilman (1993:7) declared that the only thing "red" about the book is its cover ("Aparte de su cubierta poco hay de rojo en este libro") and in a subsequent critique in *Antiquity* he dismissed the work as relativistic and romantic (Gilman 1998:911–912). For both of these archaeologists Marxism is a single coherent theory of society that provides a rigorous methodology for getting at the "truth" of the past. At best these critics would propel debate into the arcane realms of what Marx really said or did not say; at worst they propose that there can only be one approved interpretation of Marx. The power of Marxism for social analysis, critique, and action is that Marx can be read in different ways and his basic and profound insights about society have provided people with tools that they can fit to the needs of their own times. We have also seen where debates over the correct or approved interpretation of Marx can lead. On this road lies the transformation of Marxism into an oppressive state ideology, dogma, and Stalin (Klejn 1993).

Both Marxist and processualist critics lamented the lack of a materialist, scientific approach in A Marxist Archaeology. Elizabeth Brumfiel (1994) found much of use in the book but disagreed with its abandonment of positivism. In a Spanish review Luis F. Bate and Francisco Nocetè (1994) took the epistemology of the volume to task for being idealist. In both cases the critics failed to understand a realist philosophy of science, the dialectic as a relational concept, and Marxism as a theory of internal relations. They see the world in terms of oppositions—materialist versus idealist, objective knowledge versus relativism, or consciousness versus experience. From the position of a Hegelian dialectic and a realist philosophy of science, these oppositions are false. Realism accepts that there is a real world independent of scholars, our senses, and our consciousness and that scholars can gain empirical knowledge of that world. But it recognizes that our knowledge of the world is nevertheless imperfect and diverse because human thought conditions it. Thus knowledge is neither the "truth" nor simply made up, but rather a complex social product that entails both reality and consciousness.

WHAT I MISSED IN THE BOOK

The summary of Marxist approaches to archaeology in *A Marxist Archaeology* was not meant to be exhaustive. Indeed, a comprehensive international review of Marxism and archaeology would be another book in itself. This book focused on Marxism in Anglo-American and Latin American archaeologies for two reasons: first, as a North American archaeologist these are the languages and the literatures that I control; and second, at the end of the twentieth century, these were areas of highly creative and productive thought about Marxism and archaeology. The volume does contain a brief consideration of Soviet archaeology that would have been greatly improved if Klejn's (1993) history of Soviet archaeology had been available when I was researching the book.

Unfortunately I was unaware of Marxist developments in Spanish archaeology when I wrote the book. In spring 1999 I spent four months teaching at the Universitat Autónoma de Barcelona on a Fulbright Fellowship. This experience helped me to understand the contributions of Spanish archaeologists to a Marxist archaeology and based on these I am now rethinking the methodological discussion in *A Marxist Archaeology*.

In Spain the explicit development of a Marxist archaeology only became possible with the death of Franco in 1975. At that time a very empirical culture history dominated Spanish archaeology and there was only slight interest in the Anglo-American "New Archaeology." As in Latin America, Marxist archaeologists formulated their theory both in reaction to an entrenched cultural historical approach in their country and to the New Archaeology. In this context Marxism became a major theoretical movement in Spanish archaeology with research groups in many Spanish departments of archaeology. One of the most creative and internationally influential of these groups has been at the Universitat Autónoma de Barcelona. This group has adopted an explicitly scientific archaeology that focuses on the history and evolution of socioeconomic formations, the levels of development of productive forces, and the complexity of relations of production. In this work they have integrated Marxist and feminist approaches into a theory of the production of social life (Castro et al. 1998).

This theory begins with the assumption that social life requires the existence of three objective conditions: men, women, and material objects. They use an all-inclusive notion of production that views men and women as both the products and the producers of society. Men and women are products of society both in terms of their own social and biological production and in the social relations into which they enter as social beings. They are producers of society because as social agents they allow and shape the reproduction of society. Their theoretical framework is highly structured with a typology of types of production that includes the basic production of human beings, the production of objects such as food and other products intended for consumption, and maintenance production that increases the social value of objects without altering their use value. In order to understand the dynamics of social change, they consider the problem of how products are distributed and consumed. They argue that economic exploitation exists when some part of the product does not revert to the group or individual producer but instead is appropriated by others as surplus value. They posit a dialectical relationship between production and property that forms the internal dynamic driving social transformation.

As an explicitly scientific approach, much of the work of the Barcelona archaeologists has focused on how to observe and measure the social relations that they define in the archaeological record (Castro et al. 1998). They pose two questions to direct their analysis: "Who participates in the social production of men, women, objects, and in the maintenance of all of these things and how do they do so?" and "Who benefits from the products so produced?" They have developed a series of archaeological (or methodological) theories that allows them to answer these questions, identify exploitation, and define the nature and degree of this exploitation using archaeological observations.

The members of the Barcelona group (Castro et al. 1998) have made several contributions to Western Marxist archaeology. They have gone further than others in developing the archaeological implications of their theory and consequently have produced an impressive corpus of substantive works applying that theory; they have also developed a theory that integrates considerations of gender and class. They have accomplished the latter by including gender relations as part of the basic objective conditions of social life and by viewing the social and biological reproduction of people as an integral aspect of production.

THE STATE OF MARXISM IN ANGLO-AMERICAN ARCHAEOLOGY TODAY

Perhaps it is not surprising that A Marxist Archaeology has received more attention and citation overseas than in the United States. The biases against Marxism in the U.S. run long and deep. In Great Britain the book's focus on pluralism and the construction of knowledge fit with leading trends springing from both a postprocessual archaeology and the critique of this archaeology (Gamble 2000; Johnson 1999). In the Spanish-speaking world—both in Latin America and Spain—a "gringo Marxist" is somewhat of an oddity and worthy of attention for this reason if no other. In this world Marxism has also become an established theory that is currently under attack and some students have found the theory of internal relations in the book a welcome option to traditional Marxism, postprocessualism, or more right-wing alternatives.

It should also not be surprising that the clandestine history of Marxism I describe in the book continues in North American archaeology. Many of the issues and approaches that were radical in the early 1990s have entered mainstream research. World-systems theory flourished during the 1990s and continues as a widespread approach today (Chase-Dunn and Mann 1998; Kardulias 1999; Peregine and Feinman 1996). Numerous archaeologists have embraced a Marxist definition of ideology as a socially necessary illusion that serves as an instrument of domination and a locus of power (Pauketat and Emerson 1997; Seeman 1995; Whitley 1994). Still others have asked questions about exploitation and how benefits from social relations accrue to some individuals and not to others (Arnold 2000; Diehl 2000). Despite the popularity of these and other Marxist-derived ideas and approaches, most U.S. archaeologists have been unwilling to adopt the dialectical epistemology of a Marxist approach or the political costs of explicitly labeling themselves Marxists. As has been the case since the beginning of the twentieth century, some scholars adopt these ideas and approaches with an explicit nod to their Marxist origin but most seem unaware of where they came from.

In the last decade of the twentieth century, Marxism has become more established in North American archaeology than it was in the 1970s and 1980s. The core group of scholars that I identified in 1992—including Bruce Trigger, Thomas Patterson, Allen Zagarell, Mark Leone, Philip Kohl, Robert Paynter, Antonio Gilman, Charles Orser, and Dean Saitta—continues to be active and productive. These scholars have been joined by the first generation of North American graduates to be trained in a Marxist archaeology.

Bruce Trigger (1995a:349) has said, "Classical Marxism attracts me because in my opinion it accounts better than any other theory for human behaviour as I understand it." Numerous archaeologists in North America share his view and they have recently produced productive substantive, historical, and theoretical studies. Antonio Gilman (2001) has continued his research on the Copper and Bronze ages of southeastern Spain and engaged the Spanish tradition of Marxist archaeology. Jon Muller (1997) has published a comprehensive Marxist interpretation of the material conditions underlying and stimulating political development during the Mississippian period in the southeastern United States. Thomas Patterson (1995, 2001) has published critical social histories of both American archaeology and anthropology. Bruce Trigger (1998) presents a Marxist appraisal of the concept of social evolution in social theory.

There has been a marked expansion in the number of North American archaeologists explicitly applying a critical or relational theory of Marxism to their studies. Indeed, I cannot attempt to cite all such studies in this brief prologue but I will highlight some of the more important ones. This Marxist presence is much less evident in studies of the aboriginal past of the Americas than in historical archaeology, which explores the modern (i.e., post-AD 1500) era.

Marxists have established a small but pervasive presence in the substantive debates about the prehistory of North America. In general these studies have raised issues of power and exploitation in social relations as alternatives to ecological and technological explanations for change in these societies (Nassaney and Sassaman 1995; O'Donovan 2002). Dean Saitta (1994, 1997) has developed a theoretical approach that argues for the relative autonomy of power and labor relations in the social life of middle-range societies and has applied it to both Cahokia and Chaco Canyon. Bradley Ensor (2000) has used the notions of social formation and Modo de Vida from Latin American social archaeology in a study of the prehistoric Hohokam of the Phoenix Basin in Arizona. In the eastern United States Marxist-oriented studies have considered a range of issues from the replacement of stone vessels by ceramic pots (Sassaman 1993) to the introduction of the bow and arrow (Nassaney and Pyle 1999) and the political economy of stone hoes in the Mississippian (Cobb 2000). In each of these analyses the authors have sought to demonstrate the inadequacies of diffusionary or evolutionary models and have instead argued for the importance of understanding technology in the context of social relations, social power, and human interaction.

Marx's theory of capitalism has found its strongest North American following within the archaeology of capitalism; currently Marxists represent a major school of thought in historical archaeology (Johnson 1996; Leone and Potter 1999; Little 1994). This should not be surprising because in this history class exploitation is clearly fundamental (Walker 2000) and Marx's analysis of class is plainly most applicable (Wurst 1999). Moreover, archaeologists studying capitalism are themselves embedded in capitalist class relations (McGuire and Walker 1999). Even historical archaeologists who have not explicitly embraced Marxism now find it necessary to discuss labor in terms of social relations rather than simple economics (Silliman 2001). Much of the explicitly Marxist work builds on the concept of ideology that Mark Leone and his students developed in their critical archaeology (Burke 1999; Leone 1995; Potter 1994; Shackel 2000). Both external and internal critiques have led the Annapolis project to move away from the study of elite architecture and ideology to the study of the African-American working-class community of that city (Leone 1995; Mullins 1999; Shackel, Mullins, and Warner 1998). Other archaeologists have found a dialectical notion of power useful in the study of plantation slavery (Thomas 1998). Historical archaeologists working in the Marxist tradition have by and large rejected a totalizing notion of Marxism and have used class and Marxist analyses as entry points for studies that also consider race, gender, and ethnicity as loci of oppression (Delle 1998; Delle, Mrozowski, and Paynter 2000; Nassaney et al. 2001; Wood 2002).

WHAT MARXISM OFFERS THE STUDY OF ARCHAEOLOGY

The application of Marxist theory to archaeology should stand or fall based on how well it allows archaeologists to comprehend the realities of human history (Trigger 1995b:325). I argued in *A Marxist Archaeology* that Marxism addresses these goals through the logic of the dialectic, a theory of social development, and praxis. In my own work since finishing the book, I have tried to realize these goals.

A Hegelian dialectic helps archaeologists to escape many of the oppositions that frequent debates about archaeological theory; it also provides a method for archaeologists to study change. The oppositions include science versus humanism, objectivity versus subjectivity, the material versus the mental, and evolution versus history. A Hegelian dialectic leads us to examine how these poles are interconnected rather than seeing them as irresolvable opposites. Scholars are connected to the social world that they study and thus must critically examine their role in that world. The dialectic as a method for studying change also emphasizes the interconnectedness of human society and examines this interconnectedness for the contradictions that shape society. These contradictions provide a source for the cultural change that is internal to the society and springs from the social relations of real life.

A dialectical approach rejects either/or choices and instead of asking categorical questions inquires how dialectical relationships drive culture change. At the end of the twentieth century, southwestern/northwestern archaeologists were embroiled in a heated debate over whether the late Prehispanic Pueblos should be seen as ranked or egalitarian societies. From a dialectical perspective what is interesting about these societies is that they incorporated both egalitarian and hierarchical social relations; hierarchy and equality existed in a dialectical tension that drove change in Prehispanic Pueblo societies (McGuire and Saitta 1996). These observations shift the study of these societies from debates about evolutionary classification to questions about the relationship of equality and hierarchy in Pueblo societies.

Marxism is a rich conceptual source of models and theories for the study of cultural change. Marx's basic—and often somewhat ambiguous—observations have been interpreted anew by many others in light of the conditions of economic development of their own times. This fruitful tradition of scholarship has produced a copious body of theories, concepts, ideas, and insights on human history. Marx's focus on the role of socially constituted labor in the production and reproduction of real life—and his realization that these social relations are objectified in various ways, including through material culture—is compatible with the craft of archaeology (Shanks and McGuire 1996). Thus the archaeologist V. Gordon Childe (1944:1) noted that material culture reflects and participates in the social relations that produce it and that we can therefore study these social relations using material culture.

Marxism is also a theory of praxis. Praxis refers to theoretically informed practice (or agency). Praxis is the human activity through which people transform the world and themselves. The ultimate goal of Marxism is a praxis that transforms both people and society. As a dialectical concept praxis implies that our agency, both as scholars and more broadly as social beings, must lie in the interconnections between human free creative agency and the material (i.e., concrete) conditions of human existence.

Praxis implies an archaeology that can be a form of political action. In southern Colorado in 1914 the Colorado National Guard opened fire on a tent colony of striking coal miners and their families at Ludlow, killing twenty-four people including eleven children and two women. The Colorado Coalfield War Archaeological Project seeks to gain a richer and more systematic understanding of the everyday life experience of the Colorado miners and their families that led to the strike (Ludlow Collective 2001). Our study of the Colorado Coalfield War seeks to transcend the traditional middle-class community that archaeology usually serves. The United Mine Workers maintain a memorial at Ludlow and union people and the children and grandchildren of the survivors still gather once a year to commemorate the event. Our project is actively involved with this community of working people and their struggle. The project integrates archaeological research with a community of working people by asking questions that are important to them, about events that are meaningful to them, with the goal of working together in the struggle for rights and dignity for working people.

The unique contribution that Marxism can make to archaeology comes from the integration of these three parts to gain knowledge of, critique, and take action in the world. If we accept a dialectical approach to Marxism, then this integration is an ongoing, dynamic, and never-ending process. My starting point for this process is to be found in *A Marxist Archaeology* and I hope that other archaeologists will find my efforts helpful as they begin their journey.

REFERENCES

Arnold, Jeanne E.
2000   Revisiting Power, Labor Rights, and Kinship: Archaeology and Social Theory. In *Social Theory in Archaeology*, edited by Michael Brian Schiffer, pp. 14–30. University of Utah Press, Salt Lake City.

Bate, Luis F. and Fancsico Nocete Calvo
1994   Un Fantasma Recorre la Arqueología (No Solo en Europa). *Arqritica* 7:8–10.

Brumfiel, Elizabeth M.
1994   Review of *A Marxist Archaeology*. *American Antiquity* 59:157–158.

Burke, Heather
    1999   *Meaning and Ideology in Historical Archaeology: Style, Social Identity,
            and Capitalism in an Australian Town.* Kluwer Academic/Plenum, New
            York.

Castro, Pedro V., Sylvia Gili, Vicente Lull, Rafael Micó, Cristina Rihuete, Roberto
Risch, and Encarna Sanahuja Yll
    1998   Towards a Theory of Social Production and Social Practice. In *Craft
            Specialization: Operational Sequences and Beyond,* vol. 4, BAR Inter-
            national Series 720, edited by Sarah Milliken and Massimo Vidale, pp.
            24–29. Archaeopress, Oxford.

Chase-Dunn, Christopher and Kelly M. Mann
    1998   *The Wintu and Their Neighbors.* University of Arizona Press, Tucson.

Childe, V. Gordon
    1944   *Progress and Archaeology.* Cobbett, London.

Cobb, Charles R.
    2000   *From Quarry to Cornfield: The Political Economy of Mississippian
            Hoe Production.* University of Alabama Press, Tuscaloosa.

Delle, James A.
    1998   *An Archaeology of Social Space: Analyzing Coffee Plantations in Ja-
            maica's Blue Mountains.* Plenum, New York.

Delle, James A., Stephen A. Mrozowski, and Robert Paynter (editors)
    2000   *Lines That Divide: Historical Archaeologies of Race, Class, and Gen-
            der.* University of Tennessee Press, Knoxville.

Diehl, Michael W. (editor)
    2000   *Hierarchies in Action.* Center for Archaeological Investigations Occa-
            sional Paper No. 27, Southern Illinois University, Carbondale.

Ensor, Bradley E.
    2000   Social Formations, Modo de Vida, and Conflict in Archaeology.
            American Antiquity 65:15–42.

Gamble, Clive
    2000   *Archaeology: The Basics.* Routledge, London.

Gilman, Antonio
    1993   Historia y Marxismo en la Arqueología Anglo-Sajona. *Arqritica* 6:6–7.
    1998   *The Communist Manifesto* 150 Years Later. *Antiquity* 72:910–913.
    2001   Assessing Political Development in Copper and Bronze Age Southeast
            Spain. In *From Leaders to Rulers*, edited by Jonathan Haas, pp. 59–81.
            Kluwer Academic/Plenum, New York.

Johnson, Matthew
    1996   *An Archaeology of Capitalism.* Blackwell, Oxford.
    1999   *Archaeological Theory: An Introduction.* Blackwell, Oxford.

Kardulias, P. Nick
    1999   *World-Systems Theory in Practice: Leadership, Production, and Ex-
            change.* Rowman & Littlefield, Lanham, MD.

Klejn, Leo S.
    1993   *La Arqueología Soviética: Historia y Teoría de una Escuela Descono-
            cida.* Crítica, Barcelona.

Leone, Mark P.
    1995   A Historical Archaeology of Capitalism. *American Anthropologist* 97:
            251–268.

Leone, Mark and Parker B. Potter Jr. (editors)
    1999   *Historical Archaeologies of Capitalism.* Kluwer Academic/Plenum,
            New York.

Little, Barbara J.
    1994   People with History: An Update on Historical Archaeology in the
            United States. *Journal of Archaeological Method and Theory* 1:5–40.

Ludlow Collective, The
    2001   Archaeology of the Colorado Coal Field War, 1913–1914. In *Archae-
            ologies of the Contemporary Past*, edited by Victor Buchli and Gavin
            Lucas, pp. 94–107. Routledge, London.

McGuire, Randall H. and Dean J. Saitta
    1996   "Although They Have Petty Captains, They Obey Them Badly": The
            Dialectics of Prehispanic Western Pueblo Social Organization. *Ameri-
            can Antiquity* 61:197–216.

McGuire, Randall H. and Mark Walker
    1999   Class Confrontations in Archaeology. *Historical Archaeology* 33:159–
            183.

Muller, Jon
    1997   *Mississippian Political Economy.* Plenum, New York.

Mullins, Paul R.
    1999   *Race and Affluence: An Archaeology of African America and Consumer Culture.* Kluwer Academic/Plenum, New York.

Nassaney, Michael S. and Kendra Pyle
    1999   The Adoption of the Bow and Arrow in Eastern North America: A View from Central Arkansas. *American Antiquity* 64:243–264.

Nassaney, Michael S., Deborah L. Rotman, Daniel O. Sayers, and Carol A. Nickolai
    2001   The Southwest Michigan Historic Landscape Project: Exploring Class, Gender, and Ethnicity from the Ground Up. *International Journal of Historical Archaeology* 5:219–261.

Nassaney, Michael S. and Kenneth E. Sassaman (editors)
    1995   *Native American Interactions: Multiscaler Analyses and Interpretations in the Eastern Woodlands.* University of Tennessee Press, Knoxville.

O'Donovan, Maria
    2002   Grasping Power: A Question of Relations and Scales. In *The Dynamics of Power*, edited by Maria O'Donovan. Center for Archaeological Investigations Occasional Paper No. 30, Southern Illinois University, Carbondale, in press.

Patterson, Thomas C.
    1995   *Towards a Social History of Archaeology in the United States.* Harcourt Brace, Orlando.
    2001   *A Social History of Anthropology in the U.S.* Berg Publishers, Oxford.

Pauketat, Timothy R. and Thomas E. Emerson (editors)
    1997   *Cahokia: Domination and Ideology in the Mississippian World.* University of Nebraska Press, Lincoln.

Peregrine, Peter N. and Gary M. Feinman
    1996   *Pre-Columbian World Systems.* Prehistory Press, Madison, WI.

Potter, Parker B., Jr.
    1994   *Public Archaeology in Annapolis: A Critical Approach to Archaeology in Maryland's Ancient City,* Smithsonian Institution Press, Washington, DC.

Saitta, Dean J.
  1994   Agency, Class, and Archaeological Interpretation. *Journal of Anthropological Archaeology* 13:1–27.
  1997   Power, Labor, and the Dynamics of Change in Chacoan Political Economy. *American Antiquity* 62:7–26.

Sassaman, Kenneth E.
  1993   *Early Pottery in the Southeast: Tradition and Innovation in Cooking Technology.* University of Alabama Press, Tuscaloosa.

Sayer, Derek
  1987   *The Violence of Abstraction: The Analytic Foundations of Historical Materialism.* Blackwell, Oxford.

Seeman, Mark F.
  1995   When Words Are Not Enough: Hopewell Interregionalism and the Use of Material Symbols at the GE Mound. In *Native American Interactions: Multiscalar Analyses and Interpretations in the Eastern Woodlands*, edited by Michael S. Nassaney and Kenneth E. Sassaman, pp. 122–143. University of Tennessee Press, Knoxville.

Shackel, Paul A.
  2000   *Archaeology and Created Memory: Public History in a National Park.* Kluwer Academic/Plenum, New York.

Shackel, Paul A., Paul R. Mullins, and Mark S. Warner (editors)
  1998   *Annapolis Pasts: Historical Archaeology in Annapolis, Maryland.* University of Tennessee Press, Knoxville.

Shanks, Michael and Randall H. McGuire
  1996   The Craft of Archaeology. *American Antiquity* 61:75–88.

Silliman, Stephen W.
  2001   Theoretical Perspectives on Labor and Colonialism: Reconsidering the California Missions. *Journal of Anthropological Archaeology* 20:379–407.

Taylor, Timothy
  1993   Archaeology with a Small "m." *Antiquity* 67:925–928.

Thomas, Brian W.
  1998   Power and Community: The Archaeology of Slavery at the Hermitage Plantation. *American Antiquity* 63:531–551.

Trigger, Bruce
   1995a   A Reply to Tilley and Nencel. *Critique of Anthropology* 15:347–350.
   1995b   Archaeology and the Integrated Circus. *Critique of Anthropology* 15:319–335.
   1998   *Sociocultural Evolution: Calculation and Contingency.* Blackwell, Oxford.

Walker, Mark
   2000   Labor History at the Ground Level: The Colorado Coalfield War Archaeology Project. *Labor's Heritage* 11:58–75.

Whitley, David S.
   1994   By the Hunter, for the Gatherer: Art, Social Relations and Subsistence Change in the Prehistoric Great Basin. *World Archaeology* 25:356–372.

Wood, Margaret
   2002   Labor of Love: Women's Domestic Labor and the Struggle for Transformative Social Change. In *The Dynamics of Power*, edited by Maria O'Donovan. Center for Archaeological Investigations Occasional Paper No. 30, Southern Illinois University, Carbondale, in press.

Wurst, LouAnn
   1999   Internalizing Class in Historical Archaeology. *Historical Archaeology* 33:7–21.

                                                        Randall H. McGuire

CONTENTS

LIST OF TABLE AND FIGURES

TABLE

FIGURES

PREFACE

*But if the designing of the future and the proclamation of ready made solutions
for all time is not our affair, then we realize all the more clearly what we have
to accomplish in the present — I am speaking of a ruthless criticism of everything
existing, ruthless in two senses: The criticism must not be afraid of its own
conclusions, nor of conflict with the powers to be.*

Letter from Karl Marx to Arnold Ruge, September, 1843

*Without general elections, without unrestricted freedom of the press and
assembly, without a free struggle of opinion, life dies out in every public
institution, becomes a mere semblance of life in which only the bureaucracy
remains as the active element . . . a dictatorship, to be sure, not the dictatorship
of the proletariat, however, but a dictatorship of a handful of politicians.*

Rosa Luxemburg (1961:71–72)

In the 1990s we find the theoretical house of Anglo-American archaeology in
considerable disorder. The consensus theory of the 1970s — a loosely knit processual archaeology that advocated a natural sciences model — was besieged in
the 1980s by a host of alternative archaeologies: poststructuralist, feminist, and
marxist. By the end of the decade it was not possible to identify a clear consensus
view, although an essentially processualist approach remained the majority
strategy in the United States, if not in Great Britain. Many archaeologists find
the highly contested terrain of archaeological theory very confusing both because of the welter of claims and counterclaims and because they do not understand the larger philosophical issues that lay behind much of the debate. It is
doubtful that the 1990s will witness a resolution of these debates or the formulation of a new consensus. I would also suggest that we should not wish it so;
for in these debates lies a powerful dynamic that forces us to constantly question
and defend our assumptions about the world and our practice of archaeology.

A wide variety of archaeologists have explicitly adopted marxist theories, and
marxism has had significant, but often hidden, influences on all the other major
positions in the debate, including the processualist. Currently, no other English
volume provides a comprehensive summary of marxism in archaeology. This

volume was written by an archaeologist for archaeologists to discuss the role of marxism in archaeology today. It assumes that the reader has a good understanding of archaeology and theory in archaeology but little or no knowledge of marxism. Marxist scholars may find the book of interest as an exploration of what marxist theory can say about issues of long-term human history. The volume briefly examines the development of a Western marxist intellectual tradition over the last 100 years, and it reviews the various ways that marxist theory and ideas have been used by archaeologists in the Soviet Union, Latin America, and the English-speaking world. The core of the volume develops the dialectical notion of marxism as a theory of internal relationships, and it discusses in detail the implications of that theory of marxism for the study of long-term human history. A case study, drawn from Southwestern archaeology, examines both the issue of primitive communism and the application of a dialectical marxism to archaeological research. A dialectical approach requires that we critically examine our own practice as well as the past. In the United States, most archaeology concerns the study of Native American pasts; for this reason the volume reflexively looks at the relationship between U.S. archaeology and Native Americans. It concludes with a brief discussion of the implications of a dialectical marxism for the practice of archaeology.

I am convinced that I have completed this volume at a moment that is both too late and too early; too late after a decade of conservatism and the collapse of the Soviet "Empire" have blinded the minds of many in the West to radical theory and socialist ideals; too early before the "end of history" is revealed to be a shimmering mirage, and free market promises the delight of a few and the ruin of many. Archaeologists may rightly ask why they should seriously consider marxism at this moment. There are two answers to that question: one that addresses the place of marxism in the twilight of the twentieth century and the second that addresses the value of marxist theory to the practice of archaeology. The first answer raises issues that go far beyond the scope of this volume or my expertise as a scholar, but I feel compelled to address them at least briefly in this preface. The second answer is that marxism is a rich intellectual tradition that offers archaeologists a way around many of the seemingly irresolvable theoretical oppositions that beset us and as such deserves a place in the theoretical and substantive debates of archaeology. This second answer is the theme of the volume.

Marxism is many things. It is at once a way to know the world, a critique of the world, and a means to change the world. The tension between these three goals warns us away from a sterile scholasticism, a nihilistic skepticism, and the exercise of power for power's sake. This tension also makes it very difficult for any of us to ever stand exactly in the middle of these three poles. The Russian Bolsheviks, in the morning light of the twentieth century, emphasized marxism as a way to change the world. They proposed that a dictatorship of the proletariate would hold the other two goals in trust until necessary changes had transpired. Once in power, this dictatorship passed into the hands of a state bureaucracy that made the defense of the state the first priority and marxism the state ideology. They forbade marxism as a critique of the world and constrained it as a way to know the world. The political success of the Bolsheviks inspired most of the revolutionary movements in the first half of this century to adopt some variant of their program of political action before critique and knowledge.

It soon became apparent to many marxists that something had gone terribly wrong as a result of the Bolshevik resolution of this tension. In 1918 Rosa Luxemburg (1961) was one of the first to speak out, and she warned prophetically that the course of revolution could follow the road of totalitarian dictatorship. In the 1920s, marxists in Western Europe developed a tradition of Western marxism that stood closer to the poles of critique and scholarship than did the Bolshevik program. In the 1950s and 1960s, this developed into a scheme of political action commonly called the New Left, which opposed the tyranny of both capitalism and Soviet communism. Since the dissolution of the New Left in the early 1970s, Western marxists have struggled to build theories that maintain the tension of knowledge, critique, and action in terms of the changing context of the world around us. Many in this tradition of Western marxism welcome the fall of the Soviet "Empire," but there are fears that it will be replaced by nationalistic, fascist dictatorships that are even more abusive of the welfare and rights of their peoples.

Most marxists living in the West today came to marxism through their experience in the New Left or through the critical searching for new direction that followed that movement. They came to Western marxism because it was a critique of power and oppression, a critique of East and West. There is little in the events of the last few years that discredits marxism as a critique of capitalism (the West). Within the United States, over the last decade the rich have grown richer and the poor, poorer. One of every five American children now lives in poverty and, for the first time since the Great Depression, rates of home ownership are declining and inequalities in wealth and income are increasing. In the third world, the 1980s have brought even greater misery. In Latin America an ancient scourge, cholera, stalks the land, spread by the decline of sanitation and living standards to nineteenth-century levels. The collapse of Soviet state communism has freed Western marxism of a great albatross; it has not, however, transformed the ills of capitalism.

The notion that archaeology can change the world, that it can alter capitalism, or in any serious way challenge it is simply absurd. Archaeologists do not have that kind of power or influence, and I honestly wonder if any of us would want it. Archaeology is, however, part and parcel of the larger world. Our history and ideology are tied up in that world. For this reason the stories archaeologists tell about the past are seemingly more believable when they fit the assumptions of that world. Our practice of archaeology requires less effort and is more likely to be praised or rewarded when it rests snugly in the order of the larger world. When the stories do not fit and our practice does not rest snugly in the order of the larger world, we challenge that order, and we are able perhaps to lead people to think critically about it. Doing so makes our practice controversial and difficult.

Why, then, do I advocate an explicitly marxist archaeology, knowing that the time is not right and that the words alone may provoke more controversy than what I am trying to say? I could mask the origin of these ideas under commonly used aliases. Many of the positions that I arrived at in this book can also be reached via other routes; for example, in Chapter 8 I praise a number of archaeologists from around the country for the way they work with Native American people. None of these archaeologists is, to my knowledge, a marxist. I could pick and choose from marxist thought and try to discard the offensive labels along with the nasty bits and other baggage that lie within, using only the decorously disguised good bits.

Because the positions reached in this volume are a direct result of my systematic reading of marxist theory, history, and archaeology, it would be intellectually dishonest for me to hide the marxist origin of my thought. My primary reason for beginning this project was to force myself to come to a comprehensive understanding of marxism. This reading has led me to many positions that can be reached by other routes, but all of the positions that I have come to cannot be connected by any other road. Knowledge comes not just from the destinations but also from the journey. The theory of marxism is greater than the sum of its parts, and the nasty bits and baggage are better jettisoned by developing new theory from the diversity of the old theory and by synthesizing insights from other intellectual traditions, rather than simply pasting together unconnected good ideas. Finally, I believe that as scholars one of our goals should be to get our students, colleagues, and whomever else might read or listen to what we have to say to think critically about what we have said, about themselves, and about the nature of the world. When critical ideas are disguised in circumspect labels they invite the reader to reach safe conclusions and not to critique.

ACKNOWLEDGMENTS

This volume has been a labor of five years, and in that time I have benefited greatly from the help and assistance of many people. Conversations and correspondence with Immanuel Wallerstein, Catherine Lutz, Jane Collins, Robert Paynter, Eric Wolf, Russell Handsman, Sarah Elbert, Ian Hodder, Mark Leone, Michael Shanks, Barbara Bender, Joan Gero, Michael Rowlands, Kristian Kristiansen, Michael Gebühr, Maurizio Tosi, Martin Wobst, Thomas Patterson, Matthew Johnson, Charles Merbs, Jan Hammil, Ernest Turner, Maria Pearson, Peter Ucko, Jane Hubert, Roderick Sprague, Glen Rice, Rick Effland, Weldon Johnson, Liz Brumfiel, George Armelagos, Dean Saitta, Bill Marquart, Philip Kohl, Susan Kus, Tim Murray, Iraida Vargas, Felípe Bate, Alain Schnapp, Alison Wylie, Carol Crumbly, and Walter Echo-Hawk were instrumental in the formulation of my ideas. A large number of people read earlier drafts of the various chapters and offered me valuable suggestions on improving them, not all of which were taken. These people included Michael Schiffer, Vincas Steponiatis, Emlin Myers, Margaret Conkey, Catherine Lutz, Jane Collins, Susan Pollack, Cynthia Woodsong, Parker Potter, Ian Hodder, Jonathan Hill, Mark Leone, Linda Cordell, Thomas Emerson, Michael Shanks, Larry Zimmerman, William Isbell, Albert Dekin, Matthew Johnson, Clifton Amsbury, Timothy Earle, Antonio Gilman, Eric Wolf, Joan Gero, Robert Paynter, Chris Chippendale, Roger Anyon, Bill Marquart, and Bruce Trigger. I must especially thank Tom Patterson who read and commented on all but two chapters in the volume.

Four people gave special assistance in the preparation of Chapter 7 and 8. Judy Brunson provided me with a copy of her dissertation on the Los Muertos burials and Doug Mitchell sent me copies of papers he had written on Classic Period burials in Phoenix, Arizona. John Anderson kindly supplied me with the information on the Casas Grandes pageant. I would expressly thank Cecil Antone for the dialogue we initiated in Denver in 1985 that reawakened my awareness of Native peoples' concerns with what we archaeologists do.

My students at the State University of New York at Binghamton have been a constant source of inspiration and critique. They patiently let me try most of this volume out on them in the classroom, the halls, or over beers. I would particularly thank Tammy Bray, Andy Black, Lynn Clark, Louann Wurst, Nancy Chabot, Catherine Anderson, Jessica Van der Feen, Edwardo Bedoya, Lon Bulgrin, Jeff McCafferty, Cheryl Coursey, and Mark Cassell for their comments, critique, and friendship. Jane Riquelme helped prepare the manuscript for publication.

The Department of Anthropology at State University of New York at Binghampton provided me with institutional support while I was preparing the volume. The office staff of the department, Peg Roe and Ann Pierce, helped me in too many ways to iterate here. The University provided me with a sabbatical leave in the fall of 1990 that I used to work on the volume.

My family has been a constant source of support, attention, and help. Thanks to Deborah, Kathleen, and Austin just for always being there.

Finally, I must thank Bill Woodcock. Bill was an editor at Academic Press when I began this project and he had faith that I could undertake and complete this project. His support, help, confidence, and expertise were invaluable.

CHAPTER 1

Introduction

Galileo: Truth is born of the times, not of authority. Our ignorance is limitless: let us lop one cubic millimeter off it. Why try to be clever now that we at last have a chance of being just a little less stupid?

(Life of Galileo, *scene 4; Bertolt Brecht, 1987:14*)

In his play *Life of Galileo*, Bertolt Brecht grapples with the fundamental contradictions that beset scholars as seekers of knowledge and as social beings. Brecht's Galileo defies the role of authority in the production of knowledge, seeks knowledge from the study of the real world, recognizes that this knowledge is socially created in the context of *the times*, realizes that all knowledge is embedded in social and political relations that it either supports or challenges, and, in the end, submits to the political forces that he has confronted. As archaeologists, we struggle today with the same issues that vexed Brecht. Theoretical debate has focused on fundamental oppositions between science and humanism, evolution and history, materialism and mentalism, and determinism and relativism. In an overly simplistic way, this debate has often been represented as an opposition between a processual and a postprocessual archaeology. This volume enters this debate from a position not described by these oppositions. It does not resolve the debate or the oppositions that lie at the heart of the debate. Rather, it argues that the font of knowledge lies in the tension created by the debate and in the ambiguities implied by the oppositions that drive the controversy. This tension and ambiguity is the dynamic that inspires us to lop off our ignorance a cubic millimeter at a time. The argument derives from a tradition of marxist[1] scholarship and continues that tradition by advocating that our approach to archaeology be dialectical and historical.

ARCHAEOLOGICAL THEORIES

The labels, processual and postprocessual archaeology, often lack a precise definition within archaeology, despite their frequent use as an opposition. Any attempt to characterize the diversity and richness of theory in archaeology will have to over-simplify that theory. Such contrasts are easily overdrawn and can never capture the complexities of thought that lie in the heads of individual researchers. They are, however, useful for comparing and contrasting theoretical and philosophical positions at the broadest level. The categories or labels that we use in these types of discussions are not given but are devised by the author of the discussion. The simple opposition of processual and postprocessual, and the equation of these poles with science and humanism (Redman, 1991), creates a seemingly irresolvable antagonism that archaeologists must choose between. The opposition obscures alternative spaces in the theoretical terrain that finds unity in such oppositions, spaces occupied by feminism (Conkey and Gero, 1991) and marxism.

Processual archaeology broadly refers to an explicitly scientific approach that seeks to model archaeology after the philosophy, theory, and practice of the natural sciences (Redman, 1991). This approach originated in the so-called *New Archaeology* of the 1960s that was catalyzed by the arguments of Louis Binford (1962, 1972, 1983) in the United States and David Clarke (1968) in Great Britain. Few, if any, archaeologists would identify themselves today as *New Archaeologists*, but the New Archaeology's emphasis on a positivist approach to explanation, a systemic view of culture, and building methodology as the primary goal of theory, became, and remain, the mainstream paradigm within U.S. anthropological archaeology. Considerable variation exists within this mainstream as individuals debate issues such as the relationship of method and theory (Schiffer, 1976, 1988), the relative importance of causal relationships in systemic change (Flannery, 1972), and the relationship of biological and cultural evolution (Dunnel, 1989). Since the 1980s, the consensus of the processual archaeology has been challenged by several alternative archaeologies that are frequently lumped together under the tag of postprocessual archaeology.

The most prominent of these critiques originates in the work of Ian Hodder (1982a, 1986, 1990) (who coined the term postprocessual archaeology) and his students at Cambridge (Miller, 1982, 1987; Shanks and Tilley, 1987a; Tilley, 1990; Bapty and Yates, 1990). This theory grew out of larger discussions of poststructuralism and postmodernism in France and Great Britain. The Cambridge critics argue that processual archaeology has paid insufficient attention to the social context of archaeological research and has focused too much attention on method, ignoring meaning and progress, both in the past and in the present (Patterson, 1990:191). I have restricted my use of the term, postprocessual, to refer to these archaeologists and not to all nonprocessual theory in archaeology.[2]

An explicitly feminist archaeology appeared in the mid-1980s with critiques of androcentric biases in the practice of archaeology (Gero, 1983, 1985) and in archaeological interpretations of the past (Conkey and Spector, 1984). Feminists in archaeology challenge processual, postprocessual and marxist archaeologists for failing to recognize gender bias in the conduct of archaeology, failing to recognize women in prehistory, and for failing to critically evaluate western culture's underlying assumptions about gender (Conkey and Gero, 1991:5). Feminist critiques of science, including the positivism of archaeology, seek to move beyond the male bias inherent in science to a feminist philosophy of science (Wylie, 1989, 1991).

All of these approaches, processual, postprocessual, and feminist, have borrowed and used marxist social thought. As Patterson (1990:198) argues, an archaeology grounded in marxism overlaps and disagrees with aspects of all of these positions, but still defines a theoretical space that none occupies. Exploring this space allows us to resolve some of the theoretical dilemmas that archaeologists face. It is not the only theoretical space that archaeology should inhabit; the development of theory in this space will facilitate the critical evaluation and development of archaeology because it gives us a different perspective on the oppositions that bind us and the concrete world that we study.

ARCHAEOLOGY AS A FIELD OF STUDY

In the development of archaeological theory, a key concern must be how we position archaeology *vis à vis* other approaches to the study of the world. Willey and Phillips' (1958:2) oft-repeated dictum that "archaeology is anthropology or it is nothing" captures the most commonly held opinion in the United States on this issue (Binford, 1962; Watson, 1986; Spaulding, 1988). Some Americans have, however, argued that archaeology should set itself apart from anthropology with linkages to history (Noel Hume, 1982), evolutionary biology (Dunnell, 1989), or some other discipline. In England, Europe, Australia, and most of the rest of the world, these debates ring strangely because in these countries archaeology is most often constructed as a separate discipline. In reality, however, this debate transcends national boundaries because the real issue is where archaeology should find its theory. Over the last two decades archaeology has drawn on a host of sources for theory to interpret the past, including cultural anthropology, geography, general systems theory, chaos theory, decision-making theory, biological ecology, evolutionary biology, economics, and so on (Schiffer, 1988:466). A number of archaeologists have seen this situation as problematic and have argued that archaeology needs to develop theory on its own (Dunnell, 1989; Hodder, 1986; Yoffee, in press). Concurrent with these debates are exchanges that disagree as to what subjects should be included in archaeology. Should archaeology be restricted to the study of a prehistoric past, extended to include the study of all pasts, or be defined as the study of artifacts to include past and present?

The issues that are raised in these debates are false ones, and they splinter the study of the social world in a way that obscures and interferes with our understanding of that world. The breakdown of social knowledge in academic departments, each with its own matter, goals and methods, shatters society and makes it difficult to understand it as a whole (Ollman, 1976:232). Thus, economics treats the economy as separable from politics, the realm of political science. Society is broken down into parts that are seldom brought back together in an understanding of the whole, because common processes that shape all of the parts will be judged by different and sometimes contradictory criteria in each discipline.

This division of scholarship is an artifact of the nineteenth century. By the end of that century, the study of the economy had been assigned to economics, history to history, society to sociology, government to political science, and so on. The study of the non-European peoples of the world fell largely to anthropology, and since these people were thought to be more primitive than Europeans, anthropologists were expected to study all aspects of their society. In this division of labor, archaeology was fragmented (Trigger, 1989a). In the United States and throughout most of the rest of the Americas, anthropology arose as the study of Native American peoples and included four domains: their culture, their biology, their languages, and their history. Since most New World peoples lacked writing, the study of their history[3] fell to the spades of the archaeologist (Willey and Sabloff, 1980). Around the world we see a plethora of archaeologies including classical archaeology, anthropological archaeology, prehistoric archaeology, historical archaeology, and medieval archaeology. In U.S. universities we find archaeologists in departments of anthropology, classics, history, American studies, etc. In the division of the academic world that exists today, archaeology does not form a unity or a separable discipline.

We should try to escape this academic division of the world and the distortions that it brings to our studies of society. As Lukács (1971) notes:

> For Marxism there is not, in the last analysis, any autonomous science of law, of political economy, of history etc.; there is only one science, historical and dialectical, unique and unitary, of the development of society as a whole.

There can therefore be no marxist theory of archaeology separate from marxism as a whole. For practical reasons, it may be necessary to consider only parts of the social whole in our theory, but only with the recognition that such considerations are incomplete and unfinished unless they are integrated into the whole.

The variety of archaeologies and disciplinary homes for archaeologists clearly suggests that archaeology is best thought of as a craft (Shanks and McGuire, 1991) As a craft, archaeology is more than a set of methods or techniques (Gummerman and Phillips, 1978). It is instead a unified practice with a range of endeavors from the interpretive to the technical, to the practical, to the creative. Archaeologists study social process by examining the material residues of human action.[4] The craft of archaeology lies in the interpretation of this mute evidence. As such, archaeology should not have a unique theory. It requires a unique methodology and a distinct set of techniques for making observations of the world, but theoretically needs to address the development of society as a whole. Archaeology is the only direct method for studying much of human history and, therefore, is particularly concerned with those aspects of theory related to long-term processes of social change and development.

MAKING THEORY IN ARCHAEOLOGY

Many archaeologists are quite troubled that archaeology's theoretical house is in disarray. Some harken to a dimly remembered past when all archaeologists shared a set of goals and assumptions about the world (Dunnell, 1986:29). They wish to assert a new theoretical unity to our efforts. Alternatively, many archaeologists just want to get on with their digging and be done with the *sturm und drang* of polemical debate. Still others wish to avoid the limitations of any given theoretical perspective by constructing theory from bits and pieces drawn from many sources. Each of these perspectives is flawed and each would deny us the philosophical and empirical understanding that we gain from the struggle between different coherent theoretical perspectives.

A variety of theoretical approaches and programs exist in archaeology today. The index to Bruce Trigger's (1989a:478) recent book on the history of archaeology lists eight such perspectives: cultural–historical archaeology, social archaeology, contextual archaeology, behavioral archaeology, symbolic archaeology, critical archaeology, theoretical archaeology, and structural archaeology. To this list could easily be added feminist archaeology, marxist archaeology, postprocessual archaeology, and poststructuralist archaeology. This diversity can generally be distilled to three or four major distinctions (Watson, 1986; Binford, 1986; Patterson, 1989a), but no matter how we cut it, considerable and fundamental disagreement exists on what theory should be in archaeology.

Many scholars regard this disagreement as a problem that limits archaeology's ability to study the world (Dunnell, 1986; Schiffer, 1988). The lack of a single over-arching paradigm or theory for archaeology is often cited by processualist archaeologists as evidence of our field's underdevelopment as a science. The implication is that if archaeology could unify around a single paradigm or theoretical scheme, we could solve most or all of the empirical issues that face us. Scholars that express dismay at the diversity of approaches in archaeology generally wish to establish a hegemonic position that will structure all archaeological inquiry (Trigger, 1985a; Hodder, 1986; Gilman, 1989; Dunnell, 1989; Binford, 1989). The argument is that only one theoretical perspective will allow us to answer our empirical questions, or that one perspective will better serve our needs than all others. From this position, the building of abstraction (theory) becomes the goal of archaeology instead of the understanding of the concrete (real) world that archaeologists study.

Theory structures how we see the world. It shapes our perceptions and, in so doing, it both defines what questions we will ask about the world and bounds the range of phenomena that we will observe in the world. Without theory, we have no way of ordering or making sense of the great variety that we encounter. Knowledge is made in the dialectic between our theory and the world that we observe. No knowledge is possible outside of this dialogue, and those that claim to study the world without theory simply fail to recognize the theory that guides their study. Theoretical debate is important because it leads us to examine critically the conceptual structures we apply to the world. It helps us better understand the role of these structures in the complex process that creates knowledge.

Knowledge is made but it is not simply made up[5] (Haraway, 1991). A major premise of this volume is that archaeologists can learn things about the past, and that we have. In a Kuhnian sense, a theory is useful as long as it allows us to learn new things about the world. For many years diffusionism was a prominent theory in U.S. archaeology. This theory led archaeologists to look at the distribution of artifact types and styles. As a result of several decades of research under this theory, archaeologists gained an in-depth knowledge about such distributions. One of the reasons for abandoning this theory was that we had exhausted what we could learn from it. Along the same lines, the emphasis on cultural ecology in the 1970s and 1980s defined a set of questions about subsistence that were applied all over North America. Archaeologists now have far better methods for reconstructing subsistence, and we know far more about how prehistoric peoples made a living than we did 20 years ago. In both these cases, the types of information that each theory sought (artifact distributions and subsistence reconstructions) remain essential for archaeology, but the defining questions of each theory have declined in efficacy, as increasingly, the answers archaeologists gave to them became redundant, and the debates they engendered became narrower and narrower.

Changing our perspective on the world can change what we know about it; we will remake our knowledge of the world. A good example of this can be found in the reconstructions of social organization at the Hohokam site of Snaketown in southern Arizona. Research carried out at the site in the 1930s and the 1960s had come to the conclusion that there was little or no internal organization to the site (Haury, 1976:77). These researchers worked with a normative view of culture as a shared set of rules, or norms for behavior. They therefore focused on variations in the distribution of artifacts between sites and regions, but not on variation within the site, since the traits they were interested in were, by definition, those that were shared in the site. In the final publication on the site, the overall site map was cut up and printed on several pages. In 1980 David Wilcox reexamined the data from the site, but this time with a different theoretical focus (Wilcox et al., 1981). He saw culture as a system and was interested in the internal variation within that system. He therefore pasted the pages of the map together and looked for variation in the distribution of features within the site. What he found was a central plaza in the center of Snaketown surrounded by platform mounds and two ballcourts. He also found that houses tended to be organized in groups of two to four facing small courtyards. These observations resulted from an examination of the data from a new perspective and launched a plethora of studies that looked for similar patterns and attempted to explain Hohokam social organization. Haury's theory had not led him to look for patterns in the data, and he structured his analysis in such a way that such patterns would be difficult to ascertain. Wilcox's theory did lead him to look for patterns, and by restructuring Haury's data, he was able to find patterns Haury had not seen, therefore adding to the knowledge already produced by Haury.

The conclusion that I draw from these observations is that a diversity of theory in archaeology is desirable and essential, rather than a problem, to both the making of knowledge about the past and the development of new theory. Our knowledge of the past is made through the tensions created by different theories, through debate and struggle. This debate and struggle occurs both in terms of conflicts between different stories that attempt to account for some aspect of the past and in the debate between different conceptual schemes that structure how we view and study the world. The struggle goes on simultaneously in the making of knowledge and the making of theory. It directs us as to where and how we will observe, and what observations we will make of the world, and it leads us to critically examine the conceptual schemes that structure those observations. Through this debate, archaeologists make new knowledge and make the new theory necessary to continue the struggle. From this perspective, our knowledge of the past is cumulative; we amass more and more, but theory is not cumulative. Our theories do not get better and better; we exhaust their insights on the world, they groan and break under the weight of the realities that they seek to abstract, or they become irrelevant or offensive to the concerns of the world we live in. They are transformed both by the debate between different theories and the new knowledge of the world that we make through that debate. The development of the field, therefore, lies in the inconsistencies and tensions created by the juxtaposition of different theories in archaeology and not in the resolution of these tensions (Wylie, 1991:44). Such a resolution would be a disaster — emotionally comfortable, perhaps, but intellectually sterile.

This endorsement of a diversity of theory in archaeology should not be taken either as an argument for unbridled theoretical relativism (one theory is as good as another), or rampant theoretical eclecticism (archaeologists can pick and choose bits from among any number of theories). The making of knowledge and useful debate requires a dialogue between coherent, informed, and logically consistent theoretical positions (Patterson, 1990:197). Not all theories are acceptable. A theory may be or become unuseful, lacking in insight, logically incoherent, or pernicious. Extreme relativism precludes us from transforming such theory and making new theory through synthesis. The ambiguities that drive our research should lie in the complex dialectic between theories and the real world, and not in our failure to articulate coherent conceptual schemes. Nothing is learned when the ambiguities spring from fuzzy thinking or logical contradictions born in eclecticism.

Most archaeologists do not seem to be ultimately interested in theory; they are instead fascinated by the pasts that they study. They often build this study by eclectically melding notions from various possible theoretical positions. This approach would be defensible if a conscious effort were made to apply one coherent approach to a specific problem or area and another coherent approach to a different problem or area. But an archaeological practice built up of conceptual shreds and patches from here and there, applied in an unspecified manner to write history, presents real problems. The theoretical principles applied to one aspect of the history do not necessarily link up or interpenetrate with the principles used in another aspect of the story. This can easily give rise to inconsistencies, unsupported or unrealized assumptions, and logical contradictions in the histories archaeologists write. It also precludes a critique of the wider implications of the theoretical positions that are taken. We find it difficult to evaluate how the study of specific pasts relates to other cases or the implications of such studies for the social context of the researcher.

In many ways, the eclectic making of theory is more problematic than an eclectic practice of archaeology (Patterson, 1990). All theory, including that presented in this book, suffers limitations. All social theory that asks questions about the basic character of social life has implications for social practice, and it picks up pernicious baggage from its abuse in practice. It is tempting to try to build theory through a method of bricolage, whereby the unuseful and pernicious bits of each theory are discarded and the good bits pasted together to make a new theory. Such a bricolage may also be touted because it allows us to escape the hegemony and constraints of a single theoretical position (Shanks and Tilley, 1987a:11,28). The coherence and usefulness of a theory does not, however, lie in its parts but in their interrelationship; the abstract theory makes sense out of the concrete world it confronts by structuring and interrelating the bits and pieces of that world.

This method of bricolage appears in the postprocessual archaeology. In their book *Reconstructing Archaeology Theory and Practice*, Shanks and Tilley (1987a) draw their theoretical bits from a diverse and contentious bunch of sources, including Walter Benjamin, Anthony Giddens, Pierre Bourdieu, Michel Foucault, and Louis Althusser, among others. They contend that archaeologists should make a theory from a diversity of ideas that will confront us with the contradictions and ambiguities in our study. They seem to confuse logical and dialectical contradictions, and are therefore willing to accept logical inconsistencies in their own scheme. As example, on facing pages they embrace Anthony Giddens idea of structuration and Louis Althusser's notion of structural overdetermination without note of the fact that the first idea is a critique of the second (Shanks and Tilley, 1987a:121, 128, 129). The idea of structuration rests on a notion of the individual as a knowing actor, while the notion of overdetermination denies the ability of individual action to shape events because such action is overdetermined by structural causality. Such bits do not fit snugly together and they create confusion and logical inconsistency in the conceptual scheme they help to form.[6]

The contrast to bricolage as a method of making theory is synthesis. Synthesis focuses on the interrelationship of theoretical notions and ideas and builds on existing conceptual structures. The method is not to simply pick the good bits from the nasty bits, but rather to carefully examine the compatibility of ideas with an eye to a conceptual whole. The reason for such examination springs from the confrontation between the theory and other theories and the real world. Through the process of synthesis, conceptual schemes change and develop over time and occasionally are transformed into something entirely new. The process of synthesis has no resolution; it requires that we constantly examine and alter our conceptual schemes as the dialectic between theory and the real world continually shifts.

It may be useful to think of theory by making an analogy to the mixing of paint. When I worked in a theatrical scene shop, the shop foreman taught me how to mix paint from glue, water, and pigment. A measure of skill and subjective feel for the process was required. If too little glue was put in the paint, it became chalky and would not stick to the flats. If too much glue was put in the paint, it became brittle and harsh in color. If the wrong pigments were mixed together, or if too many different pigments were added, the paint turned a muddy brown color. The most pleasing shades were gained by adding small amounts of pigments to basic colors. Like the paint, the archaeological study of the past requires the glue of theory, but it becomes brittle and harsh if we make it with too much glue, make it too dogmatic, and seek a final truth rather than a constant process of synthesis. Like the pigments, all ideas do not mix together well, and the eclectic mixing of ideas gives us only the muddy brown of confusion. A scene shop mixed paint to build sets. Archaeologists build theory to make knowledge about the world and ourselves. A set would lack depth and detail in only one color, and the process of making knowledge would be quite impoverished without many competing theories.

MARXISM

Marxism is not a single, coherent theory of society that can be hitched to our purposes or dismissed in a few terse sentences. It is, instead, a philosophy, a tradition of thought, a mode of theoretical production, which has produced, and will produce many theories. It is a vibrant palette of many colors. Each of these theories is historically and developmentally linked through a process of synthesis within this tradition so that they differ by degree and blend one into the other. What the many theories, or readings, of marxism share is this tradition, history, and process of development; not a set doctrine or creed.[7] As a tradition, it has been loosely bounded, has freely drawn on ideas developed outside of it, and has contributed ideas to other traditions.

Karl Marx was one of the major intellectual figures of the modern world. He attempted to develop a theory that would encompass the whole of capitalism at a time when it was still new. To do this, he pondered the basic questions of social life. Like many other great thinkers, Adam Smith, Charles Darwin, Emil Durkheim, and Max Weber, he did so in tentative and often paradoxical ways. Each of these thinkers formulated a grand theory that incorporated a philosophy, method, programmatic, and fundamental postulates about the nature of the world. Unlike most of the others, however, Marx's grand theory actively sought to transform the social world that it studied.

Today scholars cannot escape the basic questions that these earlier thinkers raised. We keep subdividing the whole and examining it in more detail, but still we return to the basic questions and grand theory of these thinkers. In marxism, this return has led to the development of a rich tradition of thought that exceeds Marx's own formulations. As Sayer (1987, ix) notes: "Marx's thought lives insofar as it is interpreted anew by others, in the light of their changing needs." The basic questions remain, but the context in which we ask them and the ends we seek to achieve change so that we always read the grand theory in a new light. The reading of marxism that I present in this book is but one possible reading, and it is at odds with many other possible readings.[8]

The Political Nature of Marxism

Probably none of the other great thinkers of the modern world inspires feelings as strong, pro and con, as Marx. This is because Marx saw his scholarship as a means of transforming a capitalist system that exploited the vast majority of the people in the world. "The study of Marx can be a coded form of social criticism (in East and West alike), it can be snivelling apologetics, but it can hardly be politically innocent" (Sayer, 1987, vii). Most American readers are uncomfortable with Marx because marxism is ultimately a critique of power in the modern world and most especially of the power of capitalism. It questions the most basic assumptions that underlie the taken-for-granted world that surrounds us.

The political nature of marxism is always clear in a capitalist context because it challenges these assumptions. The ideas of marxism do not fit comfortably into the normal categories that Americans use to order the world, but instead prick and gouge at our consciousness so that we cannot ignore their political content. The ideas of liberal thought do rest comfortably in these categories, and their soft and fuzzy veneer belies their political content. The observations that archaeologists make to describe the reality we study, such as the distribution of artifacts, the temper of pottery, the stratigraphy of a site, or the shape of a pithouse are not, in and of themselves, political. However, when archaeologists start to build stories about the past around assumptions, such as that culture is a system, that people will maximize gain and minimize effort, that elites manage resources to benefit their followers, or that settlements will be located to maximize access to resource, we are making politically loaded assumptions about the nature of human behavior, social structure, and cultural change (Scholte, 1972:432–440). My examples may not seem political because they neatly fit the economic rationalization of modern American society. I can replace them, however, with a set of assumptions that are more overtly political because they challenge this rationalization: culture is made up of competing interest groups that stand in contradictory relationships to each other; people will seek to reproduce their social position; elites gain power through the exploitation of their followers; and regional relations of power, dominance, and resistance determine settlement location.

The children of the Cold War (and most of us in archaeology today are) learned the language of the Cold War. This was a political discourse that reduced marxism to an ugly caricature liberally drawn from the most pernicious aspects of Stalinism. This dialogue portrayed western economic rationality as based in a scientific understanding of the world and marxist theory as driven by ideology, and as ignoring the realities of the world. Simply put, marxism was political and false and capitalist thought, scientific and true. I hope that the political nature of this attack is clear in retrospect, but the caricature remains a familiar one that can be subtly invoked by a word, a phrase, or a style of critique. Like a ritual incantation, this red-baiting raises a host of images and bogeymen, so that the critics do not have to confront the real substantive and philosophical questions raised by the people that they criticize.

This highly political form of attack has become common again in American and British society and in archaeology. Interestingly, it has been primarily aimed at postmodernist scholars, such as Hodder (1986), and Shanks and Tilley (1987a), who eclectically borrow from a marxist tradition, among others, but do not fit within that tradition and avoid the label, marxist. The critics label them *neomarxists*, and once so tarred, feather them with the Cold War epithets (Binford 1987:403). Schiffer (1988:469) accuses such neomarxists of social engineering and expresses distress that "some investigators wishing to use archaeology as a means to further unspecified political ends, will subvert the scientific process." Renfrew (1989:39) skips the neomarxist label but warns us that Shanks and Tilley (1987a) lead us "at worst to an Orwellian world where poststructuralist gurus offer us guidance upon politically appropriate 'correct' thinking." He goes on to equate Shanks and Tilley's thought with Stalinism. Thomas (1990a) worries that someday leather-jacketed commissars will awaken him from his sleep and force him to account for his view on the Wessex culture. Binford,

Schiffer, and Renfrew contrast the neomarxist political positions to their own "objective" science.[9]

These debates show that there is no politically neutral position on the nature of society or questions of how scholars study society. We do not gain understanding, however, from debate waged by caricature, cheap shots, and innuendo. We gain understanding by honestly considering the political nature of our thought. We do this by critically examining how our knowledge of the world is made, both from what we can observe in that world, and from the social context in which we observe the world.

The Dialectic and History

There can never be one marxism, only different readings of Marx. Indeed, if only a single reading of Marx had been possible, then the essays of Marx would lie forgotten in the dusty archives where many of the works that he disputed now suffer the gnawing criticism of the mice. Marx's basic, yet complex, observations on the world have inspired many readings, formulated in different intellectual and social contexts, and in response to different questions. This work is a dialectical reading of Marx arrived at in the context of modern western Hegelian marxism and in the social world of the twilight of the twentieth century. It addresses the concerns and questions of a primarily Anglo-American archaeology in this context. It does not pretend to be the only possible plan for a marxist archaeology, nor the only correct, true, or useful plan.

There is no simple, unambiguous definition of what the dialectic is and, indeed, the logic of the dialectic deflects us from imprisoning complex and dynamic ideas in staid, lifeless definitions. The Hegelian dialectic that forms the philosophical and epistemological foundations of this volume focuses on the internal relations that structure the social world, both the world of the pasts archaeologists study and the world we live in. These relations are made up of contradictions that bind individuals and groups with opposing and conflicting interests together, and because small changes in any part of this social whole will alter the structure of relations, this whole is always in flux. This change is not simply quantitative or qualitative in nature, but a complex process of both types of change. When qualitative changes occur, they always work on and transform what has gone before, so that every social form carries within itself the seeds of its own transformation, the basic building blocks of what it will become. To understand the dialectic we should examine how it is used in our study of the world. In this sense this entire volume is a study of the dialectic.

Most archaeologists find the dialectical approach to the study of the world very foreign and unsettling. To the question, can scholars truly know the world? It answers, "kinda." The dialectic offers us no destination or resolution to our quest, but only an ongoing process of dialogue between ourselves and the archaeological record, a dialogue that builds understanding through a never-ending series of approximations of the past (Kohl, 1985:115). It forces us to abandon absolutes; absolute truth as well as absolute relativism. This is a very disquieting thing to do. It propels us onto a very unstable terrain where our knowledge and practice is always uncertain and constantly changing as the empirical and conceptual ground we walk on never ceases in its trembling. In place of absolutes and sure wisdom, it leads us to examine the ambiguities and contradictions that surround us to continue the process of understanding.

From a dialectical perspective, it becomes clear that our most taken-for-granted and solid notions are built on ambiguities and contradictions. They melt away under our critical gaze. For example, time is one of the most basic of such notions for archaeology (Shanks and Tilley, 1987a:7). Archaeologists treat it as a given, a natural phenomenon that exists independent of our study. In fact, however, we construct time in our study and choose between different idealized notions of time in order to do our scholarship. Sacred notions of time among many Native American groups make time a sacred circle that repeats itself so that the past can only exist in the present (Zimmerman, 1987). Anthropology and archaeology have often used concepts that spatialize time. Evolutionary time places societies in a timeless ethnographic present and then orders them based on their *primitiveness* or complexity (Fabian, 1983:144–147). Or, time may be lost all together as cross-cultural generalizations are drawn from societies frozen in the ethnographic present. Alternatively, historical time implies a relational notion of time that orders societies chronologically and studies their development in this sequence.

The dialectic finds its proper dimensions in historical time, that is, in the study of history, because the dialectic is above all the study of becoming and transforming (Murphy, 1971:116). History gained a pejorative reputation in archaeology two decades ago when it was critiqued by an evolutionary paradigm that used an evolutionary notion of time. The goal of this paradigm was not the study of real historical sequences; rather, it sought universal theories (abstractions) that predicted cultural change. The debates of over 20 years ago set up an opposition between a particularistic history and a generalizing evolution. This opposition was and is a false one. The choice is not between particularism and generalizing theory, but rather a debate over how the concrete (the particular) and the abstract should be related in our theory and practice. The dialectical history advocated in this volume is ultimately historical, but it is unlike the caricature of particularistic history that many archaeologists hold. A dialectical history begins with the premise that the study of the social world should start, and end, with the real-life experience of human beings. Abstractions are necessary tools for this method, but they are not the goal or end point of our study. Such abstractions are generalizations grounded in specific cases that constantly change as we shift from case to case. This method is not new; for over 30 years some archaeologists have engaged in a similar historical study of evolutionary (developmental) change called multilinear evolution.

In writing this book, I have tried not to be clever, but to seek clarity. I have generally assumed that the reader of this book has a basic familiarity with archaeology and little or no knowledge of marxism. The price of clarity is simplification, and this price has been paid on every page. Some, I am sure, will argue that I have paid too high a price, and others that I have paid too little. The language of marxism is often alienating to archaeologists because they do not understand the meaning of terms, and they find the style of discourse odd. Despite this fact, I have not attempted to cleanse this book of a marxist language for two reasons: (1) ideas that challenge existing modes of thought will not succeed if they use the language of the modes they challenge, because the reader will tend to find the familiar meanings in the text, and (2) to understand marxist theory, one must understand the language. My discussion will use the language of marxism when necessary, but try to do so in a way that introduces this language to a novice reader. One reason that many readers find the language of marxism odd is because it is dialectical. Terms obtain their meaning from their context of use and, therefore, are not reducible to staid definitions. To understand a term, we need to examine the development of its meaning and how it has been used in the shifting contexts of debate and empirical study.

Dwelling on the subtleties of theoretical and philosophical debate does not necessarily give understanding. We are, after all, archaeologists and not philosophers. In the end, the measure of our theory is not how well it fits some school of thought, how erudite and sophisticated it is, or how it reflects all the nuances of a philosophical debate. In the end, our theory should be judged by how well it allows archaeologists to deal with a real world — the real world of what happened in the past, the real world of how archaeologists create an understanding of that past in the present, and the real world of how our interpretations of the past serve the interests of the present.

ONE READING OF A MARXIST ARCHAEOLOGY

The theory of archaeology that I develop in this volume springs from a tradition of marxist thought that is dialectical and historical. A label for the larger font of this theory, for those readers who must have labels, would be marxism as a theory of internal relations (Ollman, 1976; Sayer, 1987). It is also a personal product. It is my reading of this tradition and of archaeology, the harvest of my insights on marxism and theory in archaeology. The tradition of marxism that I draw on, the archaeology that I wish to address, and my own intellect are constantly changing phenomena. As a result, this is not the volume that I set out to write, nor does it accurately reflect my thought at the instant that you are reading it. This book is but a moment in a larger process of the development of theory in marxism, archaeology, and my consciousness.

Marxism as a theory of relations addresses the current theoretical needs of archaeology in four ways:

1. The dialectic offers us a way to escape the oppositions that define so much of the theoretical debate in archaeology (as well as social science in general). These are the oppositions between science and humanism, evolution and history, materialism and mentalism, and determinism and relativism. Scholars escape the trap of these oppositions not by resolving them, but by recognizing that a dynamic understanding of the social world lies in the tension that they create and not in one or the other pole that they offer.

2. The dialectic also offers us a method for studying change. It is a method that finds the dynamics of change in the contradictions that exist in all human relations, with each other, and with the natural world.

3. Marxism is a rich source of theories, concepts, ideas, and insights into the nature of cultural change.

4. A dialectical approach to theory and practice leads to a self-reflexive praxis. It allows us to examine how archaeologists make pasts and how those pasts derive both from the reality of the past and the social context of the researcher. Such knowledge is intricately made and not reducible to either the subjectivities of the researcher or the reality we study.

The main dialogue of the volume follows in four unequal parts. The first part in two chapters examines the development of marxist and archaeological theory. The second part, in three chapters, forms the theoretical core of the volume. The third part, in one chapter, applies this scheme to an example of archaeological research. Finally, the last part, in two chapters, critically examines archaeology and its practice.

Archaeologists have tended to look at the history of our discipline primarily in terms of itself. The chapters on marxism and archaeology survey the development of marxist theory and its influences on archaeology in this century. The discussion of archaeology focuses primarily on Anglo-American archaeology with some reference to Latin American and Soviet archaeology for contrast. This discussion shows how these developments come together in this book and gives some indication of the range of different marxist approaches to archaeology that exist outside of this book. It is necessary to talk about the development of marxist thought both to position my theory *vis à vis* this tradition, and because few English-speaking archaeologists have much training in this tradition of thought. They often hold a stereotyped view of marxism as a doctrinaire ideology of state socialism that does not capture the true nature of variety and debate in the tradition. Some understanding of this debate is also crucial to understand the use of terms such as history, evolution, class, agency, dialectic, and mode of production in a marxist theory. These terms gain their meaning from use in the context of intellectual debate. To use them we must have some idea of how these meanings were created and how they have changed through the ongoing synthesis of theory.

Three chapters develop the theory of the volume in an abstract way and contrast that theory with existing positions within Anglo-American archaeology today. The first of these chapters, "The Dialectic – Marxism as a Theory of Relations," lays the philosophical and epistemological base for what will follow. The second chapter, "The Making of History," discusses where archaeologists have looked for the motor of history. It works from a general discussion of determinism to a look at the different forces, e.g., the environment, technological change, and social structure that archaeologists have invoked as the motors of cultural change. It concludes that there is no motor other than the action of people, and that this action is both determined by and determining of many factors. The last of these three chapters examines the opposition of history and evolution and attempts to lay out an approach for the historical study of developmental change.

The next chapter applies the theory developed in Chapters 4 to 6 to an archaeological case from the U.S. Southwest. "Death and Society in an Hohokam Community" looks at the social structure of the Colonial and Sedentary Period (AD 700–1150) Hohokam society in southern Arizona. It specifies some of the contradictions that structured that society and how change in Hohokam social organization developed from those contradictions. This chapter also allows me to further develop the concept of class in the analysis of a concrete case.

We do not practice our research in a social and political vacuum. In the United States, most archaeology is the study of Native American pasts by members of the dominant society that subdued the native cultures. This relationship makes U.S. archaeology inherently political, yet few archaeologists recognize the political nature of what we do or how our practice fits in a larger history of white domination and Indian resistance. Chapter 8, "Archaeology and the Vanishing American" examines the place of archaeology in this larger struggle with an eye to understanding the current state of relations between archaeologists and Indian people. It also explores how we might alter our practice of archaeology to transform these relations. The concluding chapter of the volume ponders the implications of marxism as a theory of internal relations for archaeology. It seeks to critically examine our practice and show how the theory developed here modifies that practice to create a praxis of archaeology.

The main dialogue that runs down the pages of the volume is not the only dialogue to be found in this work. There are several more circumspect dialogues that run through the endnotes of the volume. Throughout, I have used the endnotes in a familiar way to round out, elaborate, or qualify points made in the text. In the substantive chapter the endnotes present a discussion of why I chose the reconstructions of the past and note the competing points of view that were not chosen in the stories I present. They also contain a third dialogue, which is my own examination of why I say the things that I do in the text. In this dialogue, I try to make explicit the social context and experience that formed my voice.

Our ignorance will always remain limitless. We cut away at it a millimeter at a time through a process of engagement and debate; engagement with theory and the real world, and debate between different conceptual schemes. Through this process, archaeologists learn more about the pasts that we study; we make knowledge of history. This knowledge, however, is never more than an approximation, and is always embedded in the social context of the times. We have the chance to be a little less stupid as long as we abandon the hubris that we can truly know the past and the fear that it is unknowable.

ENDNOTES

1. The reader will note that contrary to convention I have not treated the terms marxist and marxism as proper names and capitalized them in the text. I have abandoned this convention for two reasons: (1) the other major theoretical and philosophical positions discussed in the book, such as positivism, feminism, structuralism, and postprocessual, are not capitalized, and (2) marxism is a 100-year tradition of thought that starts with, and frequently returns to, the work of Karl Marx, but is now far greater and more diverse than the writings of its founder.

2. Many authors lump the critical archaeology of Leone (1982, 1986), Handsman (1980, 1983a), and Potter (1989), with the British poststructuralist's. This critical archaeology has its roots in the marxism of the German Frankfurt school and I have treated it as a marxist approach.

3. Eric Wolf (1982) has written about how anthropology has denied the so-called *primitive* peoples of the world a history by studying them as if they existed outside the events that created their cultures. An aspect of this denial is the separation of history and prehistory. The pasts of civilized peoples of the world are history, while the pasts of primitive peoples are prehistory. This defines the primitive past in terms of what it lacks — writing — and suggests that that past is in some way less than history or simply a prelude to history. My *Random House College Dictionary* gives eight definitions for history, only one of which requires written documents. All people have a "past that is full of important, unusual, or interesting events" (definition 5), these "acts, ideas, or events will or can shape the course of future events" (definition 6), and we can write a "systematic narrative of [these] past events" (definition 2) (Stein, 1984:628). All people have a history recorded in the archaeological record.

4. I hope this rather broad notion of archaeology allows for the wide range of things that archaeologists actually do. In the last 2 decades archaeologists have increasingly directed research toward the study of the modern world either as a way to generate theory and methodology for the study of the past, eth-

noarchaeology, or to understand processes in the present. The emphasis of this volume is on the study of the past, both because this is where my own interests lie and because the vast majority of archaeologists continue to make this the primary emphasis of the field.

5. I first heard this expression from Donna Haraway in a lecture at SUNY Binghamton in the spring of 1990.

6. My critique here is perhaps too harsh. Michael Shanks and Chris Tilley have protested to me in correspondence and in conversation that the logical inconsistencies that I accuse them of are not present in their work. For example, Michael Shanks (personal communication, 1990) wrote to me saying that their use of the term *overdetermination* "was an attempt to get at/express the duality of structure that is the medium but also outcome of practice: but also that people are necessarily born into structure, hence its priority in the last instance." In conversation with them, I am able to see the logical connections to their ideas, but I have trouble doing so in their books (Shanks and Tilley, 1987a, 1987b). This is, in part, a matter of word usage. They modify the concepts that they draw from other sources slightly, but continue to use the same labels for them. Seeing the synthesis that they make requires that the reader read behind and between their words. At best, this expects too much of the reader and, at worse, the eclectic use of terms is simply confusing. Much of what they have to say is compatible with this volume, differing primarily in emphasis, but real differences do exist. One of these is in my insistence that theory is best made within the context of an ongoing tradition of theory production, and theirs, that we must challenge all existing theoretical traditions in a radical pluralism.

7. As is true of any theoretical tradition, there has been much debate over what marxism is and whether or not this or that theory is truly marxist. When governments have transformed some variant of marxism into a state ideology, such debate is usually repressive, intended to stifle any thought that does not fit the dictates of state doctrine. In an open exchange of ideas, such debate serves much the same purpose as debates over what is science or what Darwin really meant. When well done, such critical discussion can lead to a new understanding of the theoretical tradition and a swelling of the boundaries of that tradition. When poorly done, it becomes a dogmatic appeal that limits the tradition and inhibits further synthesis and growth.

8. It is a characteristic of all grand theory that it can be read in numerous ways and that some of these ways will be pernicious. Darwin's grand theory of natural selection was transformed into the theory of social Darwinism in the late nineteenth century and, as such, it was used to legitimate the near genocide of the Tasmanians and Australian aborigines (Lubbock, 1869). Similarly, Marx's theory was transformed in the third decade of this century into Stalinism and used to legitimate the slaughter of millions of people. Postmodernist philosophers such as Michel Foucault would have scholars abandon the grand theories because of these abuses. But what postmodernism offers instead is often ni-

hilistic and anarchistic, offering us no recourse, other than critique, to the conditions we find ourselves in.

9. Some might argue that Hodder, Shanks, and Tilley are deserving of such attack. The tone of their assault has not always been measured and balanced. They have taken a critique of *scientism* to similar levels, transforming the term into a caricature of what most processual archaeologists actually do, and then dismissing the caricature. They do not, however, make any claims that their position is politically neutral or objective. Moreover, what they argue for is a radical pluralism of thought; not the dogmatic, authoritarian, imposition of theory from privileged sources. If anything, the major flaw in their theory is that it is too eclectic and lacking in structure. More important, in the United States and Great Britain, no one has ever been denied a job, imprisoned, or hounded from public view for scientism. Political purges of the academy in these countries, have (and recently have) begun with red-baiting. When three of the most powerful intellectual figures of our discipline bring this kind of critique to bear, the specter of such purges is raised.

CHAPTER 2

A Brief History of Marxism

All I know is that I am not a Marxist.
(Karl Marx, 1882; Mehring, 1962:530)

Most intellectual histories create a past that inexorably leads to the views of the author. This history too, will end with my own position. It does so not out of the hubris that my views are an inexorable product of that history, but rather because the creation of my theory grows from the reading I have made of that history, and my theory is not intelligible in the absence of this reading. The theory and the history are one. The dialogue between marxism and archaeology leads to many different theories of which the position taken in this book is but a single example. My history of this dialogue seeks to show the wealth of thought that can be drawn from the tradition of marxism, to reveal the historical development of key concepts in that tradition, and to locate my own position within this richness.

The history of the dialogue between marxism and archaeology is a complex one. It involves a dialectic developed in diverse contexts and at many levels – a dialectic between ideology and science, between theory and data, and between scientific practice and political practice (Palerm, 1980:33). To understand this dialectic, we have to examine how the development of marxism and archaeology have met at different times and in different cultural, social, and political contexts. In no situation have archaeologists been able to ponder marxism in a totally free community of ideas. Politics have profoundly structured this dialogue; the Soviet state required archaeologists to adopt a marxist theory (Trigger, 1989a). In Latin America, archaeologists took up marxism as an extension of political struggle against the established order (Bate, 1984). The politics of the United States and Great Britain have marginalized, or at times repressed, an active intellectual engagement with marxism. Marxism, and archaeological interest in it, has both shaped and been shaped by the undulating political currents of the modern world that have, at some times, raised socialist ideals and have, at others, submerged them. I have organized this complex story in two parts. The first part, contained in this chapter, briefly traces the history of marxism. The second part, in the chapter that follows, traces the development of marxist archaeologies in the Soviet Union, Latin America, and in Great Britain and the United States.

In 1882, Karl Marx denied he was a marxist to divorce himself from his sons-in-laws' (Paul Lafargue and Charles Lonquet) efforts to transform his theory into the creed of a French *marxist* workers' party (Mehring, 1962:530). He rejected the effort of his followers to make his work into a doctrinaire, comprehensive world view, and the dialectical nature of Marx's thought suggests that he would have denied that a final, complete statement of his theory was possible or desirable. Marx did seek to create a theoretical system, an integrated way of looking at things, but in his hands this theory was always tentative and open ended. Marxism, like all other grand theories, becomes pernicious when dogma replaces a tentative and open-ended searching for understanding, when truth replaces doubt. It behooves us to join in such a search and to welcome a pluralism of marxisms.

Most U.S. archaeologists have little or no first-hand familiarity with marxist theory. It is possible, and commonly happens, in the United States that a student gains a Ph.D. in a social science discipline, such as anthropology, without ever reading Marx. A lack of understanding of marxism has led many western archaeologists to treat it as a single thing that can be dismissed with an isolated contrary example or simplified theoretical failing. From this assumption, the variation and conflict between different currents of marxist thought are seen as confusion and a lack of coherence (e.g., Wenke, 1984:19–21). The vitality of marxism, however, comes from the fact that it is not a single theory, but a rich tradition of interrelated and often competing theories. For these reasons, this chapter assumes that the reader has a basic understanding of Anglo-American archaeological and anthropological theory and directs more effort toward building an understanding of marxism.

The development of marxism has proceeded dialectically — that is, not in a straight line of progressive evolution, but instead in intricate spirals of political action, crises, intellectual synthesis, and action. In this process, theory and practice are intertwined in what marxist authors commonly refer to as praxis, that is, theoretically informed practice. Through the process of praxis, salient ideas shape social, scientific, and political action, and this action alters the social, scientific, and political context of life. Such action also brings on resistance, because it will be opposed by other forces, and crisis, because action reveals the contradictions and weaknesses of the theory. Such struggle and crises lead individuals to rethink and remake their theory, and then to engage the world again, continuing the dialectic of praxis. In this rethinking, the theory is remade from the diversity of ideas present in the previous period; dissenting ideas are moved to the center, and people explore what had been undeveloped themes in the theory. During its history, marxism was never hermetically sealed; its praxis has always drawn ideas from nonmarxist theory, and nonmarxist theory has taken ideas from marxism. The broad changes in marxist theory over the last 100 years not only reflect a dialogue within marxism, but are also part of broader shifts that transcend Western thought (Bocock, 1986:23).

Since the beginning of this century we have seen three complete spirals of salience, resistance, and crisis in international socialist praxis. Marxist ideas gained prominence in the first 2 decades of the century and culminated in the Bolshevik revolution of 1917. This revolution spawned a massive repression of radical thought and action throughout Europe and the United States in the years 1919 to 1920. The contradictions and weaknesses of bolshevism were realized within the Soviet Union during the 1920s, and this crises led to the political transformation of bolshevism into Stalinism.[1] In the world-wide depression of the 1930s, marxist ideas once again gained salience and peaked in the late 1940s with the defeat of Hitler, the rise of a Soviet *empire*, and the triumph of the People's Army in China. This led to widespread repression of socialism outside the Soviet bloc in the 1950s and early 1960s, particularly in the United States and those regions such as Latin America where the United States exerted considerable political and economic influence. Within the Soviet bloc, Stalin's death and the revelation of the contradictions and weaknesses of Stalinism in the 1950s resulted in Maoism in China and other parts of the Third World, Khrushchev's attempts at reform in the USSR, and western marxism in the West. In the 1960s and early 1970s, these dissenting theories gained salience in the West, starting with the Cuban Revolution and concluding with the Nicaraguan Revolution. Repression of radical ideas and action followed in the 1970s and 1980s, and, with the collapse of the Soviet Union and the massacre in China, marxism finds itself in crisis again.

MARX

Karl Marx died on March 14, 1883. The legacy of works that he left can be read in many ways. He was an honest scholar, and he revised his ideas and theory as new data became available to him. He stated his ideas cautiously, subtly, and often a little ambiguously. He made and remade his theory all during his life; it was never finished, but he rarely said explicitly how his ideas had changed. For Marx, scholarship was a process of self-education and self-clarification, a give and take between theory and data that could not stop or stand still (Avineri, 1968; Kamenka, 1969; Ollman, 1976).

Marx was not a university professor. He pursued scholarship as an integral part of his work as a radical activist. He knew that the oppressive conditions, poverty, and exploitation that he saw around him in the slums of London and the streets of Paris sprang from a powerful and complex set of social relations. To fight these relations, he sought to understand how they had begun and why they held such sway over both the exploiters and the exploited (Bloch, 1985:2).

Marx died with much work yet undone. His leadership of radical political organizations took up much of his time and effort. Many of the longer works that he began were never finished. Marx did not finish his last great work, Kapital. Only the first volume was published while he lived, and Frederick Engels completed the second two volumes, publishing them in 1885 and 1894. Engels (1972) also used Marx's notes to write *The Origins of the Family, Private Property, and the State*, printed in 1884.

Much of Marx's scholarly work was not put in print until the middle of this century. In 1883, most of his publications were newspaper articles, political tracts, and speeches. Almost all of the early papers, the essays of the young Marx, were not in print. These included major books, such as the *Economic and Philosophical Manuscripts of 1844* and the *Grundrisse*, which did not appear until the late 1930s and the 1940s. Owing in part to the disruption of normal society by the Second World War, these works did not spark serious discussion until the 1950s. New pieces by Marx continue to be printed, but they are mostly letters and notes, such as Krader's (1971) publication of Marx's ethnological notebooks. The philosophical debates within marxism over the last 30 years have often focused on how the newly available sources should be read and how important they are to marxist theory. When marxist theory has been in crisis, scholars have turned to the newly available works for fresh insights and new themes.

Marx and Engels made very little use of archaeology in their research. Their knowledge of archaeology was slight and consisted mainly of a vague awareness that prehistoric artifacts had been found in caves and that ancient cities had been excavated in the Near East (Kohl, 1983:25). They did recognize archaeological data as a possible source of information on societies in the past. The key to gaining such knowledge lay in the fact that artifacts and tools were the products of human labor and, therefore, could be used as indicators of the social conditions under which they were produced (Marx, 1906:200). As Kohl (1983:25) notes:

> *Within the Marxist tradition ethnological accounts of primitive peoples and the ancient history of Greece and Rome remained the basic sources for reconstructing primitive society and the origin of the state well into the twentieth century.*

Marx did not leave us marxism. The term was unknown during Marx's life, and Marx did not write knowing the impact or importance that his work would have 100 years after his death (Fetscher, 1970). Marxism starts with the ideas of Marx, but this school of thought has grown and branched as the social world around it and our knowledge of that world has changed.

A strong dialectical tension has existed in the many marxisms of the last 100 years. The worth of marxism lies in these tensions; in the struggle to make marxism, at once, a way of knowing the world, a critique of the world, and a guide to action (praxis) in the world. It is the tension between these goals that warns us away from the pitfalls of each; away from the fallow illusion of pure knowledge, away from the nihilistic doubt of the skeptic, and away from the blunderings of ill-conceived endeavors.

All marxist intellectuals have tried to steer some kind of course between the classic oppositions that structure western views of the social world. These oppositions should be quite familiar to anthropological archaeologists because they cross-cut modern western thought and they are currently at the base of theoretical debate in archaeology. They are humanism versus science, history versus evolution, mentalism versus materialism, and relativism versus determinism. Individual thinkers struggle (often with themselves) to chart a course through these oppositions that does not reduce their theory to one or the other of the two poles.

Despite this effort, they have tended to choose courses that lie more to the right pole of the oppositions (science, evolution, materialism, and determinism) or to the left pole. Right marxists have tended to claim great authority for their theory and to argue that through the correct application of that theory, marxists, as a vanguard party, could transform the world. Left marxists, on the other hand, have tended to argue that social transformation cannot be made by a vanguard party or intellectual elite, but must spring from the consciousness of the people. In their hands, marxism is a method of critique that seeks to build such consciousness. Right marxism has tended to be the more politically successful approach, but its authoritarian nature has, in the extreme of Stalinism, led to the stupefying of marxist thought in party dogma and great oppression in the name of that dogma. Left marxism runs the risk of being overly nihilistic and of being politically ineffective because, in the extreme, it lacks any firm guide for action. The course between these poles is not a straight, narrow, middle road, but a constant struggle in thought and action to define, in the tension between the poles, a tortuous path that avoids the perils of either pole. The unity of knowledge, critique, and action lies on this path and not in the resolution of the tensions that shape the path.[2]

THE MARXISM OF THE SECOND INTERNATIONAL

Workers in London and Paris formed the International Working Men's Association (IWMA), the First International, to express solidarity with the 1863 revolt in Poland. The IWMA included a wide range of socialist, communist, and anarchist groups, all of which worked to increase the power of labor, mainly in Europe but also in the United States and in Australia. Rent from within by debate and dissent, the association moved its office to New York in 1872. By 1876, the IWMA had ceased to exist.

The Second International began in 1889, and by 1904 had grown to include labor parties and unions from more than 21 countries. For 25 years the Second International was the center of world radicalism. In this crucible of revolutionary action and ideas, a small group of scholars forged what we now call *traditional marxism*. Engels dominated this theory from the group's origin until his death in 1895. After Engels, many people tried to shape the theory of the group, including Paul Lafargue, Karl Kautsky, George Plekhanov, Nikolai Bukharin, Vladimir Lenin, Rosa Luxemburg, and Leon Trotsky. The Second International gained in strength and influence during the first 2 decades of this century. In 1914, the Second International fell apart when most of its member unions and parties opted to abandon the idea of internationalism and choose instead to fight for their nation states in World War I.

The Bolsheviks, under the leadership of Lenin, broke with much previous marxist theory and argued that a vanguard party could lead Russia from a near-feudal monarchy to socialism without an intervening period of bourgeois capitalism. The success of the Bolshevik revolution in 1917 and the end of World War I brought a wave of revolutionary actions in Eastern Europe. From the left, Rosa Luxemburg questioned the theory of bolshevism and argued that it would lead to a dictatorship. The western powers, the United States, France, and Great Britain, unsuccessfully intervened in the Russian Civil War in 1918 to 1919, but defeated the socialist movements of Eastern Europe, overthrowing a socialist government in Hungary. Rose Luxemburg was among the socialist leaders killed in Germany.

The theorists of the Second International tried to create a scientific marxism that would give them a truer knowledge of the world than would other theories. This theory drew on many ideas common in Europe at that time. The Second Internationalists avidly advocated modernism. In Diego Rivera's mural *La lucha de Clases*, Marx points away from the chaos and exploitation of the capitalist world to a future of tidy mechanized farms, orderly cities, and neat factories. The new Soviet state used modern art, particularly the work of the constructionalists, Tatlin, Lissitzky, and Kolli, to set down its ideals with radically abstract images (Hughes, 1981:82–97). The Second Internationalists had faith that a rational and scientific approach could remake the world for the better. They defied the social order of the early 1900s, but not the basic evolutionary and modernist milieu of the time.

In his speech at Marx's grave, Engels observed: "As Darwin discovered the law of evolution in organic nature, so Marx discovered the law of evolution in human history." (Mehring, 1962:531). Engels, Lafargue, and Kautsky not only equated Marx's accomplishments with those of Darwin, but also sought to merge the ideas of the two men into a unified theory of social and natural evolution (Bloch, 1985:100–101). Engels came to Darwin after Marx, while others found Darwin first. Many have argued that Kautsky's theory was more a radical social Darwinism, drawn from Darwin and Spencer, than a marxism (Bloch, 1985:101). Like most others of their time, the Second Internationalists mixed Darwin's ideas of natural selection with a theory of given, ordered stages in social evolution (Bloch, 1985:63).

The Second International sought to build working-class organizations that could take effective political action. To do this, they simplified marxism and stripped it of much of its ambiguity to build a strong platform for political action. The commitment on the part of many of these theorists to dialectics and the relativity of truth was compromised by a fear of shaking the convictions of working-class marxists, who believed that Marx's theory was truth and a clear way to betterment of their own social conditions (Kolakowski, 1978).

Engels

Engels' ideas fit in with the larger positivist world view of his times. This world view sanctioned science as the best way to know about the world and equated science with the theory and method of the natural sciences. Scientific laws expressed the unity of life, and these laws joined both biological and social evolution. In this milieu, Engels tried to systematize Marx's ideas using the natural sciences as a model (Engels, 1927).

Engels added a theory of matter to Marx's basic premises. Matter was the physical world as directly perceived by the senses. Engels rejected the idea that matter and consciousness were separate and, instead, argued that consciousness began in matter. This led him to the position that common laws ruled subjective thought and the objective world. Thus, ideas could not deny matter.

Engels felt that his epistemology led to true consciousness, that is, a unity of ideas and matter, a true knowledge of reality (Engels, 1927; Gorman, 1982:33). Engels evaluated truth by looking at the match between ideas and matter; true ideas agreed with matter. Knowledge consisted of true ideas. For Engels, the goal of marxism was to gain useful knowledge of society and nature and to test that knowledge in practice. Useful knowledge is practical. It allows people to satisfy real needs, and scientists to predict and mold change in both the natural and social world. We can gain such useful knowledge of nature and culture only by applying the method of marxism as stated in the *laws* of the dialectic (Engels, 1954:62). Engels tried to reduce the ambiguity in Hegel's dialectic and make it a method for gaining true consciousness, that is, useful knowledge, of both the social and natural world.

Engels was not, however, a positivist. He rejected the then-fashionable positivism of Comte, and his ideas do not fit easily with the more recent positivist theory of Hempel, Binford, and others. His laws of the dialectic are not laws in the positivist sense. They do not take the form of *if A, then B*. Engels was a little more pessimistic than most positivists are about our ability to know the world. We saw knowledge as only a reflection of actual things and processes, as "merely the conscious reflex of the dialectical motion of the real world" (Engels, 1954:47).

An emphasis on matter linked to an epistemology of true consciousness complemented Engels' materialistic view of human evolution. He began with a building-like metaphor of society entailing an economic foundation or base, and an idealistic superstructure. Culture interacted with matter to create the economic base, that is, the economic structure of a society including a wide variety of things such as technology, technical knowledge, and the social organization of work. The economic base could take various forms called modes of production. The ultimate cause of social change lay not in peoples' beliefs and ideas, but in changes from one mode of production to another (Engels, 1954). For Engels and those who came after him, objective *a priori* principles govern the entire universe (Gorman, 1982:35).

Engels rejected those forms of simple economic determinism that do not allow for any change outside the economic base, because for him the base determined change only in the last instance or the last resort. He knew that there was more to social life and social change than bread alone. He, like Marx, talked of a superstructure, the various forms of social consciousness such as the state, ideology, religion, and the law that rested upon the base. The superstructure developed out of and alongside the base, but for Engels, it could have its own laws of motion. For a short time, it could even define change in the base. The superstructure could not, however, rule for long, and always in the long term, in the last instance, in the end, the base decided social change.

Second International Marxism after Engels

Most theory in the Second International began with Engels' reading of Marx and tended to reify and extend the materialistic, scientific, evolutionary, and deterministic tendencies in Engels' work. The theory leaves little room for human action as a force for long-term social change. There were also dissenters on the left, such as Luxemburg (1913, 1961), who shied away from the authoritarian trends in the theory.

All of these theorists saw tool use and technological change as basic to humans and as the key to understanding human history (Lafargue, 1910). They began with the idea that the process of natural selection created human beings, and that tools and language gave humans an edge in this selection. A leading theorist after Engels' death was Karl Kautsky, who stated that because the origin of humanness lay in tool use; an inner, material dynamic pushes humans toward progress (Kautsky, 1908, 1909; Gorman 1982:38). The German anthropogeographical school of Ritter and Ratzel influenced the father of Russian marxism Georgii Valentinovich Plekhanov to imbue marxism with environmental determinism (Plekhanov, 1961; Bloch, 1985:106–107). He said that the quality of the tools and the environment they were used in shaped the characteristics of an era.

The scholars of the Second International took much from Darwin's theory, but they used his ideas to form a radical social Darwinism, as much derived from Spencer or Morgan as from Darwin (Gorman, 1982:37; Bloch, 1985:100).

Human history was a story of progress. Engels (1972) wrote the story using a series of stages based on Morgan's work. Social evolution had moved along a single road from primitive communism to ancient or slave society, to feudalism, to modern capitalism, and it would one day reach the peak of true communism. The Russian Bolshevik Bukharin (1969:74) proposed the law of equilibrium to make plain the motion or manner of change from stage to stage. The motion of history was a constant process of disturbing and restoring equilibrium, and only communism would bring a true and final equilibrium.

Human action played little part in this motion. Changes in the material realm of technology and environment drove this process, and human actors could not will these changes, nor could they control or alter them (Bloch, 1985:103). Laws of nature such as Engels' laws of the dialectic and Bukharin's law of equilibrium accounted for the course, form, and speed of the motion. Men made history, but material conditions shaped their actions and left almost no room for them to make it just as they pleased.

Proper use of marxism vested scientists with a privileged access to knowledge and permitted them to attain true consciousness, that is, the ability to see the reality of social life. With this clear vision, they could direct change. Kautsky argued that only social scientists who grasped revolutionary theory could forge a real working-class consciousness (Gorman, 1982:38). Lenin (1908) wrote that idealism led to a bourgeoisie ideology that hid reality, while materialism freed workers with objective truth. It was the duty of the vanguard party to create an authentic working-class consciousness and use it to lead the workers, to make the revolution. Bukharin (1969) acquiesced to a dictatorship in Russia as long as scientists that knew the laws of motion, ruled.

Not all of the thinkers in the Second International agreed with the authoritarian nature of most of the group's theory. Rosa Luxemburg (1913, 1961) argued that human actors, the workers, have the larger role in changing the world. She rejected the strong determinism of others and doubted that the elite of a vanguard party could, in fact, bring about beneficial social change. She felt that social change must result from the candid action of people. People are knowing actors. Their actions spring from an awareness of the conditions of their lives and from some idea of how to change those conditions. True working-class consciousness must come from within that class and cannot be caused or forced by a scientific elite. Luxemburg spent World War I in prison, and in 1919 she died at the hands of right-wing assassins.

From 1914 on, Lenin developed a more reflexive, less authoritarian view of marxism. His *Philosophical Notebooks* were published after his death (Lenin, 1972), and in them, he relaxed the harsh materialism of his prior work. He still felt that idealism gave too much power to consciousness and staved off social change. He now argued that neither reality nor consciousness could be seen as a simple result of the other, but rather that both were infinitely complex and interconnected. In these essays, Lenin moves toward a theory of human action.

Leon Trotsky made the revolution with Lenin, but often disagreed with the party leader. He did not accept the false claims of marxism as a universal system that was the key to every problem in nature, art, and culture. Trotsky's theory of uneven and combined development broke away from the Second International's theory that human history moved along a single path through universal stages (Trotsky, 1962). Less developed social forms advanced by skipping stages, not by following the same path of more developed social forms. The motion of history was a permanent revolution, not fixed steps. Change was the result of a series of interconnected and interdependent social, political, and economic upheavals taking place at many levels and in varied social structures at different times. This theory was introduced to U.S. anthropology by Elman Service (1962) as the law of evolutionary potential. In the 1920s, Trotsky would find his ideas opposed among the Bolsheviks by Bukharin and Joseph Stalin.

COMINTERN MARXISM

The success of the October revolution gave great prestige to the Bolshevik interpretation of Second International marxism and in 1919, Lenin founded the Third International, the Comintern, in Moscow. For the first time, marxism became a state ideology, and the international organization of socialism, an aspect of state foreign policy. Through the 1930s and the beginnings of World War II, the western powers continued to suppress socialist thought both within their borders and abroad. In this milieu, all intellectual activity within the Soviet Union, including archaeology, was forced into a marxist mold, while in the west, established scholars vilified Marx and all those who advocated marxism.

The Russian Civil War ended in 1920 with the defeat of the western-supported White forces, leaving the Bolsheviks with the chore of building socialism in a ravaged land. In 1921, Lenin initiated the New Economic Policy (NEP), which encouraged greater economic, social, cultural, and intellectual pluralism than had been allowed during the Civil War. Lenin and the left wing of the Bolshevik party grew more and more concerned that the vanguard party was becoming an entrenched bureaucracy, a new ruling class (Ray and Sundaram, 1990), and in 1922, Lenin moved against this trend. During the NEP there was a flowering of intellectual activity, social research, and culture in Russia. The agricultural economist Chayanov studied peasants in eastern Russia and formulated principles of peasant economics that Sahlins (1972) would introduce into U.S. anthropology in the 1970s. The economist Kondratief developed a theory of cyclic economic change in capitalism that Immanuel Wallerstein (1980a) would incorporate into his notion of World Systems Theory.

Lenin died in 1924, and from that year until 1929, a power struggle ensued between Stalin and Trotsky. This struggle pitted the rising bureaucratic class led by Stalin against the left communists who sought to continue the NEP and limit the authority of the party (Bettelheim, 1976). In 1929, Stalin exiled Trotsky from the Soviet Union, and in 1940, a Soviet hit-man entered the garden of his Mexico City home and crushed his skull with an axe. During the 1930s, the bureaucratic class consolidated its power under Stalin. In 1929, Stalin ended the NEP and initiated a program of industrialization funded by tribute extracted from the peasants. In 1936, Stalin instituted a series of purges, which ended any open intellectual discussion in the country. Bukharin was executed in 1938, and both Kondratieff and Chayanov died in the terror.

The world-wide depression that started in 1929 witnessed an increase in socialist action and thought throughout the world in response to both the declining economic situation and the rise of fascism in Europe. In Germany, Italy, and Spain, socialist movements were defeated, and fascist governments gained power. The Spanish Civil War of 1936 to 1939 was a focal point in this conflict, pitting German-backed fascists against Soviet-supported republicans. Socialist volunteers from many western countries joined the republican forces. In the United States and Great Britain, socialist labor movements gained increasing power, and in 1936, socialist labor unions paralyzed France in a massive strike. With World War II, Stalin first made an alliance with Hitler and later joined the Allies, and anticommunist efforts in the west went on hold.

MARXIST SCHOLARSHIP IN EASTERN EUROPE

While marxism was forged as a state ideology in Russia, a critical and creative development of marxist theory and research occurred in Eastern Europe, primarily in Germany. In this crucible, a number of scholars drew on both marxist and nonmarxist theories and ideas in their research. They demonstrated a willingness to confront marxism and even to oppose it. These were not archaeologists, but they addressed issues of long-term historical change and primitive economics that would influence western anthropological and archaeological theory in the 1960s and 1970s (Palerm, 1980:18). Among these scholars were Karl Polányi (1944) and Richard Thurnwald (1932), whose notions of primitive economics would be taken up by numerous anthropologists and archaeologists. Polányi's intellectual circle in Germany included Ernst Bloch and György Lukács. Polányi has been variously labeled as either a marxist or a nonmarxist by more recent authors (Dalton, 1961; Harris, 1968). Thurnwald drew on Engels' *The Origin of the Family, Private Property, and the State* to develop his concept of primitive economics. Karl Wittfogel (1957) was on the staff of the Frankfurt School and later wrote about the asiatic mode of production. This theory and his notion of oriental despotism and hydraulic society would influence a generation of archaeologists. Finally, Paul Kirchoff (1959), whose paper "The Principle of Clanship in Human Society" defined the opposition between egalitarian and stratified clans, would become a major figure in Mexican anthropology

(Dahlgren, 1979). American archaeologists have been greatly influenced by these scholars, but the archaeologists remain largely ignorant of the context and discourse the Eastern Europeans were a part of.

WESTERN MARXISM

Marxism faced a crisis in the years separating the First and Second World Wars. The success of the 1917 October revolution fanned the flames of left wing radicalism in Europe and the United States, but by 1921, right wing forces had quickly and brutally put them out. The world-wide revolt failed. The rise of fascism and Hitler in the late 1920s led to an increasingly reactionary working class in the core states of Europe. During the 1930s, word of Stalin's excesses leaked into Europe, and his Comintern sought to control, direct, and dictate policy to socialist parties around the world.

In this crucible a new marxism broke away from the theory of the Second International and tried to write a critique of Soviet marxism, as well as of capitalism. This western marxism was born in the 1920s, grew in the universities of Western Europe, and found a mass following in the New Left of the 1960s and early 1970s. A varied group of men forged the new theory, and they shaped it to fit their time and place. Korsch and Lukács restored Hegel to marxism and tried to wed his ideas to Lenin's. Gramsci, the only nonacademic, fought fascism in Italy, defied Stalin, and, while in prison, wrote his theory of hegemony. The Frankfurt School fled to New York City to escape German fascism and elaborated their *critical theory* while in exile. All sought to build a new vision of the social world.

This new vision began with Marx. These university professors read Marx, especially the newly issued works of the young Marx, and gave special notice to his ideas about culture, class consciousness, and subjectivity. They gave the study of Marx's ideas a new focus, turning it away from political economy to debate on the state, art, philosophy, the media, the novel, social norms, sex, and mass culture. They forged a marxist course between the classic oppositions of western thought that came closer to the poles of humanism, history, mentalism, and relativism than the Second International had. They rejected the idea of objective science, the notion that human history followed a set series of stages, the primacy of the economic base, the search for laws of motion, and true consciousness. The western marxists drew from many nonmarxist theories current in their time. The social theory of Weber and Simmel found a place in the work of Lukács (Anderson, 1976:56). The Frankfurt School worked concepts of Freud's such as eros, sublimation, and ego into their theory of the social world (Adorno, 1950; Marcuse, 1955).

Western marxism helped to usher in an antimodern intellectual milieu that grew after World War II and peaked in the late 1960s. Their desire to write a critique of both capitalism and Stalinism led them to challenge the belief in modernism and positive science that they saw at the base of both these doctrines. Marcuse (1955, 1964) denied the modernist's faith in the machine, sought to reconcile culture and nature, and became a major font of New Left ideas in the 1960s. In turning away from modernism and positive science, western marxism also left behind the pervasive faith in the future that was so much a part of Second International theory (Anderson, 1976; Gorman, 1982:259). An over-arching pessimism pervades most of western marxism, a basic doubt about our ability to know the world or to alter it for the better. Stalin, Hitler, and the atomic bomb made any faith in the future appear, at best, naive. At worst, such faith sprang from a belief in modernism and positive science, the ideology that gave birth to Stalinism, fascism, and the atomic bomb.

Lukács and Korsch

Lukács and Korsch did not wish to rewrite the theory of the Second International. In many ways, their work was an extension of the theory of Rosa Luxemburg and Lenin's *Philosophical Notebooks*. They expand the theme of human action drawn from these authors into a full-blown theory of human action based on the ideas of Hegel. The traditional theorists had, by and large, purged Hegel from marxism. Lukács and Korsch broke with these theorists by reinstating him.

György Lukács was born in Hungary in 1885, and took his university education in Germany from 1906 to 1917. He studied under Georg Simmel and Max Weber and was a close friend of Ernst Bloch and Karl Polányi. His early work used Plato, Kant, and Hegel to develop a theory of art, drama, aesthetics, and the novel. In 1918, he became an activist and leader of the communist party in Hungary and had to seek asylum in Russia following the fall of the Hungarian socialist government in 1919 (Heller, 1983). Also in 1918, he published a book of eight essays under the title of *History and Class Consciousness* (Lukács, 1971). From Russia, Bukharin condemned the book, and in a series of intellectual autodafé's, Lukács (1950, 1954) renounced the errors of his early work. Despite his recantation, these essays became the basic work of western marxism (Merquior, 1986:73).

Lukács (1971) wrote that marxism is not a set of laws that give true knowledge of the world, but a method, the dialectic. He ruled out Engels' dialectics of nature and argued for a return to Hegel (Merquior, 1986:73). He denied that the base determined the motion of history in any other epoch than the capitalist, and he asserted that the superstructure could be primary even in class societies. He dismissed Lenin's (1908) reflection theory that knowledge is but the image of reality. True theory both reflects the world and changes it and thus, theory is both knowledge and praxis, and praxis, both consciousness and action (Merquior, 1986:75). Praxis is that uniquely human ability to knowingly make and change both the world and ourselves.

Lukács thesis turned on his reading of Marx's concepts of alienation and class consciousness. To arrive at his own theory, he merged Marx with Simmel's idea of reification and Weber's notion of rationalization (Anderson, 1976:56). Lukács noted that capitalism makes human relations into things and that this leads to alienation, the result of practices and ideology that separates humans from their own works and each other. For example, all humans have the power to labor. Capitalism takes from people the means (tools and resources) they need to labor so that they must sell their labor power for wages to live. Thus, labor appears as a commodity, a thing, to be bought and sold and not as a power of each person. Such ideology is not a simple bias in the service of class interests, but rather results from the way in which class position structures and limits the mind. Lukács (1971:50–51) argued that only workers occupy a class position that permits them to see labor as a commodity and at the same time as their own life, and that only they can grasp the totality of society. Once they gain this class consciousness, it will become praxis. It will lead them to throw off their chains. The vanguard party cannot make the revolution for the workers because only the workers can have true knowledge of their conditions; they must make the revolution for themselves. Alienation severs workers one from another as they must compete with each other to sell their labor power, to get jobs, and this ideology denies them true class consciousness. Before praxis can exist, they must first be aware that they share a common bond. The cadre of the vanguard party studies theory in order to set the revolution in motion by revealing to the workers their true class consciousness (Lukács, 1971).

In the summer of 1922, Lukács met Karl Korsch. Korsch was born near Hamburg in 1886, took his Ph.D. at Jena, fled Nazi Germany during World War II, and died in the United States in 1961 (Goode, 1979). Korsch's (1970a) 1923 *Marxism and Philosophy* is often linked with Lukács *History and Class Consciousness* as one of the founding works of western marxism (Merquior, 1986:82). He read Hegel in Marx and used Fabian ideas in his work. He argued that human action and consciousness were the source of change in history, and he set aside the determinism of Engels and Lenin. Like Lukács, the party cast out Korsch for his heresy. Unlike Lukács, he never repented it, and in his last essays, he saw marxism as a broken vessel that could not be mended (Korsch, 1970b).

Neither Lukács nor Korsch built on the trends that they began, but the impact of their ideas was great. In the 1920s, both wrote articles for the journal of the Institute for Social Research in Frankfurt, and their work became a major source of inspiration for the new critical theory (Jay, 1973:4–12; Anderson, 1976:32). Lukács' (1971) book took on a new life in the 1960s, when it joined the canon of the New Left (Merquior, 1986:86).

Gramsci

While Lukács and Korsch tended to their studies in Germany, Antonio Gramsci had dropped out of the University of Turin and stood at the barricades in the

Turin revolt of 1917 (Hoare and Smith, 1971: xxxii). Of the founders of western marxism, Gramsci was the only one who came from the working class and who never became a university professor. He was born in Ales, Sardinia, on January 22, 1891, and after his father was sent to jail in 1900, his mother raised the family in dire poverty. In 1911, he won a scholarship to attend the University of Turin, and by 1913 he was active in socialist politics. In 1921, he helped start the Italian Communist Party. The fascists arrested him in 1926, and he lived all but the last two remaining years of his life in prison. He died in 1937.

While in prison, he wrote a series of essays. These hand-written notes were often read by the prison censor and smuggled out by his friends. In these essays, Gramsci laid out his theory of marxism as a "philosophy of praxis," but not as clearly as we might wish. He often wrote cryptically to pass the censor, and he wrote the essays as a series of comments on specific debates, not as a whole integrated work. Publication of the notebooks did not began until 1948 (Gramsci, 1971).

Like Lukács and Korsch, Gramsci imbued his philosophy of praxis with Hegel's dialectic (Mouffe, 1979; Merquior, 1986:93–109). He saw base and superstructure as two parts of a social unity or totality, and thus, it was silly to speak of the base determining or creating the superstructure. One could not exist without the other.

> *Since there cannot exist quantity [base] without quality [superstructure] or quality without quantity (economy without culture, practical activity without intelligence and vice versa) any opposition of the two terms is, rationally, a nonsense (Gramsci 1971:363).*

Gramsci cast off the materialism of Second International theory (Gorman, 1982). He argued that knowledge stems from the social relations of a given time and that it does not derive from matter. We need to study the observable world (matter) as the link between the way we think and the way that we organize production. Material conditions do not decide this linkage in any direct or simple way, and it is possible for two societies with the same material conditions to differ culturally. Thus, ideas create matter. For this reason, a truly objective social science cannot exist because the physical world is not directly perceived by the senses, but can only be known through the mind of the observer.

Gramsci (1971:53–120) argued that specific historical conditions call human action, symbols, and ideas into being. With this antievolutionist stance, he put aside the notion of a set series of stages in human history and the idea that forces external to the consciousness and action of people guide the motion of history. He said that marxism is true because it permits us to better understand the historical conditions of change and not because it gives us a grand scheme of change based on laws of motion.

Gramsci took a humanistic view of marxism. Once the relationship between base and superstructure is cast dialectically, then the study and understanding of the superstructure takes on an importance equal to the study of the base. In

Gramsci's hands, the superstructure became the key to social change; he devoted much of his effort to ideas about the state, culture, and civil society.

He wrote about the crises that faced Europe. He argued that capitalism in inter-war Europe had forged a superstructure that did not permit people to even realize that they were being exploited. Power lay in the superstructure and not in the base. The Tsar's power had come mainly from the base. His rule was naked for all to see. The party in Russia could, therefore, exploit the discontent over this rule and lead a *war of movement*, a violent revolt to do away with it. Such a plan of action could only fail in the west. The power of modern western capitalism lay in its hegemonic world view; this power could be challenged only via a *war of position*. The world view of the west had to be exposed and a new unity formed before people could or would act.

Gramsci took the idea of hegemony from the work of Lenin and Plekhanov, but he used the concept in a new way, making it an active force in social change (Bocock, 1986). He used the term to specify a dominant world view that permeates all facets of society from base to superstructure. It allows the ruling class to go beyond its own interests by winning the consent of a variety of allies to form a social block, and thereby to give cultural permanence to the power of the ruling class. In capitalism, where few hold hegemony over many, it not only makes might right, but also makes it common and taken for granted. Such hegemony can be upset only by forging a social block, based on active consent and a collective will, that unites the exploited groups of a society.

Gramsci set aside Kautsky's notion that an elite group of intellectuals could create a true working-class consciousness. He argued that intellectuals are social actors that work and live in a social context and that they can not detach themselves from this context to gain an objective knowledge of the social world (Gramsci, 1971:3–23). They are part and parcel of what they study. Gramsci (1971:323) felt that "all men are philosophers." All people can think and reason. He sought to wage the war of position by laying bare the hegemony of the ruling class and nourishing a new hegemony, a new social bloc among the masses.

The Frankfurt School and Critical Theory

In 1923, a new center for the study of the German labor movement, the Institute for Social Research, opened its doors in Frankfurt. Its early staff included Friedrich Pollock and Karl A. Wittfogel (Jay, 1973; Merquior, 1986:111). In 1931, a new director, Max Horkeimer, shifted the work of the institute away from the labor movement to focus on a new theory of *kulturkritik*, which would become the basis for critical theory (Horkheimer and Adorno, 1972). In 1933, the school fled the Nazis and came to New York City. After 20 years in exile, it returned to Frankfurt in the early 1950s. Critical theory had its major impact in the years after World War II, when it became the main idiom of western marxism and, later, a major force in the New Left of the 1960s (Merquior, 1986:111).[3]

None of the critical theorists were important party members or active in the labor movement. They were, by and large, part of an academic elite, and they concentrated on the study of modern art, music, literature, psychology, and law. All lived out their lives in the west. Critics have often found their work nihilistic, elitist, arcane, and filled with obscure language, but their focus on emancipation and human freedom still strikes a responsive chord in the modern world (Anderson, 1976; Held, 1980; Merquior, 1986).

Critical theory sought a theory that would emancipate people from domination, in both the forms that they saw in the modern world. Like Gramsci, the critical theorists were impressed by capitalism's ability to permeate every part of the social world and to become so commonplace that people are not even aware of its existence. They found the power of modern capitalism in the superstructure. It is an unseen part of every action, idea, and belief. They felt that the mass culture of movies, radio, television, art, books, and magazines subverted the minds of people so that they could not act on their own behalf. The left had lost ground in the west because people could not reach a true understanding of their class interests. They could not see their chains. Critical theorists also looked on the Soviet Union with dismay. They saw that Stalin had made traditional marxism into a repressive state ideology that denied individual freedom, legitimated the power of a bureaucratic elite, and lacked the active consent of the masses. It was little more than a new set of chains.

They argued that domination in the modern world grew from the twin roots of positive science and modernism that fed both capitalism and Stalinism. They felt that through *kulturkritik*, cultural criticism, they could build a truly emancipatory critical theory. They opposed this critical theory to science. Whereas science is overly empirical and leads not to knowledge, but to domination, critical theory is contemplative and gives us an understanding that frees people from the rule of a false ideology. They put aside the notion that the scientist can arrive at an objective knowledge of the world free of social or class bias. In their minds such a goal is itself a bias. They cast off modernism and the notion of progress. "No universal history leads from savagery to humanitarianism, but there is one leading from the slingshot to the atomic bomb" (Horkeimer and Adorno, 1972:320).

They used the logic of Hegel's dialectic to build their theory. This logic is antireductionist. It denies that the base can decide the superstructure, since one cannot exist in the absence of the other. We must study the social world as a whole, not as parts. Matter cannot determine consciousness, because people can know matter only through their minds. Matter cannot, in any simple way, cause action. Humans are knowing actors; they must think before they act; and in the end, human action, not natural laws, determines the motion of history.

Critical theory stands on two ideas, ideology and domination. The Frankfurt

School's notion of ideology rests on an analogy between psychoanalysis and social theory that talks of *collective representations* in groups, as if they were the same as the psyche of individuals (Geuss, 1981:19–20). An ideology is a system of beliefs and ideas that people accept without being able to state the reasons why they accept them (Habermas, 1971:311). It is a *socially necessary illusion* (Geuss, 1981:15). Such a system serves to legitimate or extend domination, that is, the ability of one group in a society to rule over another (Habermas, 1974:19). Ideology does not come just from capitalism, but rather, exists in all social forms, even marxism. Ideology springs from the polarization of subject and object and can be overthrown only by laying bare the subverting myths of a culture.

Both positivism and traditional marxism split the subject from the object, and for this reason, they must both lead to domination.[4] They place scientists outside of the social world they study and argue that their method allows the scientist to make objective observations about that world, free of their own social role or context. They treat people as objects to be studied and not as subjects that take action. Scientists judge their statements by how well they fit the observable social world, and because they do not look at their own place in that world, they can only rationalize and justify human interests. This theory is instrumentalist. People use it to pursue their chosen ends, to gain power over what they study. Such theory gives those in power tools to hold sway over nature and people.

Critical theories unite the subject and the object as parts in a single whole (Adorno, 1973b; Geuss, 1981:55). In critical theory, scientists are both subjects that study the social world, and objects, part of the social world that they study. The people they study also embody these two poles. They are at once the objects of study and the subjects that make history. Most important, all people contemplate (study) their own action in terms of their own chosen ends; their behavior (praxis) flows from the same duality of thought and action as the behavior of the scientist. No theory can give the scientist a privileged knowledge of the social world, not privileged by a lack of bias or privileged in that it grants its proponents an exclusive access to truth. Knowledge cannot be free of bias because scholars are part of what they study, and the objects of study, humans, engage in the same process of understanding that the scholar does.

Critical theories seek to strip the power from ruling ideas. They run close behind them to reveal their tracks and expose their origin. Critical theories look at the observable social world of institutions and practices, but they also ask about social knowledge. Where does it come from, and whose interests does it serve? A critical theory can never be universal or neutral (Geuss, 1981). It can speak only to a specific time and place, and it cannot transcend the social context of its making. It must fit the observable social world, but we cannot judge it solely by this fit. The test of a critical theory is in its power for consciousness raising. If the theory reveals to people a new understanding of their domination, and they act on that understanding to resist that domination, then their action verifies the theory.

Critical theory breaks from prior marxist theory. It bears a crushing burden of pessimism that sets it off from the ever-present optimism of the Second International (Anderson, 1976:88–89). The Frankfurt School held little faith in the working class. In Europe, labor had joined the fascist cause. In the United States, labor had sold out for cars, houses, and radios. This lack of faith sprang from and reinforced an elitism that stains all of the Frankfurt School's work and that manifests itself in its arcane and reified language. (Anderson, 1976:53–55).

POSTWAR MARXISM

The second half of the 1940s saw a dramatic increase in the number of socialist states with the Soviet conquest of Eastern Europe, and with the success of the Chinese Revolution in Asia and the establishment of marxist states in North Korea and North Vietnam. On the international scene, the United States reacted to these advances by actively trying to subvert left-wing gains in Latin America and Asia. In part because of this U.S. pressure, there was a strong move to the right in Latin America. A military dictatorship ruled in Peru from 1948 to 1963, and in Mexico the right wing of the ruling party, dominated by northern and central industrialists, took power. In Western Europe, socialist parties gained in prestige, especially in France, because communists had made up most of the resistance movement against the Nazis during the war.

Dramatic changes also occurred in the intellectual climate of the world. Stalin died in 1953, and Nikita Khrushchev sought to reform Stalinism and create a more open intellectual climate in the Soviet Union. This shift called for a measure of objectivity in research and a greater congruency in method and approach between western and Soviet scholarship. As the intellectual climate thawed in the Soviet Union, it froze in the United States. During the 1950s, red baiting and the search for left-wing subversives culminated in McCarthyism, with many individuals hounded from their jobs and from public view. Open and public discussions of marxist ideas were actively repressed, and American academics worked in virtual ignorance of the developments in marxist theory in England, France, and the Soviet bloc.

THE NEW LEFT

The crisis of marxist theory that followed in the 1950s gave rise to a structuralist neomarxism in France and the development of a an empirical school of marxist history in England. Two major intellectual perspectives dominated French thought after the war, structuralism and marxism. Most anthropologically

trained archaeologists are familiar with French structuralism through the theory of Claude Levi Strauss. A neomarxism was also being developed in the
French universities at this time, initially with direction from Jean-Paul Sartre
(1936, 1960, 1972) and Maurice Merleau-Ponty (1947, 1955). In the 1960s these
two perspectives, structuralism and marxism, would meld in the work of Louis
Althusser (1969, 1971), Maurice Godelier (1977), and Claude Meillassoux
(1981). The English historians, including E. P. Thompson (1963, 1978), Eric
Hobsbawm (1967, 1975), Rodney Hilton (1976), and Christopher Hill (1975,
1982) developed their approach to marxism apart from, and often in opposition
to, the French.

A number of events reflected and contributed to the growing salience of
marxism in the 1960s. In 1959 the Cuban Revolution occurred, installing the
first marxist regime in Latin America. This revolution was just one of many that
began in reaction to right-wing domination in Latin America, and they would
continue through the successful Nicaraguan revolution in 1979. In the United
States, the Viet Nam war divided the nation and radicalized a generation of
students. In Europe many established and splinter left-wing parties moved away
from an association with the Soviet Union to an independent Eurocommunism.

The New Left of the 1960s would draw on neomarxism and the works of
Lukás and the Frankfurt School to build theory around the notion of freeing the
individual from oppression – cultural, political, and economic. Unlike earlier
marxist movements that were built with workers, the highly intellectualized
New Left found most of its adherents among students. The New Left as a
world-wide movement peaked in 1968, and a number of events mark this crest.
In the United States, thousands of demonstrators besieged the Democratic
convention in Chicago, and although the country grew increasingly disen-
chanted with the Viet Nam war, it also elected Richard Nixon to two terms on
law-and-order platforms. In Mexico the student movement staged a giant rally
in Tlatelolco Plaza in Mexico City; the army opened fire on the plaza, killing
300 to 500 people. In May of 1968, French students and workers staged a
massive nation-wide strike that eventually fell apart, as a long-term alliance
could not be formed. The Soviet Union invaded Czechoslovakia in 1968 to put
down the Prague Spring, an attempt to reform party socialism by giving more
freedom to the individual and allowing greater pluralism.

Repression of leftist thought in Latin America grew with the 1973 assassina-
tion of Salvadore Allende, the elected socialist president of Chile, in a CIA-
backed coup. In many nations of Latin America, such as Argentina, El Salvador,
and Guatemala, socialists had to go into exile or underground. In other countries, such as Mexico and Peru, they had to restrict their activities to the universities. In every country of Latin America during the 1970s, right-wing death
squads kidnapped leftist activists. Many were simply killed and others became
desaparecidos (disappeared ones), never to be heard of again.

The New Left set in motion a fresh climate of intellectual debate in the world. In the late 1960s and through the 1970s, marxism became admissible on U.S. and British campuses. French structural marxism became popular in U.S. and British universities and was followed in the 1970s by a revival of interest in Gramsci and his theories. In France, poststructuralism had its beginning, in part, from the reaction of scholars like Jacques Derrida and Michel Foucault to the failure of the New Left in May of 1968 (Poster, 1984:1). The theories of these scholars found many adherents in the U.S. and British academies in the late 1970s and into the 1980s. As intellectual debate became more open in the United States, it was restricted in the Soviet Union. In 1965 Khrushchev was deposed, and more conservative forces took charge. They maintained a pragmatic approach to science, but insisted that an iconographic respect be paid to the existence and validity of the tenets of party communism. This situation allowed empirical research to continue, but would not allow intellectuals in the Soviet Union to entertain the theories of the New Left that challenged those tenets (Feher and Markus, 1983).

Existential Marxism

Both Sartre and Merleau-Ponty sought to reinterpret Marx in terms of a philosophy of existentialism and a Hegelian dialectic. This radical break with Second International marxism focused on the individual, regarded human existence as not understandable in scientific terms, and stressed the freedom and the responsibility of the individual. It countered the party ideology that characterized so much marxism by focusing on the individual and the subjective, unique experience of each individual in any ethical, religious, or political situation. Like the Frankfurt School, their emphasis was on marxism as a form of critique that would raise the consciousness of individuals to realize their repression in a context of domination.

Existential marxism has not found a large number of adherents in archaeology with the notable exception of Susan Kus (1984). This approach to marxism did profoundly influence the work of a variety of other individuals who are now finding prominent advocates within archaeology. These individuals include Foucault, Habermas, and Althusser.

Structural Marxism

Louis Althusser set forth the theory of structural marxism in France during the 1960s as a response to critical theory and to the French existential marxism of Sartre and Merleau-Ponty. He sought to put science back into marxism and renew it as a revolutionary theory to direct human action. To purge marxism of its humanism, he threw off Hegel's dialectic and put structuralism in its stead (Althusser, 1969, 1971; Merquior, 1986:146; Gorman, 1982:138–154; James, 1984).

Althusser's theory starts with his distinction between the works of the young and the mature Marx. He faulted the humanists for paying too much attention to Marx's early philosophical tracts such as *The Economic and Philosophical Manuscripts of 1844*. Althusser noted that Marx had left these earlier musings to the "gnawing criticism of the mice" and he felt that modern scholars should do the same. Like the theorists of the Second International, he built his theory on the few works published before Marx's death, mainly *Kapital*. Althusser's focus on the mature Marx did not, however, lead him to accept a traditional marxism, which he dismissed as economism. He adopted Freud's notion of overdetermination to mean that the social world is irreducibly complex and that the process of interaction among social variables does not leave the original interacting variables unchanged. Therefore, causation is difficult, if not impossible, to see (Merquior, 1986:149). He agreed with the traditional marxist stance that the economic base is causal to social change in the last instance, but said that in the real world the "last instance never comes" (Althusser, 1969:113).

Althusser built his theory on the idea of structure. He argues that the form of any particular society (a social formation) does not arise from an integrated center or core, but rather, from a hierarchy of structures or practices. These structures interact with each other, but they remain distinct and separate. Human actors do not create these structures, but rather, the structures shape and decide human action (Althusser and Balibar, 1970:180). People do not make history; the motion of history lies in the structures of a society. Althusser argues that social formations are made up of different levels, or types, of practice, each with its own mode of human labor. Each mode comes with its own laborers, objects of labor (raw material), means of labor (tools), and products of labor (output). He names four such modes: (1) the base or economic level, (2) the political level, (3) the ideological level, and (4) the scientific level. The base or economic level matches the usual notion of base, the political and ideological levels make up the superstructure, and the scientific level lies outside both the base and superstructure. In all cases the base level determines the shape of the social formation, but it is not always dominant. In a given case, one of the other levels may rule. The base always gives motion to history, but the other levels can decide the form of this motion.

Traditional marxism tended to see the base as a coherent integrated whole at the center of the social world. Althusser, however, envisioned a more fragmented base made up of multiple modes of production. These modes of production are the different economic forms that can exist in a base. The modes that make up a social formation articulate with each other, but each is a discrete entity. All modes of production have their own means (tools and techniques) for transforming nature (for making things), and their own social relations to organize work and the distribution of the product. Each is a whole. The form and interaction of the modes of production that make up the base decide which level of practice (base, political, ideological, or scientific) will dominate in a specific social case.

The varied levels and modes that make up a social formation do not always fit together well; contradictions arise between them. Two modes of production may need the same workers at the same time of year. A political system of feudal estates may conflict with the need for free labor to serve the looms and mills. The dynamic motion of history resides in these structural contradictions; they would shred the social fabric, except for the mediation of ideology. When the ideology fails to mediate, revolutionary change occurs, and new social formations and modes of production come into being.

In this theory, ideology is a set of beliefs needed to adapt or to socialize people to a society (Althusser, 1971:153). In specific ideologies, this function is overdetermined to create a false consciousness that hides the real nature of social relations from the people of that society. We cannot do away with ideology. It must exist for humans to become social beings. It shapes people to accept their role within the social form.

Althusser sets science apart from ideology. By removing science from ideology, he allows that the structural marxists may come to a true knowledge of the social world that transcends their place in that world. He rejects Hegel's claim for the unity of subject and object (Althusser and Balibar, 1970:40, 156). He argues that matter and thought are distinct and that the object of knowledge is, in fact, not the same as the real object. Scientists produce knowledge through theory, apart from matter, and then use this knowledge to understand the world and to direct human action in that world.

Althusserian structural marxism gained great popularity in Great Britain in the 1970s (Hindess and Hirst, 1975). It appealed to scholars who sought a radical, rigorous science of society, but could no longer accept traditional, Second International theory. In this context, during the late 1970s, there occurred a vigorous debate between English structuralists and an already established English tradition of marxist history. By the end of the 1970s, many of its advocates were looking for ways to retain the rigor of structuralism but include some meaningful notion of human agency in their theory (Hindess and Hirst, 1978).

The English Historians

In 1946, a British economist, Maurice Dobb, published a marxist interpretation of the transition from feudalism to capitalism, *Studies in the Development of Capitalism*. This work was largely ignored by established British historians, in part because of hostility toward marxist ideas and in part because it did not fit the highly empirical, descriptive approach to history popular in Britain at that time (Hilton, 1976:10). The book was critiqued by an American economist Paul

Sweezy (1950) in the journal *Science and Society*. A spirited debate followed in the pages of this journal and elsewhere (see Hilton, 1976). One of the consequences of this debate was the development of a marxist historiography in England, which sought to link historical research and the evaluation of broader theoretical propositions about the nature of social change. A descriptively rich study of specific cases marks the work of all these historians. All put the relationship of class to culture at the center of their study. The most well known of these authors is E. P. Thompson.

E. P. Thompson (1963, 1978) spent most of his life studying the origin and development of the English working class. Thompson (1978) had little use for the rigorous, but highly abstract, thinking of French structuralism. In a witty and slightly sarcastic book, he laid out a classic argument against attempts to understand society in terms of abstractions, and for a study of the concrete, the real-life experience of people. He set aside the distinction between the base and superstructure as a false split that does not allow us to see both these things as different parts of a single whole. With this split removed, he then looks at the idea of class. He rejects the idea that class is a thing, a part of the machinery of a mode of production. He views class as a social and cultural phenomenon that can only exist in relation to other classes. People make class. It does not simply fall out of the technology. Thompson wants us to look at both structure and agency because agents remake structure even as that structure shapes their action.

The English historians imbued their work with a strong sense of culture, but not a sense exactly like that of American materialist cultural anthropology. For the British, culture is at the heart of the notion of consciousness, in that consciousness is both a product of the existing state of affairs and, conversely, makes it possible to alter that state of affairs. More recently this idea has been manifest in the work of Raymond Williams (1973, 1990), who has studied how culture and consciousness are created and transformed in specific, local cases, and how these cases fit in the larger hegemony of capitalism.

MARXISM IN A POSTMODERN WORLD

There can be no question that the twilight of the twentieth century finds marxism in crisis. Latin America has been in the grips of an economic depression through the 1980s, and as this decade drew to a close, military dictatorships founded in the 1970s yielded power to elected governments in many countries, including Peru, Argentina, and Chile. The leftist Sandanista government of Nicaragua won an election in 1984, but went down in an electoral defeat in 1990. This shift has meant greater intellectual freedom in many countries, especially Chile and Argentina, but has also been accompanied by free-market policies that have thrown Latin America open to foreign economic control, such as has not been seen since the beginning of this century. Leftists guerrillas continue to be active in a number of countries, most notably El Salvador and Peru, but generally the left has not been weaker politically since World War II. The 1980s witnessed the policies of *glasnost* and *perestroika* in the Soviet Union, which led to greater intellectual freedom and economic reform. The Soviets have given up their control of Eastern Europe, unleashing a general rejection of marxist thought in Eastern Europe. As the decade closed, the USSR appeared close to political fragmentation and economic collapse. In China, economic reform was followed by political repression and the massacre of students in Bejing in 1989. In the United States and Great Britain, the 1980s were marked by a pronounced shift to the right in terms of both politics and social policy. The strength of leftist ideas in the universities in both countries caused alarm, and there has been a massive assault on the academy. In Great Britain, this has meant reduced funding, the abolition of tenure, and a profit-motivated restructuring of the academy. In the United States, there have been reductions in student and research support, attempts to censor academic freedom by private groups such as Accuracy in Academics, and attacks on efforts to build multiculturalism in the universities through red-baiting, allusions to thought control, and mind police by groups such as the National Association of Scholars.

The last 15 years have also witnessed radical critiques of marxism, most notably from poststructuralism and feminism. These critiques share marxism's dissatisfaction with the capitalist world, but like the Frankfurt School of a generation ago, they are distressed by authoritative, party communism.

The poststructuralist critique developed in France, in large part, as a commentary on French structural marxism. As such, it is as much a critique of structuralism as marxism. The principal authors of this approach include Foucault (1979, 1984), Derrida (1978), and Bourdieu (1977). A strong anarchistic tendency characterizes all of these authors, each of whom stresses the subjective nature of knowledge claims and question the authority of the scientist as an observer. Their approach is interpretive, and emphasizes how power structures discourse and, in the end, determines what will be true. They study the world as a text with many meanings and interpretations depending on the reader. In the end they reject any totalizing world view that attempts to account for all of human experience.

The feminist critique developed in the United States in part as a result of women's experience in the New Left. Here feminists found that the proposed liberation did not include the abolition of gender inequality and that their interests were trivialized or ignored (Taylor, 1990). In the 1970s feminist authors penned a series of critiques of marxism (Sargent, 1981; MacKinnon, 1982) that culminated in Hedi Hartman's (1981) "The Unhappy Marriage of Marxism and Feminism." Marx did not focus on the relations between men and women, or on the structure of the family (Collins, 1990:10). His interpreters tended to regard women's domestic work as unproductive, and therefore as an unimportant factor in the study of social change (Conkey and Gero, 1991:100–101). Feminists argued that the marxist focus on class expressed a male bias that obscured gender inequalities. Gender was, in marxism, a historical concept, so that even as class relations changed, gender relations might stay frozen in a "natural" state (Haraway, 1991:140). In contrast, feminists have noted that the transformation of class relations that the New Left desired could be accomplished without transforming the nature of gender inequality.

Debate on marxism has continued, and has been made all the more important by the current crises. There has been a shift in the locus of theory. Whereas French scholars tended to be the most prominent in the 1950s and 1960s, the 1980s have witnessed a flowering of marxist scholarship in England and, to a much lesser extent, in the United States. This has been true in most of the humanities and social sciences, among them philosophy (Anderson, 1976, 1980, 1983; Ollman, 1976; Cohen, 1978; Sayer, 1979, 1987), history (Thompson, 1978; Hobsbawm, 1978–1982; Hobsbawm and Ranger, 1983), classics (de Ste. Croix, 1982), political science (Jessop, 1982), anthropology (Wolf, 1982; Bloch, 1985; Mintz, 1985; Roseberry, 1988), and sociology (Wallerstein, 1974, 1980a; Chase-Dunn, 1989). A number of summaries and textbooks on marxism have also come out in the last decade (Agger, 1979; Gorman, 1982; Bottomore, 1983; Merquior, 1986). Some now speak of a *postmarxism*, but the label means very different things to many different people (Merquior, 1986:192; Laclau and Mouffe, 1985; Bocock, 1986:21), and no one movement or school of thought stands out as defining the decade. There has been a continued engagement with a Second International tradition and an ongoing Hegelian tradition that builds from the work of the Frankfurt School and Gramsci.

In the Tracks of the Second International

Gerald Cohen (1978:x) has authored the most unabashed defense of "old fashioned historical materialism" to come out in recent years. He updates the traditional view with a modern style and tries to precisely define all terms and ideas. He seeks to give the theory more clarity and rigor. His view rests on a notion of the base and the superstructure as discrete but functionally related social phenomena and has become the embodiment of traditional marxism for many current critics.

Perry Anderson is best known for his avid attacks on those who would follow a winding detour from the goals of a traditional marxism. His essays have taken on the work of Gramsci, the Frankfurt School, structural marxism, and the British marxist historians (Anderson, 1976, 1977, 1980, 1983). Anderson (1976:96–106) builds his own theory on the work of Leon Trotsky. Trotsky's work appeals to Anderson, and many others in the West, because of its unique role in the growth of Second International theory. Trotsky's credentials as an orthodox marxist and a political activist are clear. He was also a pariah. Stalin exiled him from the Soviet Union and had him hunted down and killed. He had written one of the first critiques of Stalinism and had done so within the bounds of Second International theory. His work is of the Second International, but is free of the taint of Stalin. Anderson argues that Trotsky left a legacy that lies at the polar opposite of modern marxist theory in the West. Trotsky's pupils write about politics and economics and not about philosophy. Most important, this legacy calls for a unity of theory and working-class practice that Anderson argues is basic to a true marxism.

Anderson (1976:119–120) uses Second International theory critically, taking issue with some ideas of both Trotsky and Marx. He questions Trotsky's notion of permanent revolution, deeming it unproven as a general theory for all times and places. He praises Trotsky for his analysis of the fascist and bureaucratized state but notes that Trotsky did not generalize his analysis enough beyond his cases of German fascism and Stalin's Russia. Anderson (1976:114–130) also spells out three areas in which Marx's thought was "centrally uncertain." First, Marx's prophecy of a breakdown of capitalism has not come to pass. Second, Marx's labor theory of value is of little use. Finally, Marx did not build a theory of power, the state, and nationalism. Anderson (1983:98,100,104) directs us to focus on the institutionalization of power in the social world and not on how value is created.

The Belgian economist Ernst Mandel also follows in the footsteps of Leon Trotsky. His major work *Late Capitalism*, seeks to find the laws of motion in modern capitalism (Mandel, 1978). He adapts Marx's theory to the modern state of the social world. Mandel puts aside all forms of simple material determinism, among them Second International theory and French structural marxism. He argues for a dialectical method based in observations of the real world and a unity of the abstract (theory) and the concrete (history). He feels that most of western marxism fails because it does not, in fact, use a dialectical method and seeks instead to reduce the concrete to the ideal.

Two ideas lie at the core of Mandel's view. He takes from Trotsky the notion of unequal and combined development and from Kondratieff the notion that the capitalist economy is cyclic with long waves of growth and decline. This leads to a new view of the laws of motion in the modern world. The search for profit leads to, and is driven by, both uneven economic development in the world and technological innovation. This search leads to a boom-and-bust cycle. The rate of profit grows until the world economy suffers a realization crisis when production goes over demand, and the rate of profit must decline. Not all areas of the world suffer as much from the loss of profit. Some areas gain from the decline of profits in the core states and are able to grow, leading to a new pattern of unevenness and a new growth cycle. Mandel's theory shows both how capitalism is flawed and why it has been so resilient to collapse.

Immanuel Wallerstein's (1974, 1980a) *world system* theory draws on the ideas of Ernst Mandel, marxist dependency theory (Frank, 1967; Amin, 1974), and the

French *annales* school of history (Braudel, 1979, 1980). From Mandel he took the idea that the capitalist economy is driven by cycles of boom and bust; from dependency theory, the notion that the developed and underdeveloped nations of today are developmentally and systematically linked; and from the annales school, the conviction that social change is understandable only over the long *duree*, that is, periods of hundreds of years. His view shifts the focus of study from types and modes of production to types of exchange. Wallerstein sees capitalism as the production of goods for profit via market exchange and thus, makes the type of exchange the key factor that defines capitalism. This market exists in a world economy that is driven by uneven development and an international division of labor. Social change occurs as a result of alterations in the international division of labor.

Wallerstein's theory forces us to look for the causes of change in a larger world system and not in discrete nation states or societies. Wallerstein wrote his theory with a limited goal in mind. He wished to account for the origin of the modern world system. His theory has been used by some as a universal model of social change (Schneider, 1977; Kohl, 1987b; Rowlands *et al.*, 1987). Others have proposed world system theories alternative to Wallerstein's, and among these authors, Hall (1989) and Chase-Dunn (1989) have sought an active engagement with archaeologists.

Hegelian Marxism

Many modern marxists still keep Hegel's dialectic at the center of their theory and method. They tend to view Marx's concepts in cultural terms and see human action as the source of motion in history. The work of some of these individuals came to influence archaeology at the close of the 1980s. Laclau and Mouffe's (1985) Gramscian marxism has influenced a number of marxist and postprocessual archaeologists in Great Britain. In the United States, Bertell Ollman & Derek Sayer's reading of marxism as a philosophy of internal relations has influenced the work of William Marquardt (1989, in press), and provides the philosophical base for my own work.

Laclau and Mouffe (1985) try to move away from a traditional focus on the working class as the force that will transform capitalism. Rather, they start with the notion of hegemony that makes them a part of a much larger revival of Gramscian theory. Human actors make history, and hegemony is both the spur for this action and a result of it. Their book has inspired a lively debate (Geras, 1988; Mouzelis, 1988).

Laclau and Mouffe (1985) shy away from the idea of essentialist categories, that is, the idea that social categories are given in the social world and that they exist independent of both theory and the discourse or debate about them. We create social categories; we do not find them in the social world. Laclau and Mouffe argue that social categories cannot have a fixed definition because the language that we use to discuss them can never be theory-neutral. There is no way to free them from theory and use data to test whether they exist.

Laclau and Mouffe are most concerned with class, and their theory reflects the radical critiques of feminism and poststructuralism. They argue that classes are not given in the economy, but are called into being by the political action of human agents. Subordination may be political, social, and/or cultural, and it involves not just classes but also ethnic groups, women, blacks, homosexuals, and others. In the modern social world these latter groups maybe more potent agents of change than a class. Hegemony, like class, must be built, and this action begins in the realm of symbolism. Laclau and Mouffe assert that a society does not have a single hegemonic center. Instead, the connections that join groups must be constructed, articulated, and maintained. They do not automatically emerge from the mode of production. Nor does the mode of production spring from the economy; it is, rather, of the symbolic realm, a conceptual, social construct that originates in beliefs such as private property. The groups that form a society are also constructed in the symbolic realm. This theory makes the symbolic realm the main locus of struggle for social change.

The work of Bertell Ollman meshes with the legacy of western marxism, but he does not appeal directly to the theorists of that tradition or identify his work with it. Ollman begins with Marx. He retains a grounding in material relations that has been lost or down-played in the work of many modern theorists. He seeks a theory of internal relations that gives weight to both the ideal and the real.

Ollman's major work is his study of alienation (Ollman, 1976). He begins his book with one of the most lucid discussions of Marx's dialectic that is available in English. Ollman argues that Marx did not give his terms a simple direct meaning. Marx's use of terms directly reflects his dialectical view of reality; that is, he saw the world in terms of relations and not in terms of things. Such relations are not fixed, but are in constant flux. We can only imperfectly reduce relations to words because our terms (value, master, state) refer only to the observable things that result from relations. Our terms hide more than they reveal. Different relations may lead to observable things that seem the same, so that the meaning of a term must vary to fit the actual set of relations present in the case.

Ollman (1976) argues that it is people who make history, people who struggle in class conflict, people who sell their labor, and people who buy it. The human agent gives motion to social change. A universal human nature or set of wants does not decide the action of these agents, but rather biology and the circumstances of individuals' lives forge human nature and wants. Ollman sees Marx's notion of alienation as the key to understanding the nature of people in capitalism. Alienation refers to the separation of humans from their own work and from each other, a split that transforms the individual into an abstraction.

Derek Sayer (1987) takes much from Ollman, but he, also, reads Marx anew.

Like Ollman, he sees Marx's theory as one of internal relations, and he also accepts the situational nature of Marx's concepts and terms. He emphasizes the *historicity* of these concepts. They do not exist external to the social relations that they express, but rather they are historical and transitory products that refer to different things in different times and places. There is no place for us to stand outside of our social context and use concepts that are not part of the social reality they seek to depict.

Sayer applies this view of Marx's terms to three of the key concepts of marxism: (1) forces of production, (2) relations of production, and (3) superstructure. Each of these is traditionally defined as a distinct level of the social world. Sayer argues that they are, in fact, different facets of the same social totality. The forces are people's capabilities for work, the relations are the social relations in which people produce, and the superstructure is the form that the base (the forces and relations) assumes in people's consciousness.

If we sunder the unity of these ideas, we reify them. We make them into things, or fetishes, that exist outside of any real context. Such fetishized ideas can never give us good insight into a noncapitalist social world because they allow us to think of that social world only in capitalist terms. They impose capitalist forms on that world and mask the relations that do exist. For example, it is quite meaningless to single out *noneconomic institutions* (for example a church, a women's soldality, or an age grade) as the superstructure in social and historical cases "where a clearly isolatable 'economy' itself does not exist" (Sayer, 1987:143). Such ideas also lead us to false understandings of capitalism. They suggest we can transform capitalism by seizing and using the social forms (the state, law, etc.) we see rather than by transforming the relations that create these forms.

With a theory of internal relations, many of the classic oppositions of Western thought melt away. It keeps the production and reproduction of real life at the center of our study, but it leads us also to look critically at our own role in that study. By using context-defined general categories, we can let the real world into our study; we do not simply create our study in our mind. This is an empirical approach but not an empiricist one. It does not separate the object from the subject; it admits that we are part of what we study and that the subjects of our study are the active agents that make history. It does not give us true knowledge. Our knowledge of the social world is the complex result of a dialectical interplay between what we bring to that study, both our social context and theory, and the actions of the people that we study.

Either modern marxist theory is in utter disarray, adrift in a chaotic sea of contradictory ideas, or it is alive with vigorous debate, a crucible from which we can draw an infinity of fresh insights. If we desire marxism to be an instrumentalist theory that directs our action, then the variety of opinion and debate in marxism can be only dangerous chaos. If, on the other hand, we see marxism as part of the world that we study, then it must also be a locus of struggle, of debate. This debate affects our actions; we are part of it. This debate is a dialectical interplay of ideas and actions that structures our knowledge of the social world and our actions in that world, even as our actions and ideas transform the debate and the world. It generates new knowledge of the world and gives us new insight into how to act in that world. Without the variety of views and debate, marxism would cease to be a productive way to know the social world or a basis for critical action. Archaeology's dialogue with marxism has been conducted in the context of this debate.

ENDNOTES

1. One thing that should be clear in this discussion is that dialectical change does not automatically lead to a more humane or "better" theory, action, or social life. Praxis is made by people, and they may succeed or fail in making a more humane world.

2. Feminist writers have come to a similar appreciation of the importance of dialectical tensions for scholarship, critique, and action. These are discussed for an archaeological audience by Gero and Conkey (1991) and Wylie (1991).

3. Critical theory has meant different things to its varied adherents (Held, 1980). The staff of the Frankfurt School, among them Max Horkheimer (1947, 1974), Theodor Adorno (1973a, 1973b), Erich Fromm (1942, 1961), and Herbert Marcuse (1955, 1964, 1979), formed the core of the theory, but an outer circle of the school included scholars like Walter Benjamin (1979). In recent years Jürgen Habermas (1974, 1976, 1984) has kept critical theory alive and sought to shape it to his own image.

4. The use of the terms *subject* and *object* in these debates is often confusing. This is because in common usage, a person who is part of a scientific experiment is called a subject. The terms are used in this debate with the same meaning that they have in a sentence. In a sentence the subject is the noun that refers to the performer of action and the object the noun that refers to what is acted on.

CHAPTER 3

Archaeology and Marxism

It is only since the mid-1970s that an appreciable number of Western archaeologists have stated their interest in Marxist theory. There have of course been many other "closet" or "hidden" Marxists in archaeology: those using theories clearly derived from Marxism but who have chosen not to identify the source of their ideas. It is not my intention to "expose" these authors but included among their number are several of the better-known archaeologists of the 1960s and 1970s.

(Spriggs, 1984:7)

The history of marxism in Anglo-American archaeology is a hidden one (Gilman, 1989). For most of the last 100 years, U.S. intellectuals who advocated marxist ideas in any field have been discriminated against, and only in the 1910s, the 1930s, and the late 1960s to 1970s have such ideas been well received. In this context it is important to distinguish between the influence of marxist views in archaeology and the presence of marxism as a philosophical system (Trigger, 1985a:122). Spriggs (1984:7) correctly points out that, with the noteworthy exception of V. Gordon Childe, western archaeologists have explicitly used marxism as a philosophical system only in the last decade and a half. Marxist views have, however, been around in western archaeology for most of the last 75 years, and have had a profound impact on the field. In examining the development of these views and the relationship of this development to the growth of marxism, it is not my intent to expose or label some of the better-known archaeologists of the past as marxist, but rather to ask how the social and political contexts of archaeology affected the use of marxist thought in archaeology. This process is explored by an examining Soviet and Latin American archaeologies as comparative cases to the Anglo-American.[1]

WRITING HISTORIES OF ARCHAEOLOGY

In the second edition of their book *A History of American Archaeology*, Willey and Sabloff (1980:189) summarize the last 50 years of American archaeology in a figure that suggests a Greek column. The base of the column is formed by a series of individuals who provided "major intellectual stimuli," C. Kluckholm, L. White, Kroeber, and J. H. Steward. From the center of this base, a broad column of "dominant trends" rises to the top of the figure. Along the lower half of the column, various secondary trends arise as thin lines from the base and point upward; all of these minority lines converge on L. R. Binford in the center of the column and join the dominant trend in a processual archaeology. This Greek-column view of intellectual history treats the development of archaeology as an evolutionary progression, whereby new ideas emerge and bad ideas are thrown on the ash heap of history. The Greek-column view assumes that theory production is cumulative (our theory gets better and better) and linear. As Patterson (1986:7) notes, "to present the history of archaeology as cumulative and linear is to support one group at the expense of another." Authors usually build the Greek column around a core of ideas and theories that forms their own position and point it toward future directions that they wish to pursue. The Greek column sanitizes the intellectual history by eliminating or co-opting trends that do not fit in the column, celebrates the achievements of the elite of the discipline, and ignores the social and political contexts of that history (Patterson, 1986; Pinsky, 1989; Trigger, 1989a; Gero, 1989).

Marxist scholars in archaeology, most notably Bruce Trigger (1989a) and Thomas Patterson (1986), have challenged the Greek-column account of intellectual history. They write histories of archaeology that are not about the march of science, but instead examine archaeology as a practice situated in social and political contexts. They recognize the cyclic or spiraling nature of theory, that theory is not cumulative. Rather, theory is a dialogue that returns to the same concerns over and over again, but with a slightly different perspective each time, remade in terms of ongoing theoretical debate and the social context of that debate (Wolf, 1987:113). The knowledge that we make through this dialogue is cumulative, but the dialogue itself meets no resolution. My analysis follows the path laid out by these scholars and looks at a minority trend that lies hidden behind Willey and Sabloff's Greek column.

A reader of *A History of American Archaeology* would have to assume that marxism had no role in the development of American archaeology.[2] Willey and Sabloff mention marxism but once, in reference to Morris Opler's red-baiting attack on Betty Meggers in the 1950s (Willey and Sabloff 1980:184). But a close examination of their Greek column figure reveals an interesting oddity (Willey and Sabloff, 1980:182, Fig. 120). On the lower half of the figure, and to the left of the column, float three boxes, not anchored to the major intellectual figures at the base of the column. These three hovering boxes contain five names, Childe and Wittfogel each in a small box with arrows pointing to the larger box with Armillas, Sanders, Palerm, and Wolf. With the possible exception of Sanders,[3] a major intellectual stimulus for these scholars is Karl Marx.

The influences of marxism are not new in western archaeology, but they have rarely been overt, so that there are no straight lines of development leading to one or more marxist archaeologies in the west. The connections between marxism and western archaeology are complex, often disguised, and subject to multiple interpretations. An explicit engagement with marxist theory is a recent phenomenon that involves a minority of archaeologists in the west, but despite the newness of this engagement, most of the major, current, theoretical trends in marxism can be found in western archaeology.

It has long been recognized that strong regional traditions structure how archaeology is done in the world (Trigger, 1989a:8–9). In addition, Trigger (1984) defines three different orientations to archaeology that cross-cut regional traditions: (1) nationalistic archaeology that seeks to establish and enhance claims of a national heritage; (2) colonialist archaeology that seeks to downplay or denigrate the heritage of conquered peoples; and (3) imperialist archaeology in the power centers of the world that seeks world-wide generalizations and processes. The practice of archaeology is structured both by regional traditions and by the orientation of the local archaeology. The influence of marxism on archaeology depends in part on these factors, but more important, it is contingent on the institutional setting of archaeology, the political salience of the academy in national life, and the role of marxism and left political forces in the politics of the nation. In order to examine the role of these factors in the relationship between marxism and archaeology, I shall consider three contexts: (1) Soviet archaeology in the USSR, (2) Latin American archaeology, looking in most detail at archaeological practice in Mexico and Peru, and (3) Anglo-American archaeology, the archaeology of the United States, Great Britain, Canada, and Australia.

A number of archaeologists have argued that modern archaeology is primarily a middle-class pursuit and that it most commonly expresses the ideology of that class (Trigger, 1989a:15; Patterson, 1986; Kristiansen, 1981). By *middle class*, these marxist scholars do not mean the common U.S. equation of the term with middle income. In marxist usage, the middle class are those individuals that stand between the owners of the means of production and the workers. These are the managers, administrators, professionals, and small-business owners. Marxist scholars have sought to understand the development of archaeology in terms of the development of middle-class ideology and the conflict between different fractions of that class in this development. In looking at the influence of marxism on archaeology in the Soviet, Latin American, and Anglo-American settings, we can clearly see the linkage between the middle class and archaeology, but the relationship between this class, the academy, and marxism is very different in each case. In the United States, Great Britain, and Latin America, marxist theory challenges middle-class ideology and privilege, and it is exposed by individuals that are alienated from their class position.[4] The practice of these individuals differs between the United States and Great Britain, and Latin America because in the Anglo-American setting, academics are largely isolated from participation in practical politics, while in Latin America, academics play a central role in the political life of each nation.[5] In the Soviet Union, the state bureaucracy stands in the same structural position as the middle class does in the West; it controls the productive forces of the country and directs the activities of the working class (Bettelheim, 1976; Ray and Sundaram, 1990). Arguably, this is the class position of Soviet archaeological practice. As is true of western middle classes, regionally and functionally based factions exist within this class, but my concern in this chapter is not with the internal variability of Soviet archaeology, but with a comparison of it to marxism in western archaeology. A major factor that separates Soviet uses of marxism in archaeology from western uses is that in the Soviet Union, the theory has been constructed to support the class interests of the archaeologist, while in the West, the theory challenges those interests.

In the previous chapter, I identified a rough, heuristic periodization for the development of marxist theory, based on alternating periods of salience, crises, and resistance (1900–1919 salience, 1919–1920 crises, 1930s salience, 1950s resistance, 1960s–mid-1970s salience, late 1970s crises, 1980s–present resistance). In a broad sense, these fluctuations have structured archaeology's dialogue with marxism. The application of marxism to western archaeology has come primarily after periods of salience, when resistance to these ideas has prevented or limited political action. This dialogue has played itself out differently in each region because each region stands in a separate relationship to the rest of the world; marxism occupies a different place in the social life of each region; and because each region has its own tradition of archaeology.

SOVIET ARCHAEOLOGY

In 1918, the Soviet Union became the first marxist state in the world. In the context of this state, Soviet archaeology has been highly centralized with planned, long-term excavations that span decades at individual sites. By 1945, a distinctive Soviet archaeology developed, which dogmatically adhered to the evolutionary schemes of Stalinism. Following World War II, and especially after the death of Stalin, archaeologists were given greater freedom to pursue their research as long as they paid homage to a marxist theory of social evolution. Like U.S. archaeology, Soviet archaeology grew greatly in the 1960s and 1970s and become more methodologically and technically sophisticated. In the last 5 years, the turmoil and general decentralization in the Soviet Union has been reflected by a greater decentralization of archaeology and a theoretical challenging of marxist theory in archaeology.

The Birth of Soviet Archaeology to 1945

Russian archaeology had been institutionalized in the middle of the nineteenth century with the establishment of an Imperial Archaeological Commission in

Saint Petersburg, and subsequently, a regional structure for research. (Miller, 1956). Initially, most archaeologists worked on Classical sites in the Black Sea and Siberian tombs or kurgans, as agents of the imperial government (Soffer, 1983:92). By the end of the century, interest had expanded to include prehistoric sites and medieval Slavic sites. This paleolithic archaeology was commonly associated with more radical anti-imperial elements of Russian society (Soffer, 1983:93). In the 1980s, the founder of Russian paleolithic archaeology, F. K. Volkov, was briefly exiled for his political activities. At the beginning of the century there were two major theoretical camps within Russian archaeology: (1) the formalists, like Vasily Gorodtsov and the Swede Oscar Montelius, who were mainly concerned with building typologies and chronology, and (2) an empirical school led by Aleksander Spitsyn and Aleksandr Miller, that stressed the detailed and accurate description of artifacts (Miller, 1956). Little or no archaeology was carried on during World War I or the Civil War that followed.

In 1919, the Bolsheviks reorganized the Imperial Archaeological Commission and it eventually became the State Academy for the History of Material Culture (GAIMK) (Trigger, 1989a:212). Nikioay Marr, a linguist with archaeological interests, was appointed as the academy's director. He believed that language changed in response to social organization, so that linguistic variation reflected the different stages of evolution occupied by various societies. This theory was not derived from Marx, but fit roughly with Second International notions of evolutionary change. A student of Volkov, P. P. Efimenko, headed the paleontological section of the GAIMK, and he made Leningrad the center for paleolithic research in the Soviet Union. In the mid-1920s, a communist party-controlled archaeological center was organized in Moscow as the Archaeology section of the Russian Association of Scientific Institutes of the Social Sciences (Shapiro, 1982:89), and also in the 1920s, many regional science organizations (including an archaeological component) sprang up around the country (Miller, 1956:44–45).

During the New Economic Policy (NEP), archaeology remained in the hands of prerevolutionary scholars. The state supported a great deal of archaeological work with an emphasis on formal typology, diffusion, and migration. Russian archaeologists maintained contacts with the rest of the European archaeological community, and the theory of archaeology still reflected European trends. Much of this work was published in a Finnish journal *Eurasia Septentrionalis Antiqua*, edited by A. M. Tallgren. Classical archaeology remained highly historical, while paleolithic archaeology remained closely tied to the natural sciences and to Darwinian notions of biological evolution (Soffer, 1983:93). Archaeology appears to have been outside the intellectual ferment of the NEP and little changed from its prerevolutionary practice (Trigger, 1989a:216).

After 1924, intellectuals allied with Stalinist forces demanded a cultural revolution to bring all scientific, artistic, and scholarly work in Russia into line with party discipline. Scholars who were not party members were purged and at least 20 archaeologists were exiled, including Aleksandr Miller. Vasily Gorodtsov was dismissed from his post. The party disbanded the regional scientific organizations and brought the Moscow archaeology center under the control of the Leningrad state academy. From this point on, archaeological research in Russia would be centrally organized and directed. In Leningrad, Vladislav I. Ravdonikas led the intellectual attack on traditional archaeology with the support of A. V. Artsikhovski in Moscow. They dismissed the formalist as making fetishes of artifacts and as practicing bourgeois idealism. They and their students laid out a new program that would use archaeological data to illustrate the laws and regularities of historical process to prove the accuracy of an evolutionary reading of Marx, in the style of Plekhanov, Bukharin, and Stalin. They sought to explain, in Stalinist terms, what had happened in prehistory (Bulkin *et al.*, 1982:275).

They shifted the focus of research away from typology, chronology, diffusion, and migration to the study of prehistoric social organization and social change (Trigger, 1989a:223–228). In some ways this shift parallels the shift in U.S. archaeology that came 40 years later with the New Archaeology (Klejn, 1977). Excavations increasingly sought to reveal the lives of ordinary people and the digging of dwellings became, for the first time in Europe, a major thrust of work. These archaeologists adopted an excavation strategy of opening up massive horizontal exposures exposing, for the first time, entire Neolithic villages. Researchers even sought to define matrilocal residence patterns using ceramics, and fingerprints on sherds were examined to argue for female production of pottery (Childe, 1944:6).

Theoretical positions favored by individuals in power gained an unquestionable status in archaeological research. Stalin (1938:34) formalized the notion of evolutionary stages in his book *Dialectical and Historical Materialism* in terms of five fixed, unilineal stages of development: primitive communal, slave, feudal, capitalist, and socialist. The asiatic mode of production that figured prominently in much of Marx's writings was dropped and could not be discussed in scholarly debate. These stages were *dogmatized* in the mid-1930s (Klejn, 1977:12). The Soviet archaeologist P. P. Efimenko proposed replacing the standard European three-age system (stone, bronze, and iron) with pre-clan, gentile, and class formations (Kohl, 1983:26). He interpreted *long houses* excavated at several Upper Paleolithic sites as evidence of matrilineal clans, whereas contemporary small round houses found at other sites were discounted (Soffer, 1983:95). All archaeological research had to be fitted within this theory of stages. As director of the state academy, Marr had great power, and his linguistic theories were unchallenged until Stalin publicly rejected them many years after Marr's death. Marr saw linguistic variation as a manifestation of unilineal evolution, and therefore, discouraged the study of ethnic movements and boundaries in both linguistics and archaeology. All developments were seen as having been in place, and evolutionary in nature.

During Stalin's reign, severe constraints were placed on archaeological research, but archaeologists were able to carry on original and important studies within these bounds (Trigger, 1989a:227). These constraints made Soviet archaeology unique in the world, and Soviet archaeologists addressed issues that western archaeologists would, by and large, not consider until 30 years later. The knowledge they created of Russian prehistory was different from that of western archaeologists. The prehistories that they wrote emphasized internal social dynamics, were optimistic about human creativity, and explicitly rejected racism (Trigger, 1989a:227). Paleolithic archaeology offered a potential refuge from ideological constraints because Marx and Engels had paid the least attention to primitive society; researchers could be daring and foster some theory in this area (Soffer, 1983:96). Large amounts of research were done with over 8,000 archaeological monographs written between 1919 and 1940, and an average of 300 archaeological expeditions were put in the field each year during that time (Bulkin *et al.*, 1982:276). There was also change in theoretical direction. In the late 1930s, with the threat of German aggression looming from the West, a new interest developed in ethnogenesis, that is, how ethnic groups are formed and change (Miller, 1956:135–144; Bulkin *et al.*, 1982:277).

Soviet Archaeology after World War II (1945–1960)

Soviet archaeology, like the rest of Soviet society, suffered great losses during World War II. Leningrad, where the state academy was located, suffered from one of the most intense battles of the war and a prolonged siege. Several leading archaeologists were killed in action or died of starvation in Leningrad (Bulkin *et al.*, 1982:291). After the war, there was a massive increase in the amount of work done, so that by 1955 there were over 500 projects a year, and publication rates had increased by 1.5 times the pre-war level (Bulkin *et al.*, 1982:277). With the loosening of the intellectual climate under Kruschev, archaeologists could make more use of foreign sources and theories. As Bulkin *et al.* (1982:278) discuss, this did not "mean the end of ideological struggle, it gives it new character. It becomes less sharp in form but more profound in substance."

In the postwar period, the origin of human beings (anthropogenesis) and the origin of societies (ethnogenesis) became important areas of research. The study of human origins drew on Engel's idea that labor played a decisive role in the evolution of humanness (Engels, 1895; Bromlei and Pershits, 1985; Semenov, 1985). These theories shared much in common with the tool-making theories of human origins popular in the United States at about the same time, probably reflecting a common origin in the theories of Darwin (Washburn and Lancaster, 1968). The study of ethnogenesis that began in the late 1930s intensified after the war. This interest reflected a greater interest in history and a more multi-pathed view of evolution that became popular in these years (Bulkin *et al.*, 1982). Other trends also continued with the publication in the late 1940s of S. P. Tolstoff's settlement pattern studies from the 1930s.

The postwar years also saw an increased interest in the study of technology. S. A. Semenov's (1964) *Prehistoric Technology* was the fruit of this emphasis and has become, in the West, the best known study of Soviet archaeology. This pioneering research on lithic use wear was first published in Russian in 1957. Extensive studies of irrigation networks in Soviet central Asia that began in the 1930s were continued (Trigger, 1989a:236). There was also great interest in developing various dating techniques such as ^{14}C and archaeomagnetism, and in material characterization techniques such as x-ray diffraction and spectrographic analysis (Bulkin *et al.*, 1982:283).

Soviet Archaeology since 1960

Developments in Soviet archaeology since 1960 have paralleled the New Archaeology in many ways, but also differ significantly from the western tradition (Klejn, 1977). This convergence was largely a result of the New Archaeology that moved U.S. archaeology closer to the theoretical and empirical concerns that had dominated in the Soviet Union for 3 decades. This movement was, at least in part, a consequence of the marxist influences on the materialist theory of the New Archaeology. Similarities included an increased interest in production, that is, both the technology and social organization necessary for people to make a living, which was seen as a primary motor of social change and cultural evolution (Klejn, 1977:13). The differences that separated these two traditions remained, however, as marked as the similarities. Soviet archaeology lacked the New Archaeology's hypotheticodeductive method, simplistic notion of material causality, and environmental determinism. It included a theory of internal causes for change through contradictions, and the idea that social change is law governed and chance formed (Bulkin *et al.*, 1982:279). It has also remained firmly wedded to history.

Bulkin *et al.* (1982:279) identify seven major trends in Soviet archaeology from 1960 to the 1980s. These trends can be gathered into two groups, those that Bulkin and his co-authors consider established trends versus those that they consider innovative trends. This interpretation of trends in Soviet archaeology is useful, but it should be recognized that it represents the view of a specific theoretical community within Soviet archaeology.

The established group includes three trends that seek a theoretical foundation for archaeology from outside of archaeology — from history, linguistics, or sociology. Some Soviet archaeologists see "archaeology as history armed with a spade," and they are oriented toward reconstructing the historical past through involvement with history, art, folklore, and linguistics (Bulkin *et al.*, 1982:279). These archaeologists commonly use archaeology to reconstruct regional histories of people within the USSR. Interest continued is archaeological ethnogenesis, that is, research on the ethnic origins of various groups, and this study is linked to historical linguistics. These authors tend to equate archaeological assemblages with ethnic groups. The third trend draws on the theory of sociology. It is the aspect of Soviet archaeology most like the New Archaeology because it regards society as a system and assumes that patterning in the archaeological record reflects the systemic organization of society.

The trends that Bulkin *et al.* (1982) regard as innovative prefer to build uniquely archaeological methods and theories. Descriptive archaeology focuses on the characterization of the archaeological record, with an emphasis on issues of classification, typology, and seriation. It seeks a rigorous methodology for describing archaeological materials. A trend that first appeared is archaeotechnology, with an emphasis on the technical and functional analysis of materials. In the archaeological ecology trend "ancient societies and the sum of their artifacts are considered as a single system that was once in dynamic interaction with its environment" (Bulkin *et al.*, 1982:283). The emphasis of this group begins with social production rather than the environment as the starting point of analysis. Finally, the trend with which Bulkin *et al.* (1982) identify their own work is theoretical archaeology. They stress the uniqueness of archaeological data and seek to build both a unique methodology and a theory of archaeology.

Western archaeologists tend to dismiss Soviet archaeology as dogmatic and ideological even in the face of conflicting empirical evidence. What is most striking about Soviet archaeology in the last two decades is the parallels between it and U.S. archaeology rather than the ideological differences. These parallels have several sources. As archaeologists, scholars in the USSR and in the United States face broadly similar problems in reconstructing the past from mute evidence. The two traditions also share much more in terms of social theory than Cold War rhetoric would allow us to believe. Both draw on European traditions of social thought on philosophy, language, culture, and society. There has also been a far greater exchange of ideas and theory between the marxist tradition of the Soviet Union and western social theory than those of us in the West commonly recognize.

The practice of archaeology in the Soviet Union differs from that in the United States both because of theoretical differences and because of differences in the funding and organization of research (Kohl, 1986). One of the overall results of Stalinism in the Soviet Union was a highly centralized top-down organization of all productive activities, including economic, cultural, and intellectual production. This is also the case in archaeology, in which researchers work full time at research centers, and the directors of these centers decide what projects will be done rather than a competing for grants. A boon of this system is guaranteed funding for long periods. This funding includes not only field work, but also analysis and publication support so that publication is rapid and extensive. In the USSR, excavations run for tens of years with an emphasis on the accumulation of massive amounts of information and not on flashy studies based on quick results. Both this guarantee of secure funding and an emphasis on the total reconstruction of society lead to broad horizontal excavations that uncover entire sites or large portions of sites. This centralization and lack of competition for funds tends to make interpretation conservative. It is easier to productively imitate older and higher-placed scholars than to innovate. This contrasts markedly with the United States and Britain, where innovation seems to often be valued above serious empirical work, and the field's direction is charted by a progression of Young Turks.

The advantages of the centralized system can be seen in the work of E. N. Chernykh (n.d.). His metallurgical laboratory in Moscow has conducted decades of spectral analyses of Bronze Age artifacts from throughout the Soviet Union. The results of this work led to major re-evaluations of Bronze Age metallurgy in Europe.

At the present time, Soviet archaeology, like Soviet society as a whole, is in a state of flux. There are about 1200 professional archaeologists in the Soviet Union, and declining economic conditions are greatly hampering research (Dolitsky, 1989). The system of regional archaeological centers that all report and take direction from the Institute of the Academy of Sciences in Moscow has become more decentralized. Regional centers have been given more autonomy and freedom of action. On the down side, this means less reliable and more insecure funding for research, but on the up side, it has allowed more innovation and creative research (Philip Kohl, personal communication, 1991).

LATIN AMERICA

Archaeology in Latin America has always been heavily influenced by core state archaeologists, especially those from the United States that work in the region. This influence has never been a simple matter of Latin American archaeologists mimicking core state archaeology. Rather, Latin American archaeologists have taken an active role in formulating their own theory and practice, often in opposition to the core state archaeologies. In the early part of this century, Latin America was locked in a neocolonialism that left each state nominally, politically independent yet economically under the control of core states, primarily Great Britain and the United States. The first third of this century saw a widespread reaction against this neocolonialism, revolutions, and populist nationalism in many areas of Latin America. In the 1940s, conservative forces tied to core states' interests gained control of most of the countries in the region. Starting with the Cuban revolution in 1959, a wave of mainly marxist revolutions swept Latin America, and by the mid-1970s, these had been largely put down, and leftist thought and individuals were widely persecuted.[6]

The Beginnings of Archaeology in Latin America

Early Latin American archaeology was heavily influenced by U.S. practitioners. Americans helped to establish the institutional base for Latin American archaeology, especially in Mexico and Peru. The major archaeologist of this period in Mexico, Manuel Gamio, trained with Boas at Columbia and later brought Boas to teach in Mexico. While in Mexico, Boas helped to found La Escuela Internaciónal de Arqueología y Entología in Mexico City and both he, and later Alfred M. Tozzer, directed the center. Alfred Kroeber (1925) did research and published on both Mexico and Peru. By the 1920s, however, distinctive national traditions of archaeology had appeared and U.S. and Latin American researchers were often at odds in how they did archaeology and interpreted the pre-Hispanic past of the region. In 1914, the Carnegie Institute began work in the Maya culture of lowland Guatemala (Bernal, 1980:173–176). These U.S. researchers argued that the Maya represented the highest level of civilization in Mesoamerica and downplayed or dismissed the importance of the highland Mexican cultures that the Mexican archaeologists studied (Patterson, 1986:12). This growing split reflected the political relationship between Latin America and the United States. After nearly 50 years of neocolonialism, that is foreign, primarily American, economic and political domination of the region, the nations of Latin America started to assert themselves. In Mexico, the revolution began in 1910, pitting nationalistic, neocolonial, worker, and peasant interests against one another. By the end of the revolution, populist nationalists had taken control of the country. In the rest of Latin America, the involvement of the United States, Great Britain, and France in World War I allowed for greater local autonomy, and a wave of nationalism swept the region, lasting until the 1930s.

A major manifestation of this nationalism in Mexico and Peru was the Indigenismo movement. Indigenismo was a romantic nationalist movement that glorified an Aztec past in Mexico and an Inka past in Peru to give a unique, indigenous identity and legitimation to the respective states. The movement was most successful in Mexico, where it continues as the cornerstone of a nationalist ideology today, and less successful in Peru, where it died out in the 1940s. In its beginnings, the movement drew on a wide variety of populist, anarchist, and socialist ideas that it mixed together to prepare a nationalistic stew.

The study of the major Aztec and earlier sites of the Valley of Mexico fit well with a nationalistic desire to glorify a pre-Hispanic past. One of the major early spokespersons for Indigenismo in Mexico was the archaeologist Manuel Gamio. He worked at Teotihuacan to make the site a focal point of national integration; he helped to make Teotihuacan into the Mexican Williamsburg. To do this, he tried to develop an archaeology that would have mass appeal (Lorenzo, 1982:199–200). He, along with Alfonso Caso and Ignacio Bernal, advocated a historical approach to archaeology that embodied anti-imperialist, socialist, and anarchist ideals (Fowler, 1987:234). This archaeology increasingly deviated from the Boasian archaeology of the United States and from the importance that U.S. researchers gave to the Maya. In the 1920s, expatriate artists Diego Rivera, David Alfaro Siqueiros, and José Clemente Orozco returned to Mexico and emblazoned the walls of Mexico with the creed of Indigenismo, often using reconstructions of ancient Indian life drawn from the archaeologists. Diego Rivera had become a marxist while studying art in France. In the 1930s, he influenced the socialist president of Mexico, Lázaro Cárdenas, to grant asylum to republican refugees from the Spanish Civil War and later to Leon Trotsky.

Indigenismo developed in Peru at about the same time. One of the major architects of the theory here was the marxist José Carlos Mariátegui (1943). He equated Indigenismo with socialism. He resurrected arguments, originally made by the marxist writer Cunov at the end of the last century, that the Inka had been a primitive socialist state. He used this reconstruction as a model for the transformation of Peru. Indigenismo in Peru was not, however, chained to Mariátegui's socialism. As in Mexico, the essentially nationalistic character of the ideology made it appropriate for a wide-based populism that could swing to either the left or the right, and primarily served to mobilize the mass of the people to support the interests of a national middle class contrary to international capitalists. The archaeologist Julio C. Tello, who would come to dominate Peruvian archaeology until the 1950s, was an early advocate of Indigenismo with strong ties to Augusto Leguía, president of Peru from 1919 to 1930. He advanced the theory that the Peruvian high civilizations appeared first in the Andes through a process of internal development. This put him at odds with the earlier theories of Max Uhle that placed the origins of Peruvian civilization on the coast and stressed the role of diffusion from the outside in this development. Uhle's collections were in Berkeley, and U.S. archaeologists, under the leadership of A. L. Kroeber, retained the temporal and spatial schemes of Uhle while forming a circle of scholarship distinct from the Peruvians, under the leadership of Tello (Patterson, 1989b). Leguía lost power in Peru as a result of the depression, and Tello found himself out of a job. In 1937, he established ties with Nelson Rockefeller, who helped him to found the Institute for Andean Research (Patterson, 1989b).

Latin American Archaeology (1945–1960)

In Latin America, the close of World War II found most of the nations of the region in the hands of repressive right-wing military regimes. These regimes were actively trying to roll back the left-wing gains of the 1930s, and marxist scholarship was limited or denied. In archaeology, there was a rapprochement between U.S. archaeology and the national traditions of Latin America.

In Mexico, U.S. researchers continued to work in the Maya lowlands, but a new generation of U.S. scholars began work in the Valley of Mexico. Among the leaders in this movement were Eric Wolf, Angel Palerm, Pedro Armillas, Pedro Carrasco, William Sanders, and Rene Millon. This led to an emphasis of cultural ecology in this region and, for U.S. advocates of the primacy of the Valley of Mexico over the lowlands, as a center of cultural development. Mexican archaeologists such as Caso and Bernal continued to investigate the great ruins of the highlands, and emphasized their place in the heritage of a Mexican national state. Bernal assumed a number of important governmental posts in this period, among them as ambassador to the United Nations and to France.

Tello died in 1946, and Peruvian archaeology became a highly contested terrain. Within Peru, Larco Hoyle, a wealthy coastal sugar plantation owner, took up and supported a theory of coastal origins for Peruvian civilization. He had read Gordon Childe's work and tried to apply Childe's notion of cultural evolution and the Neolithic Revolution to Peru (Patterson, 1989b). The Viru Valley project and Hoyle's interaction with Willey led to a cultural evolutionist perspective that understood cultural change in terms of movement through a succession of stages (Patterson, 1989b). In the late 1950s, John Rowe launched a concerted critique of the evolutionary position, arguing instead for a narrative history that replaced the evolutionary succession of stages with a purely chronological framework (Patterson, 1989b). In this atmosphere, much of the romanticism that had characterized archaeology and Indigenismo was lost, and earlier ideas, such as the Inka as a primitive socialist state, put aside.

Latin American Archaeology (1960–1980)

A self-consciously marxist archaeology in Latin America sprang from the leftist revolutionary movements of the 1960s. In Peru, a restaurant owner, Emilio Choy (1960), befriended many archaeology students and invited archaeologists to his restaurant after professional meetings and symposia. He began to write about Inka history in a marxist (maoist) light and, both because of the force of his ideas and his support for students, he had an immense impact on the young Peruvian archaeologists of the late 1950s and early 1960s. In 1966, Tabío and Rey (1966) published their *Prehistoria de Cuba*. This Soviet-style archaeological study of Cuba had a profound effect on a generation of Latin American archaeologists, who saw in it a way to link their revolutionary politics with archaeological practice.[7] These students also turned to the works of V. Gordon Childe as they constructed a marxist archaeology. In 1969, the Chilean scholar Marta Harnecker published a theoretical work that became the primary statement of French structural marxism in Spanish. This work inspired a debate among Latin American intellectuals about the relative worth of Soviet marxism, Maoism, Althusser, and the Frankfurt School. After the massacre in Mexico City in 1968, repression of left-wing ideas spread across Latin America, ending any discussion of marxist ideas in countries such as Argentina. When the military overthrew the Allende regime in Chile, several prominent archaeologists, among them Felipe Bate and Julio Montané, fled the country under threat of arrest. Mexico became a refugee center for radical intellectuals forced out of other Latin American countries, and these included many archaeologists. For this reason, Mexico became a focal point in the development of marxist archaeology, especially at the Escuela Nacional de INAH in Mexico City. Most radical archaeologists came from middle-class backgrounds and they were allowed to develop their theories in the universities of Mexico, Peru, and Venezuela, but not in many other countries such as Chile and Argentina. The former countries generally tolerated marxist thought in the universities, but sought to suppress it among the general population.

The 1970s saw a series of very important books and conferences on marxist theory in archaeology. The Peruvian Lumbreras (1974) drew on Emilio Choy, V. Gordon Childe, and Harnecker's reading of Althusser in his book *La Arqueología como Ciencia Social*. In Venezuela, Sanoja and Vargas (1974) used Tabío and Rey as an inspiration for their *Antiguas Formaciones Modos de Producción en Venezuela*. From exile in Mexico, the Chilians Felipe Bate (1978) and Julio Montena (1980) produced book-length engagements with these earlier works. Starting in 1970, a series of three conferences was held in Mexico, culminating in the 1975 "Reunión de Teotihuacan," which sought to layout a radical program in archaeology (Lorenzo *et al.*, 1976).

These works of the 1970s were conducted within the framework of the overarching intellectual debate in Latin America about Soviet marxism, Maoism, and French structural marxism. Much of the archaeological theorizing concerned itself with how to apply the positions in this debate to archaeology and with the redefinition of the terms used in the debate for archaeology. They also expressed a profound concern for the social and political role of archaeology in the world. As Panameno and Nalda (1978) asked, the issue was "archaeology for whom?" This strong social consciousness preceded similar concerns in Anglo-American archaeology by a decade and led to discussions of who was the proper audience for archaeology and how this audience might be reached and given a voice in archaeology (Lorenzo *et al.*, 1976). By the end of the 1970s, little resolution was evident in the larger debate on marxist theory, and many intellectuals were becoming weary with the rhetoric (Lorenzo, 1982:204; Palerm, 1980:32–33).

The 1960s and 1970s also witnessed a growing alienation between U.S. and Latin American archaeologists. On a theoretical level, the Latin Americans resisted the tenets of the New Archaeology. The particularly American style of the theory and its emphasis on politically neutral science did not fit well with the socially and politically conscious archaeology, then current in Latin America. The Latin Americans tended to feel that the North American's search for universal laws and emphasis on generalized changes in history, such as the origins of agriculture, were imperialistic concerns that insulated them from the scientific community of Latin America and from their concern with their own history (Gandara, 1981; Murra, 1984:651). In the mid-1960s the U.S. Camelot project was revealed. This project had enlisted anthropologists, knowingly and unknowingly, to gather information for the CIA for use in counterinsurgency campaigns in Latin America and Southeast Asia. The revelation of the Camelot program only served to heighten the distrust between Latin American and U.S. archaeologists because the scandal cast doubt on the actions of archaeologists as well as anthropologists (Palerm, 1980:27).

In Mexico, the archaeological debates of the 1970s led to the re-evaluation of the relationship between Mexican and North American archaeologists (Lorenzo, 1976). The quality of work done in Mexico by North Americans was questioned, as was their record of publication (Lorenzo, 1982:201–202). More important, Mexican archaeologists were concerned that the North Americans were bringing superior resources to bear in Mexico and using them to engage in academic debates that were irrelevant to Mexican concerns. The North Americans carried these debates out in English language journals and showed little interest in, or respect for, the concerns and work of Mexican archaeologists. The result of this re-evaluation was the institution of stricter permitting requirements in Mexico and the denial of permits for many North American archaeologists, including some very prominent individuals in the field.

El Grupo Oaxtepec

In 1983, a group of archaeologists who had been exploring a marxist approach to archaeology met at Oaxtepec, Mexico, and formed the Grupo Oaxtepec to try to synthesize a new approach for a marxist archaeology. The group included Felipe Bate, Iraida Vargas, Luis Guillermo Lumbreras, Julio Montane, Manual Gandara, and Mario Sanoja. These scholars sought to formulate an over-arching marxist theory of archaeology. They publish primary in the journal *Boletín Antropolgía Americana*. Also in the mid-1980s, a collective of faculty and students called the Grupo Evenflo began meeting at the Escuela Nacional de INAH in Mexico City to explore methods of observing and drawing inferences from the archaeological record in the context of a marxist archaeology.

The Grupo Oaxtepec began with a fundamental dissatisfaction with the Latin American debates of the 1960s and 1970s about marxism. They eschewed both a dogmatic marxism and any eclectic borrowing from nonmarxist thought. Rather than once again reworking Second International marxism, French structural marxism, or Maoism, they returned to the works of Marx and Engels to build their theory from the ground up. They strongly rejected French structural marxism, especially its idea that modes of production can exist as separate entities that come into articulation. They sought instead, a theory of social totality that will situate diverse particular propositions.

They began their theory building with the base–superstructure opposition and the relations defined by this opposition between traditional marxist categories, such as modes of production, social formations, and ideology. To relate these abstract categories to the concrete realities that they observe, they introduced the notions of mode of life and culture. Unlike French structural marxists who treat social formations as concrete, real, societies, they regard a social formation as an abstraction. Each type of social formation has an economic base and an ideological superstructure. This base includes a set of modes of production (the technology, technical knowledge, and social organization of production), and a set of modes of reproduction (family organization, kinship relations, and marriage rules). The superstructure links these various modes of production and reproduction under a shared set of cognitive rules for behavior, beliefs, notions of cognitive models of institutions, laws, religion and so on. The key relations that define a social formation are those of property, that is, how people gain access and have rights to the means of production (tools, technical knowledge, land, etc.). A social formation manifests itself in a mode of life, a concrete, real, social form that archaeologists study. Each mode of life may include multiple cultures.

Using this theoretical scheme, an archaeologist can define a tribal mode of production based on communal or kin-based rights to property, and in which nature is the object of production (that is, it is transformed in production via agriculture or herding). This mode of production gives rise to a tribal social formation. This abstract tribal social formation can manifest itself in many different concrete modes of life, such as a pueblo mode of life in the U.S. Southwest. This mode of life includes a number of cultures, among them the Hopi, Zuni, Keresan, Tewa, Tiwa, and Towa.[8]

The work of the Grupo Oaxtepec has influenced archaeology throughout the Spanish-speaking world (González Marcén and Risch, 1990; Nocete and Ruiz, 1990). The influence of this group is only partially a result of common language. Many Spanish and Latin American archaeologists find the radical archaeologies of the English-speaking world, marxist and postprocessualist, as superficial and primarily concerned with political struggles within the academy rather than with the development of alternative theories of society (González Marcén and Risch, 1990:97). They find the theory of the Grupo Oaxtepec much more firmly grounded in meaningful political practice in Latin America and in the scientific practice of archaeology. The research of this group has largely been ignored by English-speaking archaeologists, with a few notable exceptions, such as Bruce Trigger and Thomas Patterson.

ANGLO-AMERICAN ARCHAEOLOGY

The development of archaeology in England and the United States tended to be markedly different from developments in the Soviet Union and in Latin America (see Trigger, 1989a). This is especially true when the dialogue between marxism and archaeology is considered. Despite the fact that marxist thought had a significant impact on Anglo-American archaeology throughout this century, an explicit marxist archaeology is a recent phenomenon. The hidden history of marxism in Anglo-American archaeology denied those that defined an explicitly marxist archaeology as a clear route to such an archaeology or a well-known intellectual lineage to build on. As a result, most current marxist archaeologists came to their marxist theory outside of archaeology, and then tried to reconcile the two.

Childe (1921–1945)

The Australian V. Gordon Childe is probably the best known and most cited archaeologist of the twentieth century. He is also the first archaeologist in the West to use marxist theory in his work.[9] Childe took his undergraduate degree at the University of Sidney and later did graduate work in classics at Oxford. In 1916, he returned to Australia where he engaged in various types of left-wing political activities until 1921 (Trigger, 1989a:169). In 1921, he went to England as a research officer for New South Wales. The defeat of the Australian Labour Party in 1921 left Childe in England without a job, and he once again returned to archaeology, his calling. (Gathercole, 1989). He helped to introduce the notion of an archaeological culture to European archaeology, and his work through the middle 1930s was characterized by a historical study of diffusion and migration. In the increasingly politicized context of 1930s European archaeology, these studies were a direct challenge to the racial theories of a growing fascist archaeology in Germany and elsewhere (Arnold, 1990).

In 1935, Childe visited the Soviet Union, where he was impressed by the extent of state support for archaeology and was profoundly influenced by the theory of Soviet archaeology. Childe labored under a different set of constraints and in a different social context than those of his colleagues in Russia. He was not constrained by Stalinism, which he would later call "the marxist perversion of marxism" (Childe, 1989:15–17). He did not have to fit his theory to a rigid, set series of stages, but he was also not free to openly and fully develop marxist ideas in his work. He rejected unilineal evolution, maintained an interest in typology and diffusion, and chided Soviet archaeologists for assuming in advance what they needed to prove (Childe, 1951a:28–29). In this way, he built a marxist archaeology that was stimulated by, yet distinct from, Soviet archaeology. Since he did not have to conform to a state ideology of marxism, he was able to view archaeology as a means for testing and refining marxism's observations on the long term of human history. His work was attacked in England for its involvement in Soviet archaeology and his use of marxism (Clark, 1939, 1952, 1976). As late as 1982, Glyn Daniels (1983) introduced a new edition of Childe's *Man Makes Himself* by downplaying and denying the influence that marxism had on Childe.

In four books, *Man Makes Himself* (Childe, 1951a, orig. 1936), *What Happened in History* (Childe, 1946a, orig. 1942), *Progress and Archaeology* (1944), and *Scotland Before the Scots* (Childe, 1946b), Childe laid out his own marxist, materialist view of European prehistory (Childe, 1989:15–17; Trigger, 1989a:256–259). In these works, he introduced a multilinear notion of evolution, within which changes in technical knowledge affected social, political, and economic changes. He imbued these works with a sense of dialectical contradictions that served to both impede and encourage change. For example, he argued that elite power depended both on the ability to compete with the elite of other societies and the ability to maintain the inequalities within society that were the internal basis for power. Technological change threatened to alter the relations of inequality within their societies, so they must oppose it but, on the other hand, technological change was necessary so that they could continue to compete with the elites of other societies. He tended to view superstructural factors as having a negative or conservative influence that worked against social change.

U.S. Anthropology and Archaeology (1918–1945)

The development of archaeology in the United States during the inter-war period tended to be quite different from that in Europe. An emphasis on typology, classification, chronology, diffusion, and migration continued to dominate U.S. scholarship until well after World War II. In the virile anticommunist atmosphere that flourished during the Red Scare of 1919–1920 and continued through the 1920s, any materialist or evolutionary social theory was branded as marxist and thus, dismissed. Within anthropology, Lowie (1937) framed a caricature of marxism as a theory of economic determinism and unilineal evolution that endures in the minds of many in the discipline to this day.

Some scholars, however, began to formulate materialist alternatives to the shreds-and-patches view of culture and cultural change that dominated in U.S. anthropology and archaeology. During the 1920s, Leslie White became increasingly interested in social evolutionary theory as a result of his contact with the work of Lewis Morgan. In 1929, he visited the Soviet Union and he returned to the United States quite impressed by the twilight of the NEP (Barnes, 1960:xxvi). He began to formulate a theory of cultural evolution based primarily on the work of Morgan, but in many ways comparable with Second International evolutionism, which had its origin in Engels' (1972) reading of Morgan. In the 1930s, Julian Steward began to formulate his theory of cultural ecology, which he would apply to both cultural anthropology and to archaeology (Steward, 1937, 1955). He was joined in this enterprise by archaeological colleagues at the Smithsonian Institution, William Strong (1936) and Frank Setzler (Steward and Setzler, 1938). The materialism and multilinear evolution of this theory converges with aspects of marxism, but apparently Steward was not directly influenced by a reading of Marx, Engels, or the later Second International theorists (Wolf, 1987).

Childe (1945–1957)

Following World War II, Childe moved away from Soviet archaeology because he came to question the quality of work done under Stalinist domination. To further develop his own marxist theory, he went back to Marx and readings in marxist philosophy (Trigger, 1989a:259–263). This interest gave rise to his most theoretical works, including *Social Evolution* (1951b), *Society and Knowledge* (1956), and *The Prehistory of European Society* (1958).

His theory in these books parted company with the theory of Soviet archaeology but stayed within the tradition of the Second International. He kept the primacy of the base in relationship to the superstructure, but rejected the idea that the base, in any straightforward way, determined the superstructure. He saw laws as general descriptions of what is observed and as limited in their application. His theory mixed history and evolution. He thought that general trends existed because cultures with the same type of mode of production tended to become more similar over time, but that this process occurs in historical contexts. Therefore, convergences are never complete and general trends, never adequate to the understanding of real cases. He became very concerned about what knowledge is and how we, as scientists, create it. He thought that true consciousness is possible when the scientist's idea of reality fits the reality that he or she can observe. He further maintained that such consciousness was common in technical knowledge, but rare or absent in our knowledge of social relations and ideology. Therefore, archaeologists can truly know about the technology of the past, but not the social and ritual aspects of the past. As a consequence of this view, he never developed an effective technique for studying prehistoric social and political life (Trigger, 1989a:263).

In a retrospective article in *Antiquity* he summarized his approach to archaeology:

> *I invoke no agencies external to the observed data, no external laws transcending the process as empirically given, but historical conjectures of well-established environmental circumstances and equally well-known patterns of human behavior, legitimately inferred from their archaeological results (Childe, 1989:18).*

U.S. Anthropology and Archaeology (1945–1960)

During the 1950s, a noticeable chill fell on U.S. intellectual development as public discussion of socialist philosophy was seriously curtailed and actively repressed by the federal government. This limiting of intellectual debate insulated U.S. social scientists from the theoretical debates of continental Europe, which took a markedly marxist turn at this time. The war had left the United States with an economic, political, and cultural hegemony in the world. In this context, U.S. social theory developed in distinct ways, different from intellectual currents in Europe and Latin America.

These general trends manifest themselves in anthropology and archaeology. In 1961, Morris Opler lashed out with a red-baiting attack against White, via the comments of one of White's students, the archaeologist Betty Meggers (1960). In it he charged "apparently the practical tool kit Dr. Meggers urges upon the field anthropologist is not quite so new as she represents, and its main contents seem to be a somewhat shopworn hammer and sickle" (Opler,

1961:13). As Harris (1968:639) notes, Opler was "fully prepared to expose and jeopardize his colleagues before the political passions of the times." Given that White's theory was not particularly radical, or marxist (Bloch 1985:128), and that its interest in building a universal theory of technological determinism was consistent with the promotion of U.S. political and economic hegemony (Trigger, 1989a:291), we can only wonder how Opler would have savaged a marxist theoretical perspective. We need not wonder why there were no prominent candidates on the American horizon for him to attack.

In the 1950s and 1960s, Steward's theory of cultural ecology and White's neoevolutionism gained adherents in U.S. anthropology and archaeology. In this context, Childe's marxism was not well understood, and he was generally embraced as an evolutionist, but often wrongly characterized as a unilineal evolutionist (Steward, 1955:12). White's students built a materialist, unilineal theory of cultural evolution that Marvin Harris (1968, 1977, 1979) appropriated as Cultural Materialism. Up until the mid-1960s, however, this theory was less influential in archaeology than was Steward's theory of cultural ecology and multilinear evolution. Steward's own interests in archaeology and his work with the archaeologists Strong and Seltzer involved archaeologist with his ideas for over a decade before they would seriously take up White's. Archaeologists continued to put most of their effort into the study of classification and chronology, but increasingly, most reports included a discussion of subsistence and ecology. Inspired by Steward, Gorden Willey (1953) introduced settlement pattern studies to archaeology. Childe did not exert a strong influence on American archaeologists, but gained significance later because of his impact on the thinking of Robert Braidwood (1989:90) of Chicago's Oriental Institute.

Steward and his students picked up on the ideas of an older generation of marxist-influenced Eastern European scholars who fled to the United States during the war. Many of these scholars were disillusioned with marxism both because of the Stalinist terror and the defeat of the republicans in the Spanish Civil War. Steward (1955) adopted Wittfogel's idea of a hydraulic society, and this notion became a focal point for archaeological debate into the 1970s. Polányi taught a series of seminars at Columbia, commuting back and forth from his home in Canada, because the U.S. government labeled his wife a political subversive and would not allow her into the country (Terence Hopkins, personal communication, 1988). His notion of reciprocal and redistributive economies was introduced to archaeologists by Sahlin's (1972) book *Stone Age Economics*. Paul Kirchoff went from Europe, first to Mexico, and after the war, joined Steward at Columbia. In the 1950s, he would write the seminal papers defining the Southwestern and Mesoamerican culture areas.

In the early 1950s, a cohort of younger scholars with radical backgrounds and largely trained after World War II, entered archaeology and anthropology. Some of these, such as John Murra, Elman Service, Pedro Armillas, Pedro Carrasco, Angel Palerm (in Mexico) and Jose Cruxent (in Venezuela), were veterans of the republican cause in the Spanish Civil War. In New York City, a radical circle of students called the Mundial Upheaval Society formed at Columbia (Wolf, 1987:107). Its members included Eric Wolf, Morton Fried, Elman Service, Stanley Diamond, Sidney Mintz, Daniel McCall, and John Murra (Eric Wolf, personal communication, 1990). Wolf (1987:109) commented that "all of us were some variant of Red . . . a Marxian stew but not necessarily with any commitment to a particular party line." In a Chicago steel mill, Robert McCormack Adams worked as a labor organizer in the late 1940s. Braidwood asked him to come with him to Jarmo in Turkey because Adams knew some auto mechanics. When they returned, Adams devoted himself to the study of archaeology (Adams, personal communication, 1989). These scholars, by and large, did not adopt an explicitly marxist philosophy in the 1950s. Many were disillusioned with marxism, either because of experiences in the Spanish Civil War, or because of the revelation of the Stalinist terror,[10] but as important, McCarthyism limited the theoretical and political positions a U.S. scholar could publicly take. Some of these individuals suffered from various forms of harassment. For example, the U.S. government tried to stop John Murra's naturalization as a citizen, and even after he became a citizen in 1950, would not issue him a passport until 1956 (Murra, 1984:639).

Their work was generally perceived as expressions of Steward's cultural ecology. Steward's notions of cultural ecology and multilineal evolution came close enough to the marxist background of many of these writers that it became a shield for them. It allowed them to pursue a materialist research strategy and ask questions that they wanted to about the world without exposing themselves to red-baiting critiques. They tended to bring a historical approach to their work that was lacking in Steward's ecological functionalism. These authors also had a broad and temporally deep vision of social change, which could have been derived from Steward or Marx, and this vision led all of them to blur the lines between anthropology, history, and archaeology. The impact of this cohort on archaeology also led to direct collaborations between members of the cohort and archaeologists. In 1960, the Valley of Mexico project was initiated with Pedro Armillas, Pedro Carrasco, Angel Palerm, and Eric Wolf. They worked with archaeologists, including Michael Coe, William J. Mayers-Oakes, René Millon, Jeffery Parsons, Richard Blanton, George Cowgill, and William Sanders, who used various forms of materialist theory (Wolf, 1976). In this milieu, Adams (1966) prepared his classic work on multilineal evolution, comparing the development of urbanism in Mesopotamia and Mesoamerica. This work paid explicit debts to Steward, Braidwood, and Childe, and it also drew on the work of the Soviet Assyriologist, Igor Diakonov. Very deftly, these scholars laid the foundations for an anthropological political economy.

Anglo-American Archaeology (1960–1980)

In the 1960s, marxist scholars challenged the direction of American anthropology. A number of the young radicals of the 1950s, among them Marshall

Sahlins, Morton Fried, Stanley Diamond, and Eric Wolf, took explicitly marxist theoretical positions in their work. Also, Eleanor Leacock recognized the short shrift gender had been given in traditional marxism, and she began to articulate a marxist–feminist approach to anthropology starting from Engels' *Origins of the Family, Private Property, and the State*. The revelation of this project raised questions about the role of anthropologists in the world and their relationship with informants that threatened to rip the discipline apart. In the 1960s, Marshall D. Sahlins edited a series of classroom readers for Prentice-Hall called the Foundations of Modern Anthropology Series, which included books by Robert Adams, Elman Service, Eric Wolf, and Peter Worsley. These readers were widely used in undergraduate anthropology courses through the 1970s and formed a common part of the education of a generation of American archaeologists.

Also in the 1960s, a distinctively Anglo-American approach to archaeology was forged in the United States and Britain (see Trigger, 1989a:289–328; Willey and Sabloff, 1980:181–264). In the United States, it had its origin in the work of Louis Binford and his students. This New Archaeology combined the evolutionary theory of White (1949, 1959) with an extreme brand of logical positivism drawn from the work of Carl Hempel (1966). It co-opted the earlier engagement with cultural ecology, and involved a variety of loosely related, even conflicting (Flannery, 1972), theoretical strands that shared a systemic view of culture, a materialist notion of causality, and a strong sense of functionalism. In England these broad schemes showed up in the work of David Clarke (1968), who advanced his idea of an analytical archaeology, and of Colin Renfrew, who drew freely on Clarke's work and the New Archaeology of the United States. This research was not philosophically marxist, but drew on marxist elements either through the filter of cultural materialism or from marxist anthropologists such as Fried, Sahlins, and Wolf.

Not all U.S. archaeologists embraced the New Archaeology. Many continued work in cultural history with a little cultural ecology on the side. Several archaeologists shared the New Archaeology's dissatisfaction with traditional archaeology, but disdained the evolutionary deterministic approach of the New Archaeology. Some of them came to marxism as an alternative. Others turned to structuralism.

The marxists were all self-trained in their marxism. Bruce Trigger (1978) went to the works of V. Gordon Childe, and found there the critical dialectic between history and evolution, theory and data, and mentalism and materialism that he thought lacking in the New Archaeology. In the early 1960s, Thomas Patterson (1973, 1989b) began his studies in Peru by examining the territorial organization of work in a perspective that derived, in large part, from neoclassical economics. In Peru, he came into contact with marxist political thought and increasingly saw it as a useful theoretical perspective for archaeology. In the 1970s, he found it difficult to find people in archaeology involved with marxism.

Mark Leone trained as a processualist archaeologist at the University of Arizona, but came into contact with Althussarian structural marxism when he taught at Princeton. He used this approach in historical archaeology to interpret the meaning of Mormon town fences and the Mormon temple in Washington, D.C. In the 1970s, marxism remained a concern of only a handful of individuals in U.S. archaeology. By 1974, when Philip Kohl and Antonio Gilman sought to organize a session on marxist archaeology at the American Anthropological Association meetings, they had great difficulty identifying U.S. archaeologists who were marxists (Gilman, 1989:63).

The structuralism of Levi-Strauss influenced a small group of archaeologists, most of whom worked in historical archaeology. The most prominent of these individuals was James Deetz (1977), who drew on Henry Glassie's (1975) structuralist study of folk housing in middle Virginia to interpret Puritan material culture. Many of Deetz's students took up this structuralist program and established a small, but vibrant structuralist interpretive community within historical archaeology (Yentsch, 1975; Beaudry, 1980). Apart from these historical archaeologists, Margaret Conkey (1978) drew on French structuralist theory to interpret Magdalenian portable art from northeastern Spain.

During the 1970s, marxism became much more prominent in the British academy than it had in the United States, where French structural marxism was the dominant perspective taken, rather than the strongly cultural and historical approach of the British marxist historians. Within British anthropology, a major focus of debate concerned modes of production and how they were to be defined, e.g., did they exist as abstract models, independent of empirical cases, and what aspects of society should be included in the mode of production, and what aspects, excluded (Seddon, 1974; Hindes and Hirst, 1975; Wolpe, 1980; Kahn and Llobera, 1981). British archaeologists that turned to marxism did so within this structural tradition. A U.S.-trained cultural anthropologist, Jonathan Friedman (1974, 1979, 1989), challenged the structural causality of Althusser and argued for a more historical approach in which scholars account for the existence of a given social form by exposing the structural transformation that created it. He worked closely with two British archaeologists, Michael Rowlands and Barbara Bender, and a Dane, Kristian Kristiansen. These four individuals articulated a non-Althusserian structural marxist approach to archaeology (Friedman and Rowlands, 1978).

Alternative Archaeologies in Great Britain and the United States Today

It is one of the curious aspects of contemporary U.S. and British society that while the general tenor of each country became more and more conservative during the 1980s, there was a flowering of radical thought in the universities. There are at least three reasons for this trend: (1) many of today's professors were radicalized in the New Left movement of the 1960s, (2) during the 1960s, radical ideas became legitimate within the academy, whereas previously, they had been actively suppressed, and (3) the governments of both countries have made a concerted attack on the academy that has further alienated scholars from the capitalist society in which they live. Within archaeology, this radicalism has manifested itself in the critique of the positivist basis of the New Archaeology, and of the generalized approach of processual archaeology that it spawned. These alternative archaeologies include a variety of approaches, among them feminism, poststructuralism, and marxism. All of these approaches are sometimes misleadingly lumped together under the label of a postprocessual archaeology. These alternative archaeologies have been far more successful in Great Britain, where they clearly dominate theoretical debate (Baker and Thomas, 1990), than in the U.S., where they remain distinctly minority positions. These alternative archaeologies have inspired a spate of responses and critiques from processual archaeologists that are considered throughout this book (Binford, 1987; Earle and Preucel, 1987; Schiffer, 1988; Spaulding, 1988; Renfrew, 1989).

In Great Britain, the structural marxist approach to archaeology created by Friedman, Rowlands, Bender, and Kristiansen continued into the 1980s. Barbara Bender (1981, 1985a, 1985b, 1989) developed a social perspective on the transition from gathering to farming that stressed the importance to the shift of internal relations within the society. Michael Rowlands (1987, 1989) carried out a long-term research project in west-central Africa, where he focused on the structure and contradictions of ideologies of legitimacy. Kristian Kristiansen (1984, 1989) examined the ideologies of legitimation and the formation of tribal systems in the European Bronze Age. The models of prestige goods exchange and a lineage mode of production advanced by the structuralists have been picked up by a number of researchers working in Europe and North America (Haselgrove, 1982; Pearson, 1984; McGuire, 1986, 1989a; Thomas, 1987). The emphasis on structures and the circulation of goods that permeates so much of this work, led many of these structuralists to adopt Wallerstein's World Systems theory for the study of archaeological cases (Ekholm and Friedman, 1982; Rowlands et al., 1987). Structural marxism has come under attack in British archaeology both by marxists, who wish to reject the structuralism in it (Saunders, 1990), and by poststructuralists, who object to it as a totalizing world view (Thomas, 1989, 1990b). The marxists among these critics have often adopted the historical and cultural theory of the British marxist historians, especially from the work of Hobsbawm (1964, 1975), Thompson (1963, 1978), and more recently, Williams (1973, 1990).

The 1980s saw a growth of marxist thought in British medieval and Post-medieval archaeology (Saunders, 1990; Williamson and Bellamy, 1987; Williamson, 1990). These researchers tend to follow in the highly empirical tradition of the British marxist historians, whose early debates on the nature of the transition from feudalism to capitalism, established a set of key research problems and a research agenda for the study of the medieval period. Some of these scholars have addressed these debates using archaeology (Saunders, 1991). The detailed, long-term, historical community studies of the late British marxist historian Raymond Williams (1973, 1990) sparked a growing interest in a community-focused archaeological study of the medieval and postmedieval periods (Saunders, in press).

The most dramatic development in British archaeology during the 1980s was the unfolding of a postprocessualist or poststructuralist approach to the discipline. This movement began and has remained centered at Cambridge University. It is also embedded in the intellectual debates of Great Britain over the relationship of structuralism, science, history, and a general challenge to the notion of modernism that originated in the poststructuralist movement of France. The meetings of the Theoretical Archaeology Group (TAG) in Great Britain provided a focal point for much of the debate engendered by the appearance of a postprocessual archaeology. These meetings originally started in 1977 by processual archaeologists seeking a forum to discuss archaeological theory in Great Britain. In the last few years, they have been increasingly dominated by debates between feminist, marxist, and poststructuralist theorists (Fleming and Johnson, 1990).

Ian Hodder (1982b, 1984, 1986, 1990) launched this line of theory based on his dissatisfaction with processual archaeology, structuralism, and marxism. He emphasized that the search for meaning in the archaeological record is an interpretive process subject to varied readings. Most recently, he sought to highlight the personal (that is, the role of the author) in the writing of archaeologies (Hodder, 1990), and turned more attention to the empirical aspects of data collection. His first generation of students produced some of the key works of this approach (Miller, 1982, 1987; Shanks, and Tilley, 1987a, 1987b). These archaeologists actively engaged the marxist tradition and sought to build archaeology as a theory of material culture with an eclectic borrowing from Althusser, poststructuralism, and critical theory. Some advocates of a postprocessual approach drew their theory more strictly from the work of the poststructuralists such as Derrida (Bapty and Yates, 1990) and Foucault (Thomas, 1989, 1990a, 1990b).

The labels postmodernism and poststructuralism, in fact, subsume a bewildering array of theoretical positions within archaeology, but they do tend to share certain basic beliefs. They typically place the study of the past, and of material culture, in a textual analogy. Archaeologists read the past like a text and, like a literary text, many readings of the past are possible. The reality of the past constrains the choice of a reading, an interpretation, but this choice is ultimately made according to the concerns and power relations of the present. Archaeologists need to be aware of these relations, and need to use their expertise to struggle against the existing social order. Significant disputes do arise within the bounds of these tenets. Hodder (1989) challenged the work of Shanks and Tilley (1987a, 1987b) and they responded (Shanks and Tilley 1989). He questions how well they deal with the nature of dialectical thought and, with others (Nordbladh 1989; Olsen 1989), asks how radical their ideas can, in fact, be, since they speak from the position of an educational elite and are supported by prestigious academic presses. In a similar vein, a 1988 conference at Cambridge, on poststructuralism in archaeology, gave rise to two competing collected volumes. One from a prestigious academic publisher (Bapty and Yates, 1990) advances a poststructuralist (in the style of Derrida) agenda. The other, desk-top published at Saint David's University College in Lampeter, Wales (Baker and Thomas, 1990), challenges both the theory and the agenda of the first as a Cambridge attempt to establish a new hegemony in British archaeology.[11]

The 1980s witnessed the formation of an alternative interpretive community in U.S. archaeology. Seminal to this process were a series of seminars, the RATS meetings, held from 1982 to 1986 at the University of Massachusetts Amherst, State University of New York (SUNY) Binghamton, and the City University of New York. These meetings mainly involved individuals living in the northeastern United States, but served as a focus on interaction that linked people from across the United States and England. They also provided a forum outside of the national meetings, where radical theory could be discussed in depth without the need to confront processual archaeology.[12] Most of the individuals that make up this community were originally trained in processual archaeology and are self-taught in their marxism and feminism. The lack of a common origin point or single line of development is reflected in the great diversity of thought within this relatively small group of individuals, each of whom came to a theory by a different path. U.S. archaeology has seen the development of several different strands of marxism, and a growing body of feminist theory (Conkey and Gero, 1991), but only slight interest in poststructuralism (Beaudry et al., 1991). A processual approach remains dominant in U.S. archaeology. Of the approximately 100 U.S. and Canadian universities that offer the doctoral degree in anthropology, no more than 15 have overtly marxist or feminist archaeologists on their staffs.[13]

The handful of individuals that pioneered a marxist archaeology in the 1970s continue to develop this tradition. Most of these people do substantive research in the Old World; in southwestern Europe (Gilman, 1981, 1984), in west Asia (Kohl and Wright, 1977; Kohl, 1979, 1989; Tosi, 1984), Mesopotamia (Zagarell, 1986), and in Eastern Europe (Tringham, 1971). Several of these archaeologists argued that a radical rethinking of U.S. archaeology requires a critical examination of the history of the discipline. They have undertaken such revisionist histories that challenge the progressive *great men and ideas* format that has characterized most prior intellectuals' histories of archaeology (Kohl, 1981, 1983; Patterson, 1986, 1988, 1989b; Trigger, 1980a, 1984, 1985b, 1986, 1989a; Pinsky, 1989). These efforts culminated in Bruce Trigger's (1989a) monumental work, *A History of Archaeological Thought*, which traces the social, intellectual, and political history of western archaeology from the Middle Ages to today.

The development of a postprocessual archaeology in England has often been linked to the growth of a critical archaeology in the United States (Gero *et al.*, 1983; Leone, 1986; Earle and Preucel, 1987; Patterson, 1989a; Pinsky and Wylie, 1989). This linkage is appropriate because the two groups of scholars interact frequently, both groups reject the pervasive positivism of processual archaeology, both seek an understanding of meaning in the past, both stress the interpretive nature of archaeology, and both are concerned with the political implications for the present of our study of the past. (Leone, 1982, 1986). Critical archaeology moved from an engagement with structuralism, both Althusserian structural marxism (Leone, 1972, 1977) and Levi Strauss (Handsman, 1980, 1981), to a use of Frankfurt School critical theory. The key concept in critical archaeology has been Althusser's notion of ideology as the taken-for-granted assumptions that people use to structure their awareness of the world (Leone, 1986). This can be a form of the dominant ideology thesis that argues that ideology shapes the consciousness of people in such a way that it constrains, or even determines action. Like the theorists of the Frankfurt School, these archaeologists are impressed with the power of capitalism to permeate every aspect of daily life and to subvert a true knowledge of a class consciousness. The research of these archaeologists has been devoted largely to revealing the role of ideology in the past (Leone, 1988; Handsman, 1981; Little, 1988), or in critiques of the way in which modern ideology permeates museum exhibits and other public presentations on the past (Leone, 1981; Leone, *et al.*, 1987; Leone and Potter, 1984; Handsman, 1983b; Handsman and Leone, 1989; Chabot, 1988, 1990). The basic assumption of this approach, that an elite ideology will dominate or shape the consciousness of nonelite individuals, has been questioned by a number of authors (McGuire, 1988; Thomas, 1990b, Paynter and McGuire, 1991; Beaudry *et al.*, 1991).

Immanuel Wallerstein's World Systems theory enjoyed a widespread popularity among U.S. prehistoric archaeologists during the 1980s (Upham, 1982; Plog *et al.*, 1982; Blanton and Feinmon, 1989; Whitecotten and Pailes, 1986; Kohl, 1979, 1987b, 1989; Dincauze and Hasenstab, 1989). Most of these researchers appropriated the theory's functionalist view of long-range economic dependencies between regions, without reference to the marxist philosophy and economic theory that provides the basis for Wallerstein's thought. Stripped of its marxist foundation, World Systems theory in archaeology becomes little more than an economic reading of the old notion of interaction spheres. The work of Philip Kohl (1979, 1987b, 1989), however, approaches world systems from a marxist tradition; he critically uses the theory as a starting point for empirical studies of the relationship between global and local relations in the process of state formation in ancient west Asia.

World Systems theory has also had a major impact on U.S. historical archaeology (Lewis, 1984; Paynter, 1981, 1985; Green and Perlman, 1985). Here the theory is more clearly applicable than it is in prehistoric or ancient cases because the archaeologists use the theory to study the periods it was written for, and not as a source of generalization to earlier, very different times. Robert Paynter (1981, 1985) sought to develop complex understandings of the history of the Connecticut Valley in Massachusetts that integrate far-ranging world systems interactions and local histories. Also in historical archaeology, Charles Orser (1988) tried to introduce marxist-derived concepts of the economy and power into the study of southern plantation society.

Some U.S. archaeologists look to the French tradition of western marxism for their inspiration. Susan Kus (1982, 1989a, 1989b) draws on French existential marxism and its notion of objectification to understand how the rulers of the Imerina Kingdom of Madagascar organized space to legitimate their rule. Dean Saitta (1987, 1988, 1989) uses a notion of class derived from the work of marxist economists Resnick and Wolff (1987) to interpret economic integration and development in the ancient past of the New Mexico Zuni Indians.

The late 1970s and early 1980s witnessed the fruition of a historical approach to political economy in U.S. cultural anthropology (Roseberry, 1988, 1989). This approach was heavily influenced by both the cultural tradition of U.S. anthropology and by the British marxist historians. It offered an alternative to the functionalism of Worlds Systems theory, which reduced anthropological subjects to pawns in a world system, and an alternative to the sterile abstraction of the modes of production debates (Roseberry, 1988:169–173). It has its roots in the anthropology of the young radicals of the 1950s; that is, in the theory and empirical research of Eric Wolf (1959, 1969, 1982), Sidney Mintz (1974, 1985), Stanley Diamond (1974), Eleanor Leacock (1972, 1981), and June Nash (1979, 1981). Wolf, Mintz, and Diamond brought a strong sense of history to the study of anthropological cases, a history that sought to understand these cases in terms of the intersection of local and global processes. Leacock and Nash made feminist concerns central to political economy; Leacock through her emphasis on the origins of inequality and the effects of colonization and state formation on gender inequality, and Nash, with her interest in the division of labor within and between families.

The attempt to situate anthropological cases in the intersection of local and global histories creates a useful theoretical and methodological tension that defines anthropological political economy (Roseberry, 1988:174). Such studies must avoid the pitfall of explaining all change in terms of local adaptation or regional cultural histories, and at the same time must not make global processes and long-range interactions overly deterministic. This tension cannot be resolved by a theoretical abstraction such as the articulation of modes of production; thus, the focus of study must always remain on real people and on what they do. This focus allows the researcher to productively integrate concerns often seen as distinct and/or conflicting, such as gender and class, and production and reproduction (e.g., Collins and Gimenez, 1990).

Much of current marxist scholarship in U.S. archaeology, including my own, is part of this tradition of anthropological political economy. Robert Paynter's (1985, 1989) studies of historical archaeology and his concern with inequality and power, build on this approach. Crumley and Marquardt's (1987) multiscale, historical analysis of a Burgundian landscape explicitly confronts the tension of an anthropological political economy, as does Marquardt's (1988, 1989) research on the archaeology and ethnohistory of the Calusa of Florida. The critiques by Jim Moore (1983) of information theory in archaeology and Art Keene (1983) of optimal foraging theory in archaeology, reflect this tradition. Elizabeth Brumfiel has (1980, 1983, 1988, 1991) examined the Aztec State in terms of class and gender relations. An anthropological political economy leads archaeologists to ask about the historical processes that create ethnic groups (ethnogenesis) (Patterson, 1987; Beauregard, 1989; Robinson, 1990), relationships of class and ethnicity (Clark, 1987; Cassell, 1988), and ideologies (Wurst, 1991).

The centrality of feminist concerns to anthropological political economy has inspired a spate of ethnohistorical studies of gender inequality and state formation (Rapp, 1978; Silverblatt, 1988; Moore, 1988). Leacock's championing of Engels' position that the original form of inequality in society was in the oppression of women by men, and his linkage of this oppression to private property and the rise of the state has inspired much of this work. The global process of the rise of the state is linked with the local process of gender relations in households (Gailey, 1985, 1987). These studies have addressed the effects of state formation on gender inequality among the Inca (Silverblatt, 1987), the Aztec (Nash, 1980; McCafferty and McCafferty, 1988, in press; Brumfiel, 1991), and the archaic states of northwest Europe (Muller, 1985, 1987). These studies are of considerable significance for archaeology, both because they address a key issue in archaeological research, state formation, and because they deal with substantive cases of archaeological interest.

A second prominent issue in a feminist anthropology is the origin of gender roles. Many scholars have sought, and found, the origins of modern gender roles in the primordial pasts of humankind, in the origin of humanness, or in surviving hunter-and-gatherer societies (Washburn and Lancaster, 1968; Issac, 1978). Feminist scholars have answered these studies in a number of ways. They have challenged theories that find the origins of humanness in male hunting with a set of theories that find this origin in female gathering (Slocum, 1975; Tanner, 1981; Zihlman and Tanner, 1978; Hrdy, 1981). More important, they direct us to examine how these origin tales embody mythic structures common to western culture (Landau, 1984; Fedigan, 1986:61; Harding, 1986:92–110). They have also undertaken in-depth studies of women's roles in hunter-and-gatherer societies (Dahlberg, 1981) that seriously challenge how we, as archaeologists, have viewed such societies (Strathern, 1987).

Feminism in archaeology effectively begins with Joan Gero's (1983, 1985) critiques of the sociology of the discipline and Margaret Conkey and Janet Spector's (1984) critique of male bias in our study of the past. Gero identified a division of labor between low-valued women's work (laboratory processing and logistical support) and higher-valued men's work (field excavation and survey) within the discipline. She argued that this division of labor relegated women to positions of lesser importance and prestige within the discipline. Conkey and Spector cogently show that the assumption that gender relations are given in nature led archaeologists to consistently recreate modern gender stereotypes in the past, even when the empirical data did not support these stereotypes.

More recently, Alison Wylie (1989, 1991) introduced archaeology to feminist critiques of the male bias inherent in science and to a feminist philosophy of science (see also Moore, 1988; Harding, 1986; Haraway, 1989, 1991). Much of this work seeks to understand how the construction of knowledge and both historical and social contingencies have produced and maintained androcentric biases in archaeology (Joan Gero, personal communication, 1991). Like much marxist theory, it advocates that scholars view the world from specific standpoints or social positions. Most Marxists have advocated the standpoint of the proletariate as the most appropriate one, while many feminists have argued for a female standpoint as the privileged one (Taylor, 1990:35). Wylie (1991:43) points out that such theory is unstable because it assumes a universal standpoint. She argues that if diversity is to be taken seriously, then scholars must recognize that alternative standpoints may divide them from among themselves as well as from white males. She concludes that we should learn to live with the inconsistencies and tensions that are created by different approaches (Wylie, 1991:44).

Conkey and Gero (1991:5) identify three goals of a feminist archaeology: (1) to expose gender bias in archaeological inquiry, (2) to find women in the archaeological context and identify their participation in gender relations, gender ideologies, and gender roles, and (3) to challenge underlying assumptions in western culture about gender and difference. They argue that engendering archaeology involves much more than finding men and women in the past. It requires that archaeologists try to understand how gender works. A feminist archaeology requires a radical realignment of research priorities, a reconsideration of the systems of periodization in prehistory (does the Magdelenian–Solutrean boundary mean anything in terms of changes in women's experiences?), and a questioning of our grand paradigms such as the technoenvironmental model of cultural change and adaptation.

Discussion of feminism and archaeology has increased in both the United States and Europe with numerous recent conferences and several new volumes of collected works.[14] Many of these efforts have been critical considerations of how to build a feminist archaeology (Sorensen, 1988; Dommasnes, 1990; Taylor, 1990; Gero and Conkey, 1991). There is also a growing corpus of empirical studies of gender relations in the past (Dommasnes, 1982; Therkorn, 1987; Gilchrist, 1988; McCafferty and McCafferty, 1988; Ehrenberg, 1989; Pollock, 1991; Spencer-Wood, 1991; Watson and Kennedy, 1991; Classen, 1991; Yentsch, 1991). These feminist studies challenge a wide range of thinking and practice in archaeology, including the devaluation of female labor (Gero, 1991; Hastorf, 1991; Wright, 1991), gender bias in research and public presentation (Dobres, 1988; Chabot, 1988, 1990; Handsman, 1991; Spector, 1991), and gender discrimination within U.S. archaeology (Kramer and Stark, 1988). Feminism, as constituted in these debates, questions the epistemology, practice, and sociology of modern archaeology and it confronts processual, marxist, and postprocessual archaeologies.

WHITHER A MARXIST ARCHAEOLOGY

One of the most powerful tensions in marxism has been between marxism as a totalizing theory for social action and marxism as a theory of critique. Marxists on the right see marxism as a totalizing theory that explains, predicts, and provides an instrument for directing the course of social change, and for shaping the consciousness of people to fit that change. Marxists on the left believe that democratic change must come from the will and action of people; they see marxism as a form of critique that will help people to form a critical awareness of the world necessary for that action. The current crisis of marxism clearly shows the limits of marxism as a totalizing theory and the need for a pluralism of views (both marxist and nonmarxist) and for critical debate. Scholars should not, however, loose the tension because, just as an overly deterministic marxism can lead to Stalinism, an overly critical marxism can lead to nihilism.

Within the great variety of views that characterize marxism in Anglo-American archaeology, there is a set of general principles that all or most of these views share (Trigger, 1984; Spriggs, 1984):

1. Each claims Marx as an important intellectual ancestor and as a source of inspiration. In all of these archaeologies, his work is a starting point, not an end point. Each participates in a marxist intellectual tradition that is greater than the works of Marx.

2. All seek to account for sociocultural change in terms of a similar theoretical and philosophical framework. This framework puts social relations at the core of our research and seeks to break down the oppositions that bedevil our research; oppositions between mentalism and materialism, humanism and science, history and evolution, and relativism and determinism.

3. Each treats society as a whole, a totality, that should be ultimately understood as such. They reject the idea that scholars can come to a better under-

standing of social process by reducing social phenomena to their parts and examining those parts.

4. All emphasize contradiction and conflict as vital features of human society and internal sources of change in those societies. As such, they reject functionalism, the notion that social phenomena can be adequately understood in terms of how they function to maintain society or allow it to adapt to an environment.

5. Each takes a human-centered view of history that gives human action or praxis some significant role in the process of history. They therefore reject any form of determinism (environmental, material, or technological) and the idea of abstract knowledge divorced from the action of people.

6. All recognize that our knowledge of the past is created in a social and political context, that people make knowledge. And, that this knowledge can never be merely a reflection of the reality of that past, nor should scholars simply make it up to fit our own political and social agendas.

7. Each shares in a commitment that the power relations and structure of the modern, capitalist-dominated world is unjust and destructive to people. All advocate some form of socialism as the alternative to this system.

These principles can be used to contrast marxism as a way of knowing the world, as a critique of the world, and as a means for action in the world, with the other theoretical approaches current in Anglo-American archaeology.

A processual archaeology using either the cultural ecology and cultural materialist theory that dominates current U.S. archaeology shares many empirical concerns with marxism, but differs greatly in terms of the method used to know the world, as a critique of the world, and as a means for action in the world. These common empirical concerns spring, in large part, from the covert and overt transfer of ideas from marxism to American materialist approaches in anthropology and archaeology. The processualists' interest in knowing both how people made a living in the past and how they organized their societies overlaps greatly with the empirical interests of most marxists (Gilman, 1989:72). The extent of overlap increases when processual archaeologists recognize that relations of exploitation are embedded in these social arrangements (Wright, 1984; D'Altroy and Earle, 1982; Kirch, 1984; Haas, 1982; McGovern, 1980; Brumfiel, 1980; McGuire, 1983a). Marxists, however, reject the processualist's faith that, through a scientific method, archaeologists can come to an objective understanding of social processes, or that such an understanding is ever possible. This means that they also reject the processualist's illusion that we can engage in a politically neutral study of the past or, alternatively, the early belief of some processualists that through an objective knowledge of the laws that determine social process, social scientists can engineer social change for the better (Wobst, 1989).[15]

The alternative archaeologies that were introduced in the 1980s, postprocessual (poststructuralist) and feminist, share a political position with marxism both in the sense that they are identified with a radical left and in that they attack an established processual archaeology. With marxism, they all reject the idea of a value-free objective science, and stress that active, knowing subjects have a considerable impact on social processes (Patterson, 1989a:561). These overlaps are especially pronounced where postprocessual theorists draw theory from a marxist tradition (i.e., Shanks and Tilley, 1987a, 1987b). But as Frederick Baker (in Baker *et al.*, 1990:2) has commented:

> Below each "ism" is a real issue, and a committed archaeology is doomed to failure if it mistakes the two. Behind feminism is the problem of sexism, (read sexual inequality), behind marxism is the problem of poverty (read economic inequality). Which real issue does poststructuralism address?

Most marxists feel that poststructural archaeology pays too little attention to knowing the world and focuses too much on critique, thereby limiting its efficacy as a means to action in the world. Many U.S. marxist archaeologists are as critical of poststructural archaeology as they are of processual archaeology (Trigger, 1985a, 1989a, 1989b; Kohl, 1985, 1988; Patterson, 1989a, 1990; Gilman, 1989).[16] They attack the poststructuralists for being too subjective, overly intellectualized (over-theorized), and too eclectic in their theory. They share the fear of many processual archaeologists that the relativity of postprocessual archaeology denies the validity of any knowledge of the past. They feel that this relativism makes it impossible to empirically refute pernicious uses of the past, such as the Nazi, or the use of the past to confront injustice.

The poststructuralist critique, especially when drawn from the work of Foucault, creates a tension that helps warn marxism away from an overly deterministic or totalizing path. But such a tension can also be created from the standpoint of a critical archaeology that keeps the underlying real issue of marxism in view. Most marxists are uncomfortable with a postprocessual archaeology that views the critique of Cambridge lectures as a more important, and a more radical, form of practice than political advocacy in support of gender, ethnic, racial, and class struggles.

A feminist archaeology places women at the center of our study of the past, whereas marxism places economic relations at the center of our study (Moore, 1988). If scholars adopt a totalizing theory of marxism that treats class as the sole explanation for social change, then a serious conflict must exist between marxism and feminism. One of the major flaws of Second International marxism was that it subsumed all other forms of inequality — gender, ethnic, and racial — under class, and saw class as the origin point and determinant of all inequality. The feminist critique clearly shows the error of this approach and the exploitation that it hides. People do not, however, experience gender or class separate from the other social relations of their lives, such as ethnicity and race. Rather, people make their lives within the total web of these relations. If archaeologists wish to study the human experience as it is lived by people, then we cannot study any one of these relations in isolation, nor can we *a priori* decide what relation (if any) will be primary in all cases; that is a substantive question. Our ability to grasp this whole as scholars is, however, limited by both our cognitive skills and by the practicalities of doing research. We cannot look at everything at once.

In order for us to understand the whole web of social relations, researchers must choose an entry point, a place to start our analysis, and move from that point toward an understanding of the whole. Marxists will find that entry point in the social and ideological relationships of production and reproduction; feminists will find it in gender. The analyses that each writes of the past should overlap and gain from the insights of the other; they have the potential to complement each other. Anthropological political economy has benefited greatly from the engagement of marxism and feminism, especially in the work of scholars like Nash and Leacock and their students. Feminism has an important role to play in advancing critical, and political economic theory in archaeology. This theory depends on the examination of distinctive social–economic interest groups, in which gender always plays a major role – social groups inevitably adopt gender as a central organizing principle for social and economic life. A gendered archaeology has to produce finer-grained social and economic studies of the past that eschew overly generalized patterns of adaptation in which everyone is purported to do the same thing. The basic program of feminism substantially overlaps with the marxist approach that is taken in this book.[17] It is clearly possible, and productive, to be a marxist–feminist or a feminist–marxist.

My argument should not, however, be taken to mean that either marxism should subsume feminism or feminism, marxism. Gero (1990:1033) argues that "placing women at the center of prehistory should revolutionize the views we have of our past," and she is correct. Such revolutionary views are possible only if feminism maintains a theoretical space of its own. The dynamic tension between marxism and feminism has challenged and transformed each tradition over the last 20 years, and we would do well to nourish that tension.

The varied marxist archaeologies of today are the product of a long tradition of social thought that begins with Marx and grew over more than 100 years. The dialogue between marxism and archaeology has been a complex one, carried out in shifting political and social contexts that have helped to shape that dialogue. Today marxism defines a theoretical space in archaeology that both overlaps and differs from the other major theoretical traditions of our discipline. By occupying that space, archaeologists can critically examine these other theories and create a dynamic tension that fuels our efforts to make knowledge of the past in the present. The rest of this book examines the use in archaeology of one strand of the marxist tradition, marxism as a theory of internal relations.

ENDNOTES

1. My goal in examining different regional traditions of Marxist archaeologies is to make comparisons that illustrate processes, not to provide a comprehensive survey of all regional traditions of marxist archaeology. Not included in these discussions are regional traditions in China, Eastern Europe, non-English-speaking Western Europe, and Japan.

2. While I was completing this book, Willey and Sabloff were also finishing the third edition of *A History of American Archaeology.* Jerry Sabloff has indicated to me that this third edition will not include the Greek-column figure and will directly address the influences of marxism on American archaeology.

3. Why Willey and Sabloff include Sanders with Wolf, Palerm, and Armillas as an intellectual descendent of Childe and Wittfogel is a mystery. Sanders clearly and explicitly draws his theory from the work of Julian Steward. He shares with Wolf, Palerm, and Armillas a materialist evolutionary approach and field work in the Valley of Mexico.

4. The process by which an individual becomes alienated from class position is a complex one and not reducible to simple generalizations. In all cases it must involve some process of self-awareness that makes individuals conscious that their experience is structured by class, that it is not universal, and that it breeds dissatisfaction with that structure. Two events stand out in my own process of alienation. The first of these was the divorce of my parents that transformed my childhood household from that of a middle-class military officer to that of a working-class government clerical worker. Suddenly, the middle-class images that surrounded me on television, at church, at school, and in Boy Scouts, felt strange and uncomfortable. My dissatisfaction grew as I watched my mother struggle to maintain a middle-class existence for my sister and me on a GS-4 salary. The second event was my experience during the Vietnam war, first in the army, and then in the antiwar movement.

5. Few, if any, of the archaeologists advocating Marxism in the west today could be described in Gramsci's terms as organic intellectuals, that is, intellectuals that come from and advance the interests of oppressed classes. When individuals have entered archaeology from marginal class positions they tend to use archaeology as a means to join the bourgeoisie and have co-opted bourgeois ideology. An example of this would be Julio Tello in Peru, who was raised in the Andes, became the dominant archaeologist in Peru from the 1930s to the 1940s, and was a strong advocate of the nationalist, middle-class ideology of Indigenismo (Patterson, 1989b). This lack of organic intellectuals in archaeology may reflect the marginality of archaeology for practical political practice.

6. This summary was drawn from Benjamin Keen's (1988) *A History of Latin America.*

7. The impact of this book on Latin American archaeology was comparable

to the impact of Binford's "Archaeology as Anthropology" in the United States. This interest in marxist archaeology, in part, explains the Latin Americans' lack of engagement with U.S.-style New Archaeology.

8. I must thank Felipe Bate and Ireda Vargas for their attempts to explain the theory of the Grupo Oaxtepec to me at the 1989 Wenner Gren conference on "Critical Approaches in Archaeology: Material Life, Meaning, and Power" in Cascais, Portugal. My description of the group's work, due to its brevity, tends to make the theory of the group appear more mechanical than it actually is.

9. My discussion of Childe is drawn primarily from Trigger (1980b, 1989a), Tringham (1983), and Green (1981).

10. In a letter to me dated January 21, 1991, Eric Wolf commented "I have preferred using the term 'Marxian' to 'Marxist' precisely because in the mind of many people Marxist has had a univocal meaning of a political theory, usually associated with Stalinism. 'Marxian' seemed more pluralistic to me."

11. These debates are in striking contrast to the nature of theoretical debate in the United States. Recent theoretical dialogue in British archaeology starts with the consensus that such debate is ultimately political. In the short authors' biographies in Baker and Thomas (1990), many of the authors thought it relevant and important to identify their political party membership. Most American archaeologists find such overt political statements discomforting. The general style of public debate in the United States tends to mask or obscure its political content in contrast to a more politically overt style in Great Britain or Europe. American authors must walk a fine line between being honest and critical of the political nature of their work and having their work dismissed as simply political.

12. The acronym RATS has no agreed-on meaning. Several participants suggested that it referred to Radical Archaeological Theory Symposium, while others were more comfortable with Regional Archaeological Theory Symposium. All agreed that it refers to an appropriately subversive rodent.

13. These departments would minimally include those at the University of Massachusetts at Amherst, SUNY Binghamton, City University of New York, University of California at Berkeley, Temple University, University of North Carolina, McGill University, University of South Carolina, University of Florida, and the New School for Social Research.

14. Recent conferences include the 1989 Chacmool conference at the University of Calgary that took feminism and archaeology as its theme, and the conference "Women in Archaeology" held at the Charles Sturt University in Albury, Australia, in February of 1991. Since at least 1987, feminist-oriented archaeological symposia have been a regular part of the meetings of the American Anthropological Association, the Society for American Archaeology, the Society for Historical Archaeology, the Plains Conference, and the Theoretical Archaeology Group. The *Archaeological Review From Cambridge* Vol. 7(1) was entitled "Women and Archaeology." Joan Gero and Meg Conkey's book *Engen-*

dering Archaeology came out just as I was completing this book. *Plains Anthropologist* Vol. 36(1) was devoted to the papers from a 1987 symposium at the Plains Conference on gender studies in plains anthropology. The majority of papers were by archaeologists (Francis, 1991; Guenther, 1991; Hughes, 1991; Kornfeld, 1991; O'Brien, 1991). A collected volume from the 1989 Chacmool conference is in press as I write this, but I do not have access to a draft copy before completion of this book.

15. It should be noted that most processual archaeologists in the United States would consider themselves politically liberal, and many in the New Archaeology of the 1960s considered their theoretical program to be both intellectually and politically revolutionary (see Wobst, 1989, for a discussion). Timothy Earle once remarked to me the "we are all some kind of Marxists." I believe that his comment reflected both a recognition of the intellectual debt that all social theorists owe Marx and the personal commitment to social change that many or most of the processual archaeologists had in the 1960s and early 1970s. It is for these reasons that attacks on processualism as a conservative philosophy, which maintains the status quo, severely irritates many archaeologists, especially those that participated in the New Archaeology.

16. These critiques all include the poststructuralists and the critical archaeologists in the same box that they label postprocessual. If we look at the extent to which archaeologists emphasize political and social critique in their work, a clear continuum exists from processual archaeologists that regard it as inappropriate to those poststructuralists that devote most of their energies to such critique. Marxist archaeologists fall somewhere in between on a continuum, with individuals such as Trigger, Kohl, Patterson, and Gilman, closer to the processualists, and the critical archaeologists, among them Leone and Handsman, closer to the poststructuralists. I have argued for a more expansive notion of Marxism and believe that the positions taken by archaeologists like Leone and Handsman are essential to maintaining a dynamic tension between knowing, critique, and action in Marxism.

17. I must thank Joan Gero for her helpful comments on an earlier draft of this chapter that I have liberally paraphrased in this discussion of feminism and archaeology.

.

CHAPTER 4

The Dialectic — Marxism
As a Theory of Relations

Hegel is not the giant on whose shoulders Marx thought he had to stand, but a monkey clinging to Marx's back.

(Harris, 1979:145)

The true fundamental function and significance of the dialectic can only be grasped if the philosophy of praxis [marxism] is conceived as an integral and original philosophy which opens up a new phase of history and a new phase in the development of world thought.

(Gramsci, 1971:435)

Many archaeologists read Harris' characterization of the dialectic as the Hegelian monkey on Marx's back. Harris would have us believe that the dialectic is a metaphysical violation of the most basic laws of logic and rational thought. He would mislead us. The dialectic is not an irrationality, but instead it is a world view, a philosophy, a way of knowing the world. The positivism that Harris boosts is not simply native intelligence or pure reason, but rather, an opposing world view and way of knowing (Hesse 1980). As Gramsci suggests, we can never understand the dialectic unless we realize that it is a different way of thinking from the common analytical way of the western world.

Most people of the West find dialectical thinking arduous and difficult insofar as it may violate our sense of rationality (Ollman, 1976:5; Gramsci, 1971:419–425; Heilbroner, 1980:32). Our parents and teachers train us from childhood to think of the world in atomistic terms, in terms of distinct parts that work smoothly together in a functioning system. They tutor us to see change in that world as the result of a linear chain of cause and effect that propels us from one steady state to the next. The dialectic defies this view. It bids us to see the social world as a fluid whole, made up of relations that create the fleeting apparitions that appear to us as distinct parts. Odder still is the idea that these relations define parts in contradiction, so that the whole depends on conflict and opposition rather than on harmony and integration. So, no cause can exist apart from its effect, and change occurs in a spiral motion that springs from contradictions found within the whole.

Those of us trained as anthropologists should be aware that rationality is not given in nature but differs from culture to culture. The Navajo, who views the world as a whole, so that even the action of the dung beetle disturbs the shifting of the clouds (Kluckholn and Leighton, 1946:303–321), would have little trouble with the sense of dialectical thinking. The Chinese, Taoist, philosophy of yin and yang, the oneness of good and evil, male and female, also entails a logic like that of the dialectic (Legge, 1962). For both the Navajo and the Taoist, the atomistic view so comfortable to us violates reason.

Our rationality is codified in the rules of formal logic (Gramsci, 1971:435). Like an atomistic view of the world, these rules are not given in nature. Piaget (1954) points out that children must be taught these rules; they expend great effort to learn them, and they do not always learn them well. Everyone knows people who cannot *think logically*. What is interesting about logical thought "is that, once having been mastered, its rules master us" (Heilbroner, 1980:54). Our notion of rational discourse derives from the learned structures of common sense and formal logic. We need to set those structures aside to grasp the dialectic.

There is no simple, single, unambiguous definition of the dialectic. The logic of the approach, its own internal logic, does not allow for the reduction of complex ideas to facile, staid definitions. To grasp the dialectic, the student must examine it as a fluid whole, in the same way it bids us to look at the social world as an ever-changing totality. No universal agreement exists, either inside or outside marxism, about what the dialectic is. Some marxists, most notably Althusser (1969, 1971), have advocated a non-Hegelian reading of the dialectic that differs from the Hegelian view taken in this volume. Saitta (1987, 1988) discusses the value of the Althussarin dialectic for archaeology, and his work should be consulted for an alternative view to the one given here.

Marxists have taken three basic positions *vis à vis* a Hegelian dialectic (Bhaskar, 1983:126). A few, such as Bernstein (1909) have rejected it as nonsense and tried to put other ways of knowing in its place. Others have taken the path of Engels and the Second International and proclaimed the dialectic to be universal, applicable to both the social world and to nature (Norman and Sayer, 1980; Ollman, 1976:52–54; Levins and Lewontin, 1985). Finally, a third group of scholars, among them Lukács (1971), Gramsci (1971), the Frankfurt School, and Sayer (1979, 1987), kept the dialectic at the heart of their study of the social world, but put it aside for the study of nature.

As Levins and Lewontin (1985) argue, the dialectic does have considerable value for how archaeologists think about the natural world and for a critique of how we study that world. Their dialectical view of nature effectively reveals the fallacy of reductionism and the importance of seeing natural phenomena in terms of dynamic wholes. The oppositions (contradictions) of nature are, however, fundamentally different from those of the human social world (Kosík 1976:135–140; Heilbroner, 1980:43). The contradictions that create social entities have their origins in human consciousness, and they are socially created between like entities, humans. The existence of one pole of the contradiction always depends on the existence of its opposite. Teacher and student are social opposites, but in the absence of teachers, there can be no students and vice versa. In nature, oppositions originate in different entities, cougar (predator) and deer (prey), or genes (information) and enzymes (repressors), that are in no sense reducible to a common entity. The relations of these entities can be described in a systems language of positive and negative feedback, such as Levins and Lewontin (1985:279–283) use. Deer still exist in the absence of cougars; they do not melt away like students without teachers.[1]

This volume takes a third view of the dialectic and draws its theory most heavily from those scholars who have argued that marxism constitutes a dialectical theory of internal relations (Ollman, 1976; Sayer, 1979; 1987; Kosík, 1976). In this theory, the dialectic is both a way of viewing the world, and a method of inquiry. The dialectic obliges us to put aside absolutes, both absolute truth and absolute relativism. As Heilbroner (1980:57) notes "Ambiguity, the bane of positivism, is the very essence of dialectics." The ambiguities that exist in the oppositions between science and humanism, history and evolution, mentalism and materialism, and determinism and free will, that trouble modern archaeological theorists so much, make up the substance of the dialectic. To understand how they do this, I look at the dialectic as a way of viewing the world, as a philosophy. Such a dialectical view affects how archaeologists think about material culture and how we use it in our interpretations of the past. It also affects our epistemology, our way of knowing the world.

It is hard to express dialectical ideas in words, especially words scratched on paper. The logic of the dialectic is not linear. The physical requirements of, and modern conventions for, writing require us to string our words and thoughts in linear rows. They also require us to organize our thoughts *logically* so that questions and problems are set forth and resolved; authors are expected to reach closure. The reader should recognize that the pages of a book freeze a moment in a dialectic and, as such, can only crudely represent that dialectic.

THE DIALECTIC

My discussion of the dialectic is drawn primarily from Bertell Ollman's (1976) book *Alienation*. My goal here is not to make an original contribution to the philosophy of the dialectic, but rather, to give the reader a clear introduction to this theory of the dialectic. This introduction lays out the philosophical underpinning for the rest of this book. Unless otherwise cited, my discussions come from Ollman (1976).

The notion of the dialectic is so foreign to our idea of common sense that it is often easiest to start talking about it in terms of what it is not. It does not divide the world into clear, bounded, separate entities that scholars can define in terms of lucid, consistent, and exclusive definitions. It does not look for stability, homeostasis, or the functional integration of parts. It recognizes that these states may exist, but sees them as temporary and fleeting. It rejects the idea that the social world is inherently static, inert, or stable, thereby requiring us to invoke external causes to account for change.

The dialectic views the social world as an elaborate structure of internal relations, within which the relation of any given entity to others governs what that entity will be. This social world is inherently dynamic and conflictual, because change in any part of that world alters the whole of the relations, placing all elements forever in flux. This change is not simply quantitative or qualitative in nature, but rather, it is a complex process whereby small quantitative changes in relations lead to qualitative shifts in the social whole. A specific process of change may appear very dissimilar, even reversed, when we gaze at it from a different viewpoint or for another purpose. The dialectic tells us to search for the contradictions that both form the social world and drive this process of motion. A theory of change as the normal order fits archaeology better than steady-state models that freeze change to look for causes instead of studying the process of change.

The Language of the Dialectic

The language of the dialectic can be trying and hard to understand unless we recognize that the dialectic is a different way of thinking with its own, distinctive language. If, out of ignorance, people try to apply common-sense meanings to dialectical terms and use them in a common-sense way, the dialectic becomes nonsensical (Ollman, 1976:11). The dialectic seeks to give us a novel view of the social world that is not accessible via common sense or formal logic. Attempts to use casual terms or apply casual meanings to dialectical terms limits the reader to the common perspective.

Terms in the dialectic refer to relations in a context rather than to discrete bounded entities (Ollman, 1976:12–25). As the context of these relations changes, so can the meaning of the terms used to describe them. A thing, called by one term in one context, may be called by a different term in another, because the relation between the thing and others has changed. For example, wine sold in the supermarket is a commodity, but in the communion cup it becomes the sacred blood of Christ; sacredness is not an inherent quality of the wine but instead a characteristic it acquires from its social context of use.[2] In the common-sense view, social factors are logically independent variables, and the ties between them are contingent; that is, the ties between variables can change without necessarily altering the variable. In the dialectic the ties, the relations, are internal to the factor; when the ties change in an important way, so too must the factor. We mark such a shift by using a different term to refer to the factor.

A simple example illustrates the relational use of terms. In neoclassical economics and even in common usage, a farm tractor can be called capital because it is an asset owned by the farmer. Is status as capital is an essential characteristic of the machine that derives from its usefulness or function. The price of the machine may vary, but it remains an asset as long as it is a functioning tractor. In marxism, capital comes from value produced by a specific relation between owner and worker, wage labor (Marx, 1906:633n). A tractor is therefore capital when the farmer hires a hand to drive it, but is not capital if he operates it himself. It remains a tractor and its use has not changed, but the social relations necessary for its use have changed (see Marx, 1847:211; Ollman, 1976:15; Sayer, 1987:133).

Furthermore, the concepts that scholars use to describe the social world cannot exist independent of that world, but are themselves products of the social relations that the scholar observes and enters into as a social being. The terms and ideas scholars use are part of the social reality that we seek to know. Consider an ox used by a twelfth-century manor serf. This ox cannot be capital because the relation of wage labor was not common or dominant. And, since this relation is uncommon and minor in the twelfth century, a contemporary scholar would not think to ask if the ox was capital and would view the social context of the ox in a very different way than would a modern scholar.

The dialectic views objects as components of the social relations that produce them and of the social relations necessary for their use (Ollman, 1976:26–27). Material things are more than just the reflection or outcome of action. They express the social relations that are the conditions for their existence. They are both the products of social relations and part of the structure of those relations.

Contradiction

One of the most basic ideas in the dialectic is the notion of contradiction. Internal contradictions form unities within the totality of social forms, and the source of motion (change) within these forms derives from contradictions. "The dialectical contradiction is a concrete contradiction: it is a contradiction which exists not just between ideas or propositions, but in things" (Sayers, 1980a:7).

The contradictions referred to in the dialectic are relational contradictions and not formal logical contradictions (Heilbroner, 1980:35; Sayers, 1980a:11). Formal logic asserts that $A = A$ and that a contradiction exists if $A = $ not A. The dialectic accepts this trivial observation, but this is not what is meant by a contradiction in the dialectic. Here contradiction refers to relational contradictions, the idea that all social categories are defined by and require the existence of their opposite. The classic example of this notion is the idea of master and slave. The existence of one of these social categories necessarily implies the existence of its opposite. You can have masters only if there are slaves and vice versa. The logical opposite of master is not-master, which may or may not be a slave; the relational opposite of master is slave (Heilbroner, 1980:41).

This logic shows two opposed social categories, master and slave, to form a unity. That is, they are the observable manifestations of a single underlying relation of slavery. The existence of one necessarily entails the existence of the other, yet they are opposites and, as such, potentially in conflict. Each has different and often contrary interests, and each experiences social life differently. Motion, that is, change in the social form, springs from the conflict inherent in the nature of social relations. The goal of dialectical inquiry is not to make broad generalizations about the universal nature of contradictions, but rather to study the particular contradictory processes of a given historical case (Heilbroner, 1980:39).

Such an inquiry is not easy and can never produce a single true, correct, or necessarily best account of history. If the unity of master and slave is viewed from the position of the slave, we gain one perspective of the totality of the social form of which the slave is a part. If we approach it from the perspective of the master, we obtain a different view. If we look at the totality of a given case for a different purpose, we will find different unities because every real social form consists of a mass of interconnected relations and opposites. The questions investigators ask will decide which of these unities we can or will observe. Some of these unities may relate directly to a specific goal or question, while others will not.

In a dialectic, each social actor in an opposition has a different standpoint on the relationship that creates the social space of the actor. This standpoint affects the perceptions that the actors will have, and the actions they will take. The same is true of the scholars who study these relationships. They also occupy specific social roles and standpoints in social contradictions. Some scholars may claim that a specific standpoint will influence social actors to have a truer or more useful view of the underlying relationship. In marxist scholarship, Lukács (1971) argued that workers occupy a unique standpoint that allows them to see through the false consciousness of capitalism and the contradictions upon which it is based are revealed. In a similar vein, a growing body of feminist theory, characterized by Harding's (1986) *The Science Question in Feminism*, has argued that female scholars have a special standpoint that gives them a privileged view of the gendered nature of society. Women experience the disadvantages of these relations, while men, who benefit from these disadvantages, deny or fail to see that any such constraints exist. Such standpoints are, however, considerably more complex than discussions of simple oppositions suggest, because each person exist in a social space defined by multiple social relations and contradictions. Furthermore, each person does not experience these social relations one at a time but as a whole. A particular standpoint may give us a truer or more useful vision of one unity, but ambiguities necessarily creep into our perceptions because no standpoint can ever encompass the social whole or even the whole social space of the scholar (see also Wylie 1987). Thus, some standpoints maybe more or less useful for specific issues or questions, but no standpoint gives us a single true, correct, or best account of history.

The Laws of the Dialectic

Engels (1954) drew a series of laws from Marx's reading of Hegel's dialectic. These laws give guidance on how to look for contradictions in real social forms; they suggest how some of these relations will be connected and how change will proceed (Ollman, 1976:54). The specific laws of the dialectic are less important than the general framework that they imply. I present them here in a formal manner and follow them with an archaeological example to aid the reader in grasping this overall framework, not to advocate such formality in the study of specific cases. The laws are reducible to three main ideas:

1. The transformation of quantity into quality, and vice versa;
2. The unity of opposites; and
3. The negation of the negation.

The first law suggests to us that the nature of social change is never simply quantitative or qualitative. Quantitative change can lead to a qualitative transformation, and qualitative change necessarily implies a quantitative change. The change in the quantity of one or more member relations in the totality of relations leads to the whole having characteristics that it did not have before (Ollman, 1976:55). If the temperature of water is lowered, a quantitative change, to below 0°C, the water will turn into ice, a qualitative change. The unity of opposites refers to the idea of contradiction discussed above. Opposites, such as master and slave, good and evil, war and peace, husband and wife, and teacher and student, which appear distinct and separate, are in fact joined by a common relation that defines each pole of the opposition.

The negation of the negation refers to the process of change that results from contradiction. Not all conflicts within social forms result from contradictions. Conflict can result from the clash of wills or any one of a number of other sources beyond relational contradictions. But only those conflicts that spring from relational contradictions, that are necessary for the existence of particular processes and entities, will lead to a transformation of the social form. Such relations hold within them their own negation, the contradiction that will remake the relation into something else; likewise, these relations are themselves the negation of a prior relation or set of relations. The negation of the negation thus refers to the process whereby the negation inherent within a relational

contradiction transforms the relation or set of relations into another form —
something different.

So it is that every social form has within it the seeds of its own transformation.
These seeds will not totally destroy the old form, but rather will change it into
something that is both new and old. In this mix of the new and old are the
contradictions that will, in the end, transform the new social form. Because
development grows from contradiction, the motion of social change is spiral
rather than straight or circular (Ollman, 1976:57). Each successive form of an
entity can be seen as a reaction to the form that came before. Although ensuing
forms of an entity may look like forms that it has taken in the past, such forms
never exactly replicate their earlier selves.

I will use a simplified version of Gilman's (1981) sketch of the shift from the
Neolithic to the Bronze Age in Western Europe as an example of dialectical
change by making explicit the dialectical logic that underlies it. Gilman posits
that neolithic society was generally egalitarian and that it was, for the most part,
based on self-sustaining households that were the loci of both production and
reproduction. These households used simple technologies to build economic
works of long-term utility that enhanced the security of the household.
Among the works were plow agriculture, orchards, irrigation, and off-shore
fishing. Households added to these works slowly over the years and bit-by-bit,
became more and more dependent on them for their economic security (quantitative change). The works became necessary to the survival of the households
as entities and were incorporated into the social relations that created the
household.

These works gave rise to a contradiction that became the means for transforming the social order of the Neolithic to the social order of the Bronze Age (a
qualitative change). The continuation of a household-based, egalitarian, social
order depended on the productive security provided by these works. But the
works themselves were not secure. Because the works could be seized by force and
the household could not abandon them and survive, they imperiled the household
to predation by other, more militarily powerful households. The works that
guaranteed the economic security of the household exposed the household to
social domination; they were both the necessary conditions for the egalitarian
social organization and the seeds of change in that organization. Those households that could muster the military force to seize such works became a warrior
class with specialized training and equipment. They could extract produce from
producing households as payment for protection from raids by other warrior
households. The security of a household now depended on paying tribute to these
protectors to protect their works. The contradiction in the egalitarian social
order was negated and gave rise to a ranked social order and the new unity of
warrior (protector) households and subservient protected households.

Many people have been tempted to use the dialectic as a method for proving
and predicting things; witness the work of the Second International (Chapter 2

of this volume). As Ollman (1976) notes, this is an error. The laws of the dialectic are not laws in the positivist sense. The laws of the dialectic do not predict how variables will change, but rather create terms of reference people can use to study the world (Levins and Lewontin, 1985:268). The dialectic gives us a lens through which to see the world but it does not divine what the scholar will see there. Nor does it provide us with a method for proving or disproving our theories about the world. It suggests how and where to look, in specific historical cases, to understand change, but it does not predict the path that change will take. The value of our theories about particular historical cases lies in the entities and relations that can be observed in those cases and not in the abstraction of the dialectic (see Thompson, 1978; Sayer, 1987). Efforts to use the dialectic as a tool of prediction or proof often leads to the hoary triad of thesis, antithesis, and synthesis (Ollman, 1976:59). In undergraduate classes and in critiques of marxism, scholars present the dialectic as entailing a thesis that gives rise to an antithesis with synthesis resulting from the resolution of the contradiction between thesis and antithesis (for an example, see Wenke, 1981:95–96). This triad has no basis in Marx, Engels, or Hegel's writings (Ollman, 1976:60, 288n; Heilbroner, 1980:42).

It is fairly easy to show that the triad is inadequate either for prediction before the facts have been gleaned or proof after the facts are obtained. Ollman (1976:59) argues that using the triad for prediction:

Degrades the dialectic to a guessing game: starting from a recognized thesis and antithesis, how do we decide which of two or more suggested syntheses is the correct one? Before the synthesis has occurred, how can we be sure that what has been labelled "antithesis" is really such?

Like problems crop up when the dialectic is used to prove something. There is no method to gain consensus on what is the thesis, antithesis, and synthesis in any given case. Marx did not rest proof on the notion that an entity was the negation of the negation or that some change was necessary, given spiral development (Ollman, 1976:59–60).

The triad violates the logic of the dialectic (Ollman, 1976:59) because it freezes change in three parts and makes these parts the object of interest. It blunders by failing to consider the relation that creates the unity of thesis and antithesis. It, furthermore, implies a resolution to the contradiction of thesis and antithesis rather than a transformation of that unity. A critique of the thesis–antithesis–synthesis trinity thus cannot refute the use of a dialectics of internal relations in archaeology or in any other study of the social world.

Limitations of the Dialectic

The dialectic bids us to study the whole in order to understand its parts and shows that we can have no valid understanding of any part without reference to the whole. Yet it is not always practical or possible to study the whole. Also, unless we approach the whole at a most simplistic level, we are overwhelmed by the complexity that it presents. Both practical concerns and the desire for a rich and detailed study of history require us to carve out some piece of the whole for study. The dialectic does direct us to the study of contradictions, and this gives us some guidance on how to partition our study of the whole.

The decision of how, pragmatically, to bound our studies should be based and judged on the specifics of the case that we approach. The dialectic does direct us to reject the systems approach to the world that has dominated U.S. archaeology. This systems approach suggests that scientists can divide the whole up into distinct but articulated subsystems. As in the case of burial studies, in which mortuary data is treated as a subsystem that passively reflects the whole of the social system (Binford, 1971; Saxe, 1970; Tainter, 1978; O'Shea, 1984; Bartel, 1982), the dialectic tells us that contradictions can exist between mortuary ritual and other aspects of the social structure, contradictions that are essential to understanding that structure and how it changes (Hodder, 1982a; Pearson, 1982; Shanks and Tilley, 1982; Miller and Tilley, 1984; Kristiansen, 1984; McGuire, 1988). Whatever part of the whole scholars carve out, therefore, should include a broad range of relations and entities. It must include multiple phenomena that cross-cut the subsystems of a systems approach. It is in the contrast between these entities and relations that we will find the internal dynamics of the social structure.

A similar dilemma confronts us when scholars try to bound our studies in terms of time. If the social world is always in flux, and all social forms encompass both their past and future forms (what came before them and what they will become), we have no clear markers for where to begin or to complete our study. Once again, the pragmatic judgement should be made in terms of specific cases. We cannot, however, simply search for origins and make the explanation of those origins the point of research. To understand a qualitative transformation, we should initiate our study at a point prior to that transformation and carry through past the transformation.

THE DIALECTICS OF MATERIAL CULTURE

Adopting the dialectic affects how archaeologists look at material culture and interpret it in our theories about the past. It gives us an alternative to the two contrasting views of material culture that have been set out in current theory. The New Archaeology argued that human behavior was patterned, and that archaeologists could reconstruct this behavior by studying the patterning in material culture (Binford, 1972:136; Schiffer, 1976). More recently, postprocessualists have argued that material culture incorporates meaning and thus, is an active agent affecting behavior and culture (Hodder, 1982a; Pearson, 1982; Shanks and Tilley, 1987a, 1989).

Material Culture — Passive or Active

The processualist view of material culture is aptly summarized by Binford (1972:136):

> The loss, breakage, and abandonment of implements and facilities at different locations, where groups of variable structure performed different tasks, leaves a "fossil" record of the actual operation of an extinct society. This fossil record may be read in the quantitatively variable spatial clustering of formal classes of artifacts.

Considerable debate about how to read this record followed this statement. The critiques did not so much question the basic assumption that human behavior created patterning in material culture, but rather, they differed over how to reconstruct that pattern from the archaeological record (Binford, 1983; Schiffer, 1988). The basic premise that the patterning of material culture reflects past behavior, albeit modified by intervening processes, was widely accepted. The use of things in the material world leaves patterns to be read as distorted mirrors that reflect back to us the human behavior that created them.

The counter-position comes primarily from the work of Ian Hodder. Hodder (1982a, 1982b, 1986) argues that material culture carries meaning, so that its creation, use, and even disposal, has symbolic significance for the people involved in these activities. He argues that, for this reason, material culture is an active force in culture change.

> Material culture does not just exist. It is made by someone. It is produced to do something. Therefore it does not passively reflect society — rather, it creates society through the actions of individuals (Hodder, 1986:6).

He further argues that the meaning in material culture derives from culture and that this meaning is irreducible to anything but culture. The task of the archaeologist is to interpret this irreducible component of culture so that the society behind the material evidence can be "read" (Hodder, 1986:4). He asks us to read material culture as if it were a text left to us by the people of the past (Hodder, 1989). This idea of material culture being meaningful and of this meaning being irreducible from culture, seemingly sets meaning in a closed-off, mental sphere, separate from the practical use of these items in the material world.

In two books, Shanks and Tilley (1987a, 1987b) express a dialectical notion of material culture. "Inert matter is transformed by social practices or productive labour into a cultural object, be it a product for immediate consumption, a tool or a work of art" (Shanks and Tilley, 1987a:130). They note that material culture may operate in a number of social fields. It may have a use in the natural and social world as technology, serve as a symbolic means of communication and express power and ideology to serve as a means of domination (Shanks and Tilley, 1987a:131). Despite this explicitly broad view, the role of material culture as technology plays little part in the actual case studies they present, and their dialectical view is seemingly lost in a mentalist analysis of cases.

Kristian Kristiansen (1988:480), in a review of the books by Shanks and Tilley, points to the basic flaw in the current debate about the nature of material culture:

One can discuss how far the dichotomy between passive representation (functional, information-theory approaches) and active presentation (strategies) should be taken. The social and the cultural mediate each other in a dialectical way and are thus related to material conditions and to function. The implications of this latter perspective, however, still need to be developed. It should also be noted that the concept of material culture, as presented by S & T, is a rather narrow one, mainly linked to style. Also here an extension to include the wider social and material conditions of existence is much needed.

Archaeologists might start to forge Kristiansen's later perspective by thinking about two observations made by V. Gordon Childe. First, his comment that tools reflect the social and economic conditions that produce them and that we can, therefore, learn about these conditions from the tools (Childe, 1944:1). Second, his point that we should treat artifacts "always and exclusively as concrete expressions and embodiments of human thoughts and ideas – in a word, knowledge" (Childe, 1956:I). In these comments, Childe confronts us with two complex axioms that force us to think about material culture as technology, as a social product, and as a carrier of meaning and knowledge. He also expresses an optimism that archaeologists can learn more about material culture than just its use. We should note, however, that he felt our ability to reconstruct thoughts and ideas was greatly limited once archaeologists moved beyond the realm of technical knowledge (Trigger, 1980b:142).

Material Culture as Objectification

Neither the processualist view of material culture as a "fossil" record nor the postprocessualist notion of material culture as text captures the complexity implied in Childe's two axioms. Material culture may well be a "fossil record of the operation of extinct societies" and if it is, it must reflect the contradictions that existed in those societies. Thus, archaeologists distort that reflection when we try to read that pattern as a "systematic and understandable picture of the total extinct cultural system" (Binford, 1972:23). Material culture may also help create society, but it does so both through the actions of individuals and by structuring those actions in ways individuals may not be aware of.

Material culture entails the social relations that are the conditions for its existence. It is both a product of these relations and part of the structure of these relations. As a product of social relations, it bears the stamp of those relations and in some sense reflects them. Because it is part of the structure of those relations, it affects human action, and people can wield it as a tool to affect the action of others and the structure of relations. Thus, material culture both limits and enables action, and therein lies the key to its interpretation.

Marx (1959:69) called the process by which things become components of social relations, objectification:

The object of labour is, therefore, the objectification of man's species life: for he duplicates himself not only, as in consciousness, intellectually, but also actively, in reality, and therefore he sees himself in a world that he has created.

Marx used the term object in the sense of the object of a sentence, rather than just material things. His objects do, however, include material objects and most of the time he is referring to material objects (Ollman, 1976:78). It is important to realize that an object of labor, is something that people apply labor to. This is a relational idea that includes things like air and light as well as material things. Through objectification, people transform matter into material culture. This act of transformation both creates the objects and is necessary for the reproduction of humans and the social order. In objectification, humans transform objects of nature through social labor to create material culture. The position taken by the processual archaeologist on material culture tends to equate such labor with work. Work refers to the motion of a person using energy to create energy (Marx, 1973:104; Wolf, 1982:74). In this sense, all animals perform work, and the ability of people to do so is given in nature. Human labor entails work, but it is a more complex act than work and not universal to all creatures because it is social, conscious, and meaningful (MacKenzie, 1984:477; Shanks and Tilley, 1987a:131). As Marx (1906:198) noted:

A spider conducts operations that resemble those of a weaver, and a bee puts to shame many an architect in the construction of her cells. But what distinguishes the worst architect from the best of bees is this, that the architect raises his structure in imagination before he erects it in reality.

Human labor presupposes a web of social relations and meanings that structure work. Humans do not use or create energy outside of this web, even the act of being a hermit is a social and meaningful act. Human labor is solidified in material culture so that these objects serve as an "indicator of the social conditions under which that labour is carried on" (Marx, 1906:200).

Material culture is, however, more than a simple outcome of labor; once it comes to be, it is part and parcel of the labor process. It enters into social relations, becomes a component of them, and thereby enables and limits action. Some labor is possible without material culture, but as Marx (1906:199) observed "No sooner does labour undergo the least development, than it requires specially prepared instruments." Material culture also structures human action as it shapes the social ties that link individuals and groups. This power to shape social structure springs both from the way material culture physically organizes space and action, and from its ability to carry meaning.

Humans use material culture to transform the natural world for their social use, and archaeologists commonly refer to this aspect of material culture as technology. For the last two decades, archaeologists have been wont to see technology as a component in an adaptive system, the tools used to extract energy from nature (Binford, 1972:22). This view treats technology as though it had an existence apart from the relations it enters into and, potentially, as an autonomous force in social change. Marx (1906:ch. 7) referred to the characteristics of material culture that allow people to extract energy from nature as the instruments of labor. His notion does not equate well with the commonsense idea of technology or tools.

Instruments of labor change the form of nature's material to satisfy the wants of people; they create use value. Such instruments are themselves nature transformed, so that instruments of labor are both the subjects of labor, tools used to extract energy, and the objects of labor, the consequences of energy extraction. "Labour consumes products in order to produce products" (Marx, 1906:204). Objects can be instruments of labor or the raw materials for production. A tractor is an instrument of labor when it is used to plow a field but becomes raw material when it joins the scrap metal at a steel plant.

Things become instruments of labor only when they enter into the social relations of labor; their functions are not given in their substance or origin (Sayer, 1987:26). These factors may limit the functions of an object in labor, but they do not determine them. Each object possesses different attributes so that its use is not in any simple way inherent in the object, but is derived from the way people deploy it in labor. A screwdriver may be used to drive screws, open paint cans, or scrape paint. Nature itself is an instrument of labor, as is evident if the reader thinks about domesticated plants and animals or the use of natural waterways for transportation. A train that does not carry passengers is not an instrument of labor; a tractor rusting in a field is merely a rusty tractor.

Archaeologists should always remember that labor is a conscious action and that the architect must first imagine his structure before he can build it. V. Gordon Childe (1956) built this view into his theory of technology, which he defined as a social product rather than as a component in a system of adaptation. He always recognized that consciousness came between humans and their environment. He noted that humans do not adapt to their environment, but adapt to their ideas about that environment (Trigger, 1980b:137). Thus, to understand both the environment and the technology used on it, archaeologists should also understand the social structure and ideas of the societies we study (Kus, 1984:103–104).

Material culture not only exists in a context, but it also helps form that context. It is not just backdrop; it is, instead, the stage and props for human action. As such, it both structures human action and gives reality to the social ties that bind people together. It serves both as a model of and a model for social action. The realities that it creates may not accurately reflect the social relations it is embedded in and may instead misrepresent them. In this way, it becomes a medium for domination and the exercise of power over people.

Material culture forms the physical space that structures human interaction. Rooms, buildings, roads, and bridges channel movement, and thereby affect patterns of interaction. Rohn (1971:31–41), in his study of the Anasazi P-III (AD 1100–1280) cliff dwelling of Mug House noted a clear structure to the architecture of the site based on the patterns of movement it allowed. Suites of three to nine contiguous rooms opened up onto small courtyards that usually contained a ceremonial room, or kiva, and a row of rooms in the center of the site split these courtyards into two groups. Rohn (1971:40–41) argues that this organization reveals the social organization of the village into households, lineages, and moieties, it gives reality to this structure. Once in place, it also channels interactions within the pueblo in such a way as to help reproduce this social structure in everyday life. Thus, the architecture of Mug House is more than a passive manifestation of social organization, but instead is part and parcel of that organization.

The nature of the instruments of production can affect the overall form of social organization in a society. Turnbull (1967) observed that among the Mbuti pygmies of the Congo in the 1960s, some groups hunted primarily with nets. These nets belonged to married men, who would hold their nets in the underbrush, while the women and children drove game to it. The Mbuti felt that such hunts required at least eight nets and no more than thirty. These constraints affected the number of families brought together in a band, usually eight to thirty, and the annual cycle of activities; bands break into subgroups in the honey season. Other Mbuti used bows and arrows to hunt, and this was a solitary activity. Bow-hunting bands are smaller, groups of three to four families, and these bands come together during the honey season. These differences are not reducible to environmental factors, nor does the choice of hunting methods arise from technical knowledge. Each type of group lives in a similar jungle environment and all male Mbuti know how to make nets and bows and arrows. Each type of group has also adapted to its jungle home and reproduced itself and its culture.

The patterning of material culture gives reality to social structure, but that reality may, in fact, misrepresent the social structure. It may serve to reinforce and reproduce beliefs that mask power and domination from the people of a society. In this way, material culture becomes a vehicle for domination.

Susan Kus' (1982) work on the Imerina Kingdom of Madagascar shows how the placement of cities, and the design of these cities, legitimated state formation in the early nineteenth century. This was done by creating an image of the relation between the social order of the state and nature, which denied the social origin and character of the state. This image presented the state as something given in nature. In Imerina cosmology, the year was divided into 12 months and space into four cardinal directions. The 12 months of the year were vested with astrological import, as each had a specific destiny associated with it. The four directions were thought of in terms of opposing qualities that were united at the center. For example, north was the noble direction and south, the humble. The spatial organization of the capital was based on the twelve-part astrological system and the four cardinal directions, united at the center. Important governmental structures were located in symbolically exalted spaces ad defined by this grid. In this way, the social order of the state was equated with the natural order of the cosmos and thus, the state's social origin was denied as it was made part of that natural order.

Meanings such as this are formed in a social context and reflect this context. "Consciousness is, therefore, from the very beginning a social product and remains so as long as men exist at all" (Marx and Engels, 1970:51). Not all individuals and groups occupy the same social position in a social structure and thus, different groups will read the meaning encoded in material culture in different ways (Abercombie *et al.*, 1980). Lizabeth Cohen (1980) writes about immigrant working-class families in the turn-of-the-century United States that furnished their homes with plush drapes, overstuffed chairs and couches, thick carpets, and shawl-draped tables and bureaus. They felt that these furnishings were symbolic of their success and acculturation to the new land. On the other hand, middle-class reformers saw these furnishings as unsanitary, tasteless and un-American. They prodded workers to adopt a middle-class aesthetic with bare wood floors, wood chairs, iron beds, and simple cloth curtains. Each group read a different meaning into the furnishing of homes, and this mundane context became a locus of ideological struggle between the classes.

The process of objectification is a complex one. Material culture enables and limits human action because this process simultaneously entails social realms that are commonly split apart in archaeological theory — technology, social structure, and meaning. Dialectical relations spring from the concurrent existence and mutual interdependence of these realms, and such relations cannot be detected when scholars artificially tear these realms one from the other.

A DIALECTICAL EPISTEMOLOGY
FOR ARCHAEOLOGY

The dialectic gives an interpretive approach to the study of the social world that is neither purely empirical nor purely speculative. As Ollman's (1976) analysis of alienation shows, this approach can give us new and telling visions of that world, visions often contrary to our common sense or formal logic. It does not, however, give us dialectical tests for these visions. When archaeologists try to evaluate these visions in history, we take up the tools of empirical science (Heilbroner, 1980:50–51). The dialectic does suggest that we cannot reduce our evaluations to these tools, rather that this process of evaluation is also a dialectic — a dialectic that resolves the impasses between objectivity and subjectivity, science and humanism, that plague current archaeological debate over epistemology.

At an overly simplistic level, the debate over epistemology in archaeology has recently split between an objective, processualist, scientific approach and a subjective, postprocessualist, humanistic approach. As Rowlands (1984b: 112) notes, archaeology seems to be firmly in the grip of two intellectual positions: "Either archaeology must be explanatory, empirical and capable of obtaining objective truth or it is intuitive and particularistic and a matter of personal interpretation." The processualists assume that scientists can gain objective knowledge of the past through the use of a scientific method. The postprocessualists argue that all knowledge is relative and that our understandings of the past are constructed in the present to be statements about the present. "There is no way of choosing between alternative pasts except on essentially political grounds, in terms of a definite value system, a morality" (Shanks and Tilley, 1987a:195).[3]

Schiffer (1988:462) recently stated the processualist position. He directs us to search for "a series of basic premises, postulates, or assumptions that specify certain fundamental entities, processes, or mechanisms, often implicating phenomena that themselves are unobservable (at the time of theory formulation)." He argues that such theory is hierarchical with a small number of "high level principles logically subsuming more abundant principles at lower levels" (Schiffer, 1988:462). He also divides theory into three realms: (1) Social Theory, (2) Reconstruction Theory, and (3) Methodological Theory. These realms differ in terms of their function, but all entail the same logic and a cross-cutting hierarchy of levels from low to high. Schiffer's view of theory is, like the theory itself, atomistic and systemic. He sees theory in terms of entities that are linked within subsystems.

Hodder (1984) gives us one of the clearest and boldest statements of the relativist position in his *Antiquity* article "Archaeology in 1984." It should be noted that more recently, he has backed away from the extreme relativism of this article (Hodder, 1986:16).[4] In 1984, he argued that the statements that archaeologists wished to make about the past were unobservable and that hypothesis testing in archaeology rests on consensus rather than on the confrontation of theories with data. He notes that all data are theory-laden, and that people cannot observe the world except through consciousness. This leads him to the relativist conclusion that our consciousness determines the stories archaeologists will tell about the past. Since this consciousness develops within specific socioeconomic contexts, the stories we write about the past are specifically related to the social interests of the present.

Wylie (1985b) gives us an insightful discussion about the opposition between subjectivity and objectivity in her study of the critical theory of Leone (1981) and Handsman (1980). In this article, she rejects the positions advanced by both

Schiffer and Hodder. She notes that a recognition of the fact that interests may distort knowledge claims does not necessarily presuppose that such claims are impervious to empirical examination. She also argues that once archaeologists acknowledge such interests, we cannot accept the neat hypothetic–deductive model put forth by the New Archaeology (see also Hesse, 1980).

A number of marxist archaeologists have pointed out that the debate over subjectivity and objectivity is a false one that serves only to obscure the dialectic between reality and consciousness, past and present (Kohl, 1985; Rowlands, 1984b; Patterson, 1989a). Kohl's (1985) *Dialectical Anthropology* article "Symbolic Cognitive Archaeology: A New Loss of Innocence" clearly summarizes this position.

Kohl (1985) takes both sides in the debate to task. He notes that the processualist approach has failed to produce the results that it promised and that the goal of absolute objectivity is both elusive and false. He praises Hodder and Leone for having "fled the sterile scientific captivity of Binfordian naturalism," but deplores a relativism "which threatens to introduce chaos into that painstakingly assembled record of cultural evolution" (Kohl, 1985:111). Kohl advocates, instead, a dialectical approach, a dialogue:

> *A real past, although blurred, can be glimpsed through archaeological materials. Prehistory's logic essentially is the same as history's: active engagement in a continual dialogue with oneself and one's sources. Perfect knowledge is never attained but understanding of the past "as a rational and intelligible process" is indirectly arrived at through a nonending series of successive approximations (Kohl, 1985:115).*

Archaeology as a Social and Natural Science

Much of the debate in archaeology does not explicitly recognize that the practice of archaeology requires both dialectical and empiricist methods. Archaeology involves the study of both the social and the natural–physical world, and dialectical and empiricist methods do not fit equally to each undertaking. In the end, the goal of archaeology is to understand the social world of the past; archaeology is itself part of the social world of the present. Empiricist methods can give us a description of the physical world, but archaeologists enter a web of social relations when we try to make sense of, explain, and give meaning to, this world and how it changes.

Engels (1954) made the dialectic a universal topic for the study of humans and nature by transforming it into an analytical tool, his "dialectics of nature." He hoped that through such a dialectic of nature he could account for both human and biological evolution with a common set of dialectical laws. Lukács (1971) revealed the fallacy of this logic, and in doing so, split the dialectic from the study of nature.

The distinction that the Frankfurt School (see Chapter 2 of this volume) drew between scientific and critical theories becomes important here. Scientific theories assume a separation of subject and object. Such a separation cannot exist in the social world because scholars are part of what they study, and the objects of study, people, can reflect, alter, arrive at different understandings, or come to the same type of understandings as the scholar. This is not the case in nature. The scholar is not (in the same sense) both subject and object in this world because the objects of study lack human consciousness. They are objects (see also Hesse 1980:170–171).

To expand on this point, we can ponder the subject–object relationship as it pertains to geologists and cultural anthropologists. Geologists are defined by what they study (rocks), but the objects of their study exist independent of that study; the study of geology creates geologists, but it does not create rocks. There is no unity formed between the geologist and rocks. Without geology, a geologist (the subject) and a specimen (the object) are different entities, one is a person and the other, a rock. The relationship of the cultural anthropologist (the subject) to an informant (the object) depends on the fact that both are people. There is unity between subject and object. To be an anthropologist, one must have an informant, and to be an informant, one must have an anthropologist. Furthermore, even as the informant is the object of the anthropologist's interest, the anthropologist is the object of the informant's interest; the informant studies the anthropologist even as the anthropologist studies the informant. Thus, both are active participants in the relationship, and both are transformed by it. A geologist can never be a rock. A rock can never study a geologist.

Scientific theories are also instrumental; they are tools for solving problems. They become a form of domination only when applied to social phenomena because the split between subject and object is a false one in this situation. The social scientist conceptualizes both the problem and the solution, yet the human objects of his interest may deem the problem a benefit and find the social scientist's solution detrimental to their own interests. Indeed, they may even see the social scientist as the problem (Deloria, 1968). For all parties in this relationship, these perceptions spring from a complex dialectic between social context and confrontation with the reality of the world. The relation of domination does not exist when there is not a unity that links subject and object. Rocks do not have interests in where or how a geologist finds oil, nor do they value the quest for oil differently from the geologist.

The problem with applying the dialectic to nature rests in the notion of relational contradictions. As Heilbroner (1980:43) argues, the existence of objects in nature does not depend on such contradictions. In nature, if fleas are removed from dogs, we still have fleas and dogs. If the unity of master and slave is broken, if the slave is freed, we are left with neither slaves nor masters. But these actors are changed as a result of their historic relations. We can think of the dog as a host and the flea as a parasite, but the relational contradiction of host and parasite is created in our mind and not inherent in fleas and dogs. "Dialectics thereby has a natural application to the social world that it lacks in the physical one." (Heilbroner, 1980:43).

At this point the reader would do well to recognize that archaeology studies both nature and society. The processualist position argues that archaeologists can use the theories and methods of natural science to explain culture (Salmon, 1982; Binford, 1983; Watson, 1986; Schiffer, 1988). It errs by ignoring that the nature of the subject–object distinction is fundamentally different in the study of nature and the study of society. The postprocessualists have argued for a dialectical approach to the study of the social world (Hodder, 1984, 1986; Miller and Tilley, 1984; Shanks and Tilley, 1987a, 1987b). They seemingly either do not recognize that much of archaeology is about the study of the natural–physical world or take this aspect of archaeology as trivial or given (see Hodder, 1982a:5).

Most of the traditional field and laboratory work of archaeology studies the physical world. This is clear in the case of techniques as archaeomagnetic dating, trace element analysis, faunal analysis, and palynology. It is also the case in most excavation and survey. These are questions about the distribution of objects in space: how many levels are there in a site, what is the distribution of ceramic sherds in a site, and what is the distribution of sites in a given valley? I would further argue that questions about events and practices should also be seen as questions about the physical world. Did the people of this valley grow wheat? When was the first beam put in place in Pueblo Bonito? Did twelfth-century English farmers use oxen to plow their fields? What were Acheulean hand axes used for?

Most of the work of archaeology lies in answering these types of questions. Some form of the hypodeductive model may work well in answering such questions, and archaeologists recognized this fact long before the New Archaeology of the 1960s. A good example of such an approach were the efforts to construct a dendrochronology master curve for the U.S. Southwest in the late 1920s (Haury, 1962). Archaeologists had two curves, one extending back from the present and a second floating in the past. They needed to find wood beams that would link the two curves and create one master curve. They noted that the early curve came from sites with black-on-white pottery and the later from sites with polychrome pottery (black and white on red). They hypothesized that they would find the specimens they needed in sites with transitional pottery types between the black-and-white and polychrome types (black-on-red pottery). They dug in such a site, and connected the curves.

I am reluctant, however, to assume that the study of the physical world and the study of the social world are distinct undertakings in archaeology with clearly marked boundaries between them. It is not, as Schiffer (1988) would have us believe, a matter of lower or higher levels of theory or different functional realms of theory. Leone (1981:12) noted that artifacts do not speak; scholars have to give them meaning, and the same observation applies to artifact distributions and ^{14}C dates. Furthermore, the physical world does not exist apart from the social world either in the past archaeologists wish to study or the present within which we study it. The human presence dominates the natural world, and human consciousness mediates all of our perceptions of that world. People constitute the natural world through lenses that refract rather than mirror or reflect.

Once archaeologists make an observation about an artifact distribution, a historic event, or a cultural practice in the past, we usually assign it meaning in terms of a relational contradiction. For example Hole *et al.* (1971:272) interpret the absence of horns on female sheet in the Bus Mordeh phase (7500 to 6750 BC) on the Deh Luran Plain of Iran as evidence of domestication. The idea of domestication is not part of the physical world in the way that the presence or absence of sheep horns is. Domestication forms a unity with wild; one concept necessarily implies the other. The idea of degrees of domestication quantifies this unity, but still rests on the underlying opposition. The female sheep skeletons that Hole, Flannery, and Neely found on the Deh Luran plain either had horns or they did not, but to say they were domesticated stems from research interests and questions formulated in the present. To understand *domestication* on the Deh Luran plain, archaeologists need to engage in the dialogue that Kohl (1985:115) calls for between ourselves and what we observe in the ground.

Only in the absence of humans do objects of the natural world exist independent of the social world; once humans are present, all of nature exists in both the social and natural worlds. The ox that is used to plow the field is simultaneously of the social and natural worlds. Humans created the ox through a millennium of breeding and by castrating a bull calf. The ox also figures in social relations beyond his use as a beast of burden and gains meaning in the social world. He may be an object of wealth, bride price, a ritual sacrifice, or a blue ribbon animal at the county fair. In this way, the ox becomes a component of one social relation or another (Ollman, 1976:26).

Gilman (1981:5–6) discusses such oxen in his paper on the transition from the Neolithic to the Bronze Age in Western Europe. He marshals empirical evidence to show that cattle were present, that they were castrated, and were put to pulling a plow. Having made these observations on the physical world, he then moves into a dialectical web of relations. He notes that plow agriculture stores labor in land and oxen. Because of this relation, the ox becomes a valuable social object, subject to both theft and protection. It becomes a component in the contradiction that leads to the transformation from an egalitarian Neolithic social world to a ranked Bronze Age social world.

Realism

I began this section by noting that the dialectic gives us an approach to studying the world that is neither purely empirical nor purely speculative, not purely objective or purely subjective. Rowlands (1984b:113) argues that archaeology needs to achieve the integration of objectivity and subjectivity in a single field of inquiry. The dialectic offers a starting point for moving toward this goal. Archaeologists have not achieved this goal, and I offer here only a few simple suggestions on where the path to this end might lead.

A number of scholars, most notably Roy Bhaskar (1986) and Russell Keat and John Urry (1982), have argued that Marx used a realist philosophy of science in his work. Derek Sayer (1979, 1987) explicitly links this philosophy to a theory of internal relations and Ollman's (1976) notion of the dialectic (see also Bhaskar 1986:109). Alison Wylie (1981) has argued that such a philosophy underlies most of the useful research done in archaeology over the last 20 years, despite the positivist rhetoric of the New Archaeology. These works should be read for a detailed consideration of realism. Keat and Urry (1982) is the most readily available and accessible of these discussions. Bhaskar (1986:102) notes that:

> For realism, it is the nature of the world that determines its cognitive possibilities for us; it is humankind that is the contingent phenomena [sic] in nature and human knowledge which is, on a cosmic scale, accidental. In science (wo)man comes to know (wo)man-independent nature, fallibly and variously. This cognitive relation is both the theme of philosophy and a topic for science. But only transcendental realism by setting (wo)man in nature is consistent with the historical emergence and the causal investigation of the sciences and philosophies themselves.

Let me repeat these ideas in different words. Realism accepts that there is a real world independent of our senses and consciousness. It also accepts that scholars can gain empirical knowledge of that world (Keat and Urry, 1982:5). Our knowledge of that world is, however, faulty and diverse because it is conditioned by human thought. So knowledge is neither a true image of reality nor simply created in our consciousness. To understand knowledge scholars should look at both reality and the context and processes of human thought.

Realists reject the positivist model of explanation (Wylie, 1981; Keat and Urry, 1982; Bhaskar, 1986). They argue that positivism equates explanation with prediction and thus, equates cause with correlation. This error springs from the positivist dictum that hypotheses should be accepted or rejected according to how well they fit empirical observation. Such testing fails to get at the underlying mechanisms and processes that create the phenomenon that is being explained.

Keat and Urry (1982:5) state that in realism, the goal of explanation is not prediction, but rather the discovery of the necessary connections between phenomena. This is done by acquiring knowledge of the underlying relations and processes that constitute these phenomena. Realists argue that to answer a why question, scholars must answer the how and what questions (Keat and Urry, 1982:31).

> Thus, if asked why something occurs, we must show how some event or change brings about a new state of affairs, by describing the way in which the structures and mechanisms that are present respond to the initial change. To do this it is necessary to discover what the entities involved are: to discover their natures and essences.

Theories and models in realism do not attempt to reduce the unknown to the known, but rather try to use what we already know to learn about the potentially knowable (Bhaskar, 1986:60). Realist theories give us conceptual tools with which we can look at specific contexts. They do not give us general explanations of abstract phenomena. Such theories are always imperfect. They are in the words of Keat and Urry (1982:36) "attempted descriptions of structures and mechanisms."

Sayer (1979:115–117) has followed Hanson (1969) in arguing that scientific thinking is arrived at from actual observation or experimentation, that theories do not exist in the mind before, or independent of, experience. They both refer to this process of reasoning as retroduction (Sayer, 1979:116). The process of retroduction is dialectical. It involves neither induction from a series of empirical observations to a law-like empirical generalization nor deduction from major or minor premises to an outcome (Jessop, 1982:217). Instead, it rationally moves from observations of the world that do not fit existing theory, to posit one or more processes that could account for the observed anomaly (Sayer, 1979:116; Jessop, 1982:217).

It perhaps goes without saying that our theories about the past must be coherent. They should not be tautological or filled with *logical* contradictions. They also need to account for all aspects of the phenomena that the investigator wishes to understand (Sayer, 1979:117).

As Wylie (1985b:143) points out, these theories may not adhere to the neat hypothetic-deductive model originally laid out by the New Archaeology. They should not be limited only to those things that people can empirically observe, for they also need to deal with the underlying relations and ties that create the observable reality (Jessop, 1982:219).

Our theories need to fit the facts we derive from the physical world. They should be congruous with the artifact distributions, dates, events, and practices that we can infer from the archaeological record through empirical methods. Bhaskar (1986:281) argues that these facts are not reality. They are the results of both a reality that existed before their discovery and of the conceptual schemes and paradigms that governed the enquiry that found them. As such, they are both real and social. The knowledge that scholars gain will always be the complex result of theory, methods, and reality itself.

As Leone (1981) has said, archaeologists have to give meaning to facts; they do not simply speak for themselves. These meanings are made in the present and reflect social interests. Trigger (1984:292) has observed that in archaeology "much of what is accepted as true tends to be what each generation of archaeologists finds reasonable." A full evaluation of a theory should include a critical look at how social interests interact with theory, method, and reality, at how these interests shape our research, even as that research forms interests. Sayer (1979:117) notes that "the history of science indicates that as a matter of fact choices have been made on grounds which included, amongst others, the metaphysical and the aesthetic, though we would hardly wish to build these into requirements of scientific adequacy."

Realism does not lead us to one best or true theory about a phenomenon (Sayer, 1979:135; Bhaskar, 1986:60–63). Realist theories necessarily refer to underlying relations or ties that create the phenomena that we observe. I have argued that, in studies of the social world, these underlying processes are dialectical (see also Sayer, 1979, 1986). Dialectical contradictions cannot be directly observed but must be inferred from their consequences (Ollman, 1976:15). Historians can discern through documents that Afro-Americans were being bought and sold in Alabama of the 1850s, but they cannot observe the relation of master and slave. Scholars cannot test for such underlying relations, but they can secure empirical evidence that bears on the truth or falseness of the inferred relation (Sayer, 1979:141). This process of evaluation is always imperfect and can never be conclusive. Furthermore, if scholars alter their perspective on the social whole that they observe, they will find different unities that inform them in different ways.

When theories are found to be inconsistent with empirical observation, it raises the problem of how to modify the theory to resolve these inadequacies (Bhaskar, 1986:61–62). If such modification is not possible, an alternative theory should be proposed to replace the initial one. Thus, theoretical analysis is a constant process of renewing existing theories, ideas, methods, and facts. This process is much more complex than the notion that new theories can be simply tested against old ones like so many ducks in a row. All theories arise as complex amalgams of the new and the old.

A realist approach to the study of archaeology is neither purely speculative nor purely empirical, neither purely objective nor purely subjective. It allows an empirical basis for judging theories about the past. But it holds that all knowledge ensues from a complex dialectic, so that it is difficult or impossible to assess how much interest, theory, method, or reality contribute to this knowledge. Using a realist approach, some theories will be rejected, but a best theory will not, necessarily, be chosen. It provides the bases for the active dialogue with a dimly perceived real past and ourselves that Kohl (1984) has called for.

In this chapter, I have tried to present the dialectic as a world view and explore how it relates to an epistemology for studying the real world. The dialectic also affects how archaeologists account for that world, how we deal with the ambiguities that lie within agency and structure, determinism and relativism. In the next chapter I shall discuss how it gives us a way around the impasses that these oppositions have presented for archaeological theory.

ENDNOTES

1. See also Allen (1980) and Braun and Talkington (1989) for further discussions of the dialectics of nature.

2. I have chosen a material example here and stress material examples throughout my discussions because archaeologists study material objects. The relational quality of terms in the dialectic applies equally well to all social phenomena. For example, a Hopi man may be a priest and leader of a kiva, but in his wife's house he is a husband and an outsider. These social roles are not inherent in his maleness (not all men are priests or husbands), and neither is his social being reducible to one of these social roles.

3. Shanks and Tilley make many such statements in their writings to be provocative, to trouble us with the limitations in archaeology we would often prefer to ignore. They have claimed that such statements should be read as provocations and not as theoretical tenets (Shanks and Tilley, 1989). Their provocation has been successful in goading archaeologists to debate and ponder the nature of archaeological knowledge. In the spirit of this provocation I have taken them at their word in this statement, even though I know they do not advocate the extreme relativism that it asserts.

4. Ian Hodder's frequent shifts of position and changes of mind have bedeviled many archaeologists who wish to pigeon-hole him and then reject the pigeon hole. Hodder's frequent shifts of position, however, reflect a consistent philosophical approach to knowledge. It is an anarchistic philosophy that questions authority, including the authority of the anarchist, and the freezing of inquiry in any single method or theory.

CHAPTER 5

The Making of History

Men make their own history, but they do not make it just as they please; they do not make it under circumstances chosen by themselves, but under given circumstances directly encountered and inherited from the past.

(Marx, 1978:9)

In the second paragraph of *The Eighteenth Brumaire of Louis Bonaparte*, Marx briefly states his notion of how history is made. He starts from the premise that people, rather than a deity or the invisible hand of classical economics, make history, but "they do not make it just as they please." The statement is ambiguous as to where the motor of history lies. Is it in the action of conscious human actors or in the circumstances inherited from the past?

Marxist theorists have interpreted this statement in a variety of conflicting ways. The scholars of the Second International (see Chapter 2 of this volume) tended to down-play the role of human action and stress the constraints implied by the idea that people do not make history just as they want or under circumstances of their own choosing. Rosa Luxemburg (1913, 1961) and later Lukács (1971), Korsch (1970a), and Gramsci (1971), put the focus on human action, the ability of people to come to a true understanding of their conditions and then to transform them. They took from Marx the dictum that people make history. In the postwar era both the Frankfurt School and French structural marxism (Chapter 2 of this volume) returned the emphasis to the constraints on human action. For the Frankfurt School these constraints lay in a false consciousness that denied human actors the knowledge they need to act, while the French structuralists argued that structures shape and decide human action. Humanist marxists of the last decade returned the focus to human action and to how people form the consciousness needed for such action (Laclau and Mouffe, 1985; Thompson, 1978; Sayer, 1987).

Clearly, Marx's seemingly simple statement can be read in a number of ways and the differences in such interpretations lie at the heart of theoretical debate. Archaeology has also been torn by these same debates. The oppositions between determinism and free will, mentalism and materialism, deeply trouble theorists of archaeology why feel obliged to see either some condition (economy, environment, structure, or culture) or human action as the primary, or only motor of change.

As a graduate student in the late 1970s, I was taught that there were two approaches to the study of the social world. A mentalist view held that what was in people's heads, their consciousness, determined how they would act; to understand why people acted the way they did, anthropologists had to know what was in their heads. A materialist view argued that culture is human's unique adaptation; material conditions in the environment or economy determined both how people would act and what would be in their heads. I was taught that these two views were inexorably opposed, never to be reconciled, since they began from fundamentally distinct assumptions about the nature of culture and human action. In archaeology, the materialist view clearly held sway. During the 1970s, the New Archaeology had exorcised the demon of a mentalist *traditional* archaeology, and only a handful of scholars openly took a mentalist stance (Deetz, 1977; Hall, 1977).

The inexorable nature of these two positions springs from the emphasis that both place on determinism, the idea that one aspect of the social world decides the rest. Neither position tolerates the ambiguity inherent in the dialectical view of human action as both determining and determined. Yet this ambiguity is the key to a better understanding of how history is made. "Men make their own history, but they do not make it just as they please." If we accept the ambiguity of that statement, then history is the complex result of human action and the constraints on that action. Such a dialectic is possible because the constraints on human action, whether in the environment, the economy, the social structure, or the culture, are at once both limiting and enabling. Even as they limit some forms of action, they enable others; this contradiction is a internal dynamic for change. Furthermore, these constraints do not exist independent of human action but are themselves transformed by such action.

Over the past two decades, archaeologists tended to focus on material relations of the economy and the environment as the major constraints that determine the form and content of the social world. Many archaeologists (Kohl, 1981) draw the theory of cultural materialism from the work of White (1949, 1959) and Harris (1979). Harris claims to derive this theory from Marx and it reflects many of the same emphases as the economist marxism of the Second International. Other archaeologists ground their work in Steward (1955) and his notion of cultural ecology (see Kohl, 1981). In less skilled hands, this often deteriorates into a form of environmental determinism. The theory of most archaeologists today is a poorly thought out amalgam of both of these views.

Recent challenges to this dominant theoretical view in archaeology, both marxist and postprocessualist, have recognized that a dialectic exists between human action and the constraints on that action (Hodder, 1982a; Rowlands, 1982; Shanks and Tilley, 1987a; Leone, 1988). These scholars shifted the debate to a discussion of the relative importance of human agency, structure, and culture in making history. Despite a shared adherence to a dialectical view, the choice of one of these aspects as the starting point for analysis has a profound effect on how that analyses will proceed. I will argue that a true dialectical understanding of the process of change is best achieved when investigators start by examining power (the universal ability of all humans to act) and ask how power shapes all social relations.

TWO NOTIONS OF DETERMINISM

The New Archaeology of the 1960s advised archaeologists to search for causal explanations for events in the past, to look for the conditions that determined the course of history (Fritz and Plog, 1970; Binford, 1972; Watson et al., 1971, 1984; Clarke, 1968; Renfrew, 1972). Despite a hot debate on how this goal was to be accomplished, there was a broad agreement that history was to be understood as a thing that was determined (Binford, 1972; Schiffer, 1976, 1988; Salmon, 1982). The most recent essays from this quarter uphold the stress on determinism and reject radical and postprocessualist critiques of the New Archaeology (see Hodder, 1982a, 1986; Miller and Tilley, 1984; Shanks and Tilley, 1987a) because they do not yield such deterministic statements (Earle and Preucel, 1987; Binford, 1987; Schiffer, 1988). The New Archaeology seems to be little more than a straw man today, but the notion of determinism that it argued for continues, in its broad sense, to dominate modern processual archaeology (see Salmon, 1982; Watson et al., 1984; Renfrew, 1982; Kelley and Hanen, 1988).

Determinism in Processual Archaeology

The processualist notion of determinism springs from the atomistic and systemic world view that these archaeologists bring to their study of the past. They start with the assumption that culture is a system that serves in "the integration of a society with its environment and with other socio-cultural systems" (Binford, 1972:198). The functioning of this system, like the functioning of a motor, is not reducible to any single component in it. But, like a motor, cultural systems can be broken down into unique entities (parts or components) and subsystems. These social entities can exist before, and apart from their links to other social entities. Binford (1972:12) argued that "processual change in one variable can thus be shown to relate in a predictable and quantifiable way to changes in other variables, the latter changing in turn relative to changes in the structure of the system as a whole." So social scientists can speak of some variables as being causal to others, and they can identify some aspects, levels, or subsystems of the social world as determining the nature of other aspects, levels, or subsystems.

Given that all of the components in such a system are functionally related, the cause for change must be found in independent variables that lie outside the system. James Hill (1977:76) argued that "no system can change itself; change can only be instigated by outside sources." Change is not seen as the normal state of the social world but, instead, as a violation of the smooth functioning of the system that must be explained by factors apart from the system. Some theorists reacted to this stress on external variables by dismissing causality, and instead argued for systemic explanations that mapped out the internal functioning of the system (Flannery, 1968, 1972). These efforts were condemned, in part, because they did not require that archaeologists pay attention to causality (Salmon, 1982:182).

Detailed and exact critiques of this deterministic method already exist in the archaeological literature (Trigger, 1978; Hodder, 1982b; Shanks and Tilley, 1987a, 1987b, 1989), and I will limit my comments on it to two points. First, the equation of causality or determinism with prediction is logically flawed. Second, the approach has failed by its own goal. It has not led us to the deterministic laws, law-like generalizations, or general theories to account for culture change that it promised.

Processual archaeologists tend to equate explanation with prediction (Watson et al., 1984:25–26). "An explanation is not considered adequate unless the general law and the statements describing the circumstances pertaining in the particular case in question logically could have enabled the observer to predict the particular case" (Watson et al., 1971:5–7). Renfrew (1982:13) holds that explanations should be general and that archaeologists should be able to use the explanatory principles derived from one case to predict aspects and changes in other cases. Earle and Preucel (1987:511) argue that we should adopt a "behavioral archaeology" that seeks to predict the outcome of human decision-making processes to explain things like settlement patterns.

Many philosophers have questioned the parity between prediction and explanation (Kelley and Hanen, 1988:227). Salmon (1982:159) notes that explanatory theories should do more than allow prediction. Realist philosophers have gone even further to reject the idea that prediction necessarily has anything to do with explanation or causation (Keat and Urry, 1982; Wylie, 1981; Bhaskar, 1986). Predictions do not, necessarily, give us an account of the actual mechanisms through which a given effect is, in fact, produced (Sayer, 1987:124). They do not tell us how the effect came to be.

Colin Renfrew (1982:15) said that his "down-the-line" model of exchange explains "the phenomena [sic] of exponential falloff of quantity with distance for certain traded commodities." This model is a logarithmic regression equation that describes the distribution of obsidian on Neolithic sites in Western Asia. The model can be used to predict how much of a commodity will occur at a given distance from a source, but it does not explain why that amount occurs there or even why the goods are present at that point at all. The mechanisms that make the distribution described by the model could be trading partnerships (Renfrew, 1972:465–466, 1975), differential use of the goods across space (Ammerman and Andrefsky, 1982) or that people who walk farther to a source carry less stuff back and/or use it more frugally (Hodder, 1984). To fully explain the distribution of obsidian on West Asian Neolithic sites, archaeologists would need to construct a theory that describes the structures and mechanisms that generated that distribution.

Even the major advocates of a processual archaeology recognize that this archaeology has failed in its goal of finding universal laws, law-like generalizations, or general theories that explain cultural change (Renfrew, 1982:8; Salmon, 1982:140). Numerous general laws have been proposed under the heading of "Middle Range Theory" (Binford, 1981) or "reconstruction theory" (Schiffer, 1988). These principles apply to the physical–natural world and include such observations as how dogs chew up bones (Binford, 1981:35–86) and the decay processes of wood (Schiffer, 1987:163–180). Some have down-played these principles as trivial or as *Mickey Mouse Laws* (Renfrew, 1982:8), but such knowledge is essential for us to make observations on the archaeological record. Archaeologists have, however, failed to generate comparable principles or generalizing theories for the explanation of culture change. After 20 years of trying, we really should ask why archaeology does not have such theory. Does the fault lie in the immaturity of our discipline, in our inability to carefully follow the prescriptions of the right philosopher of science, or has our underlying systemic, atomizing world view played us false? Perhaps it leads us down the wrong road toward the wrong goal. It is past time we considered the last explanation.

Determinism in the Dialectic

The dialectic leads us to a different notion of determination than the one found in processual archaeology. It recognizes that society is not like a motor. Society cannot be shut off. It is always running, perpetually changing. If a motor is taken apart, it is no longer a motor, but the parts that made up the motor still exist. If the relations that create the entities we can observe in a society are broken, these entities cease to exist. A divorce does not leave a husband and a wife because these social entities exist only because of the relation that links them. The new relation created by the divorce transforms the entities into new ones, ex-wife and ex-husband. This makes it futile to split off some social entities or subdivisions of the social whole as necessarily before or causal to other subdivisions or parts of the whole. Furthermore, unlike a motor, all the parts of society do not fit together snugly but rather, their existence may stem from contradictions in the relations that call them into being. The dialectic bids us to search for change in the contradictions that these relations entail and not the functions that social entities perform.

Sayer (1987:88) argues that a sense of determination exists in a dialectical approach to marxism, but that this sense cannot be the "standard causal one, in which the related terms are seen as being merely externally or contingently related." Scholars cannot isolate some entities or subsets of the whole as determining and others as effects since the existence of the determinate entity necessarily implies the existence of the effect (Ollman 1976:17). Scholars can, however, point to the role that one entity or subset of relations has in altering one or more of the relations that make up other entities or subsets (Ollman 1976:17). In doing this, the investigator singles out an influence as being worth noting in a particular case, but does not say it was causal in the sense of processual archaeology.

The notion of prediction also comes into play in a dialectical marxism, but again, not in the same sense as in processual archaeology. A better term for the type of prediction possible in a dialectic would be prognosis (Sayer 1979:139). A prognosis is *strictu sensu* a premise as to the likely course of future events that should be based on an analysis of the mechanisms and conditions present in the case, but cannot be arrived at by simple deduction. Such prognoses may be referred to, and have been referred to in marxism, as "laws," but they are in fact statements of tendencies and not predictions or "laws" in a positivist sense (Ollman 1976:19). Such laws are derived from evidence in the real world, and they are constantly modified with evidence from the real world. They cannot be reduced to timeless and spaceless generalities.

Childe's (1947:5, 69; Trigger, 1980b:182) view of laws as "shorthand descriptions of real processes" captures the dialectical notion of a law. A classic example of such a law is Marx's (1906:Ch. 14) dictum that with the development of capitalism, the rate of profit will tend to decline. A slightly different archaeological example in Kristian Kristiansen's (1982:273) observation that "A regional system may eventually be composed of several local cycles of expansion and regression, as is exemplified by the Nordic Bronze Age."

This sense of determinism means that social change is neither determined nor the result of human free will. The circumstances inherited from the past enables some forms of change and limit others, and our theory can specify these parameters. Our theory cannot, however, specify the exact form that the change will take. The dialectical approach will reveal the contradictions that will transform the social whole, but it will not tell us the specific sequence of events that will occur (Heilbroner, 1980:40). These events are best understood in the specific contexts in which they occur. The generalizations that we make in such a theory tell us where in a specific case to look for the process and mechanisms of change, but they do not tell us what the consequence of that change will be (Ollman, 1976:19).

MATERIALISM

Archaeologists have, for the last 20 years, tended to see the constraints on human action that reside in the material relations of the economy and the environment as determining the course of history. They have been prone to reduce the social realms of social structure and meaning to inert effects, the consequences of material change. Archaeologists have drawn this theory from two main sources, the cultural materialism of Leslie White (1949, 1959) and Marvin Harris (1979) and the cultural ecology of Julian Steward (1955) (Willey and Sabloff, 1980:181–185). These two perspectives often draw on, or parallel, marxist themes, but neither captures the dynamic interplay of the material and the mental that the dialectic implies. For this reason, they lead us to a vulgar materialism that is barren and mechanical (Friedman, 1974).

Adopting a dialectical view of social change does not require that archaeologists dump all of the empirical concerns or issues raised by cultural materialism or cultural ecology. These theories do prod us to look at important material constraints on human action and social change. These constraints remain crucial to our understanding of history, but we should look at how they dialectically interact with other social realms, rather than making them the motor of social change. To do this, archaeologists need to rethink the ideas that these theories carry about the material and the mental, and about nature and culture.

The Material and the Mental

Many archaeologists have avidly embraced Leslie White's theory of cultural evolutionism (Meggers and Evans, 1957; Ford, 1962; Quimby, 1960; Binford, 1972; Willey and Sabloff, 1980:181–185), and many others have drawn ideas from White's pupil, Marvin Harris, and his notion of cultural materialism (Price, 1982; Kohl, 1981:96–101; Schiffer, 1988). Harris (1979) claims that his theory and that of White are marxist, yet they champion a severe materialistic notion of determination that is hard to find in other works of marxist theory (Bloch, 1985:129, 133).

White (1959:8) defined culture as "man's extrasomatic means of adaptation," and he further divided culture into three subsystems, the technological, the social, and the ideological. He posited that social change began in the technological subsystem, and that this change led to changes in the social and ideological subsystems. Harris (1968:4) follows a similar path and argues for a techno-environmental or techno-economic determinism.

This principle holds that similar technologies applied to similar environments tend to produce similar arrangements of labor in production and distribution, and that these in turn call forth

*similar kinds of social groupings, which justify and coordinate their activities by means of
similar systems of beliefs.*

Harris argues that the characteristics of the base or infrastructure define and
determine the rest of the social whole. He grounds this theory in Marx and
quotes Marx's (1970:21) 1859 preface to *The Critique of Political Economy* as
support for the link.

Those authors, like Harris, who wish to portray Marx's theory as a form of
materialist determination, largely base their position on the 1859 preface and
comments that Marx (1971) made in his *Poverty of Philosophy* (see Cohen, 1978).
In the 1859 preface, Marx (1970:21) states that

> *The mode of production of material life conditions the social, political and intellectual life
> process in general. It is not the consciousness of men that determines their being, but, on the
> contrary, their social being that determines their consciousness.*

In the *Poverty of Philosophy*, he gives us the now infamous dictum "The handmill
gives you society with feudal lord: the steam mill, society with the industrial
capitalist" (Marx, 1971:109).

These ideas resonate in the work of the Second International (Bloch,
1985:103). For marxists such as Bukharin, Kautsky, and Plekhanov, shifts in the
material realm of technology and environment drove social change. They tended to see the base or infrastructure as constraining human action to the extent
that changes in this realm were the primary motor of history. These authors
did, however, maintain some sense of a dialectic in their thought. They did
admit that the superstructure had some role in social change and could, in some
instances, be a determining factor. Thus, Plekhanov (1961:18) noted, "Marx
reproached the earlier materialists with having forgotten that if men are products of circumstances . . . it is men that change circumstances." And Engels
wrote in a letter to Joseph Bloch on September 21, 1890:

> *According to the materialist conception of history, the ultimately determining element in
> history is the production and reproduction of real life. Neither Marx nor I have ever asserted
> more than this. Therefore if somebody twists this into saying that the economic factor is the only
> determining one, he is transforming that proposition into a meaningless, abstract, absurd
> phrase (Marx and Engels, 1977:75).*

Harris and other vulgar materialists can read Marx's words as statements of
material determinism because they fail to grasp Marx's the notion of "social
being" (Kohl, 1981:97–101; MacKenzie, 1984). The social being of humans, the
production and reproduction of daily life, all spring from human labor. Such
labor is a form of conscious, meaningful action, and readers can interpret these
quotes as a material determinism only if they equate labor with work. This
group of theorists, however, clearly accepted the idea that changes in the material base were the primary motor for change in history.

All social theories that invoke technological or material determination rest on two assumptions (Ollman, 1976:7–8; MacKenzie, 1984:474): (1) the autonomy of the base, the idea that the material base can change independent of the social and ideational factors that it is presumed to determine; and (2) changes in material relations spawn direct and corresponding changes in all other activities and institutions of a social form.

It is very hard to argue that the material factors that make up the base, e.g., technology, economy, and demography, do not depend in some ways on the mental factors of the superstructure, e.g., religion, law, and kinship. Zagarell (1986) has written about how changes in the economy of Early Dynastic III Mesopotamia sprang from shifts in social relations between kin groups, private estates, and temple estates. In this context, production for export by the state depends on indebted female labor drawn from the kin groups. The base of ED III Mesopotamia depended on a set of social, gender, and political relations. It was not autonomous from these things.

The assertion that changes in the base will lead to direct changes in all other aspects of a social form is also dubious. Marx (1906:205) does not accept this view as he concludes his discussion of the labor process in *Kapital* by saying:

> As the taste of the porridge does not tell you who grew the oats, no more does this simple process [the labor process] tell you of itself what are the social conditions under which it is taking place, whether under the slave-owner's brutal lash, or the anxious eye of the capitalist, whether Cincinnatus carries it on in tilling his modest farm or a savage in killing wild animals with stones.
>
> As Ollman (1976:8) notes, it does not take a deep probing of history to know that Christianity and Roman law survived long after the productive relations that supposedly produced them disappeared.

A number of marxist theorists have questioned the priority of the base over the superstructure. Some, among them the members of the Frankfurt School, Lukács (1971), and Korsch (1970a), switch priority to the superstructure, at least in some historical contexts. Althusser (1969:113) accepted the priority of the base in the last instance but argued that in the real world the "last instance never comes" so that the social world is complexly overdetermined by base and superstructure.

A more radical critique arises from dialectical theorists who deny that the base may be split from the superstructure (Ollman, 1976:7–8; Godelier, 1982; Sayer, 1987). They usually begin by noting that the existence of the base depends on the existence of the superstructure; neither can exist before, or in the absence of, the other. From this stance, Gramsci (1971:363) judges that any opposition of base and superstructure is nonsense.

Sayer (1987:90–93) has argued that it is not productive to look at the base and superstructure as two different levels of realms of the social world. He notes that the base is more than simply tools, but rather, that it is people cooperating to use those tools, that is, social labor. The superstructure does not exist apart from this social labor but is the mental structure necessary for that labor. Creating or changing the base, creates or changes the superstructure; these are a single activity, not two activities.

If I dismiss the idea that marxism is necessarily or productively viewed as a theory of material or economic determinism, then I must ask whether marxism is, as Marx claimed, a materialist theory. I would answer yes to that question. It is a materialist theory but one that is embedded in a dialectical method and thus, it differs from the materialism so common in modern archaeology.

A dialectical perspective rejects the notion that either the material or the mental may be seen as before or dominant to the other. People engage in social labor, and they are only able to do so because of the unity of the material and the mental. When Marx (1970:21) noted that social being determines consciousness, he was not arguing that the material should be given primacy over the mental, but rather that the material and the mental form a unity (Sayer, 1987:84–85). Godelier (1982:19) finds that a complex body of mental representations reside inside all human relations to the material world, and that they must be there for such action to occur.

In order to understand the dynamic of the material and the mental in history, scholars must pick a starting point, a moment where they enter that motion (Ollman, 1976:292). Do they start with human relations with the material world or with the mental representations that make those relations possible? This choice of a moment is not the same as an *a priori* judgment that the material or the mental determines the course of social change; rather, it is a choice of tactics that will shape our inquiry.

The theory advocated here is materialist in the sense that it argues we should start our inquiry into the past with the material production and reproduction of everyday life (Sayer, 1987:148; Arthur, 1986:22–23). Humans must be made as living beings in order to act, engage in labor, and think. Humans must be able to live in order to make history. As Arthur (1986:23) points out "we can not create our being by some undetermined pure act or thought." Scholars cannot take ideas alone as our starting point unless they wish to assume that humans form ideas arbitrarily or that forces external to people introduce ideas into their heads (Godelier, 1982:28).

CULTURE AND NATURE

Current materialist theory in archaeology tends to find the motor of social change in the human–nature relation (Willey and Sabloff, 1980:191–194). As Kohl (1981:96) observed, this leads to interpretations that range from a crude determinism, whereby social groups only react to environmental or demographic changes, to a more sophisticated cultural ecology. This theory depends on the assumption that culture and nature can be treated as two distinct things, one determining or shaping the other. These archaeologists prefer to see the environment or ecological relations as constraining human action in such a way as to decide the nature and path of social change. They often bring population growth into their analyses as an independent variable, an inevitable force that springs from our nature as a species. This theory fails to recognize both the unity of culture and nature and that environmental change simultaneously constrains and enables human action.

Ecology and Society

Ecological theory in archaeology can be divided into two parts, a cultural ecology and a human ecology, a division also found in cultural anthropology (Vayada and Rappaport, 1968). The first group writes a cultural ecology based, in large part, on the work of Julian Steward (1955). These archaeologists see culture as a uniquely human form of adaptation that relies on learned social behavior. The second group of theories argue for a human ecology in which archaeologists can use biological theories, models, and laws to understand human action and social change in the past. These archaeologists feel that human adaptation is enough like that of other animals to apply the same theory to human and animal adaption.

Of these two theories, Julian Steward's is the most akin to a marxist approach. Both cultural ecology and marxism realize the importance of the process by which people transform nature for our understanding of history (Roseberry, 1978:27). Cultural ecology also recognizes that there is a dynamic interplay between culture and nature and that people consciously select and reject aspects of the environment (Kohl, 1981:101). In this regard, cultural ecology shares with marxism the awareness that production is at the same time a physical and a social action (Gilman, 1989:67). The two approaches differ in that cultural ecology tends to stress the technological or physical aspect of that action and marxism tends to stress the social nature of the action (Roseberry, 1978:28).

Much of the critique of Steward's theory in archaeology and elsewhere has centered on his idea of cultural core. He posited that "the constellation of features which are most closely related to subsistence activities and economic arrangements" formed a culture core and that investigators should focus on this core to understand social change (Steward, 1955:37). This notion clearly differs from the materialism of Harris because it allows that mental factors, among them social, political, and religious patterns and esthetics features, could be part of the motor of change (Steward, 1955:37). Archaeologists looking for determinate causes that they can apply across time and space often have problems with this idea because it is ambiguous about what should be in the culture core (Adams, 1966:14–15). Steward intended this ambiguity because he saw the aspects of culture in the core as differing from time to time and from place to place. Thus, aspects in the core had to be discovered anew for each case or set of comparisons, and were not given *a priori* in theory (Steward, 1955:37, 93–96).

The search for universal determinants led most archaeologists to pass over the idea of culture core or equate it with the technology (Willey and Sabloff, 1980:151). As a result, most studies that promote cultural ecology differ very little from those under a theory of cultural materialism (Kohl, 1981:102), or worse, they degenerate into environmental determinism. This is clearly seen in Sanders and Nichols (1988:33) paper on the evolution of Monte Alban in the valley of Oaxaca, México. In this paper, they claim to be using Steward's idea of cultural core, but all of their explanations make the environment primary. "In highland México and Guatemala, the microgeographic complexity and nonredundancy of other (nonsubsistence) resources favored the formation of central places which, on the one hand, facilitated exchange and, on the other, provided an additional mechanism for centralization of political authority" (Sanders and Nichols, 1988:33).

Human ecologists in archaeology routinely chide the rest of the field for not being scientific enough in theory and method and argue that archaeologists can become more scientific by using biological theories and models. A number of authors, among them Dunnell (1980, 1989), Leonard (1989), Rindos (1985), and Wenke (1981), argue that we should adopt a Darwinian theory of natural selection to account for social change in history. For example, Dunnell (1989:42) suggests that "complex society, a perennial focus of both anthropological and archaeological interests, may be little more than the manifestation of a shift in the scale at which selection is most effective." Many archaeologists studying hunters and gatherers have evoked an optimal foraging theory drawn from biological ecology to explain the action of such groups (Hawkes *et al.*, 1982; Belovsky, 1988; Winterhalder *et al.*, 1988). This theory blurs the line that splits biology and anthropology and assumes that humans will always make rational choices to optimize calorie capture in order to build mathematical models that predict human action. Winterhalder *et al.* (1988:323) conclude that the economy of hunters and gathers "has an ecological master."

Many devotees of both cultural and human ecology invoke population growth as an independent causative variable in their explanations. They start from the belief that nature controls human demographics and that human populations have an innate tendency to grow. When such growth pushes the population size above the level of available calories in the environment, the carrying capacity, then social change must result to reorganize production and boost calorie capture. A number of authors have critiqued this view, showing that population growth is not innate and but is instead as much under the sway of culture as of nature (Cowgill, 1975a; Hassan, 1981). In spite of these critiques, a number of archaeologists still see population growth as a natural phenomenon and as a (or the) motor driving long-term cultural change (Sanders and Nichols, 1988:74; Keeley, 1988:375–377; Johnson and Earle, 1987).

The Dialectics of Culture and Nature

Archaeologists find it very hard to grasp the essence of the relationship between humans and nature. On the one hand, we are impressed by the fact that people are biological organisms and that they share with other animals certain basic needs in order to survive and breed. People are a part of nature, and we must, like other animals, adapt to the rest of nature. On the other hand, we note that human adaptation depends on a number of cultural characteristics, such as tool use, language, and learning, to an extent, and in ways that the adaptations of other animals do not. From this observation, we assume that culture is something apart from nature, and we treat culture and nature as two distinct things. In the first view, human action and social change is reduced to biological principles, and in the second, either culture or nature is seen as occurring before or determining human action and social change. In a dialectical point of view, we focus on the ambiguities in the human — nature relation instead of trying to dissolve them away by reducing all to biology or by making nature and culture separate things.

Godelier (1986:1) begins his anthropological study of thought, economy, and society with a series of comments about what makes humans different from other animals — what sets culture apart from nature. He starts with the fact that humans do more than just live in society; they must make society in order to live. They invent new ways of thinking and acting. The worst architects differ from the best bees not only because they must raise their structures in their minds first, but also because they can design and build a structure that has never been built before. This action produces culture and creates history. Other animals are the products of a history; however, it is not a history that they have made, but the natural evolution of living matter. Godelier argues that humans have a history because they use social labor to transform nature, or more exactly, because they transform their relations to nature by transforming nature itself.

Godelier's discussion captures the ambiguity in the relation between culture and nature. He sees that people stand in a different relation to nature than do other animals because, as Steward also noted, our adaptations are learned and meaningful, that is, they are social. Scholars are ill advised to reduce our understandings of human action and social change to biological principles created for the study of other animals. These biological ideas do not give us access to the workings of human consciousness or to meaningful social action. On the other hand, he recognizes that culture does not exist apart from nature but rather, that culture is a transformation of nature.

The means to this transformation lies in human labor. As Young (1983:351) points out "Labour is neither nature nor culture but their matrix." Labor gives order and form to both nature and culture. Human beings are of nature, they are biological creatures, and the human capacity to work is given in our nature – the bone, muscle, neurons, and blood of our bodies. Labor implies more than just work; it is a form of conscious, meaningful, social action essential for human survival. The social quality of labor allows people to transform their relation to nature by transforming nature itself.

The ability of humans to transform nature also depends on the tools and facilities that they have to use in nature. Archaeologists have long argued that peoples with simpler technologies have less control over nature than peoples with more complex technologies. This observation lies at the heart of cultural materialism and is the basis for this theory's view that changes in technology and other material relations are the motor of history.

There can be little question that the characteristics and complexity of technology are key factors in the social transformation of nature. The fault in the materialist logic does not lie with this fact but with the idea that nature is something separate from labor, an entity to be controlled. From this view, the simpler the technology, the greater the role of the environment in determining social change, and the more complex the technology, the greater the role of the social in determining social change. The relation between culture and nature is a dialectical one, and even though the effect of each pole of this dialectic may vary with levels of technological development, the route of change is never set by one pole or the other.

The only situations in which the environment exists as a thing apart from, and untransformed by, labor are cases in which people enter previously unpopulated environments. Even in these rare cases, people at once set about to transform that environment in order to live.

The simplest tools allow people to transform the environment in vital ways. Fire not only serves to give light and heat, but is also used as a powerful tool to transform nature. Australian aborigines had a simple technology and lacked agriculture, but manipulated their environment in complex ways (Yen, 1989). They set fires to create grasslands in which plants useful to them would grow more densely and with more regularity than the same plants would have grown given the natural succession of the areas (Yen, 1898:57–58).

The least elaborate technologies for food production allow humans to profoundly alter the environment. People created the open grasslands of highland New Guinea millennia ago by cutting down tropical forests with stone tools to make open areas for cultivation. Recent farming methods work to ensure the productivity of agriculture in this environment; a nature that is the result of a prior, human caused, and irreversible deforestation (Powell, 1982:28–30; Golson, 1989:683).

Those who would set nature aside as something separate from culture tend to see the role of nature in social change as either determining or possibilistic (Vayda and Rappaport, 1968; Netting, 1971). Environmental determinism holds that the environment is a major factor that decides the form of social groups and their changes through time. The possibilistic view, on the other hand, says that the environment will permit a range of social forms and changes, but that there are always alternatives. It can never really be known which possibility will come to be. Once we recognize the dialectical relationship between nature and culture, the possibilistic versus deterministic antinomy dissolves away.

Environmental and demographic change both enables and constrains human action, and through this process, social change. The functionalist notion of adaptation that pervades much of archaeology (Kirch, 1980; Keeley, 1988) views societies as systems that adapt to an environment. Environmental or demographic change will, therefore, be beneficial or detrimental to that society. This assumes that all social groups and individuals in a society stand in the same relationship to the environment and to each other. This is rarely, if ever, the case.

In reality, environmental or demographic change will benefit some groups in a society and will be detrimental to others. This is true regardless of the technological level of the society. For example, in twentieth century northern Colorado, late summer rains benefit ranchers because the grass uses the water to make more graze on the ranges, but these same rains harm farmers because they can beat down the wheat and make fields too muddy for combines to enter. In traditional Hopi agriculture, some families have most of their fields in the alluvial fans of large arroyos, and others have them in the fans of small arroyos, or on the talus slopes of the mesas. In a dry year, the small arroyo and talus slope fields wilt, and the large arroyo fields grow green, so that some families are forced to leave the pueblo to hunt and gather, while others put away corn for the coming year (Hack, 1942).

Environmental and demographic changes affect social change because they enable the action of some social groups in a society and constrain the action of others. These changes enter into the dynamic of conflicts and contradictions that exist within and between societies and affect how these are played out. In this way, nature becomes one with human agency, social structure, and culture in social change. The outcome of such change transforms nature so that the relationship of culture and nature never reaches stasis.

AGENCY, STRUCTURE, AND CULTURE

Recent marxist and postprocessualist theory in archaeology recognizes that a dialectic exists between human action and the circumstances inherited from the past that structure that action. These scholars have shifted the debate to a discussion of the relative importance of human agency, structure, and culture in the making of history. The debate is not over which of these aspects determines social change, but the choice of one of these aspects as a starting point for analyses has a marked effect on how that analysis will proceed. Archaeologists tend to emphasize one or the other of these aspects as primary to our understanding of social change rather than beginning their analysis with a consideration of power as a relation that permeates all of these aspects.

Power

All humans have the power to act, that is, the ability to do or accomplish something. It is this ability to act, to do work, that makes social labor possible; this is labor power (Marx, 1906:197–198). Yet this sense of power is usually lost in archaeological analysis.

Typically, social scientists equate power with a force, as a quantity that some people or social groups may have and other people or social groups may lack; a sum that can be tallied. People are elite by virtue of the fact that they have more power than others. Egalitarian social groups have little power, and the distribution of power becomes an issue only if the social group is ranked or stratified. Most of us recognize in this view Weber's (1978:152) notion of power as "the probability that one actor within a social relationship will be in a position to carry out his own will despite resistance." In this view, power is ultimately an ability to thwart another, a form of negative action. Power becomes something set apart from society as a whole, a thing held by some people and not by others. Scholars can then divide social groups into the elites who have power and the common people who lack power. This is "power over" (Foucault, 1984; Miller and Tilley, 1984:5).

We can also think of power as "power to." "Power to" refers to the ability of all people to act or intervene in a set of events so as, in some way, to alter them. Such power permeates all social life, in all times and places. It is not a quantity, but instead, an inherent aspect of human being. "Power to" may involve "power over," but this broader idea of power encompasses Weber's notion of thwart as but one way among many by which "power to" involves a "power over."

Power does not exist apart from society. It has no force as an abstract quantity. Power has force only when it is exercised by persons or groups of people (Hoy, 1986). These people derive power from the network of social, material, and ideological relations of which they are a part. Power, therefore, exists only in the social relations between people and/or groups of people, and just as "power over" comes from "power to," so too does "power to" give people the ability to resist force.

Taking this broader view of power leads us to recognize that power exists in many forms, and that it is not reducible to a single source, structure, or hierarchy (Crumley and Marquardt, 1987:613–615; Paynter and McGuire, 1991). It is not a quantity that an elite horde or dole out, and it exists in the absence of an elite. Can it really be said whether the power to lead a hunt is greater or lesser than the power to initiate children, or are we dealing with qualitative differences in forms of power? Scholars err in trying to reduce all forms of power to a single tally or in trying to understand history without talking about power.

Agency

It is tempting to read Marx's comment that "men make their own history" to mean that people are free to act in any way they wish. We could then embrace the Parsonian idea that actors freely choose among a wide or infinite range of possible actions. This notion was key to diffusionary theory in the archaeology of the first half of this century. In this theory, all cultural variation began with a person using his or her imagination to create something new, that is, to invent (Haury, 1952:19). The idea of people as free agents would, however, be a serious misreading because as Marx cautioned us "they do not make it just as they please." Any discussion of human agency in history should start with the realization that human actors are not free agents and that circumstances inherited from the past both enable and constrain human action.

The strongest arguments for the importance of human agency in social change have come from Ian Hodder (1982a, 1982b) and his students (i.e., Shanks and Tilley, 1987a; Johnson, 1989). Hodder (1982a:5) has said:

> Individuals are not simple instruments in some orchestrated game and it is difficult to see how subsystems and roles can have 'goals' of their own. Adequate explanations of social systems and social change must involve the individual's assessments and aims.

Shanks and Tilley (1987a:123) decry the way that functionalism, structuralism, and poststructuralism remove the individual from our analyses in various ways. They argue that all agents are positioned in relation to other agents, social groups, and institutions, but that this positioning does not make agents simple props or parts of these other aspects.

These archaeologists derive their theory of agency primarily from the work of Anthony Giddens (1984). The basic premise of Giddens' work is that structure is a necessary condition for action, while at the same time structure is produced through action. He starts with the truism that "all human beings are knowledgeable social actors." People have the ability to discuss and explain their actions and the goal orientations that motivate them. Most action, however, is of a mundane character and is rarely subject to overt consideration, and as such, remains a nondiscursive phenomenon. Knowledgeable actors are not all knowing or all seeing. Their actions are also bounded by conditions, the unintended consequences of prior actions, and the action of others.

The theoretical stress that poststructural archaeologists put on the individual seems not to be a productive approach to the study of the past. As Johnson (1989) points out, the individual appears in their theory but not in their substantive studies. Shanks and Tilley (1987a) appear to contradict themselves as they argue for the importance of the individual agent on one page, yet on another, state that all human action is overdetermined by structures. In more recent work, Tilley seems to set aside this stress on the individual. He states that "The individual does not so much construct material culture or language, but is rather constructed through them" (Tilley, 1989:189).

This view of human agency is not a marxist one. It derives from Weber's (1978:4) emphasis on the study of social action and its meaning for individual actors. Giddens (1984) links a Weberian notion of human action to structure, but he still treats individuals and structure as separate things; human action may entail structure, but individuals exist as abstract beings free of that structure. The notion of methodological individualism creeps into Shanks and Tilley (1987a) through their use of Giddens' theory.

The idea of the abstract individual who is naturally independent of others and creates social structures *vis à vis* action is a rather recent notion dating from the eighteenth century (Marx, 1906:92, 1973:84; Foucault, 1974). The division of labor in capitalism forms people as individuals, that is, as autonomous subjects that can freely enter into contracts with others as owner or worker, that can freely act and give their own meaning to the world (Sayer, 1987:99). This view is an illusion of the modern world, since human life presupposes social structures, and the need for these structures, in fact, grows with capitalism. The more a division of labor that individualizes people expands, the more specialized the productive roles of individuals, the more socially interdependent people become, since they depend more on the products of others' labor.

As Godelier (1986:1) notes, humans "do not just live in society, they must produce society to live." Human action should not be opposed to social structure because human action and social structure form a unity. The existence of one necessarily requires the prior existence of the other (Frisby and Sayer, 1986:91–96). Humans make history as social beings, and they do so as members of social groups; it is the action and social consciousness of such groups that a marxist archaeology should contend with and not an abstract idea of individuals (Ollman, 1976:126).

Kus (1989a, 1989b) uses such an approach in her study of the long-term emergence of the Merina state in eighteenth-century Madagascar. She shows how the people were actively involved in the formation of the state, and she looks at the relationship between the state and its citizens by which consent was made and upheld. Her work parallels that of Lukcás and Gramsci in its focus on the creation and transformation of class consciousness.

Structure

Some have used Marx's critique of the autonomous individual to dismiss any notion of volunteerism or free will in marxism and to stress the role of social structure in the making of history. The best known of these theorists is Althusser, but the marxist structuralism of Jonathan Friedman has had a much wider impact on archaeologists. Both these approaches run the danger of reifying structure as a thing apart from people and thereby, leaving little room for human action in the making of history.

Althusser argues that the form of a society arises from a hierarchy of structures or practices (Chapter 2 of this volume). These structures interact with each other, but remain distinct and separate. Human actors do not create these structures, but rather the structures shape and decide human history. People do not make history; the motion of history lies in the structures of a society. Mark Leone (1972, 1977) made some use of Althusser's structuralism in his early work on the material culture of Mormons in the United States, but this idea of structuralism has not been widely accepted in archaeology.

Jonathan Friedman's Structuralism

Jonathan Friedman's (1974, 1979, 1989) work on structuralism has had a much wider impact on our field than that of Althusser. This is, in part, because of his association with archaeologists such as Michael Rowlands, Kristian Kristiansen, and Barbara Bender, and in part because Friedman himself has written on archaeological topics (Friedman and Rowlands, 1978). He rejects the structural causality of Althusser and argues instead for a more historical approach, whereby archaeologists account for the existence of a social form by exposing its origin in a structural transformation (Friedman, 1979:19).

Social structures for Friedman (1979; Friedman and Rowlands, 1978) consist of functionally related categories and a set of rules that guides their interrelations. These structural categories are more or less autonomous, and a range of intra- and inter-systemic functions link them in a whole. Contradictions arise because of the limits in functional compatibility between these categories. The way in which a specific society uses its environment will create a hierarchy of constraints that decide the evolutionary potential of the whole system. A transformation occurs when a given social system alters the means of production and creates a new set of constraints that are not compatible with the existing social relations. Such change can be explained only with reference to the prior forms. These processes of change occur as regional events linking social units in a larger system across space. Pursuit of this last aspect of the theory has recently led its proponents to employ Wallerstein's (Chapter 2) World Systems theory (Ekholm and Friedman, 1982; Rowlands et al., 1987).

Friedman's structuralism makes finding the origin of the structural transformations that created the history that we study the goal of archaeology (Friedman, 1979:19; Rowlands, 1982:165). It shares with other types of structuralism the assumption that systemic features logically come before the actions of people who transform them and that these features, therefore, shape human action (Archer, 1988:91). Structuralists also note that human action in the form of resistance to structures of domination may not change those structures but may, in fact, have the opposite effect of making them stronger (Archer, 1988:68).

Structuralism puts the emphasis in the study of history on qualitative change and fails to recognize the dialectical relationship between qualitative and quantitative change. Qualitative transformations occur because of the build-up of quantitative changes that expose, accentuate, and realize the contradictions that exist in the social whole. A focus on the origin of social structures could be read to suggest that structures exist as static entities until transformed. In reality, quantitative changes begin to modify structures from the moment they come into existence. An understanding of transformations requires that archaeologists study this dynamic. Structure is not logically before human action because it is a product of human action, and the decision to start our analyses with structure or action is an analytical one. Human action brings about the quantitative changes in structures that ultimately lead to their transformation. People do not make history just as they like. Resistance may not always transform structures of domination, but it does change them. What strengthens domination in the short run may realize contradictions and initiate new action that will, in the long run, transform that domination.

Just as the individual cannot exist in the absence of society, so too, society cannot exist in the absence of individuals. Social structures have no existence independent of the people who form them. These structures are not things, but instead are sets of relationships that link individuals (Frisby and Sayer, 1986:96). Because society is a relational network of differences, that is, a network of contradictions that define individuals in definite ways, as husband and wife or master and slave, conflict is built into these unities. Shanks and Tilley (1987a:129) note "the seeds of change need no sowing" — they are inherent in the structure. People take on certain social characteristics and consciousness as a result of their position *vis à vis* others in these sets of relationships and, for this reason, people make history as members of social groups. As Ollman (1976:126) notes, "history is the product of mass movements."

Wallerstein's World Systems Theory

Friedman's notion of structuralism meshes quite effortlessly with Wallerstein's (1974, 1978, 1980a) notion of world systems theory. Both approaches attempt to account for change by examining the origin of large-scale structures that shape the way that people live. Both approaches are systemic, stressing the functional interaction of units within these systems. Both theories see people as caught up in larger structures and historical processes beyond their control.

The theoretical value of the World Systems perspective has attracted many archaeologists. Some such as Kohl (1979, 1987b), Whitecotton and Pailes (1986), and Ekholm and Friedman (1982), have attempted to map Wallerstein's theory directly onto an ancient past. Other archaeologists find the World Systems model heuristically useful but analytically inappropriate to their cases (Blanton *et al.*, 1981; Plog, 1983; Upham, 1982).

In *The Modern World System*, Wallerstein (1974, 1980a) does not present a general theory of cultural evolution but instead, a historical theory for the rise of capitalism. Wallerstein writes modestly about the empires that preceded the capitalist world economy and extensively on the rise of the capitalist world economy. He has, however, only slight concern with the noncapitalist world economies that characterize most of human existence. More important, Wallerstein's theory is historical and not evolutionary. Wallerstein's concepts refer to specific developments in the history of the world and are not generalizable to all times and places.

Archaeologists have primarily used Wallerstein's concept of world economy as a mode of production[1] (Plog *et al.*, 1982; Plog, 1983; Upham, 1982; Whitecotten and Pailes, 1986). Wallerstein, however, made no original contributions to the study of precapitalist world economies. When he discusses world economies, he inevitably moves immediately to the discussion of the capitalist world economy. World economies derive from a functional and geographic division of labor but differ from world empires in their lack of an over-arching centralized government. Wallerstein indicates that world economies are inherently unstable and short-lived entities; the capitalist world economy is anomalous because it has lasted 500 years. Clearly, the dynamics of the capitalist world economy is markedly different from those of earlier world economies. Wallerstein does not provide us with discussions of those earlier dynamics.

Wallerstein's approach emphasizes that the core subjugates the periphery, but it does not adequately deal with the unique aspects and developments of peripheries or how peripheries affect the core (Wolf, 1982:23). Archaeological interpreters of Wallerstein identify regional interaction as important to uneven development, but accounting for how this interaction leads to particular prehistorical sequences is another matter. Archaeologists need to be able to interpret the variation in societies that are not cores. Simply identifying all such societies as peripheries obscures both the variability and the role of these societies in determining prehistoric developments.

The concepts *core* and *periphery* themselves present some problems for the archaeologist. They may have heuristic value, helping us to interpret history as the result of unbalanced interaction within a region. But how do we, as archaeologists, decide whether a prehistoric area was a core, periphery, or semiperiphery? There also exists a problem of scale. In the context of Southwestern archaeology, an archaeologist may wish to speak of Chaco Canyon as a core; but in terms of the Southwest and Mesoamerica, the entire Southwest is best thought of as a periphery. These concepts may function well at the macro level of explaining the rise of capitalism as a world-wide phenomenon, but they are too broad and imprecise for understanding the specifics of development in a region.

A more important problem with the core–periphery contrast is that it assumes that all groups and relations can be ranked. This is a questionable assumption. A great number of contrasts can be made between social groups based on linguistics, culture, adaptation, religion, etc., and these distinctions may be ranked or not (Marquardt and Crumley, 1987:11).

These, and other, problems with the use of World Systems theory spring from the attempt to account for the totality of social reality with a single theory.

These attempts reduce the rich variation of history to a handful of categories, a few processes, and a high order scale. World Systems theory takes a systemic view, that stresses the units (cores, peripheries, and semiperipheries) that are linked in the system rather than the relations that create the units. Classificatory terms such as core and periphery unite areas in terms of a specified set of similarities, but in doing so, they mask or hide important variation between regions placed in the same category. The theory identifies inequalities in the processes of economic exchange and development as the driving forces for change in history. In World Systems theory a social group becomes core because of its functional position in the international division of labor. A social group may, however, be central because of its position in a web of religious, social, economic, or political relations. One group may be the center for one set of relations, e.g., religion, while a different group is the center for another set of relations, e.g., economic. Finally, this theory derives all social change from processes that occur at the highest scale. People, however, live and act in a world of varying scales, and their relations with others change as their scale of reference changes. The processes that occur at different scales are linked, but they are not reducible, one to another (Marquardt and Crumley, 1987:2). These weaknesses in World Systems theory are accentuated when archaeologists attempt to expand it beyond the specific case of the origins of capitalism for which it was drafted.

The theory points to an important aspect of social relations, unevenness in development, and to the contradictions that occur from this unevenness. Archaeologists can take this notion of unevenness and examine it as a much more multidimensional phenomenon than World Systems theory allows. To do so, we need to avoid a totalizing theory that uses *a priori* functionally related categories such as core and periphery and that assumes that processes of social change are best understood at a single scale.[2] Instead, we need to examine the unevenness of cultural development in terms of multiple dimensions and at multiple scales (see Chapter 6 of this volume).

Culture

Culture is one of the "given and inherited circumstances" that constrain human action (Sayer, 1987:96). The culture legacy of the past is an important material part of the present that frames present experience and affects how people will perceive the world around them, while this perception affects they way they will act (Roseberry, 1989:42). Some archaeologists have argued that the motor of history lies in culture, that culture makes history. In a similar vein, others embrace a dominant ideology thesis arguing that the culture and ideas of the ruling class determine the culture and ideology of the ruled. In these ways, both culture and ideology become entities apart from real people and the lives that they lead.

In a humorous essay, Flannery (1982) argues that archaeologists should put the culture concept at the center of our study. If we take Flannery seriously, then archaeologists need the culture concept to understand the connections that exists between the things that we dig up in a site. Flannery (1982:274) sees "that body of shared customs, beliefs and values that we called culture" as the key notion to structure archaeology and our explanations of the past (see also Flannery and Marcus, 1983).

Advocates of a cultural determinism, such as Flannery, base their theory on the notion of cultural integration (Archer, 1988:2–4). They view culture as a system with an underlying unity and fundamental coherence that moves the people who share it to act in a uniform matter. Archer (1988:3) points out that this notion confuses two logically distinct elements: (1) the consistency of attempts to impose ideational order, and (2) how successful these attempts are.

As Keesing (1987:161) argues, even in the most egalitarian of societies, cultural knowledge is unevenly distributed and controlled. Culture lacks the coherence that the notion of cultural integration would give it. Culture is neither an *a priori* or a flawless cognitive structure; it is created through historical processes and it contains internal contradictions. It cannot have a superorganic existence, it must reside in the minds of individuals. Paradoxically, culture neither originates nor changes in the minds of individuals because it is a social phenomenon that lies in the relationship between people. Individuals participate differentially in these relations and with diverse interests, so that culture is a most imperfect set of beliefs and meanings, differentially shared by people and prone to inconsistencies and contradictions (Keesing, 1987:163; Archer, 1988:19).

Keesing's (1987) argument seems to conflate culture and ideology; his message appears to be that culture is ideological. Wolf (1984:399) takes a similar tack when he notes that "much of what anthropologists have called culture is 'ideology-in-the-making, rationalizations', developed to impart to the practical existence of everyday life an imaginary directionality, a fictitious resolution." It is important to recognize, as these authors do, that culture is socially created within relations of power and that it is not understandable without reference to this process of construction and power. Culture is not an autonomous system of meaning that directs peoples' actions. Something is lost, however, if we equate ideology and culture, that is, if we reduce all meaning and social relations to power. For example, the relationship of parent and child in modern middle-class America certainly involves relations of power, but it would be sterile and facile indeed to try to understand this relationship only in these terms. Just as culture cannot be understood without reference to power, so too, ideology cannot be understood without reference to meaning. To reach this understanding, we should first realize that as much dissention exists in marxism about the definition of ideology as exists in anthropology over the definition of culture.

Within marxism a consensus seems to exist on what ideology does. Most writers agree that it masks, hides, or obscures the real nature of social relations from the people in a society (Althusser, 1971; Leone, 1986; Gramsci, 1971; Lukács, 1971; Miller and Tilley, 1984). This negative view of ideology, however, is insufficient because it defines ideology in terms of its function or social use, but does not tell us what ideology is.

When scholars try to move beyond a functional definition of ideology, two meanings emerge (Larrain, 1983). The first of these is a notion of ideology as the whole of social consciousness. The second is the political ideas linked to the interests of a class (Marx and Engels, 1970). Both of these meanings are embedded in the major works on ideology, and they are rarely split (Gramsci, 1971; Althusser, 1971; Thompson, 1963; Lukács, 1971). For example, Althusser (1971:78) speaks of a "ruling ideology" that holds sway over people by means of "ideological state apparatuses" and of ideology as the givens of everyday life that form consciousness. When scholars use the first definition of ideology, they typically view ideology as a tool or instrument of the ruling class. This instrumentalist notion is particularly salient in the work of Althusser and has deeply affected a number of archaeologists (Leone, 1986; Handsman, 1983a; Miller and Tilley, 1984).

The idea of ideology as the whole of consciousness essentially equates ideology with an oft-held anthropological notion of culture, that is, culture as a system that structures thought or consciousness. Culture allows us to perceive and deal with the world because it builds order by the means of categorization. This process of categorization reduces the richness of reality into a manageable scheme, but such reduction denies us an understanding of the whole of that richness. For example, a color wheel is a continuum of hues. People order that continuum into *colors* so that we can conceptualize and speak of the natural phenomenon. The colors that are created, however, deny us a different subdivision of the whole, which would yield other colors. From this perspective, the process of perceiving the world is necessarily mystifying since it allows us some knowledge of the world only by denying us other knowledge.

Gailey and Patterson (1987:8–9, note 7) use Sapir's (1958) contrast between authentic and spurious culture to define the relationship of culture and ideology. Authentic culture exists when members of a society generate a set of symbols and meanings that they share consensually. When a powerful group or set of institutions impose symbols and meanings, they create a spurious culture that must be ideological, a tool to control the masses. This view captures the notion that culture involves more than ideology, but limits ideology to class-based societies and leaves few means to talk about the differential control of knowledge that can form the basis for power relations in egalitarian societies.

It is important that archaeologists consider culture as something greater than ideology, and both of these phenomena as socially created. The mystification inherent in perception is not limited to relations of control. As Gailey and Patterson point out, however, relationships of control must always either consciously or unconsciously provoke such mystification. Ideology, therefore, is an aspect of culture that originates in the relationship between consciousness and the attempts of people to exercise power over others. This relationship is not given in all times and places, so that specific aspects of culture (beliefs, rituals, taken-for-granted assumptions, etc.) may be ideologically loaded in one context and not in another.

Maurice Bloch's (1986) study of the Merina circumcision ritual in Madagascar traces the changes in the social context, meaning, and function of the ritual over a period of about 200 years. During this time, the ritual changes from a public, spectacular, ritual affirmation of the power of the Merina Kings, to a barbarous private ceremony that betrayed nationalist resistance to French colonialism, and finally to communal, antielite source of lower-class solidarity. Despite these changes in function and meaning, the symbols, the songs, and the dances of the ritual changed very little. This analysis shows that the forms, expressions, and content of specific aspects of culture can stay amazingly constant even while the relationship between consciousness and domination, and the ideological consequences of this relationship, change radically over time.

Locating ideology within a larger cultural structure of cognition eliminates the most simplistic reading of the instrumentalist position. This reading would empower the ideas of the ruling class to determine all of social consciousness. Few advocates of an instrumentalist ideology would take this extreme position, but all would see the ideas of the ruling class as determining the relationship between consciousness and power, and as a robust tool for controlling subordinate groups,

Abercrombie et al. (1980:1–3) have published a critique of what they define as the "dominant ideology thesis." In this critique, they challenge both the instrumental nature and the effectiveness of ideology in effecting social action. They argue that, in most historical periods, the dominant ideology serves mainly to integrate the dominant class, and that the subordinate classes reject it. They conclude that the dominant ideology is a weak instrument because they find these ideologies fractured and often contradictory. Their critique suggests that ideology participates in resistance as well as domination and that ideology will always be embedded in a larger cultural consciousness.

At the extreme, arguments like those of Abercrombie et al. (1980) suggest that discussions of ideology have relevance only for understanding the actions of an elite and tell us little about how inequalities are created and maintained. Removing ideology totally from our discourses about domination ignores the embeddedness of ideology in culture. Even in the examples of Abercrombie et al. (1980), it seems that the subordinate classes do not so much reject the dominant ideology as rework it for their own ends, and that ideologies of resistance share much with dominant ideologies. Ideology as that part of culture originating in the relationship of consciousness and power does participate in the negotiation of social relations, but not in the simple way posited by the instrumentalist notion.

As defined here, ideology may have multiple functions in the negotiation of social relations. No single ideology will exist, and the same sets of beliefs, symbols, and rituals may be given different meanings and importance in different sectors of society and at different times. An ideology is both the product of, and a prerequisite for, a group attaining a political consciousness and, as such, always serves to integrate some class or portion of a class in power struggles. In order to maintain dominance, a ruling class needs to be integrated by an ideology and will typically mystify domination by representing their interests as the common interests of the whole society (Marx and Engels, 1970:64; Larrain, 1983:24–25). This ideology may be accepted by subordinate classes, or they may rework it into an ideology of resistance. Conflict may result from the inconsistencies between the ideology of elites and the ideology of subordinates, providing the conscious basis for resistance. Change in the ideal moves people to action; this action transforms the reality, again challenging the ideal (Godelier, 1982). Subordinate ideologies, therefore, may reveal power relations but, because they are cultural, they also mystify reality. Such mystification serves only to reproduce and legitimate inequalities in society if the subordinate group comes to dominate.

Ideology does not exist just in peoples' heads, but has observable material and behavioral manifestations; it springs from the day-to-day reality of peoples' lives (Mepham, 1979:148). Social groupings, behavior, and material objects embody ideology and give it reality. The appearances created by these things fulfill the expectations of the ideology, and through this affirmation, recreate and legitimate the ideology. For example, the uniform style and size of gravestones in early nineteenth-century Broome County, New York, cemeteries legitimated and affirmed an egalitarian ideology that denied inequalities in the community (McGuire, 1988).

Individuals perceive and experience this day-to-day reality differentially depending on their own experience, so that it is not the same for all members of society. Slavery, for the African-American field hand, was an experience of hard labor, punishment, degradation, and material want. For the plantation owner, it was an experience of leisure, control, prestige, and wealth. Social relations channelize this experience; these differences are the preconditions for multiple cultures and multiple ideologies. The consciousness of the social actors is steeped in meaning, that is, culture, and this meaning confronts the reality to form perception and ideology. As Roseberry (1989:42) notes "culture is at once socially constituted (it is a product of present and past activity) and socially constitutive (it is part of the meaningful context in which activity takes place)."

HISTORY AS DIALECTIC

If archaeologists truly accept a dialectical approach to the study of history, we need to put aside the determinism of cultural materialism, the biological reductionism of human ecology, and the methodological individualism of a post-processual archaeology. Once we have done this, we are left with the idea that the dialectical interplay of real social relations and practices makes up the social whole. This leaves us with no notion of hierarchy to our explanations, determinism, or abstract definition of causality. We should instead put the production and reproduction of real life at the center of our study. Some commentators may find this notion theoretically thin (Rowlands, 1982:165), but such a focus does allow us to forge rigorous and determinate concepts and theories. As Sayer (1987:147) argues, it does so "not at the level of some general theory of history nor by virtue of philosophical virtuosity, but for substantive societies and on the basis of empirical investigation."

People made history. People painted the caves at Lascaux, people crossed the Bering land bridge, people worshiped in the great henge monuments of Europe, people died on the stone altars at the top of the pyramids in Tenochtitlán, and people dragged them to their deaths, people wove the cloth and wrapped the mummies we find in the sands of the north coast of Peru, and today, people write the story of that past. History is not, however, the sum of individual acts; it is the product of masses of people whose action as social groups stemmed from common consciousness derived from the shared relations, experiences, cultures, and ideologies that linked them to each other and to the world around them. These people were not free to make history just as they wanted. They acted in a milieu of power that sprang from conditions and structures inherited from their past, the products of past action (Marquardt, 1989:8, in press). These constraints on human action, whether they be in nature, the economy, the social structure, or in culture, were (are), in the same moment limiting and enabling. Even as they enable some forms of action, they limit others; in this ambiguity and the contradictions that call it into being, we may find the dynamic of history.

To examine this dynamic, archaeologists need to look to the nature of power in real societies, how it forms a part of the production and reproduction of real life. Power permeates all of the relations that I have discussed, culture and nature, human action and social structure, and culture and ideology. Yet archaeologists frequently wish to discuss these relations without reference to power, in part, because they embrace theories that hide power, and in part, because they define power too narrowly as domination.

Scholars search in vain for a motor that drives history. People do not make history just as they please, and neither does the environment, technology, social structures, ideology, or culture determine, in any direct or simple way, what people will do. These phenomena make up the conditions that must be in place for humans to act, but they are themselves, the results of human action. As necessary conditions for human action, they allow some forms of action even while they constrain or limit others. If archaeologists accept the ambiguity in the notion that human action is both determined by these conditions and the determinant of them, then we should seek our explanations for history in the real dialectical interplay of nature, structure, culture, and agency in the specific cases we study. This approach will be theoretically thin, a simple empiricism, if all archaeologists only describe what we can observe in those cases. If such an approach is lead to rigorous theories of the past, then archaeologists need to rethink the relationship between our abstract ideas, notions, and theories, and the concrete world of the archaeological record. The next chapter discusses a method for studying the world, a method for moving from the abstract to the concrete — that is, from an abstract notion, such as the state, to the study of historically concrete entities, states.

ENDNOTES

1. Wallerstein (1978) identifies four possible modes of production in world history: reciprocal minisystems, redistributive empires, a capitalist world economy, and a hoped-for socialist world government. In reciprocal minisystems, all able-bodied individuals engage in production, and processes of reciprocal exchange create inequalities favoring senior males. World empires contain a stratum of nonproducers who preempt the surplus of others through a tribute network controlled by a centralized political system. The nonproducing capitalist bourgeoisie secures surplus from the workers via market exchanges. In these formulations, Wallerstein draws his understandings of noncapitalist economics almost exclusively from Polányi.

2. A number of archaeologists working in Europe have proposed the notion of peer polity interaction as an alternative to a World Systems approach (Renfrew, 1986). There are dangers in framing an either/or choice between a peer polity and World systems model. Renfrew's (1986) idea of peer polity interaction is not really a theory but an argument for analysis at a certain scale, and against *a priori* assumptions of economically and politically defined cores and peripheries. It is, however, just as wrong to *a priori* assume that the polities we are dealing with in a given case are peers, as it is to *a priori* assume cores and peripheries. Our analyses need to look for both possibilities.

CHAPTER 6

History and Evolution

People, as curious primates, dote on concrete objects that can be seen and fondled.
God dwells among the detail, not in the realm of pure generality. We must
tackle and grasp the larger, encompassing themes of our universe, but we make
our best approach through small curiosities that rivet our attention — all those
pretty pebbles on the shoreline of knowledge. For the ocean of truth washes over
the pebbles with every wave, and they rattle and clink with the most wondrous
din.

(Gould, 1989:51–52)

At the fiftieth anniversary meeting of the Society for American Archaeology,
the organizing committee granted various archaeologists the podium to remi-
nisce on where American archaeology came from, to remark on the state of
the field today, and to assess where the field was going. The latter task fell,
not inappropriately, to Lewis Binford (1986:461–465) who defended the New
Archaeology against the twin evils of reconstructionism and relativism. For
Binford, reconstructionism was the old bogeyman of empiricism wrapped in the
new cloak of formation processes and relativism, the new rascality of structural
and symbolic archaeology. He urged archaeology to chart a straight and narrow
course between an empiricism mired in the muddy detail of the concrete and a
relativism, in which abstractions wafted in the vapors of political consciousness,
unsullied by the mundane detail of the archaeological record. He asked us to
play God among the detail; to reduce the din and clatter of concrete objects to
an elegant set of universal abstractions that explain culture change.

Archaeologists should, however, consider a fourth way of relating our abstractions about cultural change to the concrete reality of past cultures, a dialectical way. In the dialectic, the abstract and concrete are not separable things, but
instead, moments in our analysis, each generated by the prior state of the other.
For our consciousness to form abstractions, it must confront a reality, yet we
can have no knowledge or perception of that reality except through the abstractions that form our consciousness. To think requires a reality to think about, but
that reality can be known only through thought. This perspective would agree
with Binford that the concrete cannot be understood only in terms of itself; it

145

rejects empiricism. And it agrees with Binford that the abstract cannot exist as pure generality unfettered by the realities of the concrete; it rejects relativism. But it also sets aside the notion that the abstract and the concrete can be treated as two different things, and the reductionism that follows from this notion, that is, the idea that our understanding of the concrete can be reduced to the abstract.

A dialectical approach to archaeology is necessarily historical. It begins with the small curiosities and pretty pebbles that so fascinate Gould, moves to the building of abstractions to help us better understand the larger encompassing themes that envelope those details, and then back to a fascination with small curiosities and pretty pebbles. The ultimate goal of such analysis remains a substantive one — to understand the real, lived experience of people. This goal cannot be achieved either by reducing that experience to a set of elegant laws of cultural change or by myopically burying ourselves in the detail of that experience.

This historical approach contrasts markedly with the evolutionary themes that have dominated so much of archaeological discourse over the last quarter of a century. These themes assume that cultural change follows an evolutionary trajectory from simple to complex forms and that archaeologists can understand the past by developing universal law-like statements (abstractions) that predict this trajectory. The goal of evolutionary studies in archaeology has been to discover such universal principles of cultural change. To do this, the archaeologists treat the real social forms that people created in the past, the Inka ayllu or the Athenian state, as manifestations of abstract social types, such as the family or the state, that evolve over time.

To think dialectically about culture change requires that archaeologists examine the underlying relations and contradictions that produce the real social forms that we see. Transforming real social forms into ideal types wrenches them free of their historical context, and these relations and contradictions vanish, so that any discussion of social forms in the abstract is, at best, analogical. Generalities about the process of change always remain tentative statements that must be recast in each new substantive study. Abstraction in the dialectic shows us where to look and how to look in real historical cases of cultural change, but it does not tell us what we will find. It is a tool for understanding real, lived experience, not the goal of analysis. The study of archaeology thus requires a constant movement from abstract to concrete, and our understanding of the past comes from that movement and not from the pauses that we make in it.

THE ABSTRACT AND THE CONCRETE

The fundamental disagreement between a processualist theory and a dialectical theory is in relating the abstract and the concrete. Each argues that the archae-

ologist must actively engage both the abstract and the concrete, but they disagree on the nature and goal of this engagement.

Processual Archaeology and the Search for a General Theory

Binford's comments in 1985 spring from his conviction that the goal of archaeology should be to generate general theories that specify the causes of history
(Binford and Sabloff, 1983:408). Archaeology should be a nomothetic (law-
generating) science. This goal is also shared by Michael Schiffer (1988:462),
whom Binford wrongly labels as a reconstructionist and empiricist. Both call on
us to construct a general theory of archaeology that will allow us to predict the
processes of culture change. They study the concrete world of the archaeological record to generate and verify the abstract theories that are the ultimate
purpose of our discipline.

This approach to the study of archaeology and the relationship of the abstract
and the concrete has been discussed by many, but none treats it so clearly and
delightfully as Stanley South (1977). In a series of charts labeled "The Polearm
of Archaeology," "The Orbit of Archaeological Science," and "The Dolphin
Chart," South lays out processual archaeology's reduction of the varied detail of
the past into theory.

He argues that "the ultimate goal of archaeology is to explain laws of culture
process though theory building" (South, 1977:32). These laws or generalities
allow archaeologists to predict what we will find in the empirical world. We can
therefore test these laws against what we find in the archaeological record. He
advocates that we select cases to verify these abstractions; the significance and
value of studying the real world lies in how well it allows us to test our abstractions. In his Dolphin Chart he illustrates the feedback between data and theory
that his approach entails. The archaeologist, as dolphin, leaps from a particu-
larized sea of observed facts into a nomothetic atmosphere where theories are
formulated, and then back into the sea of facts to test those theories. An "arm-
chair theorist" floats above the sea and a "blind empiricist" pilots his submarine
under the sea. Like most processualists, South places theory on a higher plane
above the concrete world. South is quite clear in asserting that the sea of facts
can be understood only in terms of the theoretical abstractions generated in the
atmosphere.

South purposefully oversimplifies his discussion of the processualist method
in the interests of clarity; the practice of archaeology rarely, if ever, fit his
simplified scheme. Many archaeologists have also questioned and rejected our
ability to generate *laws* of human behavior. Despite these two caveats, the
emphasis on building abstractions to account for the real world pervades much
of the theoretical debate within archaeology. Much of the debate has concerned
where archaeologists should find these universal generalities in biological ecology (Hawkes *et al.*, 1982; Belovsky, 1988; Winterhalder *et al.*, 1988; Keeley, 1988),
biological evolution (Wenke, 1981; Dunnell, 1989; Rindos, 1985; Leonard,

1989), or decision-making theory (Johnson, 1982; Johnson and Earle, 1987; Earle and Preucel, 1987). Other lines of debate have focused on the nature of these generalizations; must they be absolute statements about the world or can they be couched in statistical terms (Salmon, 1982; Kelley and Hansen, 1988)? But underlying all of this debate is the basic premise that we study the concrete in order to generate abstractions.

Despite the prominence of this emphasis on building general theory in polemics and in the contents of major journals, it is not clear that a majority of archaeologists ever embraced this goal (Trigger, 1989a:299–328). As Trigger (1989a:313–315) so persuasively argues, the New Archaeology bears the stamp of its history. It was a product of U.S. society, and its interest in building a universal theory of cultural process accorded well with the promotion of U.S. political and economic hegemony. As such, it did not fit well with other regional traditions in the world. It found few advocates in Europe and even fewer in the archaeological communities of the Third World, especially in Latin America. Even in the United States it soon became clear that the search for a general theory of cultural change would produce few, if any, universal generalizations that would stand up to empirical scrutiny. More important, most people did not enter archaeology to build general theories but instead, because they were fascinated by the concrete objects they could dote on and fondle. They wanted to place these objects in a history. The vast majority of archaeologists did not yearn for the clean air of the nomothetic atmosphere, but instead, continued to trawl the sea of particularistic facts to learn more about the concrete world of the past. Many of those who did invoke general theory did so because they hoped it would help them to better understand the particular past they studied and not to subjoin their study to a search for abstractions.

The Dialectical View

The dialectical approach reverses the primacy that processual archaeologists give to the abstract and the concrete. It begins with the simple idea that any study of the human condition should start and end with the real, lived experience of human beings and how that experience has changed over time (Sayer, 1987:86; Roseberry, 1989:53; Conkey and Gero, 1991:15; Wylie, 1991:34). That is the concrete. Abstraction, a necessary tool for study, is never the goal or end point of our endeavor, nor are abstractions things separate from the concrete realities in which we find them.

The processual theory treats the real world and the abstractions archaeologists create as two different things — in South's (1977) Dolphin Chart, the nomothetic atmosphere and the sea of particularistic observed facts. This separation reflects the atomistic and systemic view that subordinates the real world to an abstract predictive theory. The real relations that people enter into and the social forms that result from these relations are reified into abstract categories such as the family or the state. These categories are then treated as distinct, preexisting variables that determine or are determined in the process of cultural change.

From the perspective of a theory of relations, the social forms that the processualists reify into categories and variables are not distinct entities, but instead are manifestations of underlying social relations. The observable form of a tractor does not tell us whether that tractor is capital or not; the form of social institutions, like the family and the state, does not necessarily reveal the culturally constructed relations between people that create these institutions. Social institutions with similar forms may result from very different sets of social relations. Scholars reveal the social relations that create social institutions in two ways: (1) by looking at how such institutions and the people that make them up are interconnected, that is, by placing them in their broader context; and (2) by examining the changes in these inter-relationships, this context, over time. The processualist program elevates the formal consequences of social relations to the main object of analyses and seeks explanation for this form by atomizing the contexts in which social relations exist.

In a dialectical study, therefore, social categories such as family, class, tribe, state, etc., must refer to specific realities. The abstract notion of the state is not separable from the concrete reality of a specific state. The use of the term *state* to refer to a variety of real social forms — the French state, the Inka state, the Aztec state etc., — does imply certain commonalities of scale and form between these concrete social forms. Such a categorization, however, ignores the multitudinous differences between these real cases and accounts for only a small part of their makeup. What defines these states in their real existence are precisely those features that they do not share with other members of the class, *states*. We do not adequately define these entities in an empirical sense by identifying them as states any more than we can adequately define a lemon by calling it a fruit (Sayer, 1987:55). Since social categories can never adequately define a phenomenon, any explanation that makes them the explandum cannot possibly account for change in real social phenomena.

In a dialectic, cover terms like *the state* refer to "things and their interrelations" (Ollman, 1976:4). Abstractions acquire substantive definition and meaning only from the particular contexts in which they are applied (Sayer, 1987:21, 126). Social categories do not exist in the absence of the real social phenomena that scholars label, any more than fruit exists in the absence of apples, oranges, peaches, and pears. The meaning of the term changes with the concrete reality that it seeks to signify. An abstract social category has significance only in a specific case. Every abstraction requires both a general and a specific referent.

In a dialectical approach, the archaeological study of the past needs to be both contextual and historical. Archaeologists learn little by reducing the lived experience of people to abstractions and then treating those abstractions as the subjects of our investigations. People must make society in order to live. They make society by entering into social relations with each other, and these relations manifest themselves in social institutions. The innermost nature of this web of social relations is dynamic and conflictual, because a change in any part of this web alters the whole of the relations, placing all elements, relations, and institutions forever in flux. In other words, people live in a particular context, and this context is constantly changing. It has a history.

People dwell among the details. The qualitative changes that archaeologists see in the past spring from small, sometimes imperceivable changes in the mundane lives of individuals and groups. These subtle changes in the entities that make up the social whole lead to the whole's having characteristics that it did not have before. When these quantitative changes heighten the conflict resulting from relational contradictions inherent in the web of relations, they can lead to qualitative change, the transformation of the social whole. Our study of this process should reflect the reality of the process. It should concern itself with the details of people's lives and mirror the relational and historical reality of the process (Sayer, 1987:23; Conkey and Gero, 1991:15). Abstraction serves us in this study, but the process archaeology studies is not an abstract process and needs to be understood ultimately in the concrete.

Archaeologists often contrast a historical and contextual approach to studying the past with an evolutionary approach. They make the argument that history deals only with particularistic description, whereas cultural evolution allows us to explain the process of cultural change. In a broad sense, this contrast is a false one because a dialectical approach to history engages both the abstract and the concrete, and therefore, cannot be reduced to simple description or particularism. The dominant notion of evolution current in Anglo-American archaeology is antithetical to a dialectical history because it seeks to reduce the study of the past to the study of abstractions.

CULTURAL EVOLUTION

Probably no abstraction holds more powerful sway over the thought of contemporary archaeologists than the notion of cultural evolution. Many scholars have identified explaining cultural evolution as the preeminent goal of archaeology (South, 1977; Dunnell, 1980; Wenke, 1981; McGuire, 1983a; Johnson and Earle, 1987; Spencer, 1990). This abstraction has been a major structuring principle of Anglo-American archaeology since the early 1960s (Willey and Sabloff, 1980:182–183). As such, it has become a force in the discipline, guiding our choice of research questions, constraining archaeologists' view of historical sequences, influencing funding decisions, directing our data collection, and framing our interpretations both within the academy and to the public. It has so permeated our thinking that many archaeologists do not know how to distinguish cultural evolution from history (Yoffee, 1979).

Cultural Evolution and History — Two Examples

Johnson and Earle (1987) have produced a major work of cultural evolution, *The Evolution of Human Societies*, which seeks to integrate archaeological and ethnographic data into an overall theory that accounts for cultural evolution. They start by asserting that cultural evolution is a fact and that the only issue that confronts us is how to explain that fact. "The evolution of human society is most dramatically seen in the growth of the polity from the camps and hamlets of family-level society to the empires and nations of state societies." (Johnson and Earle, 1987:313). The family or household level of organization becomes their earliest stage of evolution, and it survives as a remnant in all of the later stages. The five levels of polity that follow it are the local group, the Big Man collectivity, the chiefdom, the archaic state, and the nation state. They identify three interlocked processes of evolution, all of which involve some increase in quantity or degree, subsistence intensification, political integration, and social stratification. They conclude, however, that a single cause underlies these three processes: "Fundamentally it is population growth that propels the evolution of the economy" (Johnson and Earle, 1987:5).

Johnson and Earle's (1987) volume is a major work with much to recommend it. It contains many aspects that fit comfortably with a dialectical theory of internal relations. They put human agency at the center of their arguments, and they recognize the dialectical tension between the individual and society (Johnson and Earle, 1987:320). They appreciate the dynamic between quantitative and qualitative change and the fact that cultural change must be understood in ideological as well as material terms. They seek to integrate cultural ecology and cultural evolution in their study, and when they historically analyze specific cases, their approach greatly resembles the one advocated here. The real differences show up when they string these case studies together using the abstraction of cultural evolution. They have given us a sophisticated neoevolutionary study that illustrates how the notion of evolution structures our study of the world in a way very different from a notion of history.

Johnson and Earle (1987:2) eschew the notion that the process of cultural evolution is one of progress and that a greater value should be given societies at higher levels of evolution. As has become common in anthropology and archaeology, they find great value in the *simple* lives of societies at the family level of organization. Despite their explicit statements and clear preference for the primitive, their discussions are peppered with adjectives and metaphors that impute progress and hierarchy in the process of cultural evolution. For example, "We see the evolutionary process as an upward spiral" (Johnson and Earle, 1987:15). The abstraction of evolution structures our thinking and, perhaps more important, our language, in such a way that the taint of progress and ethnocentrism remains even when scholars explicitly reject these ideas.

The abstraction of evolution also plays other of Johnson and Earle's perspectives false. They argue for the importance of human agency, but a general theory of cultural evolution leaves little room for such agency. It requires determinants that can be applied across time and space. The authors, therefore, lose sight of the role of human agency in their prime determinant, population growth. They put aside agency, and argue that human population has an innate tendency to grow (Johnson and Earle, 1987:16, 96). Yet it is people who have babies, and various cultural and social practices can, and did, limit population growth (Cowgill, 1975a; Hassan, 1981).

The *Evolution of Human Society* conflates time and space. The issue of long-term human cultural development, of human history, is equated with variation within the ethnographic present. A series of societies, !Kung San, Great Basin Shoshone, the Yanomamo, the Tsembaga of New Guinea, the Indians of the Northwest Coast, the Trobriand Islanders, the Hawaiians, and the Inka, among others, are taken out of their historical contexts and ordered by the authors into six evolutionary levels. In the discussion of specific cases, most notably the Reindeer herders, the Machiguenga, the Kirhgiz, Hawaii, the Inka, feudal Europe and Japan, and the Brazilian hacienda, Johnson and Earle provide detailed discussions of historical change. But when these cases are ordered, the dynamics of concrete history are lost and the societies are frozen in abstract evolutionary levels. They then discuss various parameters, such as population size, intensity of subsistence, political integration, and social stratification to show how each increases along this ordering.

Nowhere in the discussions of evolutionary change is time the thread linking cases. Johnson and Earle make only sparing use of archaeological research, and the longest discussion of prehistory comes in the consideration of the family level of organization. Here a very broad and generalized discussion of the European paleolithic follows descriptions of the !Kung San and the Great Basin Shoshone as the type societies for this level of development. The authors show concrete examples of historical changes related to population growth in their discussions of Hawaii and medieval Europe, but at no point do they show population growth to be the driving force for cultural change in a concrete historical case that moves through two or more of the six evolutionary levels. Only by taking cases out of their historical sequence can they equate population growth with evolutionary change. Their evolutionary model springs not from a reconstruction of history but instead from the comparison of variation across space.

Eric Wolf's book *Europe and the People without History* provides a historical work that contrasts greatly with the cultural evolution of Johnson and Earle (1987). Wolf's scope is also grand, but his goals are more modest than those of Johnson and Earle. He seeks to understand how capitalism developed and the effects of this development on the micropopulations that ethnohistorians and anthropologists study (Wolf, 1982:23). He shares with Johnson and Earle the aim of accounting for the variation that exists in the ethnographic record, and he discusses many of the same societies that appear in *Evolution of Human Society*.

Wolf makes use of abstractions in his study. He defines three modes of production: the kin mode, the tributary mode, and the capitalist mode, to organize variation in social forms (Wolf, 1982:73–100). These modes are not stages of development because all existed at one time, and at a given time, the existence of each mode in some way depended on the existence of the others. Most important, these modes are not the explandums of the analyses; they are, instead, tools that allow Wolf to work at a broad level of analysis and make comparisons about the processes in the real historical sequences he discusses.

Wolf does not treat the societies he studies as abstractions. He does not see them as hard-bounded objects that can be dealt with apart from the historical contexts in which they occur. He seeks instead to show how the historical processes that led to capitalism made and remade the societies that anthropologists used to create the ethnographic record. He seeks to understand the development of each in terms of the historical sequence of which each is a part. He discusses how Dutch and Bantu expansion drove the !Kung San into the Kalahari, leading to the ethnographic present in which Johnson and Earle freeze them (Wolf, 1982:41, 347–349; see also Schrire, 1980; Headland and Reid, 1989; Wilmsen, 1989). He also discusses how the European fur trade remade the potlatch, social structure, slavery, and warfare of the Northwest coast tribes into the forms discussed in *The Evolution of Human Societies* (Wolf, 1982:184–192). In Wolf's hands, these societies are not remnants of earlier eras, frozen in the amber of underdevelopment, but rather, they are dynamic entities that make history and are made by that history.

In the end Wolf does not give us a short list of universal processes or an underlying motor for cultural change. What he gives us is as rich historical account that shows how the processes of history worked themselves out to create the modern world and the ethnographic record of the anthropologist. The agents of this process are not abstractions, but people.

Cultural Evolution as Fact

Many authors treat cultural evolution as a fact, a given that must be explained, but does not have to be established (McGuire, 1983a:91; Wenke, 1981). Johnson and Earle (1987:4) assert "Whether or not cultural evolution has taken place is no longer an issue. Recent archaeological work from all continents documents the basic development from early small-scale societies to later complex societies." Such assertions relieve scholars from having to defend or examine the notion of evolution in structuring their view of the past, so that they can see change only in evolutionary terms. They also reveal a fundamental confusion about what evolution is and the difference between evolution and history (Yoffee, 1979:6, 25).

The most fundamental difference between an evolutionary approach and a historical approach lies in how data are ordered in an analysis. The notion of evolution in the social sciences has always implied something other than temporal change; it implies movement along some dimension or parameter, as is suggested by Johnson and Earle's (1987:4) movement from "small-scale societies to larger complex societies." The dimensions used for the evolutionary orderings of societies have been based on various abstractions, for example, progress or complexity. There can be only one dimension that orders a historical analysis, and that is chronological time. The notion of cultural evolution has so permeated our thinking that many archaeologists see any change through time as evolutionary.

The modern notion of cultural evolution originated in the second half of the nineteenth century, and this development is reviewed by numerous authors (Harris, 1968; Wenke, 1981; Johnson and Earle, 1987; Stocking, 1982, 1987; Trigger, 1989a). The notion of evolution exerted a powerful influence on social research throughout the second half of the nineteenth century and into the first two decades of the twentieth century. Within this larger social milieu, it even came to permeate the theory of Second International Marxists (see Chapter 2 of this volume). The underlying parameter or dimension of evolution for these early researchers was progress, from savagery to barbarism to civilization and finally to western culture. They told a story of Tasmanians evolving into Englishmen. The first generation of Boasian anthropologists, especially Lowie, attacked the ethnocentrism inherent in this idea of progress (Harris, 1968; Stocking, 1982). They also attacked evolutionism as subversive by equating evolutionism and marxism and thereby reducing marxism in the minds of most American anthropologists to the thought of the Second International.

Donald Ogden Stewart (1923) captured the ethnocentrism of this idea of evolutionary progress in his book *Aunt Polly's Story of Mankind*. The frontispiece of the book depicts "From Jelly-Fish to Uncle Frederick Or: The Ascent of Man." In this illustration, a mountain with a path spiraling to its top rises from a sea. A jelly-fish floats in the sea, while a reptilian figure crawls from the sea onto the path. An ape comes after the reptile, then a caveman, an ancient Egyptian, an Assyrian, a Greek, a crusading knight; finally, on the pinnacle of the peak stands Aunt Polly's husband, Uncle Frederick, with one hand on the protestant church and the other on the first national bank.

Modern cultural evolutionists, starting with White (1949, 1959) in the 1950s, tried to escape the obvious ethnocentrism of nineteenth-century evolutionism by seeking objective parameters or dimensions for ordering societies on an evolutionary scale. The term *progress* continued in use, through the early 1970s (Fried, 1967; Service, 1975), but the idea was to measure progress in terms of a neutral parameter such as energy use (White, 1959). Since the mid-1970s the dimension for ordering societies has principally been some notion of cultural complexity (Flannery, 1972; McGuire, 1983a; Johnson and Earle, 1987; Paynter, 1989; Rowlands, 1989).

The dimensions that have been used in evolutionary studies bear no necessary relationship to time (Shanks and Tilley, 1987a). The nineteenth-century theories of cultural evolution were not based on historical studies of change through time, but instead, on cross-cultural comparisons (Fabian, 1983; Stocking, 1987; Paynter, 1989:375; N. Thomas, 1989). They classified societies according to stages of development, with the implication that societies that were observed at lower stages of development had some-how fossilized in that stage and had not progressed to the next, whereas European societies had progressed through all stages. The use of stages in evolutionary models has been hotly contested, but the basic method of analysis has remained the same. Societies are treated as hard-bounded entities that can be taken out of their historical and cultural context and ordered by an underlying dimension, such as complexity. They can be strung like beads on a string, and like beads on a string, they can be rearranged and restrung in a new order. But no matter how the beads are strung, Tasmanians always seem to occur at the bottom of the string and Englishmen, at the top.

The notion of evolution conflates time and development (Fabian, 1983; Gledhill, 1988; N. Thomas, 1989; Yoffee, in press). Cultural evolution locks the *primitive* peoples of the ethnographic present, the !Kung San, the Eskimo, the Australian aborigines, and the highland farmers of New Guinea, in an earlier time, freezing them like flies in amber. Wenke (1984:198) declares, "Today, in the Arctic, the Kalahari Desert, and a few other places, hunting and gathering bands still follow the ancient ways, but soon they will be extinct and the 'victory' of complex societies, complete." Evolution creates a primitive other by spatializing time. It equates the primitive, those people most unlike westerners, with the early (Fabian, 1983; N. Thomas, 1989). Once time and development are so confused, an uncritical look at the world suggests that cultural evolution is a fact.

Cultural evolution is not a fact, but an abstraction created by more than 100 years of western scholarship. Developmental change did occur in a variety of historical contexts. Societies got larger, political structures became more complex, people worked harder to produce more, people learned to harness more energy, and the domination of one individual over another became institutionalized. That these changes occurred in a number of historical trajectories around the world cannot be questioned, but is this change accurately characterized and understood by labeling it cultural evolution? Calling this change evolution suggests that each instance of such change is simply a specific instance of a universal process of change. Furthermore, if a universal process drives such change, places the beads on the string, then we assume that human history had to follow the trajectory defined by the string. Cultural evolution makes the course of history inevitable.

Cultural Evolution and Historical Sequences

An evolutionary approach characterizes change in terms of a single process that accounts for only a small part of the changes we see and that ignores the multitudinous differences that exist in real trajectories of historical change. No real sequence of historical change replicates the smooth ordering laid out by cultural evolution. Developmental change does not always occur, and when it does, it alternates with collapse and involves many changes not interpretable in terms of less or more (Steward, 1955; Yoffee and Cowgill, 1988). The beads can be strung only if archaeologists ignore long periods and/or jump from one historical sequence to another. For example, Near Eastern archaeology and scholarship has been guided by a ubiquitous orientalism that holds that civilization originated in southwestern Asia (and Egypt) and was then passed to the West (Said, 1978; Larsen, 1989). The commonalities that evolution stresses obscure the differences between historical sequences that define those sequences and gives us a fragmented and delusive understanding of the past.

One of the major attractions of cultural evolution is that it gives us a means for organizing the macrolevel processes of human history, but even at the highest scale of analysis, the understandings it gives us are only partial. The notion of evolution affords us little help in understanding, and in fact, impedes our ability to understand, why civilizations and states appeared in some areas and not in others, and the timing of developmental change.

Much of the concern with cultural evolution has been with explaining the rise of the highest level of evolution – civilizations or states. Yet, this process did not occur all over the world. Generally, cultural evolutionists identify only six regions where the process occurred: Southwest Asia, Egypt, the Indus Valley, China, Peru, and Mesoamerica (Wenke, 1984:198; Gowlett, 1984:186–190; Wright, 1986:323). Although the number of areas in which the process occurred is quite limited, the areas themselves are quite varied in terms of environment, geography, natural resources, and history (Wright, 1986). Cultural evolution offers us little help in understanding why civilizations or states did not appear in other areas of the world. Most obviously, we must ask why civilization did not appear in Australia or, for that matter, why so little change, in an evolutionary sense, occurred there at all (Yoffee, 1985). The continent is not all desert, and its temperate regions cover an area larger than many of the cradles of civilization. Humans populated the continent 30,000 years before they populated Mesoamerica, and the archaeological record shows evidence of population growth (Ross, 1985; Williams, 1985). The assumption, sometimes made explicit, is that in other areas of the world, like Australia or New Guinea, the same processes occurred but did not come to full fruition (White and O'Connell, 1982). If left long enough, these regions would have also developed civilizations and states. By accepting the concept of evolution, however, we preclude consideration of the idea that each region in the world had its own historical trajectory and that once established, these trajectories led to many different ends rather than movement along a single dimension (Yoffee, in press). Interestingly, many students of Australian and Melanesian archaeology find that these *simple* societies left a rich, complex, and dynamic record of prehistoric change that is poorly reflected in theories for the evolution of complexity (Allen, 1985; Lilley, 1985).

Cultural evolution also gives us very little insight into why developmental change occurred when it did, at different rates, and different sequences. Biologically, fully modern *Homo sapiens* appear in the world over 100,000 years ago. Yet the entire course of cultural evolution occurs only in the last 10,000 years, less than a tenth of our species' time on the planet (Wenke, 1984:198–200; Gowlett, 1984:172). If human history is guided by an underlying process of evolutionary change, why did it take so long for that process to begin and why does it work for such a brief space in that history? Many scholars argue that agriculture was a prerequisite for evolutionary developments and that climatic change at the end of the Pleistocene, (about 10,000 years ago) led humans to abandon big-game hunting and turn to a broad-spectrum adaptation that leads to agriculture (Wenke, 1984:156; Gowlett, 1984:146; Henry, 1989). This scenario suggests that the condition necessary for the processes of cultural evolution came into existence only about 10,000 years ago. But was this so? Recent work in Southwest Asia and Europe suggests that the contrast between Pleistocene big-game hunters and mesolithic broad-spectrum foragers is overdrawn (Soffer, 1985:352, 1990; Edwards, 1989). If the wide-ranging exploitation of plants and animals had existed in these regions since at least the Middle Pleistocene, 120,000 before the present (BP), the supposed precondition for the development of agriculture was in place more than 100,000 years before agriculture appeared (Edwards, 1989). Archaeologists cannot use the argument of climatic change at the end of the Pleistocene to explain why it took over 100,000 years for the process of cultural evolution to warm up and take off.

THE FAMILY AND THE STATE

The evolutionary approach depends on the transformation of real human experience, for example the San family or the Inka state, into abstractions, the family or the state. It takes the social groupings that people form and turns them into things or categories, and in doing so, rips them from the context of social relations that created them. These categories of analysis are presumed to exist before and independent of the case being analyzed. The evolutionary approach studies real experience to account for the abstraction so created rather than using abstractions as tools to understand the lived experience of people.

As scholars, we have inherited these categories and continue to treat them as genera, of which each historic context produced variants or species. We think of each as having a given original form that changes under the effect of reified phenomena such as population growth, environmental change, or hypocoherence. Our attempts to study the historical variations of classes, tribes, households, and states is overshadowed by an implicit assumption of evolutionary change that makes the origins of these *things* the crucial issue, especially in a discipline like archaeology that seeks to plumb the full depth of human history.

Terminology that reduces the world to units opposes our understanding of the social relations that constantly make and remake that world. Words that should enable us to conceptualize the changing stream of reality, limit us by freezing that reality and produce confusion because they create the illusion that all who use them have grasped the same reality in them (Wallerstein, 1980b).

The problem with words lies at the heart of our effort to conceptualize social entities. There is no simple way to move from the fetters of words to a true dialectical understanding of the moving stream of human history. Such an understanding will be facilitated, however, by concepts that do not seek primordial units, stress the role of constantly changing relations in the formation of history, and allow us to account for change in each historical instance.

Archaeologists have, in the last 2 decades, emphasized a number of such primordial units as the stuff we should seek explanation for. These include the tribe, the chiefdom, civilization, the family, and the state. Here I will focus on two of these, the two that bracket the evolutionary trajectory, the family and the state. The first of these is taken as a fundamental entity for human existence and the second as the end point of cultural evolution.

The Family and the Household

Many archaeologists have identified the family or the household as the most basic aspect of human social organization: basic either as the evolutionarily original level of social organization (Johnson and Earle, 1987) or as the fundamental social unit that appears in all social structures (Wilk and Rathje, 1982). Over the past few years, archaeologists followed other social science disciplines in focusing on the household as the key analytical unit for our analysis (Wilk and Rathje, 1982; *Man in the Northeast* Vol. 28, 1984; Saitta, 1984; Wilk and Ashmore, 1988; Stanish, 1989).

Most social scientists do not currently equate the family with the household (Netting *et al.*, 1984). A household maybe greater or lesser in its membership than a kin group, the family. A family may or may not occupy a single residence (or group of adjacent residences) and, in many definitions of households, a household may or may not be coresidential (Netting *et al.*, 1984:xxvi–xxviii; McGuire *et al.*, 1986:76–78). It is generally accepted, however, that "the household cannot be divorced from the ideas that people have of the domestic group and from symbolic concepts like family and home" (Netting *et al.*, 1984:xxi). Archaeologists need to recognize that what we can study are residence groups, what Winter (1976) calls household clusters, and that these residence groups do not exactly correspond to the theoretical notions of households or families. We should not be too chagrined by this constraint, however, because most anthropological, historical, and sociological studies of households also end up treating residential units as households and families because of methodological limitations on their data collection.

As the original form of human social organization, the debut of the household has been equated with the dawn of *humanness* (Issac, 1978, 1984; Tanner, 1981; Potts, 1988). Debates seek the origins of the family by unearthing *home bases* and evidence for food-sharing households in *Homo habilis* sites in eastern Africa (Issac, 1978, 1984). Explanations for why the family appeared, have invoked male hunting (Washburn and Lancaster, 1968), female gathering (Tanner, 1981; Zihlmann and Tanner, 1978; Hrdy, 1981), or the scavaging of dead animals (Binford, 1981; Shipman, 1986) as adaptations that created the family. However, Potts (1988) questions the archaeological evidence for home bases and argues that no good evidence exits for home bases until the Middle Pleistocene, hundreds of thousands of years after the appearance of genus *Homo*.

We need to recognize that these scenarios for the origins of humanness are, in fact, origin myths that are a complex mixture of subjective judgements and empirical observations (Fedigan, 1986:57–63; Harding, 1986:92–110; Haraway, 1991:81–108). Landau (1984) has pointed out that our models of human evolution follow a standard narrative form, that of the hero story, which is a recognizable literary model in western culture. This narrative fits western notions of the family, home bases, and gender roles, to the meager data of early hominids. Fedigan (1986:61) stressed the need to understand the symbolic and subjective content of the scientific narratives that scholars write in order to better evaluate such models, as both myth and science.

Feminist critics question several aspects of the idea of households and family as units. (Mukhopadhyay *et al.*, 1988:475–479; Moore, 1988:54–67). They insist that the household encompassing family life is neither a survival from some prehistoric past nor a basic unit that varies from place to place. They note that the notion is based on the separation of production and reproduction, which is equated with the gender roles of men and women. Production occurs outside of the household, and then the products of this activity are returned to the household, the locus of reproduction. They argue that this separation is a recent one in western history, and even with their spatial segregation, reproduction and production are not separate domains, but instead, are linked by social and gender relations that define each (Lamphere, 1986; Hareven, 1984). They also question the notion that the household is necessarily characterized by egalitarian relations as opposed to power relations that structure society outside of the household (Folbre, 1985; McGuire and Woodsong, 1990). The notion of the household or the family as given units tends to universalize the gender relations found in modern western societies to societies of the past, especially when that past is at the dawn of humanness.

Several authors note that women are often left out of archaeological studies of households, although prehistoric residence units surely had to include women (Conkey and Gero, 1991; Tringham, 1991; Brumfiel, 1991). Studies that treat households as a given universal unit or as an initial stage of evolution tend to assume that gender relations in such households were universal or given — that men produced things and that women reproduced them. Archaeologists sought the forces and causes of change in the *male* realm of production and assumed that the *female* realm of reproduction changed little or only in response to changes in the male realm. This assumption systematically devalues female labor and makes gender relations a nonissue. Part of the reason for this lack of attention to the relations that form households, relations that necessarily involve gender, springs from a focus on the function and form of households.

Ashmore and Wilk (1988:4–5) argue that archaeologists should focus on what a household does, that is, on its function, rather than on its form. As Tringham (1991:100–101) points out, this focus leads us to examine the architectural remains, features, and material culture that are found with residences as evidence for an abstract functioning unit, the household, rather than as evidence for the lived experience of active, gendered, humans. She concludes that this approach "leaves prehistory hanging in a cloudy nowhere-land of faceless, genderless categories" (Tringham, 1991:101).

The focus on families or households in terms of their formal characteristics obscures the social relations that form these units, define the social roles that make them up, and structure the larger society. In a widely used introduction to anthropology, Kottak (1979:103–106) argues that the mobility of households, and the lack of ties to land in industrial societies and foraging societies, makes the nuclear family the most significant kinship group. This position equates the nuclear family of the modern United States with the family form of the Great Basin Shoshone. Although the form of these families is similar — mother, father, and children — the social relations that these individuals and families enter into are radically different. The focus on a superficial resemblance of form obscures the fundamentally different character of lived experience in these societies.

Households and families do not exist autonomously (Wallerstein, 1984; McGuire *et al.*, 1986; Wallerstein and Smith, in press). The household and the family are embedded in larger sets of social relations. They are transformed even as those larger sets of relations are, and changes in the relations that structure households also alter those larger sets of relations (Tringham, 1991:102; Brumfield, 1991). For example, Viana Muller (1985, 1987) has written about the appearance of states in early medieval Europe that transformed the relations between households and families and the gender relations within those families. As families entered into hierarchical relations with other families and states, the power of men in the household was advanced, and the sexuality of women was limited and controlled. The basic form of the family changes little in this transformation, but treating that form as an abstraction to be explained would hide from us the profound changes in lived experience that occurred.

We need, then, to look at families and households not as a stage or level of evolution, or as a fundamental social unit, but as unique historical constructs. The notion of the household as a general category is an analogy scholars draw between different real social forms in history. It is a useful analogy in defining a scale of analysis and set of issues to be examined, as long as we realize that neither its form, function, nor existence is universal in human history. It must be discovered in our analysis and not assumed to be there. Little is learned and much obscured when archaeologists treat it as an abstract category and search for its origin and cross-cultural regularities to explain its form. As Tringham (1991) has so delightfully argued, archaeologists should seek to study households with faces, households as sets of relations between real people.

The State

More important to archaeology than the notion of the household has been the idea of the state. Most evolutionary models treat the state as the most advanced form of human society, and the ultimate goal of evolutionary theory is to explain the rise of the state (Service, 1975; Wright, 1977; Haas, 1982; Harris, 1977; Johnson and Earle, 1987; Cohen and Service, 1978; Claessen, 1984). The emphasis on the state led at least one archaeologist, Philip Kohl (1987a), to suggest that the notion has been overworked to the point of being an entrenched idea that impedes useful research.

Many anthropologists and archaeologists have seen the origin of the state as the great divide in human history that separates us from our egalitarian, kin-centered past (Service, 1975; Wright, 1977; Cohen and Service, 1978; Haas, 1982; Johnson and Earle, 1987). Attempts were made to subdivide pre-state societies into stages, for example, bands, tribes, and chiefdoms (Service, 1962; Fried, 1967), and considerable attention has been given to ranking or chiefdoms as a crucial intermediary step leading to states (Sanders and Price, 1968; Renfrew, 1972; Peebles and Kus, 1977; Smith, 1978; Feinman and Neitzel, 1984; Earle, 1987; Drennan and Uribe, 1987; Kipp and Schortman, 1989). In most of these formulations, the stages of pre-state development were put forth to better explain how societies got to the great divide (Service, 1975:3–5).[1] The gap was evolutionary and not historical; the primitive peoples of the world existed in a timeless ethnographic present on the opposite side of the chasm. The cradles of civilization, Egypt, Mesopotamia, Mesoamerica, the Andes, China, and the Indus Valley, stood on the brink of the chasm linked as examples of the state to modern western societies in an ahistorical frame.

The great divide separated the anthropologist and the anthropological archaeologists from the others of social science. In the nineteenth-century intellectual subdivision of the world, the primitive fell to the anthropologist; prehistory, that is, the time before civilization introduced writing, fell to the anthropological (or in Europe, the prehistoric) archaeologist. The great divide defined a unique subject for a unique investigator and in doing so, legitimated and perpetuated an atomistic, evolutionary view of the world.

The origin of the state becomes a central issue both because of the prominence of the great divide on the intellectual landscape and because the states of the modern world, in Braudel's (1979:39) words, "filled the whole social space."

Understanding of the modern phenomenon was sought in its origin. Service (1975:21) insightfully observed:

> *Evolutionary theories about the nature of the state seem inevitably to involve an interest in its origin. A mature state has acquired in its later history so many special features and manifest functions that its* main *function, its "true nature," is often obscured. The feeling seems to be that the nature of the state is best revealed — and best discussed — in the context of a consideration of its origin and early, rudimentary functioning.*

This emphasis on the state as an evolutionary stage has been tempered by attempts to classify states into subtypes such as city states, archaic civilizations, early state modules, nation-states, etc. These subtypes, however, remain variants of a type, the state, and by implication, fundamentally different from pre-state cultures and, in some fundamental way, alike.

The most important of these subdivisions has been that between *pristine* and *secondary* states (Fried, 1967). Pristine states originated independent of existing states, and secondary states developed under the influence of existing states. Pristine states provided the best cases for studying the origin of the state because the pure and true nature of the state must originate in these cases and could not be introduced from without. Also, many people think we can learn a lot about the state by studying trajectories of the earliest states in which there is no question of an existing state apparatus being introduced from elsewhere (Isbell and Schreiber, 1978). This distinction did much to elevate the substantive importance of archaeology, because archaeology provided the only vehicle for studying the necessarily prehistoric origins of the pristine states.

In Western Europe and the United States, the development of anthropological theories to account for the origins of the state reflect the sociopolitical context of the theorists. Gailey (1985) aptly reviewed these trends, and I take my comments from her discussion. From the 1950s until the end of the Viet Nam war, anthropologists and archaeologists advanced theories that linked the rise of the state to overpopulation (Carneiro, 1970; Harner, 1970), to technological advancement (White, 1959; Wittfogel, 1957), or to some combination of the two (Sanders and Price, 1968). The theories paralleled the modernization–development movement that identified the causes of world poverty as overpopulation, inadequate technology, and rural backwardness. The origin of the state became an inevitable solution to ecologically determined problems, and cultural evolution, a process that elevated the western countries and promised the same for the Third World (Rapp, 1978:309; Paynter, 1989). In the 1970s, the academy responded to the social turmoil of the late 1960s by championing systems models that stressed the role of bureaucracies in restraining chaos by controlling information (Flannery, 1972; Service, 1975; Wright and Johnson, 1975). Such factors continue to shape our research, and the current strife in the United States over diversity, gender inequality, and the concurrent rise of U.S. military hegemony and the decline of U.S. economic hegemony in the world certainly shaped the positions that I present here.

The key issue underlying competing theories for the origin of the state is the following: did the state came into being as an integrative mechanism that maintains the stability of society, or as an instrument of an exploitative elite (Haas, 1982; Rathje and McGuire, 1982)? This fundamental debate has raged in all considerations of the state from the nineteenth century to the present, and remains central in the anthropological discourse. The debate also reflects the realities and ambiguities of the modern world, in which capitalist and socialist nation states have become, in the words of Ocatavio Paz, "the philanthropic ogre" (1972:85).

The anthropological issues and debates that surround the origin of the state are irresolvable and, to a large extent, false because of scholars' conceptualization of the state. The state is either an evolutionary stage or a widespread social form of which all empirical states are but variants. The state processes an underlying nature, organization, or essence that is the germ for the development of real states in any given historical instance (Gaily and Patterson, 1987; Kohl, 1987a; Gledhill, 1988).

The empirical diversity of historical instances included under the rubric of the state is disturbing. Shaka's Zulus and the modern nation state of Great Britain have been identified as states (Service, 1975). This identification suggests that in some fundamental way, the nineteenth-century Zulus are more like the modern British than they are like the !Kung San. This linkage seem to hide differences more than reveal similarities and, most important, it obscures the historical processes that created all three entities. The !Kung San are the archetypical egalitarian hunters and gatherers, in large part, because they were forced into the desert first by the Bantu ancestors of the Zulu and later by Europeans. The Zulus became a state in a context of European, particularly British, expansion, and all of these events are linked to larger scale processes that created the modern capitalist world and allowed the West to remodel the world in its own image (Wolf, 1982; Wallerstein, 1974).

Our conceptualization of the state derives, from a projection of the characteristics of the modern capitalist nation state back in time. The nation state is a relatively recent phenomenon, appearing at the end of the eighteenth century and becoming the most common political form world-wide only in the second half of the nineteenth century (Anderson, 1983). An error present in my own, earlier, work is to make all change simply quantitative variation on what exists today (McGuire, 1983a). Archaeologists and anthropologists often ascribe to early states characteristics of the capitalist nation state, including territoriality, control of access to land and resources, the role of coercion, and the universal domination of women (Leacock, 1983:22; Rowlands, 1984a; Silverblatt, 1988).

The evolutionary notion of the state as a stage views the state as a thing that changes in response to external stimuli, often as a necessary solution to environmental problems. Our mechanistic conception leaves little room for human action and struggle (Rapp, 1978:310; Gailey and Patterson, 1987; Gailey, 1987; Gledhill, 1988). Political structures arise from and meet resistance in the conflict between social groups. The individuals who compose such groups are conscious social actors who are motivated by a complex mixture of ideological and economic concerns. An evolutionary notion of the state denies us access to this process and tends to legitimate states as the inevitable products of deterministic forces (Rowlands, 1984a).

Much of the anthropological controversy about the state makes sense only on the false assumption that the state is a unitary phenomenon because it exists to serve the interests of a social group or perform a preordained function (Kohl, 1987a). Both the exploitative position and the integrative position are essentially functionalist, an obvious statement with regard to the integrative position, but not so the exploitative. In exploitative theories the state comes into being as an instrument of elite power; that is because it functions to advance elite power. The great debate over the great divide therefore is an argument as to the true function of the state.

This argument is in fact a false one, as is suggested by Gramsci's (1971:263) definition of the state as "hegemony protected by coercion." Godelier (1980:609) has commented that, in any situation of domination, two components are always present, violence and consent. These components give states both strength and efficacy. Consent is achieved by the dominators stressing the integrative and religious services they render the society as a whole. Thus, a state must serve the function of both advancing the interests of elite groups and integrating society in order to survive (Brumfiel, 1983). It may also have a host of other functions. Defining an entity in terms of its functions does not adequately describe the entity nor does it explain the existence of the entity, because any social entity will have multiple functions.

If we reject the idea of the state as a unitary phenomenon, the question remains, how to develop an approach to studying the empirical states that have existed in the present and in the past? My arguments here suggest that such a notion must allow us to understand each historical instance in terms of its own context and the historical processes that created it. Further, it must allow us to examine the role of human action and struggle by focusing on the relations between social groups and individuals.

Proceeding from a realist approach to science, what I advocate here is a method of articulation (Jessop, 1982:213–220; Keat and Urry, 1982), a concept of the state that allows us to deal with states as complex syntheses of multiple determinations, a theory that suggests what sets or social relations and social groups scholars should examine in a particular historical instance and that does not reduce the instance to abstract mechanistic and deterministic statements of causality. So I will now consider three tentative guidelines for constructing accounts of states.

First, states are assemblies of institutions that cannot as an ensemble exercise power (Jessop, 1982:221). States consist of a number of institutions, and the nature and unity of these institutions are not given, constant, or inherent, but are generated and recreated through historical processes of political struggle. These institutions may include an army, police, schools, a bureaucracy, courts, and temples, among others. The assembly of and relations between these institutions will vary from case to case, and some of these institutions may exist without the state apparatus.

Second, power does not lie in a state, but when a state exists, political power can most effectively be exercised through the state. Power is a relational quantity that results from human action and, as such, cannot be an inherent quantity of an institution. Political power, however, requires an institutional framework for its expression because it lies in the relations defined by such a framework. A state is both a product of social relations and a force in shaping these relations through its ideology, intervention, and structure (Jessop, 1982:221). The power that is exercised through state institutions is not, however, the only form of power that exists in society; people also have the power to act outside of the state institutions and, for this reason, the domination of a state necessarily engenders resistance (Gailey, 1987).

Third, the institutions of the state do not, even in the modern world, define the whole of the social context. The very existence of a state creates a powerful contradiction between kin and civil society. In a state, the elites are not related by kinship to their subordinates (Johnson and Earle, 1987:246). In this sense, they form a class of surplus takers that exercises civil control (often ideologized in kinship terms) over a population organized by kin relations. Civil and kin relations therefore, exist as opposites, yet they become integrated in a whole in such a way that one cannot exist without the other. A conflict is set up between the kin relations that link people within the society and the civil institutions that exercise political power in that society (Diamond, 1974; Gailey and Patterson, 1987). This contradiction is a major dynamic of change in states.

Furthermore, states may incorporate multiple modes of production, which are themselves not limited to the boundaries of the state. An economic system may link different modes of production and states into a regional or even global whole, thereby creating a unity without which those modes and states would not exist (Laclau, 1977:35). These wholes form what Wallerstein (1980b) calls "historical systems" — large-scale, long-term systems with origins, historical trajectories, and ultimate collapses or transformations, the most recent of which has been the capitalist world system.[2] The institutions, including states, that make up these historical systems are consequences of specific systems and would not exist in their absence. In this context, the formation of states can call into existence societies that would be classified by evolutionists as bands, tribes, and chiefdoms (Fried, 1968; Patterson, 1987). It can also lead to processes of ethnogenesis, whereby populations on the peripheries of states organize themselves as ethnic or cultural groups to resist domination by the state (Brumfiel, 1988, 1989; Patterson, 1987).

The state, therefore, is a set of institutions that structure and effect political power. They both affect relations of domination and resistance and are affected by them. They are the products of human struggle and constantly change in response to that struggle. They exist in the context of large-scale historical systems and have no reality or continuity separate from the relations that define such systems. In sum, we can speak of no unified phenomenon, the state, only states set in particular historical instances.

Having so defined the state, it is reasonable to question whether or not this definition makes the state a universal characteristic of human societies? If not, is it still important to ask about origins? The definition does not make the state a universal characteristic of human societies, because by the term institutions, I mean associations of people not based solely on relations of kinship. The elites of a society are no longer linked to their followers by kin relations, although kin relations may be used as a metaphor (an ideology) for these relations. Within this conceptualization, the origins of the state ceases to be an issue, but the beginning of states, in particular historical contexts, remains a matter of considerable substantive and theoretical importance. The emphasis here should be on beginnings, because state formation is an ongoing process of quantitative change that begins with a qualitative transformation, the establishment of the civic–kin contradiction (Diamond, 1974; Gailey and Patterson, 1987).

A key issue in the study of state formation remains local elites' acquiring the means, in Wolf's (1982:94) words, "to break through the bounds of the kinship order." The institutions that affect and are created by these new power relations represent state structures. These institutions will be widely variable depending on the historical system, the position of the society in that system, and the historical development of the society. They may include associations as varied as Shaka's age-graded regiments (Service, 1975:108), the manor and centenna of northwest Europe (Muller, 1985), and the forms of slave production in the Abron kingdom of west Africa (Terray, 1974). These institutions are all similar because they provided local elites with sources of production apart from the reproductive relations of kinship. In doing so, they also restructure the relations that define families and households (Brumfiel, 1991). In a social world where all social relations in a society are grounded in kinship, the family and the household are transformed.

The beginning of a state is of great importance in any historical instance. It introduces a system of domination and hegemony separated from the relations of reproduction. It establishes a fundamental contradiction between civic and kin relations. Traditionally, authors have stressed the importance of this change in terms of the formation of classes and class relations. As a number of feminist writers cogently argue, the significance of this transformation lies as much in the realm of gender relations as in class relations (Sacks, 1976; Leacock, 1983; Rapp, 1978; Gailey, 1985, 1987; Muller, 1985, 1987; Silverblatt, 1988; Moore, 1988:128–185; Brumfiel, 1991). The establishment of a civic–kin contrast creates new social relations by abstracting categories of gender and age from their particular kinship connotations and meanings to define peoples' positions in a division of labor (Gailey, 1985:79). This abstraction erodes the authority and social position of women by accentuating and rigidifying the sexual division of labor and reproducing the stratification of society in male–female relations.

I am not arguing here that the appearance of the state means the replacement of kinship as the organizing principle of a society. In most of the states that have existed in the world, kinship remains the dominant organizing principle, but as my previous discussion suggests, kinship relations are redefined and restructured through their articulation with state institutions. The survival, in most states, of communities organized by kinship provides for an internal contradiction and constant conflict as these communities attempt to maintain their autonomy and authority by resisting the state (Rapp, 1978). This internal dynamic within the context of a larger historical system shapes the development of the state.

The formation of states in a particular historical sequence is not, however, a great divide. The demise and rise of new historical systems recreates state structures, a transformation not demonstrably of lesser magnitude than the creation of states. This can be clearly seen in the literature that discusses the transformations wrought by the penetration of the capitalist world system into new areas. Wolf (1982) shows how that penetration created, destroyed, and recreated class relations and systems of domination and resistance throughout the nonwestern world. Nash (1980) and Silverblatt (1980, 1988) demonstrate that the Spanish conquest of the Aztec and Inka changed the very nature of gender relations, turning the women's universe inside out.

Dropping the conceptualization of the state as thing, a germ from which all empirical states spring, restructures archaeologists' approach to the study of human history (Gledhill, 1988). It moves us away from universal causes and prescriptions and leads us to question the historical processes that have created the historical instances we study. We can then begin to build an understanding of a moving reality rather than freezing it in our hands. Most fundamentally, it leads us to question the basic conceptualizations we have inherited from our own origins and perhaps to something other then a reinterpretation and restatement of the past.

HISTORY

If archaeologists abandon evolution and turn to history as the basis for our study of the past, we must answer several questions. What kind of history will that be? What is the role of abstraction in that history? How do we deal with developmental change as a historical process?

Kinds of History

We could approach this history like Ralph Linton (1936:326–327) at his break-fast table.[3] This approach treats culture as a thing of shreds and patches. The theory proceeds from the assumption that culture is a set of norms or rules for behavior, and the material attributes, traits we observe in the archaeological record, are material manifestations of those norms or rules. Cultural history then becomes an exercise whereby archaeologists find the origin point of the different traits and trace how they diffused in time and space. Through this exercise, we track the assemblage of traits, the shreds and patches, that we find in our sites and how they came to be there.

The New Archaeology criticized this approach to history, and it is the stereo-type of a historical approach that many archaeologists carry. As the critiques pointed out 20 years ago, it is not a very satisfying method for understanding archaeology or culture. Diffusion leaves open the crucial questions of why some traits are accepted and others are not, and how do these traits affect the societies that accept them? History in the sense of Linton is not something that explains the past or present but is instead, something that requires explanation.

One, more contemporary, anthropological approach to history also defines culture as a mental phenomenon and sees history as cultural difference (Geertz, 1980; Sahlins, 1985; Flannery and Marcus, 1983). This approach equates histo-ry with culture or structure. Study focuses on either a context of symbols (Geertz, 1980) or a structure (Sahlins, 1985), which is historically derived and to which human actors attach meaning. Human behavior is always meaningful behavior; action can occur only in the context of these symbols or structure. From this vantage point, the historically created culture that must precede any human action severely channels that action.

These contexts of symbols and structures doggedly resist change, so that shifts in culture are relatively gradual over time. Geertz (1980:5) talks of histor-ical change as a continuous cultural process with few, if any, sharp breaks. A sequential account of what people did does not capture this slow process of change in meaning or allow one to finger exactly when and where change occurred. Sahlins (1985) does not share Geertz's emphasis on meaning and action but focuses instead on the conceptual scheme or structure of history. He speaks of the relation and interaction of structure and event; any event in history depends on the contingent circumstances of structure, which mediates how people will behave. People can creatively reconsider their conceptual schemes, and they are most likely to do this when confronted by phenomena that do not fit these schemes, especially in the form of people that bear different conceptual schemes.

If history is defined as cultural difference, then the dynamic of history derives from the fact that not all groups of people share the same culture (context of symbols or structure). These symbols and structure may overlap and differ in complex ways. These differences and overlaps were historically created. The events of history take the form that they do because of the incomplete sharing and differences in conceptual schemes of their participants. To view history as cultural difference necessitates that we regard these patterns of symbols and conceptual schemes as hard-bounded entities that have histories of their own, in some sense separable from a larger history.

We can see many boundaries in the archaeological record, the distribution of pottery types, the edges of horizons, and the limits of traditions, among others. Yet we also know that this boundedness is a historical product. Much of the empirical study of archaeology has been in defining these boundaries, charting how they appear, spread, and disappear. It seems likely that the boundedness we see is more a consequence of this history than simply a manifestation of clearly separable cultures, each with their own history.

History as cultural difference also raises severe methodological problems for archaeology. It requires us to examine the contact and conflict between different conceptual schemes and patterns of symbols. This is something archaeologists are not well prepared to do. The theory lacks any significant material referent and gives us few clues on how to approach its study in history with only material culture at hand.

There does exist a third way to view historical process, that is, to look at history as a material social process (Wolf, 1982; Mintz, 1985; Roseberry, 1989), a process that involves not only changes in the relations between cultural groups, but also the transformation of whole social orders. To understand the changes archaeologists see in the past, we would ask about the connections between the social groups that constructed that past. We would ask about their commonalities and differences and the larger history in which these commonalities and differences emerged. The focus on the connections between cultural contexts examines how these connections develop within a larger, unevenly developing, but unified social process. Boundedness becomes, in this theory, a product of history and a phenomenon that requires a study of the history of the larger whole in order to understand the boundaries that we see at any given time. We would look at a process of cultural change that springs from the tension between tradition and transformation.

Archaeologists have long known that development in the prehistoric world was uneven. They speak of key and dependent areas (Palerm and Wolf, 1957), cores and buffers (Rathje, 1971), and heartlands and hinterlands (Adams, 1965). The existence of such unevenness provides the dynamic for historical processes of change. Uneven development creates within a social order social groups that have different interests. As they attempt to act in accordance with those interests, the contradictions and ambiguities of the unevenness lead to conflict and change.

When speaking of uneven development, there is a tendency to assume that the unevenness will spring from an imbalance in economics and power that favors one center over other peripheries, much as it does in the modern world. Centrality, however, may be a product of a variety of factors or a combination of factors. A social group may be central because of its position in a web of religious, economic, or political relations. One group may be the center for one set of relations, e.g., religious, while a different group is the center for another set of relations, e.g., economic. Archaeologists also tend to assume that all groups and relations can be ranked, a questionable assumption. A great number of contrasts can be made between social groups based on linguistics, culture, adaptation, religion, etc., and these distinctions may be ranked or not (Marquardt and Crumley, 1987:11).

How a social group is placed, as central or not, depends, in part, on the scale with which investigators examine the web of social relations and the aspects of the social world we choose to look at. In the context of Southwestern archaeology, we may wish to speak of Chaco Canyon as a center, but in terms of the Southwest and Mesoamerica, the entire Southwest must be thought of as a periphery. In the Hohokam Classic Period, the Phoenix basin was not a center for stylistic innovation, but it did have a more intensive agricultural system and greater social differentiation than surrounding areas (McGuire, 1991).

Marquardt and Crumley (1987:2) speak of the "effective scale" of research, that being "any scale at which pattern may be recognized or meaning inferred." Such effective scale does not exist in predefined levels but is created in the process of analysis. As investigators change the effective scale of their analysis, they frame a different web of relations. The unevenness in these relations will disappear at a different scale as a new pattern of unevenness appears. Social groups also live and act in a world of varying scales, and their position *vis-à-vis* others changes as their scale of reference changes. Our choice of an effective scale, therefore, brackets an area for study, allowing us to view a particular set of social relations, while denying us access to sets visible at other scales. Also, archaeologists will find that some theoretical models are more informative at one scale and others at a different scale, so that our choice of models in part also depends on the scale of our analysis. The prehistoric world we wish to understand was a complex product of the intersection of all of these scales; thus, our studies of history need to be multiscalar.

The Role of Abstraction in History

The study of historical process necessarily involves a concern for the detail and richness of particular human experiences. Such a concern frustrates the making of predictive generalizations from these particulars. It does not, however, preclude the search for pattern in historical process in order to make generalizations beyond a particular case. In this effort, it is probably wise to keep in mind Mark Twain's observation that history may not repeat itself, but sometimes it rhymes (Salomon, 1961:208). Four issues are raised in a discussion of historical processes and the making of abstractions: (1) authority, (2) determination, (3) generalization, and (4) contingency.

Authority

We as scholars do not live outside of history. We write from a position within a social order, and each of us sees the past differently and attaches different significance to the past depending on that position. We should be able generate a best description of the archaeological record (the distribution of objects in space) and of past practices and events. Any explanation for why these things happened or for the meaning of these events must fit this description, but such a fit would not be an adequate test of the explanation because many possible explanations could fit the description. We need to also examine why we, as socially situated scholars, might prefer one such explanation over another, a topic I shall take up in Chapter 8.

Determination

Historical determination lies in conditioned action. Human action is cultural action and requires the prior existence of conceptual schemes, social structures, and material necessities (food, tools, technical knowledge, raw materials, etc.). Human action is also constrained by the biological makeup of the species. These prior conditions determine how people may act, and limit the potential consequences of this action, but they are themselves the consequences of prior activity and thought (Roseberry, 1989:54). The starting point is always conditioned action. The prior conditions of cultural life channel historical change by ruling out a large array of actions and possible consequences. These channels are broad, and there always remains an assortment of unknown possible actions and consequences, some of which neither the actors or the scholars who study history can imagine.

The process of historical change is, therefore, both constrained and unpredictable. At any given time, the prior conditions of a historical sequence define the range of possible actions that people can conceive of and perform. Each point in time is a crossroads from which a variety of paths branch out into the mists. People never know where the paths lead, and once they have chosen one, this choice will have unintended consequences that they cannot have foreseen. We can use a knowledge of prior conditions to identify what the range of paths might be and to hypothesize on the consequences of taking one path or the other. Scholars can never, however, predict which path will be taken. Once a path is taken, the previous paths dissolve away in the mist, and a new crossroad appears. The historical factors that condition human action have been changed, and a new range of possible actions and consequences, generated.

Generalization

Generalizations about historical process can examine the pattern of process in a set of cases to determine how best to study change in other similar cases. These generalizations suggest what prior conditions, actions, and consequences we should examine to understand change in a particular case. For example, Wolf (1982:90) observed that in societies bound together by kinship, kinship may be a means of mobilizing labor or a means of controlling access to resources. In the former case, control over the reproductive powers of women will be a key aspect to understanding change, because such control grants rights to social labor. In the latter, parentage and lineage will be the keys because these define membership in the kin group and therefore, access to resources. Similarly, the observation that the contradiction between kin and civic society will be a major dynamic force in a state suggests to us what sets of relations we should look at to understand cultural change in such a sequence. It does not, however, predict what direction or path that change will take.

Such generalization may lead to prognosis rooted in the realities of particular cases. A prognosis is *strictu sensu* a premise as to the likely course of future events, which should be based on an analysis of the mechanisms and conditions present in the case, but cannot be arrived at by simple deduction. Prognoses are derived from evidence in the real world, and they are constantly modified with evidence from the real world. They cannot be reduced to timeless and spaceless generalities. Scholars can look in different historical sequences for patterns that can appear in the array of paths and for the consequences of taking a given path. This gives us a basis for deciding what the crossroads will look like in another case and what the consequences of change in that case could be. In a comparison of this sort, the differences between the cases and patterns is as important as the similarities, because these differences alert us to the variety of possible paths and consequences. This knowledge, then, becomes a guide for action, and further study and will be constantly revised through action and study.

Contingency

Gould (1989:14) captures the idea of contingency in historical process when he notes the "awesome power of apparent insignificance in history." Contingency is not, however, randomness, because each event depends on the outcome of previous events; it is contingent and dependent on what went before it. The circumstances that condition human action leave broad channels and much room for actions and consequences that cannot be predicted or known in advance. Small changes in events can cumulatively have dramatic consequences over the course of history.

Contingency warns us away from the fallacy of assuming that just because something happened a certain way in the past, it had to happen that way. As archaeologists approach each crossroad in our study of the past, we need to consider not only why one path was chosen, but also why others were not. We need to think about the possible paths that were not taken. The problem with thinking about alternative historical sequences is that they did not happen. If carried too far, this kind of contrafactual history quickly becomes absurd. However, pondering what the alternative paths might have been and why they were not taken can gives us insight into the range of possible historical sequences we might encounter, and it reminds us that the past might have been different.

The Historical Study of Developmental Change

How, then, do archaeologists make a historical study of developmental change? Processual archaeologists promised us if we would just learn to be good scientists and amass the right corpus of law-like generalities, middle-range theory, and general theory, we would be able to explain what happened in the past. They urged us to learn how to study cultural evolution, and at the 1985 Society for American Archaeology meetings, Binford berated us for failing to be good students. Archaeologists do not have to await the development of new methods and theories to engage in the historical study of developmental change. The methods for doing it have been around in archaeology, and some archaeologists have been doing it, for almost 50 years. We find them in the works of scholars like V. Gordon Childe, Julian Steward, and Richard McC. Adams.[4]

V. Gordon Childe is often mistaken for a unilineal evolutionist (Trigger, 1980b:173). In two works, *Man Makes Himself* (Childe, 1951a) and *What Happened in History*, (Childe, 1946a) laid out his views on evolution. These works resemble a unilineal model in their invocation of the notion of progress. Childe found evidence in the archaeology of southwest Asia for a general trend toward increasing control over nature that he thought would have helped people improve the material conditions of their life. Although he saw these developments as cumulative, he never thought that they were continuous (Trigger, 1980b:115). His analyses were always historical. His two most famous works discuss the broad historical sequence of change in southwest Asia, and he did not remove societies from their historical contexts to place them in an idealized evolutionary order. He was concerned with the differences between regional sequences as well as with their similarities and with why societies did not change in a developmental manner as well as with why they did. He rejected any notion of determinism in developmental change and instead looked to the specifics of historical sequences and contingent factors of diffusion and migration to explain the changes that he saw. In the end, Childe's goal was not to generate abstractions to explain cultural evolution, but to generate generalizations to help us better understand specific historical sequences. He recognized the unity of the abstract and the concrete, and argued that the significance of any generalization can be understood only in a specific historical sequence (Trigger, 1989a:260).

Many archaeologists have equally widely misread and misinterpreted Julian Steward's (1955) notion of multilinear evolution. This misunderstanding springs from their acceptance of the Sahlins and Service (1960) compromise between evolution, specific and general.[5] As Binford (1972:110–111) has recognized, this compromise is a false one because it masks the fundamentally different views that White and Steward had regarding determinism and the nature of explanation. It violates the historical nature of Steward's theory of multilinear evolution by subsuming Steward's historical sequences under the type of universal progressions and deterministic principles that White advocated. Steward (1955:18–19) defined multilinear evolution as:

> *Essentially a methodology based on the assumption that significant regularities in cultural change occur, and it is concerned with the determination of cultural laws. Its method is empirical rather than deductive. It is inevitably concerned also with historical reconstruction, but it does not expect that historical data can be classified in universal stages. It is interested in particular cultures, but instead of finding local variations and diversity troublesome facts which force the frame of reference from the particular to the general, it deals only with those limited parallels of form, function, and sequence which have empirical validity. What is lost in universality will be gained in concreteness and specificity. Multilinear evolution, therefore, has no a priori scheme or laws. It recognizes that the cultural traditions of different areas may be wholly or partly distinctive, and it simply poses the question of whether any genuine or meaningful similarities between certain cultures exist and whether these lend themselves to formulation.*

The emphasis on developing *cultural laws* in this theory springs from the context of Steward's time when anthropologists were actively challenging the particularism and antigeneralization stance of Boasian anthropology. Just as here the particularistic aspects of the historical study of developmental change are emphasized to challenge the processual archaeology's emphasis on abstraction. It is obvious that Steward's notion of a cultural law is a generalization grounded in empirical cases. He clearly sees such abstractions as being useful in the study of real historical sequences and not as ends in and of themselves. He also emphasizes that developmental change can be understood only in the context of real historical sequences where non-developmental change, digression, and diversity are as important to the understanding of change as the regularities that he seeks.

In most respects, Steward's approach to the historical study of developmental change is consistent with the ideas presented here. His views diverge from a dialectical historical approach in his emphasis on adaptation. To understand change in a historical sequence, Steward looks primarily at the functional interrelationship between humans and nature instead of looking at cultural change as historically conditioned in a dialectic between prior historical conditions, material relations, and human agency. Steward's approach to the historical study of developmental change is consistent with the present formulation, but his functionalism is abandoned.

Archaeologists have primarily used Steward's theory of cultural ecology and have made much less use of his notion of multilinear evolution. They have widely applied Steward's environmental functionalism to the study of prehistoric regional adaptations. The most widespread and in-depth use of multi-linear evolution has been by William Sanders and his students, who sought to reduce the complexities of developmental change to a very functional cultural ecology (Sanders and Price, 1968; Sanders and Webster, 1978; Webster, 1990). These authors accept the Sahlins and Service (1960) compromise. In their hands, multilinear evolution is often the application of unilineal schemes, such as tribe, band, chiefdom, state (Sanders and Price, 1968), or generalizations drawn from decontextualized, cross-cultural surveys (Webster, 1990) to specific historical sequences. Acceptance of the Sahlins and Service compromise has so confused the notion of multilinear evolution that Johnson and Earle (1987:247) label their unilineal study of cultural evolution, multilinear.[6]

The most astute and insightful archaeological study of multilineal evolution remains Robert McC. Adams (1966) *The Evolution of Urban Society*. This is a work that is still widely cited in archaeology, but, I suspect, less widely read. In it, Adams draws on the theory of both Childe and Steward to make a controlled, cross-cultural comparison of the development of urban society in Mesoamerica and Mesopotamia. He rejects the idea that urban society is a type of society that forms a unity so that the study of one urban society informs on the characteristics of the type (Adams, 1966:10). He searches for broad similarities between the two regions and sees these as parallels in the development of urban societies (Adams, 1966:37). He also argues for a fundamental cause-and-effect sequence in both cases but one grounded in "a continuing interplay of complex, locally, distinctive forces" (Adams, 1966:173). He does not reduce the development of urban society in each area to a common processual core, but instead, includes in his explanation of these developments how different they were in each area and how uneven and discontinuous they were through time. Adams' emphasis on cause and effect, and function and adaptation are not consistent with the approach advanced here but were an important part of his attack on particularism.

In a more recent work, Bender (1985a, 1985b) sought to understand the processes of change and technological intensification in the prehistoric tribal societies in the United States midcontinent and in Brittany. She gives us a detailed comparison of the two areas that highlights both the similarities and the differences between them and draws generalizations about processes of change. She finds the reasons for change in each sequence in internal processes within the societies of each case that reproduce the social configuration, that constitute authority, and that mediate social customs and rituals such as alliances, marriage, and exchange. Her analysis draws no universal causes or effects; it produces no abstractions that can be used to explain another case. It instead identifies crucial relations in her two cases, relations between humans and the environment, humans and humans, and humans and the supernatural, that should be studied to understand the process of developmental change.

As archaeologists, we have done a poor job of playing god among the details.

We have, however, done a far better job of studying the pretty pebbles that lie on the shorelines of knowledge. In many ways, my appeal here for a historical approach to the study of development is a reactionary one. It advocates that archaeologists do what we do best — study the specifics of development in historical sequences. Our generalizations should be drawn from this knowledge, and we should seek them in order to better understand such sequences. I believe that such an approach is not only intellectually superior to a search for elegant abstractions that explain cultural evolution, but is also a better description of what most archaeologists now do and wish to do.

Human history does not resemble a string of beads. It is instead a complex, vibrant tapestry, in which intricate designs appear, are interwoven with other motifs, and then disappear. Scholars are part of that tapestry, and it stretches all around us as far as we can see. We can never step out of the tapestry, and our vista is always limited to a portion of it. As we move back and forth and side to side, that portion changes, and varied motifs and patterns emerge, metamorphoze, blend one into the other, and fade from our perception. Developmental change is one thread that recurs in many motifs and in many places on the tapestry. It does not, however, form a continuous design that runs from one end of the fabric to the other. It, like the other myriad threads that form the fabric of history, emerges from previous motifs, unfolds in new designs, and then blends into fresh images. We can learn a great deal by comparing and looking for commonalities in the designs that are woven from these threads of development. We gain little wisdom by plucking the tapestry apart, laying the threads of development end to end, and stringing beads on them, and we lose much. We lose the sure knowledge that the tapestry was the work of many hands and that these were human hands.

ENDNOTES

1. It should be noted that some researchers have argued that the stages of pre-state societies are not necessarily rungs on a ladder leading to the state, but are instead alternative avenues of development (for examples, see Webb, 1975; Habicht-Mauche et al., 1987; Hoopes, 1988). These discussions depart from the positions taken in this paper by retaining the evolutionary terms, tribe and chiefdom, but otherwise reflect the direction in research that is advocated here.

2. Wallerstein defines historical systems in terms of a single mode of production defined by the economy. The concept of a historical system seems useful even if this single-mode perspective is not used.

3. Ralph Linton wrote a textbook on anthropology that was the most commonly used text in introductory classes from the 1940s until the 1960s. In this text, he takes an "all-American" breakfast of bacon, waffles, orange juice, coffee, and eggs, and shows that most of these items originated somewhere else in the

world and diffused to the United States. It is one of the most generally known expositions of the cultural-diffusion approach.

4. These archaeologists all used the word evolution and saw their approaches as historically situated studies of evolution. The term evolution has been used to identify both the notion of developmental change and the idea of a universal process of change leading to greater complexity or higher levels of development. I have limited my use of the term to the latter meaning and used the term development to refer to the former to highlight the distinction between the two meanings.

5. In this compromise, Sahlins and Service attempted to reconcile the neo-evolutionary thought of Leslie White (1949, 1959), with the historical, multi-evolutionary theory of Julian Steward (1955). They argued that White's theory referred to general evolutionary principles that were universal, whereas Steward's approach addressed change in specific historical sequences under that general evolution.

6. Obviously, many archaeologists would disagree with my characterization of multilinear evolution. I have chosen to emphasize the historical and particular aspects of Steward's theory in recognition of his influence on my own thought. Other scholars have chosen to emphasize his search for generalizations. They assume that Steward meant, more or less, the same thing as processualist archaeologists when he used the term *cultural law*. Clearly, I disagree. In the end, what is important is how we approach the study of developmental change and not who has made the most correct reading of Steward. I have not labeled my approach *multilineal evolution* because I may have misread Steward, because a generation of archaeologists have interpreted multilineal evolution in a very different way, and because I do not accept the functional cultural ecology that made up the rest of Steward's anthropology.

CHAPTER 7

Death and Society in a Hohokam Community

The history of all hitherto existing society is the history of class struggle.
(Marx and Engels, 1848)

That is all written history.
(Engels, 1888)

Maurice Bloch (1985:18–20, 54–57), in his synthesis of marxism and anthropology, notes that the concept of classless primitive societies long hampered the development of a marxist anthropology. By denying the existence of class in prehistoric societies, Engels' (1972) *Origin of the Family, Private Property, and the State* created a romantic egalitarian vision of this past and discarded the method of class analysis for most of prehistory. What was left in its stead was a rough materialism that anthropologists such as White (1949, 1959) and Harris (1979) transformed into a universal, evolutionary theory of human prehistory and history. For more than 2 decades some form of this evolutionary theory has dominated the study of archaeology. As a result, a major goal of archaeology has been to explain how stratified, that is, class-based societies, came to be. Archaeologists have seen the origin of class-based society, or its political form, the state, as the great divide in human history that separates us from our egalitarian, kin-centered past. They have assumed that egalitarian or classless societies lacked structural inequalities in power and studied these societies as functionally integrated adaptive systems. People are passive in this scheme. The nature of the environment and changes in that nature decide social forms and social change.

Recognizing that conflicting interest groups do exist in so-called egalitarian societies calls into question these assumptions and opens up these same societies to a marxist analysis. Such an analysis asks what interest groups exist in a society, and how these groups and individuals both use social relations and are shaped by social relations to maintain and reproduce power relations.

This chapter presents a dialectical analysis of a prehistoric *egalitarian* community, the Colonial and Sedentary period Hohokam site of La Ciduad, in Phoenix, Arizona. I shall use burials and houses to identify the interest groups and power relations that existed in the community, and I shall look at how mortuary ritual played an active role in reproducing these groups and the social structures they were embedded in. The village of La Ciudad was composed of linage or extended-family groups that occupied discrete clusters of houses with shared courtyards and cemeteries. The members of these groups maintained and enlarged the power and position of the group by recruiting a larger group of kin, followers, and dependents. Only the most resourceful of such groups could reproduce the social group beyond the lives of its founders. The inequalities that existed between groups and between individuals were masked by an egalitarian ideology expressed in day-to-day life. The mortuary ritual mediated tensions within Hohokam society between the egalitarian ideology and the existing inequalities of the social order by revealing and then destroying the material symbols of these inequalities.

A contradiction lay within this set of social relations. The process that reproduced these inequalities fueled quantitative change in the relations and forces of production needed to sustain the existing social structure. The means by which people exercised power depended on population growth as households gathered more labor to secure irrigation water for new fields. Once there were too many people for the water, the means no longer worked. The means failed at the end of the Sedentary period. At this time richer social groups could have manipulated the mortuary ritual and its ideology to gain a more stable, long-lasting dominance over poorer social groups. By doing so they would have effected a qualitative change in the social structure.

KIN AND CLASS

Bloch (1985:162–163) credits the French structuralist anthropologists with revitalizing the marxist study of primitive societies by extending class analysis to nonstate societies. The French concept of class derives from Marx's distinction between classes in themselves and classes for themselves. "Classes in themselves are groups standing in an unequal relation to other similar groups as regards the control of the means of production" (Bloch, 1985:163). The French structuralists have found such classes in the relations between age, sex, and descent groups. Class consciousness, that is class for itself, is rarely expressed in nonstate societies because the groups are seen as primarily products of biology and kinship, not exploitation. The value of the French approach lies in the way it opens up nonstate societies to a marxist analysis. The danger in the perspective lies in the reduction of kinship to little more than a metaphor for an overly abstract concept of class. Kinship is the structuring principle of nonstate societies, and it is more than simply something imposed from above (Bloch, 1985:167).

The work of scholars such as Diamond (1974), Leacock (1972, 1981), and Wolf (1982) point to a similar approach that opens up primitive societies to a marxist analysis without reducing kinship to class. They suggest that we can use class analysis to examine contradiction, social relations, and legitimation in kinship structures, but we must recognize that such structures are not the same as class. Kinship creates groups with differential control of the means of production but exercises this control primarily through reproduction and ideology, not control of coercive force or the instruments of production. This difference in the means of control has profound implications for the quality of life and life chances of people living in kin-ordered societies. The exercise of power in these cases can never be as oppressive or as ever present as it is in the modern world. In these cases power and inequality are qualitatively different phenomena from those we experience in our day-to-day lives. Having power may not equate with material well-being; indeed, to gain power, persons or groups may have to reduce their own material well-being (Bender, 1990; Lee, 1990; Trigger, 1990).

Primitive Communism

An alternative to the evolutionary notion of egalitarian society lies in the idea of primitive communism (Diamond, 1974; Leacock, 1972, 1981; Lee, 1986, 1990; Trigger, 1990). Primitive communism exists when groups hold the means of production — the land, game, plants, and fish needed to sustain life — in common. No one starves unless all starve. These essays argue that primitive communism existed in many if not most nonstate societies, especially those with a low level of technology, for example the !Kung and the Montagnais. Only in states does the power exist to deny people food and life. They argue that many scholars misrepresent these societies and foster bourgeois ideology by projecting on them forms and spheres of domination that are found only in states. The most debated case of such projection has been the universal nature of male domination. There is a strong moral tone to these essays. They see this social form as more humane than states.

This notion of primitive communism is basically accurate. Private property does not exist in most societies and arises in the relatively recent human past. It is a mistake to assume that power relations in kin-ordered societies are simply variants by degree of what we see in the modern world; nowhere is this more clear than in the realm of gender relations. Gender is more a locus of power in state than in nonstate societies (Silverblatt, 1988). Kin-ordered societies, especially those in which nature is the object of labor such as the !Kung, are more humane than the modern world (Lee, 1990). It is also a mistake, however, to assume that because the exercise and results of power are qualitatively different from what we know, competing interest groups do not exist in kin societies.

Like many other marxists, the theorists of primitive communism downplay ideology and reproduction as loci of power and control. The communal ownership of property does not necessarily imply that each communal group will have the same amount of property, that persons within these groups will have equal access to resources, or that some groups will not be in a position to direct or control other groups (Gilman, 1984:116; Bender, 1985a:53, 1989:84–87, 1990; Saitta, 1987:10; Saitta and Keene, 1990; Brumfiel, 1989:128–132). Inequalities can exist within and between kin groups or fractions within a class or classless social grouping (Brumfiel, 1989:128–132). Reproduction and ideology can become the means by which seniors direct juniors within a group or by which one lineage gains dominance over another. Kin groups do tend to have a *communal ethos* that spurs each person to act for the well-being of the group. This communal ethos may temper the exercise of power and soften its impact on the daily life of people, but social relations of power remain an internal dynamic of daily life and social change. We are mistaken, however, to assume that these inequalities will always have the same form or exist in the same spheres as we find in our own lives, for example in gender.

Class and Archaeology

Archaeologists have drawn a hard black line across prehistory and put kinship on one side and class on the other. Using a theory of cultural evolution, they have searched for the origin of class as a marker of stratified society, a marker that divides our modern heterogeneous world from a prior egalitarian, homogeneous world. These archaeologists have often used the idea of class in a fairly casual way to refer to craft specialization.

More recently a number of marxist archaeologists have given detailed attention to the idea of class and how to use a marxist method in the study of societies that lack class. These studies give allow us to separate class from kin but also allow us to examine relations of power and inequality in all social forms.

Many archaeologists commonly use the term *class* to refer to the functional division of labor in a society between specialists, that is, potter, chief, priest, scribe, or weaver. This notion of class implies some type of power differential. Some individuals, the chief or the priest, specialize in ruling, while others, the potter, the scribe, or the weaver, serve these rulers. More often than not, archaeologists who use this notion are not primarily concerned with power. They usually see the relationship between such classes as a mutually beneficial one in which the craft specialists and others who serve the elite gain from the elites the ability to manage resources, labor, goods, or information (Rathje, 1971; Renfrew, 1972; Johnson, 1975). These archaeologists look for the origin of class in the advent of craft specialization.

V. Gordon Childe (1950, 1951b) used a marxist idea of class that turns on the idea of social surplus. Childe speaks of a tiny ruling class that extracted a social surplus from the primary producers, who were left with only a bare subsistence level of life. Two ideas are the keys in this definition. First is the notion of social surplus, that is, the creation of products over and beyond the social and biological reproductive needs of the primary producers. Second is the idea that a ruling class sustains itself by taking this social surplus from the primary producer. Such relations do not exist in all societies.

Morton Fried's (1967) theory of social evolution has had a great influence on archaeology. In this work Fried links class and stratification. A stratified society is one that has classes. In such social forms people do not have equal access to the basic resources that sustain life.

A view that looks to the concerns of both Childe and Fried survives in the recent work of many Marxist archaeologists. Gailey and Patterson (1987:6) note that:

> Class implies a relationship of permanently or consistently unequal control over the goods, resources, and labor that ensure the continuity of the social group. In class relations, there is always a power relationship: at least one group is permanently removed from direct production and extracts goods and services from other groups in the society.

Gailey and Patterson contrast class-stratified and kin-based societies in terms of how much control direct producers have over their labor and goods. In a kin-based society the direct producers control both their labor and goods. In class-based societies, such producers must give up to an elite some part of their labor and goods. If the direct producers try to hold back this labor or goods, the elite may kill them, imprison them, enslave them, banish them, evict them, fire them, or in some other way deny them basic resources.

Gailey and Patterson recognize that the dynamics of class formation must begin in kin-based societies. They argue that elites create class by using and subverting extant forms of gift-giving and sharing normally found in kin-based societies. The elite gain charge over the gifts and the givers.

Many archaeologist share this notion that the dynamics of class must begin and have its roots in kin relations. This has led some to speak of prehistoric *interest groups* that we can study like classes (Gilman, 1984). Others have used the idea of social debts to show how unequal access to ritual knowledge and marriage could be used in kin-based societies by some to control others (Frankenstein and Rowlands, 1978; Bender, 1985a; Kristiansen, 1984; McGuire and Howard, 1987). Social debt is, in these cases, a source of power and a locus of inequality.

Saitta (1987, 1988; Saitta and Keene, 1990) draws on the work of Resnick and Wolff (1987) to argue that class exists in all social forms and that we can apply a class analysis to all societies. Saitta's notion of class turns on the idea of surplus labor. Class relations derive from the making and the taking of surplus labor. He defines surplus labor as "that amount of socially determined labor time expended beyond the amount (conceptualized as *necessary labor*) required to meet the subsistence needs of the direct producers" (Saitta, 1987:4). With this notion we can find surplus labor in all societies. Saitta (1987:62) counts labor expended for the replacement of tools, for the storage of food, for the care of children and the infirm, and for ritual as surplus labor. Since surplus labor exists in all societies, the potential also exists for some persons to gain more control over this labor than others.

Saitta distinguishes between class and communal class processes. In communal class processes the persons who take surplus (the extractors) are simultaneously the direct producers. The key distinction that he makes in his analyses of class processes is between the fundamental class process and the subsumed class process. Fundamental refers to the process of extracting surplus; subsumed refers to the process by which extractors distribute surplus to those people who help secure the social conditions that allow the fundamental class process to exist. The subsumed classes are not exploiters in the communal society — they receive surplus from the exploiters (the commune as a whole) for services rendered; political, economic, social, and ceremonial. The exploitative class is subsumed in the commune, and this fact structures and limits the nature and extent of power relations in these social forms.

In the end, Saitta redraws the same distinction between class and kin as others have, only in a more interesting way. In all of these theories, economic and power relations exist in the absence of an elite or ruling group that extracts surplus from direct producers, and the kin group structures and limits the exercise of power. His approach does escape the equation of kinship with class since Saitta thinks that all societies have class relations just as all societies have kinship. This study, like those of Childe, Gailey and Patterson, Gilman, Bender and others, does point to the need to find the genesis of class in kin relations and to look for inequalities in kin societies.

Kin and Class as Social Relations

At the heart of our views of kin and class is a desire to treat kinship and class as things, instead of the outcomes of underlying relationships. The notion of kinship and class as things does not give them a history, only an origin. They are transhistorical notions. We insist on treating kin and class as alternative means for structuring societies. One of the things must be primary, and the other, secondary or absent.

The transhistorical notion of kinship and class treats each category as if it were a genus of which the social groups that form classes or kin groups in real historic cases are but types or species. We take kinship as a given, a universal aspect of all societies that drops in consequence to the advent of class. Class is seen as a direct and necessary result of a social and material relation, private property. Since nonstate societies lack private property, they must lack class. This leads us to search for the origin of the genus in the origin of private property. We do not ask how people create classes, since class is an inevitable result of economic relations. It also tends to obscure the variety that exists in both state and nonstate societies, leaving us with an overgeneralized understanding of both.

We need to distinguish between class (or kinship) as an abstract concept and as a concrete reality (Godelier, 1986:245–248). In the abstract, class refers to social groups that are based on relations of exploitation and surplus extraction between groups. This abstract notion is useful for discussing similarities between divergent cases and to draw broad generalizations when appropriate. Classes, however, never exist in the abstract, but only in concrete social and historical contexts. That is, kin groups and classes are historically constituted by the actions of people. Thus we can never study class or kinship but instead, only classes and kin groups existing in real historical contexts that must be ultimately understood in terms of those contexts (Sayer, 1987:137–140).

From this point of view we cannot understand classes by seeking the origin of class. In all social forms members of economic classes do not simply know their interests, but they have to form ideas of them. To do so they must draw on the culture, values, and world view that they find around them, that exists before them (Bocock, 1986:103; Crosby, 1988). As Gailey and Patterson (1987) see it, class formation is a constant, ever-on-going process. Economic classes in modern capitalism will therefore differ in kind from economic classes among the Aztec, in feudal Europe, or even nineteenth-century capitalism. People make class.

If people make class, then classes can be neither universal nor utterly unique. People create classes in specific contexts, so they are in a sense unique, but they do so using ideas, values, and economic relations inherited from the past, so they are in a sense historical. The social groups we call classes and kin groups (families, lineages, etc.) do spring from different underlying sets of relationships. If, however, we look for the origin of class, we can only be disappointed, since any primeval classes we find must have developed from prior social forms and must differ from classes in other historical contexts. The first classes in any given historical sequence should be more like the social forms that came before them than like modern classes.

Kinship refers to those sets of relations that structure human reproduction. Human reproduction is never simply a biological process nor is it ever divorced from production. The reproduction of persons requires that they be socialized to behave in social groups; the reproduction of these social groups also requires that the material needs of these groups be met. Kinship is always about reproduction and production. This is the case even in the modern world, in which family structure and classes depend each on the form of the other (Thorne and Yalom, 1982; McGuire et al., 1986; Collins and Gimenez, 1990).

Kin relations can include inequalities in power and goods. When the kin group is the locus of reproduction and of most or all production, some persons

(elders, lineage heads, mothers, etc.) may use their influence on the reproductive rights of others (juniors, wives, sons, daughters, etc.) to gain some measure
of control over the process and products of production. In these cases the *elites*
are embedded in the kin group and therefore limited by the group and obligations to the welfare of the group (Saitta, 1987). In this situation there will also be
conflict between different kin groups, the fractions within the single class of the
society (Brumfiel, 1989). As Lee (1990) and Trigger (1990) have both argued, the
egalitarian nature of small-scale, kin-based societies is not given or inherent, but
rather actively maintained by social relations and ideologies that limit social
inequalities. With class the elite are no longer embedded in the kin group, but
form their own kin groups; this removes products (surplus) from the kin groups
of direct producers and does away with a major limitation on the exercise of
power. Such relations can actually increase the inequality within kin groups, as
well as between them. Production at the locus of the group and those persons
who engage in such production maybe devalued, whereas production outside
the locus of the group and those persons who engage in this production maybe
increased in value (Muller, 1985, 1987; Conkey and Gero, 1991).

What defines class relations is not the separation of production from kinship
but rather the creation of surplus production. With classes the locus of some
production may move outside the home, but even in modern capitalism, productive activities continue in the home (McGuire *et al.*, 1986; Collins and
Gimenez, 1990). Production and reproduction remain inseparable in all contexts (Tringham, 1991; Hastorf, 1990, 1991; Wright, 1991; Brumfiel, 1991).
Classes result from the operation of underlying relationships of surplus extraction. Such relationships do not exist in all places or times and appear relatively late in human history. The flaw of the notion of a great divide lies not in
its recognition of a qualitative change in human history but in its de-emphasis
of the quantitative changes that lead up to and follow this qualitative change to
class relations. The appearance of these types of relations in any specific historical case is an important transformation, but the basis for this change must lie in
the social relationships that preceded it. In many incipient cases of class formation, kin relations still structure production, and surplus extraction requires
that class relations be masked as kinship. The Inka give us an example of this
mixing of classes and kin groups (Patterson, 1986; Brewster-Wray, 1988).

In Childe's scheme the social surplus exists first, and then the ruling class
arises to exploit this surplus. This view assumes that there exists a set quantity of
stuff that is needed for social reproduction, and that once primary producers
make more than this amount, they have produced a social surplus. There does
not, however, exist a set amount of stuff that is necessary for social or biological
reproduction. The amount and quality of calories, protein, clothing, shelter,
education, and other things needed to reproduce the primary producers can
vary enormously from time to time and place to place. The division between
necessary and surplus labor reflects an underlying relationship, class, that exists

when one group, an elite class, has the power to take labor or the products of labor from another, the primary producers. This relationship defines social surplus.

As anthropologists we know that kin relations can vary enormously from place to place and time to time. We are naive to expect any less variation in class relations. The possible variety of consequences of these relations is further increased by the fact that class can never exist independent of kin. All societies must reproduce. The intersection of class and kin defines social forms in complex ways. The existence of class allows for the existence of very different kin relations in different classes. For example, Rapp (1982) found that kinship in modern America involved very different relations between individuals and structures in underclass, working-class, middle-class, and elite-class families, all of this despite a shared ideology of what family should be.

If we see kinship and class as relations instead of things, and recognize that these relations can take a great variety of forms, then we need to ask how these relations are created and recreated through human action. We should not expect the answer to this question to differ from time to time and place to place. We can, however, use a common method to address the question in all times and places. We should ask what competing groups and/or fractions existed in the society; how did these groups relate to the means of production; how were the existing power relations maintained through ideology; and how did people create new relations from those that had come before.

THE HOHOKAM AND THE SITE OF LA CIUDAD

The Hohokam are one of the major archaeological traditions of the Southwest (Fig. 7.1) (Cordell, 1984). Hohokam remains occur in the deserts of southern Arizona and along the northern frontiers of Sonora (Crown, 1990). Archaeologists frequently speak of the Hohokam region in terms of a core, the Phoenix basin, and a periphery extending from Flagstaff, Arizona on the north, south to the international border, and from the San Pedro river on the east to the Gila Bend on the west.[1]

The Hohokam range encompasses all of the Lower Sonoran desert in southern Arizona. The Lower Sonoran desert is part of the Basin and Range physiographic province, consisting of a series of drop-faulted mountain ranges divided by extensive block-faulted basins. Low precipitation (3 to 12 inches a year across the region) and summer temperatures in excess of 100°F make the availability of water the main determinant of agricultural production and reliability in the desert. Two perennial rivers, the Gila and the Salt, pass through the core area. The seasonal flow of these streams varies greatly, but they provide well-watered floodplains for agriculture, and people can extract water from either using minimal technology.

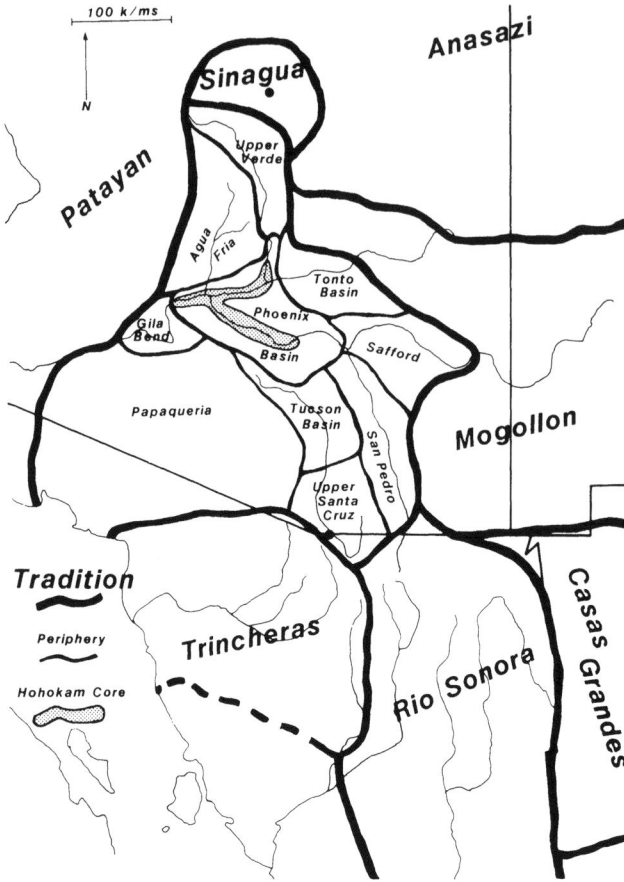

Figure 7.1   Map of the Hohokam tradition.

Archaeologists divide Hohokam prehistory into four periods; Pioneer, Colonial, Sedentary, and Classic. Considerable debate exists concerning the dating
of the sequence, and I have used Eighmy and McGuire's (1988) interpretation of
the chronology.

Pioneer period (AD 150–725) settlements appear principally in the core area,
with some late Pioneer villages in the periphery. Core villages consisted of a
handful of shallow pithouses, usually along the flood plains of the Gila and Salt
Rivers. During the Pioneer period the Hohokam began using irrigation agriculture, but wild plants and game continued to make up most of the diet
(Gasser, 1976). Hohokam potters produced a red-on-grey pottery in the earliest
phases of the period, but by the end of the period they had developed this ware
into the typically Hohokam red-on-buff style. The first evidence of marine shell

obtained from the Gulf of California appear in this period, as does the typically Hohokam ritual assemblage of censors, palettes, and long, serrated projectile points. At the beginning of the period, burial way by inhumation, but the Hohokam practiced cremation by the end of the period.

The aptly named Colonial period is usually divided into two phases, Gila Butte (AD 725–825) and the Santa Cruz (AD 825–1000). During the Gila Butte phase the Hohokam tradition spread over most of southern Arizona. Core area villages exist along major canals. They continued to be made up of pithouses, but these now tended to cluster in groups around shared courtyards with an adjacent cemetery. Ballcourts appear in this phase, and at the largest sites, such as Snaketown, capped platform mounds were built around central plazas. Cremation burial became the norm in this phase. This basic culture assemblage continues in the Santa Cruz phase as canals were extended and more and larger villages built.

The patterns established in the Colonial period continued and were elaborated in the Sedentary period, which contains a single phase, the Sacaton (AD 1000–1100). In this period the Hohokam tradition reached its greatest spatial extent and artistic expression (Haury, 1976:356). A hierarchy of settlements existed with villages lacking ballcourts, villages with a single ballcourt, and villages with multiple ballcourts, central plazas, and platform mounds. Despite the expansion of public architecture, domestic structures continued to be relatively ephemeral; shallow pithouses were little changed from the Gila Butte phase.

Dramatic changes in the Hohokam material culture assemblage and spatial distribution ushered in the Classic period, which is divided into two phases, the Soho (AD 1100–1300) and the Civano (AD 1300–1450). In the Soho, the Hohokam regional system that extended all across southern Arizona appeared to collapse, and the term Hohokam is best applied only to the core area. Despite this seeming regional retraction, during the Classic period of Hohokam expanded the canal systems in the Gila and Salt basins to their greatest extent (Fig. 7.2). Settlements became more compact, with compounds replacing the courtyards of earlier periods, and above-ground adobe rooms replacing pithouses. The Hohokam continued to build pithouse villages in marginal areas of the core and perhaps on the edges of larger settlements. During the Soho, ballcourts ceased to be used and platform mounds became residential spaces with domestic structures on them. In the Civano, some Hohokam settlements cover areas of greater than a square mile and include specialized administrative centers such as Casa Grande. Cremation continued throughout the Classic with cemeteries near compounds, but starting in the Soho, individuals were also buried within compounds and in special mortuary structures such as Clan House 1 at Casa Grande.

The large settlements of the Classic period appeared to be abandoned by the late fifteenth century. A subsequent El Polvoron phase (AD 1450–?) appears to

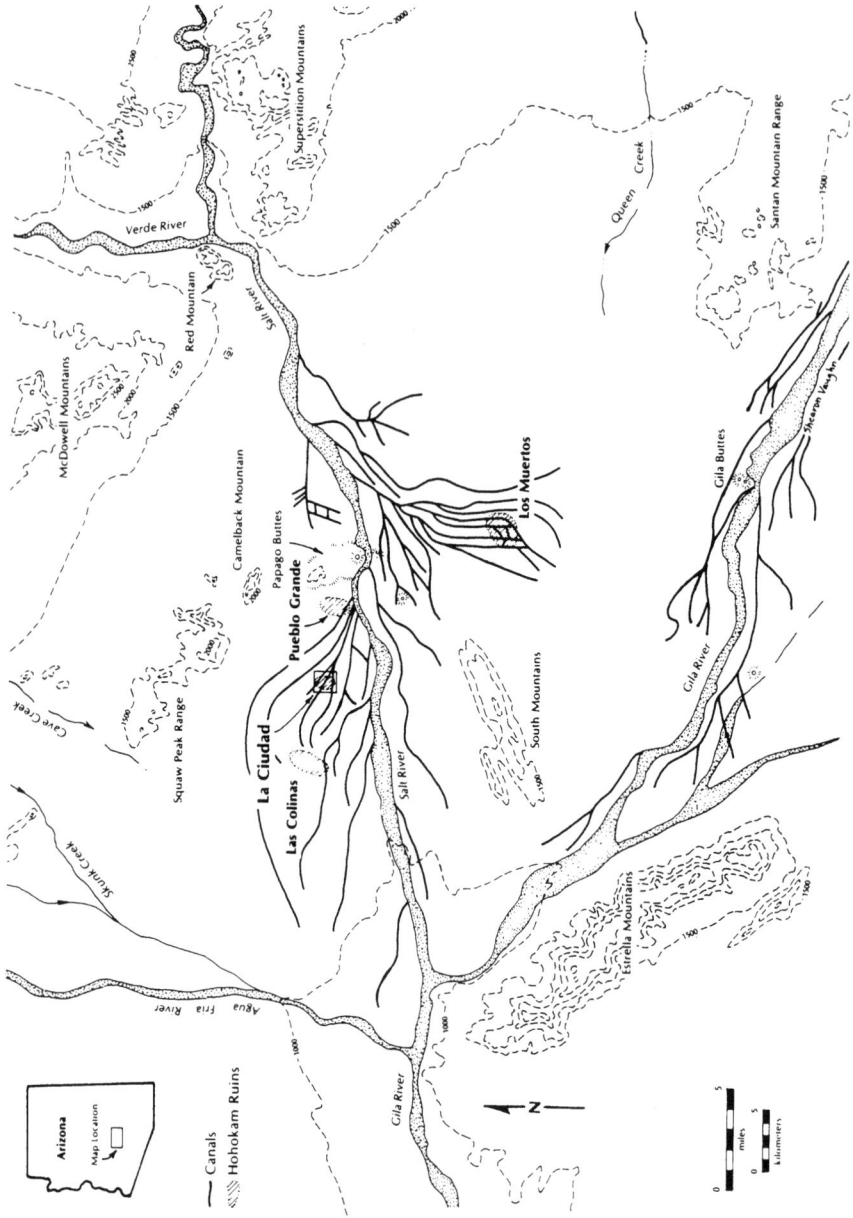

Figure 7.2 Hohokam canals and sites in the Phoenix basin, Arizona. (Drafted by Shearon Vaugh, McGuire 1987).

be the product of a remnant population, sometimes living in the ruins of the large centers. When the Spanish first entered the area in the late seventeenth century, they found the Salt River valley abandoned by settled agriculturalists and only a few villages of O'odham (Pima) on the Gila River.

The Village of La Ciudad

La Ciudad (the city) was one of over 15 major Hohokam villages in the lower Salt River basin (Fig. 7.3). The site is situated in a residential area, adjacent to downtown Phoenix, Arizona. Observations made before the expansion of Phoenix suggest that the village covered an area of approximately a square mile (Turney, 1929). The most visible part of the site was a core area of Classic period age that included a major platform mound, several compounds, numerous trash mounds, a ballcourt, and a series of canals, which were mapped and partially investigated by Frank Midvale (Wilcox, 1987). All surface indications of these and other features have been obliterated, first by agricultural fields in the early part of this century and then by urban expansion starting in the 1920s. Beneath the ground surface, however, remains a record of Hohokam prehistory from the Pioneer to the Classic period.

Starting in the fall of 1982 and continuing until late summer in 1983, Arizona State University conducted excavations in the periphery of La Ciudad. This particular area has been called the Northern Resource Zone and has been divided into a series of smaller loci (cf. Rice, 1987). The Arizona Department of Transportation and the Federal Highway Administration funded these investigations to mitigate the adverse impacts associated with the construction of the proposed Papago Freeway, Inner Loop of Interstate 10.

The Arizona State University excavations concentrated on an L-shaped area bounded by Brill Street on the north, Moreland Street on the south, 20th Street on the west, and 22nd Street on the east (Fig. 7.3). Less intensive excavations were conducted in two areas to the east and south of this northern component, and four cremations were recovered from an area one block east of 22nd Street.

The northern component was subdivided into five large loci based on the street grid in the area. These loci were named Brill, Belleview, Moreland, 21st Street, and 22nd Street.

A grid of 20 × 20-meter quadrates was laid over the entire site to provide a basis for provenance control. A project datum was established, and the quadrates were identified by their north and east coordinates, expressed as distance from the datum to their southwest corners. The provenance of each feature was given by the quad coordinates and by a nested set of northern and eastern coordinates, expressed as the distance from the southwest corner of each quad. All features were numbered sequentially, regardless of type.

The site was organized around a major prehistoric canal that cut diagonally from the southeast to the northwest across the project area and through each

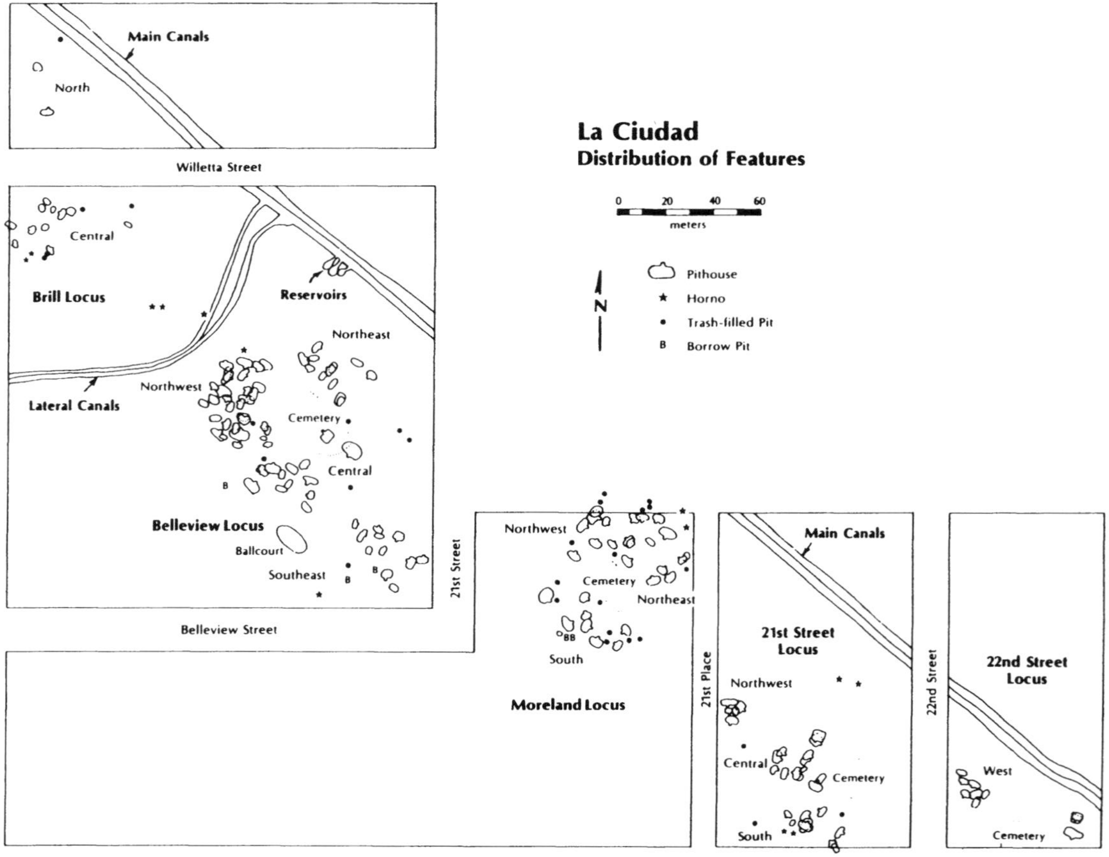

La Ciudad
Distribution of Features

meters

0 20 40 60

◯ Pithouse
✳ Horno
• Trash-filled Pit
B Borrow Pit

N

Main Canals

North

Central

Brill Locus

Willetta Street

Reservoirs

Northeast

Northwest

Lateral Canals

Cemetery

Central

Belleview Locus

Ballcourt

B

Southeast

Belleview Street

Main Canals

Northwest

Cemetery

Northeast

South

BB

Moreland Locus

21st Street

Main Canals

21st Street Locus

Northwest

Central

Cemetery

South

21st Place

22nd Street Locus

West

Cemetery

22nd Street

Figure 7.3 Map of the Hohokam site of La Ciudad (McGuire 1987).

locus. Very little prehistoric material and no burials were located to the north of the canal. The prehistoric occupation of the area was concentrated in a strip of 100 to 125 meters in width, along the south bank of the canal. This occupation extended from the Pioneer period to the Sedentary period. There was little or no evidence of Classic period occupation of the project area.

Pithouses, burials, and other features were concentrated within this linear strip, in clearly definable village segments with associated cemeteries, which corresponded to the loci defined in this analysis. Some of the loci included entire village segments, and others contained only portions. The Brill Locus contained only a portion of a village segment lying primarily to the west of the project area and no cemetery. Belleview contained almost all of the largest village segment, which included a Gila Butte Phase ballcourt and the largest of the four cemeteries at the site. The Moreland Locus contained an entire village segment and its cemetery. The 21st Street Locus contained the northern portion of a village segment and all of its cemetery. The 22nd Street Locus contained the northern portion of a village segment and a large portion of its cemetery. The Ciudad project recorded a total of 2933 features and subfeatures. These included 205 pithouses, 26 activity surfaces, 17 ovens, 189 trash-filled pits, 1 ballcourt, 2 canal gradients and 254 burials.

Hohokam Social Structure

In the last 15 years, most of the debate about Hohokam social structure has focused on what evolutionary levels to assign different Hohokam periods. At various times, social organization in the Colonial and Sedentary periods has been characterized as egalitarian (Haury, 1976), big men (Wilcox and Shenk, 1977; McGuire, 1983b; Upham and Rice, 1980), and ranked (Doyel, 1980; Wood and McAllister, 1980; Nelson, 1981). Even more disagreement surrounds the Classic period, as researchers claim social organization was egalitarian (Haury, 1976), big men (Doyel, 1980), ranked (Wilcox and Shenk, 1977; McGuire, 1983b; Teague, 1984), or stratified (McAllister, 1976). These studies have based their inferences primarily on examinations of architecture, settlement pattern, and artifacts. Only recently have burials figured prominently in such debates (Nelson, 1981; Antieau, 1981; Teague, 1984).

Recent studies of Hohokam social organization characterize this organization in terms of an evolutionary category or a single underlying dimension of complexity. In doing so they reduce an immense amount of both inter- and intrasocietal variability to an imposed unilineal order. They assume that culture is a functionally integrated system and that the different parts of culture are so interconnected or determined that the nature of one part, for example mortuary ritual, necessarily implies the existence of specific organizations, practices, and relations in other parts, for example, social organization, economy, and inequality.

On a methodological level they share a set of assumptions about the relationship of material culture and social organization that allow them to draw inferences from the archaeology of southern Arizona. They assume that the material culture record will provide a direct, but not unambiguous reflection of the cultural system, as long as the formation processes of the archaeological record are adequately controlled for. Thus, a certain mortuary assemblage corresponds to a given evolutionary stage or level of complexity and should be accompanied by a given range of architectural variability. Because culture is a system, each material cultural category should reflect the evolutionary stage or level of cultural complexity of its culture. This means that architecture, mortuary assemblages, or other material categories can be studied independently and without reference to their larger context, because each reflects the evolutionary stage or level of complexity.

This general approach to the study of Hohokam social organization has resulted in a welter of competing estimations of evolutionary stages and levels of complexity. Researchers have arrived at these varied opinions not only because they interpret the data differently but also because they have focused on different material categories, and these different categories appear to reflect different stages and levels. For example, Colonial and Sedentary period Hohokam domestic architecture was relatively ephemeral, and there are no clear examples of elite structures that would indicate high levels of inequality (Wilcox and Shenk, 1977). Cremations, however, vary greatly in the richness of their grave goods from burials with hundreds of exotic items to burials with none, suggesting real inequalities (Nelson, 1981). The current theoretical and methodological assumptions in Hohokam archaeology cannot resolve the dilemma caused by these seeming contradictions in the data.

The Ciudad analysis sought to arrive at a substantive interpretation of the historical processes embodied in the archaeological record of death, society, and ideology in the Hohokam community at La Ciudad. I have not attempted fit the data into predetermined evolutionary stages or reduced the richness of Hohokam social relations to a single dimension of complexity. The analysis treats the relationship between social organization and mortuary ritual as an empirical question. The key underlying assumption is that burial ritual was a manifestation of Hohokam ideology and that it played a role in the negotiation of power relations in Hohokam society.

This contextual approach requires that the mortuary remains be examined in the larger contexts in which it was embedded to determine how such ritual was active in the negotiation, reproduction, and legitimation of the social order. The key to this methodology is a search for contradictions between different artifact classes, such as burials and architecture, and different social contexts, such as mundane and ritual. In the processualist analysis, such contradictions are anomalies. In a dialectical analysis, they become the keys for understanding prehistoric ideology and social structure.

The conclusions of the Ciudad analysis suggest Hohokam social organization was too intricate to yield to characterizations of evolutionary stage, level of complexity, or simple oppositions between egalitarian and ranked or achieved and ascribed status. The analysis leading to these conclusions begins with a consideration of the ethnographic data on cremation and then looks at the patterns of burials and houses at the site.

Ethnographic Analogy

Cremation burial occurred commonly among Native American groups in California and in western Arizona. In all the ethnographic cases of cremation from western North America, the grave goods destroyed at the cremation rite appeared to reflect the relative status of the deceased (McGuire, 1987, in press).[2] From this fact, the formal analogy could be drawn that in cremation burial, a reasonably direct correspondence exists between the status of the dead person and property destroyed in the funeral. To accept such an assumption would be to commit the fallacy of "perfect analogy" (Wylie, 1985a:94). Just because the funerary practice was similar does not necessarily mean that the relation of the practice to social organization is also similar in each case. The relations that create this association in the ethnographic case should be examined to see if evidence of them can be found in the prehistoric situation.

In both the California and Yuman cremation rites, the funeral is not a simple statement expressing the *social persona* of the individual. It is, instead, intimately involved in the establishment and maintenance of relations between social groups. These groupings tend to correspond to extended families or lineages, and they, not the individual, establish the primary relations of social organization. These groups usually had at their core a married couple and their children but would also include other individuals, usually relatives. In rare cases the groups would be built around a polygynous household. Individuals have no status or social position independent of membership in these groups. The cremation rite is a complex statement about the status of the group, of the individual within that group, and of the relationship of the group with other groups.

The goods that were destroyed in the funerary ritual originated not just from the bereaved household but also from other comparable social groups. Behind the public display, an elaborate accounting was kept of debts being made and debts being paid. Through the presentation and receipt of grave goods, relations between the groups were negotiated. The ritual affirmed the unity and existence of the bereaved social group; at the same time, it recreated the relations of dependency and power that linked the different social groups into a larger social whole.

Yuman extended-family groups depended on a complementary mix of male and female labor to survive. Agricultural activities were shared, with men doing most of the field preparation, men and women doing the planting, and women

doing the cultivating and harvesting. Other activities were more strongly gender specific. Women wove baskets, made pottery, gathered wild foods, cooked
vegetable foods, ground grains, and spun thread. Men hunted, fished, cooked
animal foods, built structures, and wove cloth. In war men were primarily
responsible for fighting and protecting the village, but women would form a
rear rank in battle and use their staves to kill wounded enemies and drive
cowardly men back into the line. As long as vacant arable land was available, any
couple could put it under cultivation. Labor was the limited productive resource
in Yuman society, and successful extended families were those who could recruit
and hold the most productive individuals. Since labor power remained the
property of the individual, persons could change residence easily (their labor
power being in demand), and marriages were often of short duration with
frequent divorce.[3] Young adults enjoyed a special status in these relations because they had adult labor power and could move between the households of a
number of kin. A household would try to entice these individuals to stay with
the household as long as possible, while the young adults, once married and with
children, would seek to establish their own households.

Maintaining an extended-family group involved considerable social effort. A
family head, usually male, drew followers through a combination of spiritual
power and charisma. The woman was expected to bear children, enlist the help
of unmarried sisters, and establish reciprocal relations of food sharing with
other like groups. A woman could become the family head if her husband died,
none of her sons was adult, and if she could maintain the family's following. A
couple founded a new extended family by building a winter house and attracting
kin and others to provide a labor pool to advance the interest of the group.
Followers benefited from the leader's ability to negotiate relations with other
groups, his control of necessary resources such as the winter house, and his
ability to acquire and distribute valued goods. They gained from the woman's
ability to organize and direct household work, establish networks of reciprocity
that buffered against famine, and her skill as a basket-maker and potter.

Couples advanced their own position only through their ability to form and
manipulate a large household; other couples in the household could seek to
break off and form their own groups, especially once they had children old
enough to make meaningful labor contributions. The reproduction of such
groupings was a generational process linked to the life of the founding couple.
All couples could seek to establish their own households but not all could
achieve it.

Among some California tribes such as the Pomo, the extended-family groups
appear to have been ranked, with some remaining more powerful across numerous generations (Kroeber, 1925). In these situations the funerary ritual became
important in maintaining dominant and subordinate relations within the villages. The presentation of goods for destruction at the ritual reaffirmed the
relations of power between groups and guaranteed their continuance.

Among the Yumans, a variety of other adult statuses existed in addition to the family head. Higher level tribal leaders could call on the family heads to act as a tribal unit in times of war. War leaders in each village could organize raiding parties based on their reputations and charisma. There were some specialists, principally of a ritual nature, such as doctors and funerary specialists. The family/household provided the basic identity and source of power and position for all members of the society.

To evaluate the appropriateness of the Yuman analogy for the Hohokam data, we need to examine the cremation data in its larger context, to look for material patterns that correspond to the types of relations we see in the analogy. The fact that there exists considerable diversity and inequality in the grave lots is consistent with the analogy, but not sufficient to accept it.

The Moreland Locus

Based on the Wilcox *et al.* (1981) reanalysis of Snaketown, archaeologists have come to recognize that Colonial and Sedentary period Hohokam villages are made up of groups of houses facing a common activity area or residential yard (Henderson, 1987). Rice (1987:148–149) has identified an internal structure to these yards with the smallest yard being a single core house and larger yards having a core house and several support houses. He equates these yards with extended-family households. These residential yards are often clustered into larger village segments, called cemetery groups, containing several residential yards, hornos, trash areas, and a cemetery (Howard, 1985; Henderson, 1987). Anderson (1986) maintains that the cemeteries contain the dead of the village segment, that was probably a lineage group. Rice (1987:147) argues that the early Hohokam village was organized as a nested hierarchy of households, cemetery groups, and ballcourt complexes. This interpretation of Hohokam village organization allows for two to three levels of leadership: residential yard head, village segment head, and village head. No marked domestic architectural distinctions appear to identify these levels of leadership.

At least four village segments, each with its own cemetery, existed at La Ciudad; these are labeled loci. Of these, the Moreland Locus was the best preserved and most fully excavated of the four main loci. The sample of houses and cremations for this locus is as close to 100% as is possible, given currently available excavation techniques (Fig. 7.4). It therefore provides an excellent location to examine the relationship between cemeteries and architecture at the site.

Henderson (1987) has reconstructed the sequence of residential yards in the Moreland Locus. This discussion summarizes her results; the full report should be consulted for more details and discussions of methods and assumptions.

The Moreland cemetery group was founded by the construction of a single large core house, Feature 1660, at about AD 880. This house eventually burned,

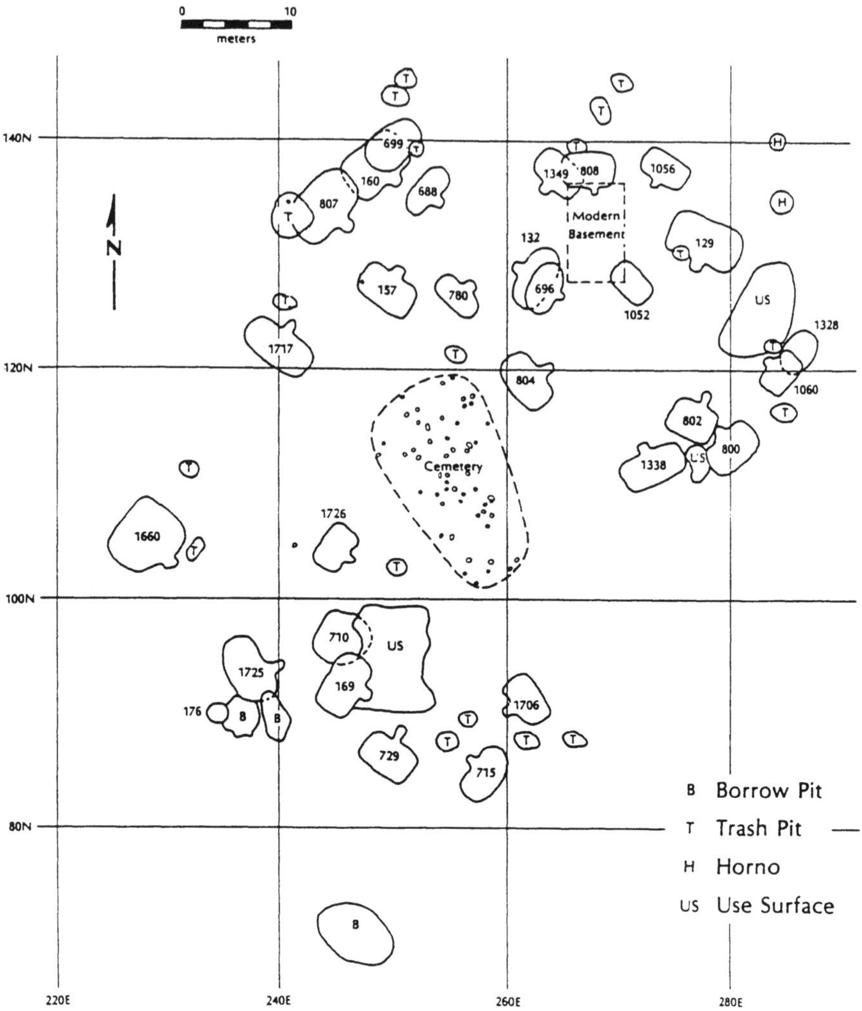

Figure 7.4 The Moreland locus at the site of La Ciudad (McGuire 1987).

and the area over it became the location of the crematorium for the Moreland cemetery. The placement of the crematorium over the original house in the village segment and the location of the cemetery near to it may not be coincidental.

In the Middle Colonial period (AD 880–960), the Hohokam established the cemetery and two contemporary residential yards, one to the northeast of the cemetery and the other to the south. The early northeast yard lasted about 50 years and includes six houses. The southern yard lasted about 40 years and grew to include four houses, then declined to a single house (Feature, 169).

Toward the end of the Middle Colonial period, a single house, Feature 160, was built in the northwest portion of the cemetery group. This house was the *founding* house for a new yard that developed in the succeeding Late Colonial period (AD 960–1000), lasting into the early Sedentary (AD 1000–1100). This yard contained seven houses, not all of which were occupied at the same time.

In the Early Sedentary period, Feature 1056 was built at a right angle to the northwest yard to establish a late northeast yard. This residential yard was occupied until about AD 1060 and included up to five houses.

Two contrasting models have been advanced to account for the growth and decline of Hohokam residential yards. Wilcox *et al.* (1981:166) and Howard (1985:314) argue that yards develop as part of the growth cycle of a domestic group. Doelle *et al.* (1986) contend that the development of a yard results from the ability of a family head to accumulate wealth and power both to maintain the cohesion of the group and to attract new members. As Henderson (1987:125–135) demonstrates in her analysis of La Ciudad community patterns, these processes are not incompatible, since one necessarily entails the other, and she argues that both appear to have taken place at La Ciudad.

The existing interpretations of Hohokam residential yards suffer from three major limitations. The first of these is a strong androcentric bias, such as is seen in many archaeological studies, especially at a household scale of analysis (Conkey and Gero, 1991; Tringham, 1991; Brumfiel, 1991). They tend to interpret courtyard development in terms of the actions of male courtyard heads, who found and develop the courtyards to advance their own position and power. Women are not mentioned in these discussions or their labor is seen as serving only male interests. Change occurs owing to the actions of men, whereas women remain passive and unchanging in their activities. My initial attempt at interpreting the La Ciudad data made this same mistake (McGuire, 1987). Second, this male-centered view interprets prehistory in terms of a modern Capitalist sense of individualism and individual striving for gain. Such individualism is a relatively recent product of the Enlightenment (Marx, 1906:92; Foucault, 1974). In all ethnographically known Southwestern aboriginal cultures, an individual existed only as a member of a social group; this membership provided the basic identity and source of position for all members of society (Eggan, 1983). Finally, existing interpretations of Hohokam residential yards treat household organization as a consequence of changes in material conditions such as population growth, irrigation technology, or exchange, rather than seeing this organization as a dynamic aspect of change affecting other levels of organization.

The full developmental cycle of residential yards at La Ciudad ranges from 30 to 100 years. It seems that some yards lasted for only a generation, while others lasted several generations. In addition, individual core houses were present at La

Ciudad that were not part of yards (six in Moreland). Henderson (1987:135) suggests that the members of these households might not have been able to "garner the support of additional families necessary for further development."

In the ethnographic case of the Yumans, the process by which individuals attempt to establish new extended-family households began with the establishment of a new separate winter house. The growth and success of this new household depended on the fecundity of the founding couple and their ability to attract new members. This process was not always equally successful. Some founding couples were more fertile, effective, and persuasive than others and attracted a larger group of kin, followers, and dependents. The increased labor provided by these individuals was both a source and a result of the household's power. Once established, these powerful households could try to maintain the household across generations and reproduce the social group beyond the life of the founders (Forde, 1931). The process of residential yard development at La Ciudad fits well with the type of dynamic process of extended-family reproduction in the Yuman example.

Evidence for productive activities at the site also supports the Yuman analogy. Kisselberg's (1987) analysis of such activities at La Ciudad revealed very little evidence for household specialization in production. Each residential cluster produced its own pottery, weaving, lithic tools, and food. Long-distance procurement of items appears to have occurred at the level of the village segment or cemetery group. Some specialization did exist of ceremonial objects, with some houses making slate palettes that were used in the cremation ritual and others making the stone or pottery censors that were used with these palettes. The level of household self-sufficiency that Kisselberg infers for La Ciudad would mean that the only effective way for a household to increase its access to goods would be to secure more labor.

The mortuary evidence from La Ciudad is also consistent with the Yuman analogy. In Yuman villages, as at La Ciudad, the people built crematoria and cemeteries associated with distinct social groups. We might also expect that the special status of young adults and household heads would be marked in Hohokam cremations.

The analysis of mortuary goods at La Ciudad used several different statistical techniques and several different organizations of the data to look for relationships between the contents of graves and the gender, age, phase, and location of those individuals buried there (see McGuire, 1987; McGuire, in press, for a detailed presentation of the analyses). Oblique principal components analysis was used to arrive at a scheme for grouping burial goods at La Ciudad. The best solution produced was a six-cluster solution. Each cremation was also assigned a grave lot value (GLV) derived from a ranking of grave goods in terms of their origin (local or foreign), relative labor requirements for manufacture, and usual context of use (mundane, ornamental, or ritual).

The analysis suffers from several limitations. The Hohokam cremated their dead very thoroughly, and may even have ground up the cremated bone before burying it. For this reason, age and sex characteristics of the bodies were very difficult to determine, with only 181 bodies assigned to age categories and only 44 to sex. Furthermore, only 4 of the sexed burials were female and therefore no conclusions could be drawn about relations of grave goods to sex. The Hohokam practice of secondary cremation also means that not all artifacts involved in the burial ritual may have been gleaned from the cremation fires and placed with the bodies. Finally, the types of artifacts placed with the burials were highly diverse.

The age category with the highest GLV and the most diverse collection of artifacts was that of subadults aged 10 to 20 years. These cremations were particularly rich in shell ornaments, bracelets, and beads. Subadults were 15 times more likely to be buried with shell beads than were adults, and five times more likely to be buried with shell bracelets. This age category was clearly marked as a special status in the La Ciudad cemeteries.

What evidence exists in the Ciudad cemeteries for the leaders of extended-family or lineage groups? If the leader's status was marked, then the number of cremations so marked should at least roughly correspond with the number of residence yard heads that would have lived in the village segment. Such leaders would presumably be adults and, given their centrality to the social group, buried in the cemetery.

A plausible estimate of the number of residence yard heads that should be in the cemetery can be generated by examining the occupational spans of the yards (Table 7.1). If each of these courtyards gained a new leader with each generation, then the number of leaders who should have been buried can be estimated by dividing the occupation span of each yard by 25 years. The sum of the products of this division for each of the four courtyards suggests that 8 to 10 courtyard heads should lie in the cemetery.

In his discussion of architectural variability at La Ciudad, Rice (1987) defined two types of domestic structures, core houses and support houses. The Hohokam constructed both houses using basically the same materials, techniques, and forms. Core houses were slightly larger and usually had a floor assemblage including evidence of manufacturing activities and a variety of special artifacts

Table 7.1 Occupation Spans of Moreland Courtyards

Courtyard	Dates	Occupation span	Number of generations
South	AD 920–969	40 years	1–2
Early NE	AD 910–960	50 years	2
NW	AD 950–1040	90 years	3–4
Late NE	AD 1010–1060	50 years	2
Total			8–10

such as palettes and censors. Rice (1987) suggests that the core houses were the homes of residence yard leaders and their wives and support houses, of their dependents. The Moreland locus contained eight definite and three possible core houses, suggesting the number of residence yard heads in the locus should be between 8 and 11.

Nine cremations in the Moreland Locus held Cluster 1 artifacts (hairpins, turquoise, turtle shell). Cluster 1 is not the only cluster to occur in the cemetery at about the right frequency for the number of residence yard heads. Cluster 1 was, however, the only cluster to show associations with adult age and cremations in cemeteries. None of the other clusters as associated with adult age or cremations in cemeteries, and they therefore appear to be bad candidates for artifacts marking household-head status.

The key artifact in Cluster 1 was hairpins; burials with hairpins tend to be richer than burials without them. A dummy variable analysis on all cremations with grave goods from the site was done to compare the mean GLV for cremations with hairpins to those without. The graves with hairpins had a mean GLV of 46.26 and those without, 17.77 ($r^2 = 0.12, p = 0.0001$, n = 125).[4] This mean also exceeds the mean for sub-adult cremations (35.58).

Bone hairpins would have been a very good symbol of residence yard head status. Hairdos would have been highly visible icons of certain meanings, and the hairpins would have reiterated such meanings. The special status of these individuals would have been apparent at a glance to all in the village.

The occurrence of a hairpin with a single female cremation is also consistent with the Yuman analogy, because Yuman women could become household heads upon the death of a husband. At La Ciudad, courtyard heads appear to have been predominantly male, but not to the exclusion of females.

Wilcox and Sternberg (1983) have postulated that the Hohokam cremation rite, like the Yuman, was the central religious ritual of the society. Evidence at La Ciudad suggest that the cremation ceremony was a public rite requiring the interaction of different residence yards or clusters for performance. The spatial identification of the ritual with the cemetery group village segment defines a group identity, whereas the execution of the rite links different clusters.

The cremation rite itself must have been a public event at La Ciudad and other contemporary Hohokam sites (Hood, 1985). None of the cemetery groups as walled, and none of the houses blocked the view of the crematorium or cemeteries from all possible sides. The gathering of people for the funeral, the destruction of property, and the secondary burial of the remains would have been visible to individuals not within the spatial boundaries of the cemetery group. The funerary pyre itself would have required a large amount of wood (in order to totally consume the body) and would have put up a plume of smoke during the day or a glow at night visible across the entire community and in nearby communities.

The specialized artifact set that appears in all of the cemeteries at La Ciudad and in other contemporary Hohokam sites was not produced in each of the residence yards or cemetery groups (loci). Kisselburg's (1987) analysis of special artifacts from La Ciudad suggests that, at each point in time, residents of only a few yards manufactured projectile points, censers, and palettes. The Moreland cemetery was rich with censers and palettes, but there is little evidence that the residents of this locus ever manufactured these items. The social groups that occupied the residence yards probably could not have assembled the necessary special items for funerals without getting many or most of them from other comparable groups.

These discussions suggest that a similar set of relations structured the Hohokam and the Yuman funerary rituals. Based on this conclusion, the grave lots in La Ciudad cemeteries did not help to mystify the social order through a process of denial. The statements made by the cremation ritual reflect both on the social group and on the individual's position in that group.

Ideology

If burial ceremonialism did not mystify the nature of social inequalities among the Hohokam through a denial of those inequalities, it remains to be determined how the funerary ritual was an active force in the reproduction, negotiation, and legitimation of the Hohokam social order. Answering this question requires returning to an examination of the cremations in their social context and a consideration of how the material culture from the site would have been used in meaningful action in that context.

In the past, it has been assumed that both architecture and burials have the same meaning for the interpretation of inequality in prehistoric contexts (McGuire, 1983a:124). This assumption is not necessarily valid and, in the case of the Hohokam, it is exceedingly misleading.

Architecture is part of an overall cultural landscape. This landscape includes other human-produced features like canals and hornos, and the human modifications of the environment. The cultural landscape forms the stage for all human action. In the context of daily life, it is part of the mundane and taken for granted. In Giddens' (1984:281) terminology, it is nondiscursive, that is, rarely subject to explicit consideration. As a nondiscursive phenomenon, architecture is crucial to the reproduction of social practice because it provides part of the mundane, everyday reality that verifies the ideology by fulfilling the expectations of the ideology.

Mortuary ritual is not, except under exceptional circumstances, a mundane, everyday occurrence. As discussed by Huntington and Metcalf (1979:23), death has the potential of having an immense emotional impact on the survivors. The reasons for this are numerous, including the shock of separation from a loved one, the fear of one's own death, anger at the powers that control death, fear of the dead person and, finally, reactions to the corpse itself. Death is the final transition in life's passage, a transition that stresses not only individuals but also the social linkages that create social groups. The position of individuals in these sets of relations determines how intensely and widely the impact of their deaths will be felt, both emotionally and structurally. The diversity of cultural reactions, rituals, and funerary rites in the ethnographic record is immense, but regardless of how frequently it occurs, death is rarely mundane (Huntington and Metcalf, 1979).

The funeral and burial of a Hohokam person was not the stuff of everyday experience but a single, limited, culturally meaningful statement. Once the ceremony was complete and the grave goods had been deposited in the ground, they were no longer visible and could not be used in a meaningful way in the society, except through the memory of people. Hohokam cemeteries may have been marked, but the types of markers suggested (large sherds, small mounds of earth, and inverted ceramic vessels), do not reveal the magnitude or nature of the grave goods contained in the grave.

The funeral ritual would have linked the living and the dead in a purposeful, discursive way. We can speculate from the data available and the Yuman analogy, that the richest funerals would have been great spectacles, with a large pyre, flame, and smoke, and the pushing forth of wealth to be destroyed in the ceremony. Songs and oratory would have filled the air. The ceremony would have explicitly called on the participants to examine the social relations that brought them together and were being recreated in the process.

The architecture of Colonial and Sedentary Hohokam sites does not overtly pronounce the inequality within and between the households that composed the society. All of the houses were constructed of similar materials, had similar functions, were relatively impermanent, and varied primarily in size. The Hohokam village resembles what Wilk (1983) has called a closed village economy, in which inequality finds expression through portable objects, not architecture.

Wilcox and Sternberg (1983) have identified some possible specialized storage houses that they think were associated with more powerful courtyard groups at Snaketown. These houses, however, differed from other houses primarily in their internal structure and would not have been ostentatious statements of wealth and power. No such structures were identified at La Ciudad.

Wilcox et al. (1981) identified a set of Sacaton houses at Snaketown inside the circle of mounds. In a large village, with a major ceremonial precinct, the positioning of houses could well indicate status differences. In the Snaketown example, the household clusters in the inner ring included the possible specialized storage structures, but again in outward appearance, would not have been greatly different from other houses in the community.

The distinction between core and support houses certainly would have been obvious to the site's inhabitants (Rice, 1987). However, each of the loci at La Ciudad had both house types, and no obvious architectural distinctions would have existed between courtyard groups.

The inequality apparent in the grave lots greatly exceeds the same among the pithouses. A Gini index calculated for the variation in floor area among all the pithouses in the site (data from Henderson, 1987: Fig. 3.4) has a value of 0.10.[5] This value is substantially less than the Gini index for the grave lot values from all cremations on the site (0.74).

The public architecture on Hohokam sites, such as the ball court at La Ciudad, is quite impressive when compared to the pithouses. These public structures, mounds, and ballcourts, were not associated with specific courtyard groups. Some courtyards would be closer to or farther from the public structures, but none was situated in such a way as to indicate a proprietary control of these edifices. Most Hohokam archaeologists interpret these structures as stages for ritual performances and/or games (Wilcox and Sternberg, 1983).

The day-to-day message conveyed by architecture on Colonial and Sedentary period Hohokam sites denied the existence of inequalities in the social order. The architecture reinforced an image of variance by degree that was linked to generational development. The lasting public architecture of the site was spatially associated with no particular social group, producing an impression of institutions shared by, and to the benefit of, all people.

The mundane, day-to-day world of the Colonial and Sedentary period Hohokam reinforced an ideology that denied inequality in the social order. I agree with Wilcox and Sternberg (1983) that an egalitarian ethos governed the everyday lives of the Hohokam in these periods. Their position acknowledges that this egalitarian ideology masked the existing inequalities in the social order.

I would suggest that the egalitarian ideology of everyday life was reproduced and legitimated in a seemingly contradictory mortuary ritual. In the mortuary display at La Ciudad, the inequalities within courtyard groups were expressed, possibly even exaggerated. On average, the richest burials were those of residence yard heads who appeared to have achieved their status in their lifetime. The richest burials, however, included subadults too young to have achieved much status; subadults, on average, had richer grave lots than juveniles or adults. The mortuary data suggest that forces archaeologists would traditionally assign to both achieved and ascribed status determined the distribution and inequality of grave lots.

The cremation ritual would have resolved the crises to the social order caused by death. The more important or extensive the dead individual's relationship to the household, and the household's relationships with other households, the greater the social crises caused by the individual's death. The death of an infant would have stressed the social structure less than the death of a prominent resident yard head; the death of an elderly person, less than that of a subadult. In the cremation rite, the property that the deceased could call on within his/her group or through obligations and relations with other groups, would be assembled and then destroyed. The inequalities in the social order were ritually revealed in the assemblage of items. Then the destruction of the items would deny the permanence of such inequalities, and seemingly limit accumulation across generations.

If the analogy to the Yuman and California cremation complexes is appropriate, this was also a process of social negotiation within and between social groups. The giving of goods for the funeral was involved in a complex system of accounting, debts being paid, and debts being made. When the head of a residence yard died, both succession to the leadership role and the relative standing of different yards would be in question. The bereaved social group could be reduced in position or possibly even destroyed by the imposition of debts it could not hope to repay or internal conflicts it could not resolve.

In the end, the Hohokam gathered up the few remaining fragments of bone and the broken artifacts, placing them in the ground. Even if a surface marker was left, the wealth of the funeral was confined to memory and the possible memorial ceremony. In the mortuary ritual, tensions between the egalitarian ideology of the Hohokam and the existing inequalities in the social order would be revealed and then mediated. The egalitarian ideology is affirmed and the social order is reproduced and legitimated.

The Sedentary to Classic Period Transition

Hohokam archaeologists have long recognized that the change from the Sedentary to the Classic period was a qualitative change, leading some to conclude that the Classic period peoples must have been a different cultural group than those of previous periods (Haury, 1945; Di Peso, 1956; Schroeder, 1957, 1979). Early attempts to argue against a theory of ethnic displacement have done so by obscuring the qualitative nature of change between the two periods (Wasley and Doyel, 1980; Grady, 1976). The most recent interpretations of the transition have tended to once again stress the qualitative changes involved (Wilcox and Sternberg, 1983). Comparison of the contextual relations of the architecture and burials of the two periods suggests that the system of social organization and the ideology supporting it had changed radically.

A shift from pithouse to adobe compound architecture was one of the most pronounced changes in the transition. In both the Soho and the Civano phases, structures differed to a much greater degree in material, permanence, function, size, and elevation (Doyel, 1974; Wilcox and Shenk, 1977; Hammack and Sullivan, 1981; Sires, 1983). At a household level what had been open residence yards and cemetery groups were reorganized into closed, contiguous roomed and walled compounds. Some social groups lived in pithouses arranged in residence yards much like earlier ones, some in adobe compounds, and others in compounds on top of mounds. The previously public, ritual edifices were transformed in the Classic. The ballcourts declined in importance and may not have been used after the Soho Phase (Wilcox and Sternberg, 1983). Social groups of the size of earlier residence yards appropriated the previously ritual and public space atop mounds for living space (Hood, 1985). At least one new type of specialized administrative site with a new structure type, the Casa Grande, appears at Casa Grande (Wilcox, and Shenk, 1977).

Inequality is no longer denied in the architecture of the Classic period. In the day-to-day context, Hohokam individuals were confronted by marked differences in the quality, permanence, and elevation of the dwellings housing different social groups. Perhaps more important, the difference in these dwellings would have created varied daily experiences for the individuals that lived in them. The compound walls surrounding the adobe dwellings would have been around 2 meters high (Doyel, 1974), effective privacy shields that denied outsiders a view of the compound interiors. The activities of social groups living in pithouses lacked such shields and would have been open for casual observation. Even among the compounds, an important distinction occurred. The residents of compounds on top of mounds could look down into the adjacent compounds, whereas those at ground level could not observe activities in the elevated compounds. The architecture hierarchically structured the access that different social groups had into the activities of other social groups.

The domestic lives of households were also probably transformed. Wilcox (1987, 1989) has argued that elite households, those resident on top of mounds, engaged in a continuous network of cross-cutting marriage ties with other elites in a Salado interaction sphere that stretched from the Phoenix basin east to Casas Grandes in Chihuahua. He also has suggested that spinning and weaving was concentrated in mound-top compounds, where elite households wove fine cotton textiles for exchange throughout the Salado interaction sphere. Among the Yumans and O'Odham of the Southwest, spinning was a female activity and weaving, an activity of older males. We have no way of knowing what the gender division of labor would have been among the Classic period Hohokam for these activities. Clearly, however, an increased emphasis on textile production would have changed the domestic regime of elite households and may have had a profound effect on gender relations in these households. Such changes would mean that the nature of domestic relations and gender relations differed between elite and non-elite households, further differentiating the lived experience of each.

Classic period architectural relations are antithetical to an egalitarian ideology that attempts to deny the existence or permanence of inequalities in the social order. The appropriation of previously ritual space by high-status social groups suggests that the ideology may have been transformed to one that naturalized the inequalities by denying their social nature and giving them a supernatural or religious origin (Hood, 1985).

The most apparent qualitative change in burials was the increased importance of inhumation as opposed to cremation. Researchers who have examined the field notes for the Hemenway burial collection have seen little evidence for lavish grave goods, other than ceramics, in the Classic period burials (Nelson,

1981; Teague, 1984; Brunson, 1985, 1989). The location of burials and the treatment of the body appear to have become the more important factors differentiating burials (Brunson, 1989:444–460; Mitchell, 1991a,b). Cremations continue to occur in well-defined cemeteries; inhumations occur in cemeteries, rooms within adobe compounds, and atop mounds; and a few individuals were buried in special crypts in possibly nonresidential buildings such as Mound I at Los Muertos and Clan House 1 at Casa Grande.

The differentiation in the type of burial and locations of burials would have also affected the public awareness of the burials (Hood, 1985). Cremations must have remained a public event owing to the large fires required to consume the bodies. The actual burial of an individual in a room could not have been a public event. The compound walls would have shielded the happening from casual observation, and a large number of people could not have fit in the room to observe it. For example, it seems doubtful that the room containing the crypt in Clan House 1 could hold more than 20 to 30 people (Andreson, 1983).

Burial ritual did not make public the inequalities in the social order apparent in the course of mundane life (that is, in the architecture), but rather, the placement of the burials and their degree of publicity recreated in the eternity of death the cultural landscape that provided the stage for day-to-day activities. The grave goods, which in the high-status burials could not have been interred in the public view, seem to have not reflected, or inconsistently reflected the hierarchical position of the individual. The burials of the Classic period did not declare the inequalities of the social order to be transitory and fleeting, but rather projected the structure of everyday life into death; in doing so, the inequalities in the social order were declared to be naturally derived and eternal.

A panoptic landscape would have structured the day-to-day village life of the Classic period Hohokam (Foucault, 1979). The everyday outdoor activities of the subordinate lineages would have been subject to scrutiny by the elites on the mounds. Those dwelling below would not even have been able to tell whether they were being observed. In death the cremation ritual of the pithouse dwellers would have been public and subject to observation. The activities of the elites, in contrast, would have been hidden from those below, and even their funerals were private matters.

These material relations create the type of social distinctions and segregation that appear in the Pima creation story (Russell, 1975:226–229; Teague, 1989). The story speaks of magicians that lived in great houses segregated from the rest of the people and of the rebellion of the people (led by Elder Brother) that overthrew the magicians and tore down the great houses.

The Process of Transformation

The qualitative nature of the transformation between the Sedentary period and the Classic period have led many researchers to posit unique events or combinations of *causes* to account for the change. These have included migration

(Haury, 1945; Di Peso, 1956; Schroeder, 1957), Mesoamerican influences (Wasley and Johnson, 1965), environmental stress (Doyel, 1980), population growth (Grady, 1976), domination by a foreign power (Di Peso, 1979), and most recently, floods (Nials et al., 1989). Such explanations are generally unsatisfactory because they fail to adequately link the cause or event with the processes of human action or the lived experience of Hohokam people (Teague, 1989). A consideration of the cremation ritual at La Ciudad in the context of changes in economic and social relations in the Colonial and Sedentary periods suggests a different type of scenario. The social organization of the Classic period had its origins in the social relations of Sedentary period villages like La Ciudad. These relations underwent qualitative changes through the Colonial and Sedentary periods, culminating in a qualitative transformation, which marks the transition to the Classic period.

Rice (1987) has reconstructed the development and decline of the Hohokam village represented by the northern resource zone of La Ciudad. His inference suggests that the settlement grew and expanded its agricultural fields until the first half of the Sedentary period, when all of the surrounding area would have been in production. He postulates that the village then began to decline because Casa Buena, a more powerful village to the north of the site, encroached on and eventually took over its fields.

The Hohokam maintained a seasonal occupation of the site area in the Pioneer period, but it was in the Gila Butte phase of the subsequent Colonial period that they extended a canal into the area and began year-round use of the area. This canal was part of a system that included the main canal feeding Casa Buena. Rice (1987) argues that during the Gila Butte phase, some Hohokam lived permanently in the site area and that specialized work parties joined them in the growing season to assist with crops.

Toward the end of the Gila Butte phase, the occupation of the village became more permanent. The ballcourt was built, and cemeteries were established. By the Santa Cruz phase, courtyards were established across the site. Population growth was rapid from the Santa Cruz phase into the Sacaton phase. Rice (1987) suggests that an area of natural desert separated the fields of the northern resource zone from those of Casa Buena. The Hohokam may have used this area to grow agave or other desert plants.

The village reached its maximal size in the Sacaton phase and began to decline. Agave roasting ceased at the site by the beginning of this phase, and Rice (1987) takes this as an indication that the Hohokam had put all of the land between the village and Casa Buena into cultivation. The abandonment and filling of the ballcourt before the beginning of the Sacaton phase suggests that the village was loosing power in the region by the start of this phase. Population peaked in the beginning of the phase and declined so that the village was abandoned by the end of the phase. At the end of the Classic period, the Hohokam redesigned their canals with lower gradients, allowing a single canal to water a larger area (Ackerly et al., 1987:117). The Casa Buena folks initiated such improvements in their canal and extended their fields over the northern resource zone. The village became one of many Hohokam settlements that were absorbed by more powerful villages when population concentrated at the beginning of the Classic period.

Given an aboriginal technology in the lower Sonoran desert, three factors potentially limit the expansion of agricultural production – labor, land, and water. Throughout most of the prehistory of the northern resource zone at La Ciudad, the major resource limiting establishment of new residence yards and cemetery groups, or the expansion of existing ones, was labor. It was only toward the end of the village's occupation that the Hohokam brought all of the surrounding land under cultivation, and since they continued to expand the irrigation network following the village's abandonment, we must assume that sufficient water was available.

The crucial problem facing households and couples wishing to found new residence yards would have been the recruitment of labor. This could be accomplished through two basic mechanisms, either by fecundity, or by attracting individuals from outside the nuclear family. Fecundity would have been the more certain recruitment strategy because children become useful workers long before they can function as socially independent adults. This process of labor recruitment is, however, slow, limited by human fertility, and subject to chance factors of infant mortality and sex rations. Since other residence yards would have also been competing for labor, non-nuclear family members and even grown children could leave a yard where they were dissatisfied to join a different one or start a new one. Households could have recruited and maintained a following through a variety of social and ritual mechanisms but would have had little economic control or cohesion. Family heads could have established social dependencies by using trade partnerships to control the distribution of exotic goods, such as shell jewelry, which would have been required for social transactions (McGuire and Howard, 1987).[6] Older men and women in the household may also have had control of ritual knowledge necessary for individual and group welfare (Wilcox and Sternberg, 1983). As is the case with historically known Yuman's, successful Hohokam family heads would have been known for their generosity as they distributed goods to establish the social debts that were the necessary for their power and influence.

An egalitarian ideology would have advanced and limited the interests of households. It would have advanced them as it obscured the existence of inequalities in the society. It would have limited them as any overt expressions of superiority, retention of wealth, or resort to cohesion would have brought social and possibly ritual sanctions.

Through a combination of factors, such as well-made trade partnerships, fortunate birth patterns, favorable agricultural conditions, luck in betting, and careful manipulation of social debts and obligations, one lineage could gain power over others. It would, however, be difficult for a lineage in this position to maintain it. Establishing social debts would have required the dispersal of property and basic food resources. Such debts could be hard to collect, and a lineage that fell too far into debt could simply melt away as members sought new associations. Finally, the death of the family head would have created problems of succession, the funeral would have been a drain on courtyard resources, and the funeral would also provide the opportunity for other lineages to absolve old obligations and establish new ones to the bereaved courtyard's disadvantage.

Inherent in this set of relations were those that would transform the system of social organization. The more individuals a household could recruit, the more land it could work, and the higher the level of production possible. A powerful stimulus would have existed to maximize fertility and draw people in from outside areas. With an egalitarian ideology, few, if any, normative barriers would prevent a wide range of individuals from trying to expand agricultural production and establish new courtyards. These relations would have spurred population growth and expansion until the limits of land or water were reached. The causes in other theories (including increased drought, flooding, or increased in migrations) would accelerate these trends while wet years and increased out-migration or death rates would slow them. I doubt the process of change would have been a smooth one, but rather an erratic sequence of tension and resolution as declining material conditions constrained growth or improved conditions encouraged it.

During the Sedentary period, populations in the Ciudad area began to experience land shortages.[7] With the declining availability of land, some lineages and villages such as Casa Buena increasingly would have been able to turn small advantages into long-term relations of dominance. With a shortage of land, indebted lineages would increasingly be unable to dissolve away, and aspiring individuals would be unable to establish new residence yards. Dominant lineages could exploit the ideology and system of social and ritual debts and obligations to acquire economic dependents and establish ranked lineages. The northern resource zone at la Ciudad lost out in this process, first with the destruction of its ballcourt and then with a lingering decline from AD 950 to 1050. By the end of the Sedentary the lineages of the northern resource zone had left, and Casa Buena extended its canals and fields over the village.

ENDNOTES

1. Crown (1990) provides the best article-length summary of Hohokam prehistory, and the articles collected in Gummerman (1991) cover the current range of issues and positions in the interpretation of this prehistory.

2. The ethnographic sources from which this summary is constructed are Forde (1931), Spier (1970), Castetter and Bell (1951), Kroeber (1925), and Kelley (1977). These sources are extensively discussed in McGuire (1987, in press).

Readers interested in a more detailed consideration of the sources should consult one of these monographs.

3. Some readers may object to my use of a Yuman analogy here because they feel that the O'odham are the descendants of the Hohokam. I would note that the gender and family relations described in this paragraph were similar among the O'odham and indeed among most lower Southwestern cultural groups (Russell, 1975; Underhill, 1939; McGuire, 1991).

4. Executing a dummy variable analysis on the presence or absence of Cluster 1 is problematical because individual cremations could include more than one cluster, violating the assumption of independence of cases. The mean value for cremations containing Cluster 1 artifacts was 43.62.

5. In an earlier article (McGuire, 1983a) I reported Gini indices for the Colonial and Sedentary periods considerably higher than 0.10. The higher indices result from the inclusion of public architecture in the earlier calculations. This lumping of domestic and ritual architecture obscures the processes and relationships that the present study seeks to discover.

6. Seymour (1988) and Crown (1991) should be consulted for different interpretations of the shell-trade data.

7. This assumption is based on Rice's (1987) observations concerning the growth of the village.

CHAPTER 8

Critical Archaeology – Archaeology and the Vanishing American

Our religion is the tradition of our ancestors — the dreams of our old men given to them in the solemn hours of night by the great spirit, and the visions of our Sachems, and is written in the hearts of our people. . . . The White Man will never be alone. Let him be just and deal kindly with my people for the dead are not powerless.

(*Chief Seattle, 1854*)

Archaeologists look at artefacts and they look at bones and, seemingly, the bones tell them a story. In what Chief Seattle says, the story is passed on from generation to generation and it is told in the heart because, in the spirit, this is the true story. That cannot be misinterpreted, and it goes on forever.

(*Ernest Turner, 1989:193*)

The lot of the archaeologist is wretched enough in fearing the spirits of the disturbed ancestors without adding the fear of armed attack by the agitated descendants.

(*Roderick Sprague, 1974:2*)

Many, if not most, archaeologists regard the past as something knowable independent of the present (Salmon, 1982; Watson *et al.*, 1984; Watson, 1986; Binford, 1987; Schiffer, 1988; Kelley and Hanen, 1988). Positivst theorists allow that social and political factors may determine what questions scientists choose to investigate about the past and what hypotheses they will entertain to answer them (Wilk, 1985), but they see method as sharply circumscribing these influences (Wylie, 1989:93). They believe that through the rigorous application of method, scientists can arrive at objective understandings of the past, independent of the social and political influences of our present. If this is true then we must wonder why the past is so often a locus of social and political struggle in the modern world (Conkey and Spector, 1984; McBryde, 1985; Layton, 1989a,b; Bintliff, 1988; Quick, 1985). Marxist scholars have demonstrated that nations spawned archaeologies (colonialist, nationalist, or imperialist) that fit with their place in a larger world economy (Trigger, 1984), and that within these traditions, archaeology most often reflects middle-class interests (Kristiansen, 1981; Patterson, 1986; Trigger, 1989a:15). Feminists have identified significant androcentric bias in scientific practice and asked, if science is self-correcting, then why have these biases survived (Harding, 1986; Wylie, 1991:41)? Indigenous peoples in various parts of the world have challenged archaeology as an aspect of western domination that appropriates their pasts, their history, to advance western interests and colonialism (Quick, 1985; Layton, 1989a,b). As Layton (1989a:4) notes "Mere protestations of objectivity cannot free the archaeologist from the political implications of research." Archaeologists need, instead, to seek a better understanding of our places in these struggles. This requires a critical examination of our history that articulates the past directly with our contemporary scholarly, theoretical, social, and political interests (Pinsky, 1989:88), and changes in the praxis of archaeology.

Native Americans in the United States have a very different notion of the past and its relationship to the present than do archaeologists (Zimmerman, 1987, 1989; Anyon, 1991a). Chief Seattle said in 1854 that "it was written in the hearts of our people." Today many Indian people, such as Ernest Turner, question the value and practice of archaeology. They see archaeology's study of Native American pasts as part of a larger history of domination and exploitation of Indian people (Hill, 1977; Hammil and Zimmerman, 1983; Talbot, 1984; Quick, 1985; NCAI, 1986; Antone, 1986; Hammil and Cruz, 1989; Turner, 1989). They are concerned that archaeologists treat Indian people as a vanished race that exists only in the archaeological record, and thus cannot have rights in the present (Deloria, 1973:49). This myth of a vanishing Indian race originated in nineteenth century attempts to construct a distinctive national identity and heritage for the United States (Dippie, 1982).

Archaeology played a historical role in the creation of a national heritage and in the myth of the vanishing American. Archaeologists rarely situate their practice in this larger history and therefore frequently fail to understand both how the Native American past became their object of study and why many Native Americans are resentful of that fact. They wonder why Roderick Sprague (1974:2) warns us to beware the dead that are not powerless and their agitated descendants. An understanding of linkage between the development of U.S. Indian policy and the development of U.S. archaeology is a starting point for a dialogue on how archaeologists might recreate their science to reconcile our disciplinary, intellectual interests and the interests of modern Native Americans.

This chapter can also be seen as a case study of a larger phenomenon within archaeology. In many ways the themes of vanishing and heritage extend beyond this case and resonate throughout world archaeology. The image of vanished cities, tribes, or peoples is a common one in archaeology, especially in popular books on the topic. The titles of such works often speak of quests or searches for lost worlds or civilizations. Fagan (1985:14) notes that "archaeologists have to be guardians of the world's dying cultures." The idea of heritage is often universalized to a "human heritage" that the archaeologist has the duty to protect (Silberman, 1982; Trigger, 1984:365). These themes take on specific meanings and affect how archaeologists do archaeology in their encounters with specific regional traditions of archaeology and in their confrontations with national pasts, such as the past of the Native American (Trigger, 1985b).

THE PRESENT IN THE PAST

A dialectical view suggests that knowledge of the past can exist only in the present and that such knowledge must therefore be a complex result of past and present. Our knowledge of the past is constructed in the present as archaeologists try to create order out of the confused and conflicting observations we can make on the past (Haraway, 1989:6; Gero, 1991). In this creative process researchers start from different sociopolitical standpoints that give them different angles of view on the observations that are made (Wylie, 1991:42). These standpoints will be diverse and divergent, leading to many different pasts and the need to examine critically the present in the past.

The Past as Object

Modern western people tend to see time as a road. It fades behind us in a haze and disappears before us into a dense fog. As people advance along the road, the fog parts and the haze fills in behind. This perspective defines three spaces along the linear continuum. The fog is the future, the haze the past, and the brief space of clarity the present.

A number of vital ideas about time derive from this view. Time is linear and directional, leading from a past, through a present, and on to a future. Each space creates a separate reality from the flow of time and allows time to be split into still smaller units (Shanks and Tilley, 1987a:110–111). Western observers always stand in the present, and the view from this place mandates how they can observe and understand the other spaces. The future is unobservable and unknowable but may be predictable. They can directly observe the present, but they are too close to it and too much a part of it to gain an objective knowledge of it. The past is harder to observe than the present, but they can be more objective about it because of the time that separates them from it. People see the past dimly but with a less biased vision. The directionality of time, moving from past to present to future, means that scholars might be able to use the trajectory of the past to predict the future.

This view of time makes the past a separate reality that can be isolated as an object of study. The past is distinct from the present. Since scholars can be more objective about the past, we can come to a truer understanding of the past than the present, and thus the past serves as a touchstone for the present. But scholars cannot fully know the past. Our inability to directly observe the past limits our knowledge of it; these limits are greatest when there are no written records, the observations of people in the past. This view makes the study of the past mainly a technical problem, a problem of observation. Archaeologists claim a role, *vis à vis* historians, in the study of the past because our method and theory allow observations of the past even when there are no documents. Archaeologists can study the most ancient past, prehistory (Daniels, 1981:13). This method and theory also gives us a unique perspective on material culture in all times and places (Rathje and Schiffer, 1982:6).

Archaeologists are rarely explicit about why we should study the past. We seem to just take it for granted that knowledge of the past has value. Introductory texts, however, commonly broach the issue, and two themes appear again and again in these books. Authors with very dissimilar theoretical points of view often share these themes but put different twists on them (Shanks and Tilley, 1987a:26). The first theme holds that the present is a product of the past. This view builds on the idea of past as touchstone. Archaeologists study the past in order to know how the present came to be (Chard, 1969:1, Hole and Heizer, 1973:10). We study the past to answer questions about our own society and ourselves (Sharer and Ashmore, 1987:8; Clark, 1970:40), or, more grandly, archaeology studies the past to grasp the nature of humanity (Fagan, 1985:15), to know "what does it mean to be human" (Sharer and Ashmore, 1987:8). The second theme says that archaeologists can use the past to pierce the fog of the future. The direction of the past gives us a means of predicting the future. Some archaeologists study the past for lessons to help us make decisions about the future (Chang, 1967:156) or to learn the laws of cultural development that will plot the course of the future (Hole and Heizer, 1973:10; Eddy, 1984:26), or to learn how to predict behavior (Rathje and Schiffer, 1982:6).

These themes give the past a power in (or over) the present. They make the past immutable. The past cannot be altered, and the rules, principles, and standards that give legitimacy to the present lie in this immutable past. The outcome of the past is also certain, and its direction is known — who won and who lost. This leads us to believe that the present is also the inevitable outcome of the past. The certainty of the past also allows the prediction of the future when the direction of the past is projected beyond the present.

The power of the past in the present means that the past can be used as a political tool, to make the political forms of today look certain and inevitable. John D. Rockefeller, Jr., built Colonial Williamsburg, and Henry Ford built

Greenfield Village in Dearborn, Michigan, to legitimize different notions of class relations in the modern United States (Wallace, 1981). Rockefeller enshrined an old-money, mercantile, planter elite in colonial Williamsburg, whereas Ford glorified the Midwestern inventor and entrepreneur in Greenfield (Wallace, 1981).[1] The Nazis rewrote the prehistory of Europe to brace their idea of an Aryan master race (Arnold, 1990). Afrikaners in South Africa have written a prehistory of Africa that equates the land claims of whites and Bantu by making both tribes (M. Hall, 1984). Mexico, Britain, and China have used the past to legitimate their states and ways of life (Fowler, 1987).

George Orwell (1949:204) commented in *1984* that "Who controls the past controls the future; who controls the present controls the past." The past can serve these ends because western thought has made it a distinct object, because we think we can know it apart from the present. None of these ends is possible if scholars cannot free the past from the present, if we cannot take the present out of the past. The past loses its immutability, its power over, when its construction is critically examined — when the scholar asks who controls the past, and what interest does that control serve?

The Critical Dialectic of Past and Present

A dialectical view forces us to question the split between subject and object, past and present. A dialectical view recognizes that there was a real past but also that the past is made in the present. Our stories must fit what archaeologists can observe in the past. The past should not be made up, but more than one story will always fit these data because the perceptions, interests, and social position of the teller also affect the telling of the story (Leone, 1982, 1986; Handsman, 1983b; Shanks and Tilley, 1987a; Haraway, 1989:6; Gero, 1991; Wylie, 1991). This suggests that multiple stories of the past will always exist and that these stories will change as the concerns and realities of the present change. The dialectic of past and present is a complex mix, a tangled skein of observation, intention, interest, bias, and belief.

Much of the recent work in critical archaeology has sought to examine archaeology's role in creating a capitalist world view or ideology (Leone, 1981, 1982, 1986; Leone *et al.*, 1987; Handsman, 1983a; Shanks and Tilley, 1987a; Handsman and Leone, 1989; Little and Shackel, 1989). These studies usually examine public programs, mainly museum exhibits, and discuss how these programs help to create and recreate capitalist ideals of individualism, the commodification of culture, and the notion of time. Some archaeologists have turned the critique into practice and developed public programs that oppose a capitalist world view (Leone and Potter, 1984; Potter, 1990).

In terms of a capitalist world view, archaeology is a very small cog in a very big machine. Although these authors clearly show that this world view has a great impact on archaeology, I doubt that archaeologists have the power to affect the larger machine very much. Other analyses have sought to lower the level of our critique from the capitalist world view to the role of archaeology in capitalism and ask about the professional interests and privileges archaeologists derive from that role. These analyses include marxist studies that examine how archaeology serves the interests of ruling classes or class fractions (Trigger, 1980a, 1981, 1985b, 1989a; Kristiansen, 1981; Patterson, 1986, 1987, 1989b), feminist analyses that highlight the gender biases of archaeology (Conkey and Spector, 1984; Gero, 1985; Conkey and Gero, 1991; Wylie, 1991), and analyses that investigate the sociopolitics of archaeology itself (Gero et al., 1983). All of these studies ask about our professional interests and how they are part of power relations.

These analyses are inevitably historical. As social beings and scholars, we inherit beliefs and social relations from the past, and these factors structure how we act. This inheritance does not enslave us, but it urges us along already set paths of thought and deed. It is easy to follow these paths without thinking about why they exist or what the unintended consequences of such a course may be, but to just accept them as given. A historical analysis dissolves the given nature of these paths and asks how were they laid out, why should archaeologists follow them, to what ends do they lead, and whose interests do they serve? Such a historical analysis is also socially made, but should not be made up. It must fit what scholars can know about history. Because it is a social product, archaeologists also need to critically think about the social and historical context of the critique.

My goals in this chapter are more modest than those of either of the two groups of researchers I have talked about. I do not wish to use archaeology to expose a capitalist world view or rewrite the history of American archaeology. My intent is less grand, yet may strike closer to home. Why is it that archaeologists study the Indian past and have power over the objects from that past? How do archaeologists lay claim to the Indian past and how does this process relate to the development of Indian–white relations?[2] The story that I present of this history is my understanding. I have woven it from what I have been able to learn about the history of archaeology and the history of Native American–white relations in U.S. history, but there may be other stories that also fit this history.[3]

ARCHAEOLOGY AND NATIVE AMERICAN PASTS

The Native American has an ambiguous and often contradictory position in the American consciousness. Whites in the United States tend to see the Indian as both a savage enemy and a romantic symbol of our heritage as a nation (Stedman, 1982). Indians appear in movies and television programs as savages decked out in feathers intent on taking the scalps of White women and children. When asked about Indians, non-Indian school children make war whoops and evoke images of killing and scalping (Stedman, 1982:4). On the other hand, the Indian can be the noble primitive, the first American, the origin point of our heritage. A sign at the entrance to the village of Deposit in upstate New York says "Deposit, the One-Time Indian Village of Koo Koose." On Thanksgiving, young school children put up a bed-sheet tepee, make paper feathers, and dance around going woo-woo-woo. The first page of the trail guide for Casa Grande Ruins National Monument in Arizona states "This area belongs to you and is part of your national heritage as an American citizen." The title of a book by William Haviland and Marjory Power (1981) proclaims Indian people to have been *The Original Vermonters*. Kevin Costner's romantic portrayal of the Sioux in his film, *Dancing with Wolves*, has become a critical and commercial success, taking seven Oscars. All about us are conflicting images of Indian people that are rarely commented on or noticed.

These conflicting images spring from two different aspects of the European American's encounter with Native Americans; the Native American as a savage obstacle to the nation's growth and the Native American as the first American. The continent of North America was thickly populated with people when the first Europeans arrived, and these Indians were *savage primitives* who had to be disposed of before Europeans could settle. As primitives, the Indians were wild and savage, but also natural and closer to the original state of humans, as conceived by Europeans (Fowler and Fowler, 1991). The Enlightenment-trained founding fathers of the United States grounded the national heritage in nature, that is, the Indians, land, plants, animals, and minerals of North America. In this sense the Indian became the First American. The contradiction between the Indian as savage and the Indian as the First American was historically mediated by the notion that Native Americans were vanishing or had vanished (Dippie, 1982). The concept of the vanishing American disarticulated Native American heritages for nationalistic and scientific purposes.

Who Controls the Past?

In the United States, archaeologists and anthropologists have been the authorities on Native American pasts, and this authority has given us power over those pasts. Courts of law and government commissions call us as expert witnesses and have often given our testimony more weight than that of tribal elders.[4] We are the ones who write about Indian pasts for the general public, and it is, by and large, archaeologists or anthropologists who control the great museum collections of objects from that past. An 80-plus-year legacy of historic preservation law, beginning with the Antiquities Act of 1906, reserves the archaeological record of Indian peoples for our study (Moore, 1989). We often assert this authority in the books, articles, and exhibits we prepare for the general public. We make the archaeologist the hero of the story and either split

Indian peoples from their past or treat them as artifacts of that past. Rarely do our public presentations give an Indian view of the past or treat that past as part of an ongoing native cultural tradition.

Archaeologists frequently argue that they are the only ones who can really know the past of Indian people (Zimmerman, 1989), as the stewards of extinct Indian cultures (Meighan, 1985; Turner, 1986). We sometimes assume that Indian people do not know their past, have no interest in that past, or are unable to preserve it (Deloria, 1973:31–33).

Brian Fagan's (1985:11) widely used textbook *In the Beginning* states a typical assertion of this type:

> *Most American Indian groups came into contact with literate Western civilization only in the past three centuries. Before European contact, Indian history was not written; it consisted mostly of oral traditions handed down from generation to generation. Archaeology and archaeological sites are the only other possible sources for American Indian history. Only as archaeologists probe into their ancestry will the first chapter of American history be written.*

Fagan goes on to laud archaeologists who work with Indian people. He indicates that by working with Indians, archaeologists can interpret the objects we find, and that we can bring the forgotten history of Native Americans "into the consciousness of the Indians themselves" (Fagan, 1985:11).[5] Like Fagan's, most archaeological claims to the Indian past seek support for that claim by making that past part of a United States national heritage. Someone who accepts this position might ask why archaeologists should be interested in the larger history of Native American–white relations, and what are the implications of that history for what archaeologists do?

Why Should Archaeologists Address the Interests of Indian People?

Many archaeologists have taken what they perceive, rightfully, to be liberal stances in regard to Indian people. They have actively worked to protect Native American sites and to promote acceptance by the general public and the powers that be in the United States that Native American pasts are a legitimate part of the American heritage; deserving of the same level of attention, protection, and understanding as our European heritage. They see their actions and concerns primarily in terms of their own intentions, in terms of debates about national heritage, and in terms of the history of archaeology. Most are honestly at a loss to understand why many Indian people do not appreciate these efforts. Most Indian people cannot escape the larger history of white–Indian relations because that history dwells in the relations of their day-to-day lives. It lives in the regulations, bureaucracies, poverty, and discrimination that deny them the ability to determine their own lives and futures. In this larger set of relations, the archaeologist's authority over Indian pasts is simply one other aspect of their selves that has been taken from their control. Understanding relations between scholars and Native Americans in terms of this larger history provides an opportunity to contextualize archaeological authority.

The American Anthropological Association (1983:1) statement of professional ethics asserts that "In research, anthropologists' paramount responsibility is to those they study." If, as anthropologists, we accept that our first responsibility is to those we study, then I must ask, who are these people and who speaks for them? By detaching the pasts of Native Americans from living Indian people, archaeologists have struck mute our subjects. Archaeologists who define our obligation as being to the people of the past or the people of the future (Meighan, 1985; Goldstein and Kintigh, 1990) conveniently identify persons who cannot speak to their interests as objects of study, leaving scholars free to express scientific interests as theirs. Archaeologists have ethical obligations to a variety of communities, to the profession, to the general public that pays for research, to students, and to the people studied. An examination of archaeology's place in a history of Native American–white relations shows that the people we study were Indian people and that archaeologists have a significant responsibility to their living descendants.

Recent legislation profoundly alters our access to and control over mortuary remains and sacred artifacts. Public Law 101-185 that established a National Museum of the American Indian and the Native American Graves Protection and Repatriation Act of 1990, both recognize the interests of Indian people in burials and sacred objects that require that scholars consult and abide by these interests. The laws in essence mandate that archaeologists will have to work closely with Indian people in the future. It will no longer be possible to engage in archaeology without involving Indian people.

The history of archaeology and the vanishing American participates in a much larger history that embodies all of anthropological practice. The splitting of the Indian image into noble versus savage savages ultimately springs from Enlightenment rationalism (Leaf, 1979). These twin images are cultural projections of a rationalist world view onto nonwestern others. Resolving the contradiction by placing Indian people in a category of "vanishing/vanished" peoples fits with general projection of Enlightenment rationalism, along with its political creation – the nation state – onto non-Western peoples. At the heart of this rationalist view is the notion that world cultural diversity was/is dying out and being replaced through the formation of nation-state melting pots by a deculturated, homogenized, high-tech world system. This notion sees ethnicity and cultural identity as relics of a preindustrial past that will disappear once people become rational. Of course the resurgence of ethnicity in the last 20 years, including the resurgence of American Indian identity, proves that human social reality is far more complex.[6] The notion of nations structures the current resurgence of American Indian identity (Deloria and Lytle, 1984), and it is as part of this struggle for self-determination that Indian people have recently confronted the archaeologist for control of their ancestors' bodies, sacred objects, and pasts.

U.S. archaeology stands at a crossroads. Archaeologists need to rethink and reforge our relationships with Indian people; doing this will require more than just an accommodation of the interest of science to theirs. It will require rethinking the object of study and rationales for research, the training of students and the conduct of research, and the dissemination of results. This will not be easy, nor will there be a simple cookbook or set of "right" or "best" answers. Archaeologists are entering into a process of negotiation, advocacy, and scholarship that will be difficult, fraught with failure, constantly renegotiated, and ultimately beneficial to the discipline. A first step in this process is to reconsider both the key concepts that have structured how archaeologists speak about Native Americans and the history of how relations between archaeology and Native Americans got to this point.

HERITAGE AND NATION

The *Random House College Dictionary* defines heritage as "something that comes or belongs to a person by reason of birth; an inherited portion." It is an owned past. People most often think of heritage as being the property of individuals, nations, or all of humankind. My focus here will be on national and universal heritage.

The idea of nation implies the existence of a people united by a common government and territory. I should note that European nations are a relatively new phenomenon. They first emerge in the late eighteenth century, and the United States along with Great Britain, Holland, and France were among the first nations to be formed (Anderson, 1983). The idea of a nation-state vested the right to govern in a people, a nation, that shared a common language, culture, and heritage. A border, a line on a map, defines each nation-state. At least in theory, the stuff that makes up these states, the culture of the nation, the authority of the government, or the history of the people, should extend evenly and completely from border to border.

A dialectical contradiction lies at the heart of the idea of a nation-state. A nation-state includes all of the people of that nation, yet this inclusion necessarily implies the exclusion of individuals and groups that are not part of that people. A nation-state seeks cultural uniformity within its bounds and in doing so creates diversity by distinctly bounding and opposing groupings that may have previously blended gradually one into the other. Further, by structuring political debate and legitimacy in terms of membership in a nation, it encourages tribalization. Tribalization replicates the political process of nation-state formation within the state by reducing complex multilingual-cultural regional systems into a simplified, monolingual-cultural, territorial discrete "tribe." These tribes then assert their legitimacy in struggles against the state by claiming to be nations, entitled to the same privilege as the nation-state they are in. This process unfolds in the reduction of Indian people to reservations and the restructuring of aboriginal cultural groups into the "nations within" the United States (Deloria and Lytle, 1984). This dialectical contradiction drives nation-states to create greater uniformity within their bounds, but even as they do, it also structures resistance to the state so that greater and harder-edged diversity results to threaten the existence of the state.

Political groups within nation-states have taken both conservative and liberal approaches to resolving the contradiction between inclusion and exclusion, uniformity and diversity.[7] The conservative approach manifests itself in the savage-savage image of the American Indian in the United States. Those that are different are inferior, even subhuman, and must be eliminated or removed from the state to protect the people. The liberal approach appears as the noble savage. The other is not subhuman, but capable of achieving the culture of the nation, becoming part of the people. But the other loses something in this process; the noble savages lose their nobility. In either case the other must vanish and be subsumed in the nation. Archaeologists have, at least since the late nineteenth century, usually taken the liberal position that Indian people are part of the nation and that their past should be part of the national heritage. For Indian people, this liberal position is a two-edged sword. By asserting that they are Americans and part of a larger U.S. heritage they can gain sympathy and support for their interests from other Americans that identify with the U.S. heritage (Emerson and Cross, 1990:571, 573). To do so, however, submerges their identity in the national identity, and undermines their status as "nations within," entitled to their own culture and destiny; it undermines their right of self-determination (Deloria and Lytle, 1984).

In the ideology of the nation-state, the people of the nation are defined by a shared history that equals a common national heritage. The nation includes those groups of people that participated in the history of that nation, and because the nation had one history, all the peoples of the nation have a common heritage. However, just because two peoples share a common history does not mean that they shared a common experience. That experience is their past, their heritage, and thus the same history creates many pasts, many heritages. The experience of nineteenth-century white settlers on the high plains was quite different from that of the Indian people that they displaced; the slaughter of the Seventh Calvary at the Battle of the Greasy Grass and the Seventh's revenge at Wounded Knee were different experiences for the white troopers and Indian people involved in each. The nation has set aside the Little Big Horn battlefield as a national monument, the primary shrine of the western Indian Wars. Wounded Knee is a barren field with a simple marker, but it lives on in the consciousness of the Lakota people today. A nation transforms the varied pasts of its history into a common national heritage by selecting pieces of that history and representing them as if they were the whole of that history.

The awareness of heritage on the part of national governments tends to focus on tangible sets of historic objects, structures, or places rather than the people who produced them (King et al., 1977; Lowenthal, 1985:238–248; Bintliff, 1988:3; Cleere, 1988). Such artifacts of the past have power in the present, can legitimate the nation, because they create the appearance of a known, given past, whereas their interpretation remains infinitely malleable. They give the official stories of the past an overt and tangible aura of accuracy because the interpretation becomes confused with the thing. In reconstructions of buildings viewers tend to assume that if the details of door hinges, window sashes, paint color, and furnishings are correct, then so too is the story told about the place. If scholars know the exact spot at the Greasy Grass where Custer fell, then other aspects of the story we tell have greater credence. These artifacts verify tangibly that there was a reality to the past, and our skill at reconstructing them confirms our ability to know that reality apart from the present. Scholars find meanings for these artifacts in the present, and these meanings are molded so that heritage always fits the interests of the present.

Lowenthal (1985:37) notes that heritage is an ambiguous notion for a nation "normally evoked with sub-lyrical vagueness." Heritage is one of the things that defines a nation, that legitimates its being; a nation can not exist without a heritage. It also, however, serves as a brake on progress because it inhibits change. In the United States this ambiguity has led to a long-standing progress – preservation debate (Mitchell, 1981). Archaeologists typically take a preservationist stand and defend heritage in the face of economic progress (McGimsey, 1972; King et al., 1977; Fowler, 1986; Knudson, 1986, 1989; Cleere, 1988).

Heritage varies in form from nation to nation and so too does the nature and content of debates over heritage. Sometimes the debate is about the commercialization of heritage, often it concerns the disposition of objects from the past, and at other times it is about who will be included in the heritage of the past. In all cases, the question of who will control the past lies at the center of the argument.

Many archaeologists in Great Britain oppose the burgeoning heritage industry that sells the past in for-profit heritage centers such as the Jorvik Viking center in York (Chippindale, 1985; Baker, 1988; Bintliff, 1988; Hatton, 1988; Merriman, 1988; Hewison, 1987; Shanks and Tilley, 1987a). Two lines of critique have emerged in this British debate. Some voice concern that this industry takes heritage away from archaeologists and puts it in the hands of guardians rather than interpreters, thus making it an object of commercial exploitation rather than of education (Bintliff, 1988). Others decry the commodification of the past, a commodification that they say serves the interests of capitalism (Shanks and Tilley, 1987a:25, 88).

Heritage is a locus of struggle in many other nations as well (Bahn, 1984, 1986; Layton, 1989a,b). In Israel the ultra-conservative Jewish Kadisha vies with a secular government over how the past of Israel and objects from that past will be used (Bahn, 1984, 1986). In Latin America controversy swirls around what the role of Indian people will be in the nation states of that continent (Males, 1989; Condori, 1989; Bate, 1984). In Australia and New Zealand, fights between archaeologists and native peoples parallel those in the United States, with aborigines and Maori trying to gain control of their ancestors' bones and their own past (Ucko, 1983; Sullivan, 1985; Mulvaney, 1985; Hubert, 1989; Ross, 1989; Chase, 1989). In South Africa, a daring few have used archaeology to indict that nation's racism and made-up history of apartheid (Tobias, 1961; M. Hall, 1984, 1987).

Nationalistic archaeologies tend to be monolithic, exposing a *party line*, whereas there can be a multitude of heritages in the history of a nation. Thus in nationalistic archaeologies, a key battle is whose heritage becomes dominent and thus isomorphic with national identity. Archaeologists have looked at the uses of archaeology in nationalism. Fowler (1987) examined the role of archaeology in the national identity of México, Great Britain, and in the People's Republic of China. Both Trigger (1980a, 1986) and Patterson (1986, 1988) have discussed archaeology and nationalism in the United States. Arnold (1990) writes about how the Nazis used archaeology in Germany, and McConnell (1989) showed how archaeology was used to help create the modern nations of Greece and Italy. Groube (1985) and Mangi (1989) discuss how archaeology is being used right now to forge a nation of Papua New Guinea.

Archaeologists will also call on the notion of a universal human heritage. The usual form of this call is to say that all archaeological remains are the property of all people (Turner, 1986). This assertion springs from the idea that the ancient past in some way speaks to our common humanity. Trigger (1984) notes that an imperialist archaeology most often clings to this view, and that such a notion is most common in Great Britain and in the United States. In the United States the idea of a universal human heritage is often linked to the notion of a national heritage. U.S. archaeologists commonly argue that the archaeological record of the United States is part of our national heritage and that it is the property of a scientific world (Knudson, 1989). This mix of the universal and the national is not new. In the first decade of this century Monsignor O'Connell evoked both ideas in his plea for the passage of the Antiquities Act of 1906 (Moore, 1989:203).

Appeals to a universal human heritage rarely adequately answer one key question: if the human past belongs to everyone, why does control over the things from that past and the interpretation of that past fall to archaeologists?

Why are archaeologists the stewards of the past? Most often these appeals contrast the interests of archaeologists only with those of pothunters, art dealers, and others who would make a profit from the past. They oppose science to greed. Profit-takers benefit only themselves, while science gives value for all. These appeals seldom write about, or often dismiss as purely political, the interests of native people, such as Native Americans, who derive their identity and belief from a very different notion of the past than that of the scientists.

If archaeological remains are part of a universal human heritage, then many voices should be heard. To let many voices speak raises a crisis of representation in archaeology that parallels reassessments of dominant ideas in many other social sciences, among them in cultural anthropology (Marcus and Fisher, 1986:7). It means that the notion that archaeology should be guided by an abstract generalizing framework that encompasses all efforts in the field must be questioned. The field should be restructured to support a diversity of interests, paradigms, and notions of the past. The problem is how to do this? Archaeologists are not the only voices speaking about a Native American past, and many of the other voices are antagonistic; the change is not one that archaeologists alone can make. Archaeologists do not know how to facilitate the interests of Indian people without translating their voices into the language of science and technology, nor do they know how to deal with the conflicts that arise when different voices disagree; not just on the substance of the past, but more fundamentally, on what the past is. Opening archaeological practice (scholarly, public, and pedological) and theory to a dialogue of many voices that will transform us as well as them is problematic.

THE VANISHING AMERICAN

Why are scholars (archaeologists, historians, and anthropologists) the stewards of Indian pasts?[8] The answer to that question lies in the relationship of archaeology to the larger history of white–Native American relations in the United States. White American attitudes about Indian people have always stemmed from a definition of the Indian as an alien and singular other (Berkhoffer, 1978:xv; Trigger, 1980a). Defining Indian people as alien placed them outside the usual rights and privileges of white society; lumping all Indian people in a single group denied them an identity except in relationship to whites. Whites have tried to characterize the *otherness* of Indian people in terms of an opposition between the noble savage and the savage savage. These ideas say more about the psyche and political debates of whites than they do about Indian people. Two more-basic ideas about Indian people, however, mediate this seemingly incompatible dichotomy. Most white observers have agreed that the Indian other was a primitive other and that this other had vanished or was vanishing.

Whether Indians were noble savages or savage savages, there was little doubt that they were savages, that is, primitives. In the western mind, primitive is a temporal notion that fashions otherness by relegating people to an ancient time, with little or no regard for their true place in time. Such people always live in the past (Fabian, 1983:18). For this reason the general public and archaeologists tend to treat Indian remains as ancient even when the remains are not (McGuire, 1989b:168).

Trigger and Patterson on Indians and American Archaeology

Bruce Trigger (1980a, 1984, 1985b, 1986) has written about how the white view of the Indian as a primitive other affected the growth of archaeology. He argues that in North America archaeology began as a colonial venture that downplayed the achievements and skills of a vanquished people to excuse the reduction and subjugation of that people.

> *Colonialist archaeology, wherever practiced, served to denigrate native societies and peoples by trying to demonstrate that they had been static in prehistoric times and lacked the initiative to develop on their own* (Trigger, 1984:363).

Trigger sees the "New Archaeology" of the 1960s as a form of imperialist or world-oriented archaeology. This type of archaeology only occurs in a few nation states that gained world-wide hegemony. He argues that the rise of the "New Archaeology" in the United States led to a shift away from the study of Indian people to a search for universal generalizations. Such theory trivializes the study of prehistory for its own sake. It is often ardently antinationalistic. The heritage claims of less-powerful nation states hinder the ability of core state archaeologists to study the pasts of those states, and to remove and curate artifacts from those states (Gjessing, 1963; Ford, 1973; Fagan, 1985:12–13).

In a similar vein, Patterson (1988) has used Gramsci's (1971) ideas about the nature of intellectuals to study United States archaeology. He remarks that in the early years of the republic, people such as Thomas Jefferson were organic intellectuals whose thought embodied and helped to form the ideas and interests of their newly formed class. By the 1830s traditional intellectuals had arisen to defend the interests of an existing ruling class and the factions within that class. At the end of the nineteenth-century technicians arose, who mastered the specialized learning, techniques, and know-how that would become modern archaeology.

Patterson argues that a debate over the nature of wealth guided the growth of scholarly knowledge about Indian people. The debate between two factions of the ruling class was over the merit of property or trade as a source of wealth. Patterson relates this debate to the expansion of the United States and the rise of U.S. archaeology in both the United States and in Latin America. He argues that the ideas that came out of it justified the taking of Indian land or the domination of Latin American countries.

I accept these analyses as being essentially correct, but I would argue that they are not complete. From them we learn how archaeology has served the interests of the ruling class, but they do not convey the often ambiguous feelings that typify white views of Indian people. They fail to show us how whites could think their ideas about Indian people were just and fair. They do show us why all tribes were banished to the evolutionary level of barbarism and why until the 1960s archaeologists failed to study Indians in terms of cultural change. They do not, however, lead to an understanding of why Indian people were made part of the heritage of the United States. To understand this I also look at the second primary image, that of the vanishing American, and at the debates that white America had over the nature of the Indian.

The Image of the Indian in the New Republic

At the turn of the eighteenth and nineteenth centuries, the new nation of the United States was forged. It was consciously built around a new concept of nation grounded in Enlightenment thought. Such a nation would have four parts: it was a people united by a common culture, language, territory, and government (Commager, 1975). Many in Europe, such as the French philosopher de Buffon, did not think that the new nation could survive (Gerbi, 1973). Pragmatists argued that the United States was too big and too socially and environmentally diverse to create the cultural unity and economic integration needed for a nation state. The more philosophically inclined said that the environment of the New World was impoverished and that a new nation founded there could only wither and fall.

At the same time the nature of relations between Indian people and the Europeans on the East Coast changed.[9] For over 150 years most Europeans had lived in frequent, even day-to-day, contact with Indian people. During the same period, the military power of native confederacies such as the Iroquois and the Cherokee rivaled that of the colonies, and these confederacies could raise large armies to strike at the colonies. These confederacies had been key players in the conflicts between French and English, and English and colonist. During the Revolutionary War colonial armies burned the towns and fields of both the Iroquois and the Cherokee and pushed their remnants aside. In the War of 1812 Federal armies met and defeated the united tribes of the Midwest and the Southeast. By 1814 Indian groups posed no threat, either real or imagined, to the security of the nation and were only a "problem" on the frontiers. The United States had broken the tribes in the East. In the early nineteenth century, the frontier moved west of the Appalachians, and the government removed, destroyed, or concentrated all of East Coast tribes. For the first time in 150 years most White Americans would have little or no first-hand contact with Indians in their lifetime. The American Indian had faded from the actual experience of most whites, and their day-to-day lives confirmed the myth of the vanishing Indian (Dippie, 1982:12–18). Scholars reinforced the popular image with a litany of lost tribes and declining numbers (Heckewelder, 1876:93; Emerson and Forbes, 1914:23). It seemed that Indian people must be fading away.

Many of the founders of the new nation, among them Jefferson, Adams, Washington, and Franklin, were urbane gentlemen of the Enlightenment. They accepted the primacy of nature and the theory that scholars could arrive at a rational understanding of the world by uncovering the laws of nature (Leaf, 1979; Fowler and Fowler, 1991). Each person was born a *tabula rasa*, and it was the environment that made each what he or she would be. Primitives stood in a special relationship to nature; they were noble savages, unsullied by the corrupting might of civilization, but such pure souls were ill prepared and unable to adapt to civilization. The evils of civilization, which the learned man could endure, would sully the nobility of the savage. So, the noble savage could only exist in the untamed wild lands of the west, and as the advance of American civilization transformed the wilderness, the noble Indian had to surely perish (Berkhofer, 1978:89, Dippie, 1982:28). The Indians that survived the advance of civilization and lived in small concentrations in the east or on the fringe of the frontier were a fact that denied the noble image. The urbane gentlemen of the Enlightenment blamed the drunkenness, beggary, and savagery of these people on a social decay resulting from their contact with civilization. They were fallen noble savages, not worthy of their heritage (Dippie, 1982:25–28).

The eighteenth-century theory of environmentalism held that differences in the natural and social environment produced the diversity of the human species. This theory held that the primitive state of the Indian ensued from the environment of the New World, raising the chance that the new American republic might in the end sink to the same state (Gerbi, 1973; Berkhofer, 1978:42–43). The theory warned of a dim fate for the nation.

Thomas Jefferson (1964) accepted the environmental theory but tried to refute the idea that the North American environment begot a lesser flora, fauna, and people. He bid army officers to shoot and mount the biggest specimens of bears, beaver, moose, and elk so that he could ship proof of a superior fauna to Europe. He charged Lewis and Clark to look for mammoths in the west. Jefferson gathered ethnographic data and dug in an Indian burial mound, being the first to disturb Indian graves for the sake of scholarly inquiry. According to Jefferson (1964:91–92) the Indians were a noble and vibrant race that had faded from the East Coast owing to the vices of civilization, not defects in the environment. White Americans with the help of the virtues of civilization could build only a great nation in this land. Jefferson and many other Enlightenment nationalists of the early 1800s called the Indian the first American to try to give the new republic its own, distinct, national identity (Commager, 1975:187). As primitives, Indians were part of nature, an aspect of the superior environment that would give rise to a superior nation, but the rise of civilization would also destroy the nobility of the Indians and erase them from the land (Jefferson, 1964:92).

The scholarly and political polemic of the late 1700s and early 1800s linked Indian people with the environment of North America both as the basis for an American nation and as a domain of scholarly inquiry. In 1794 when Peale began the first museum of natural history in Philadelphia, he institutionalized the Indian as an object of natural history (Sellers, 1980; Goetzmann and Goetzmann, 1986:15; Fowler and Fowler, 1991). Five years later the American Philosophical Society issued an appeal for data on the archaeology, flora, and fauna of the new nation. In 1812 Isaiah Thomas founded the American Antiquarian Society in Massachusetts for the study of American antiquities as well as fine and rare products of art and nature (Willey and Sabloff, 1980:29).

These acts and institutions laid the groundwork for a liberal program of study to record the nation's Indian and natural heritage before they faded away (Mitchell, 1981). This agenda thrived in the 1800s. Schoolcraft (1857) and Heckewelder (1876) talked to elderly Indian people and read old documents to try to capture the dwindling memory culture of the eastern tribes. Adventurers like George Catlin (1841) and Prince Maximillian went west to try to save with pen and brush the primitive culture of the Plains Indian before it too disappeared (Dippie, 1982:25–29, Goetzmann and Goetzmann, 1986:15–35, 44–57).

The Mound-Builder Myth

Not all Americans approved of the liberal ideal of the noble savage, and many winced at the idea of an Indian first American. The noble savage was an urbane, East Coast ideal and not accepted either on the frontier or in rural areas where whites were, or had recently been, locked in struggle with real Indian people. Enlightenment ideals also faded in the third decade of the 1800s, displaced by a new, more xenophobic nationalism (Horsman, 1967). In the West the religious fever of the Second Great Awakening molded a new vision of the American people – a vision that denied that all people were born equal. Americans were God's chosen race, and Indian people, the savage savages, were not part of the image (McLoughlin, 1986:xvi). Indian people stood in the way of the United States' manifest destiny and they were best removed, by force if need be, to the West (McLoughlin, 1986; Every, 1966; Satz, 1975). Even as the United States army drove the people west, some whites tried to rout their ancestors from the history of the nation. Those who were troubled by a savage ancestry promulgated the *myth of the mound builders*. They argued that a civilized, often white, race had built the great earthen mounds of the midwest only to be overrun by red savages (Silverberg, 1968). The whites of the United States were the inheritors of this heritage, not the Indian.

These conservative thinkers tried to build a national heritage for the United States in much the same way that Europeans resurrected Celts, Goths, Magyars, and Anglo-Saxons to legitimate their nation states (Hobsbawm, 1983; Lowenthal, 1985:337–338). One unnamed contributor to the *Literary World* noted that: "We have, what no other nation on the known globe can claim: a perfect union of the past and present; the vigor of a nation just born walking over the hallowed ashes of a race whose history is too early for a record" (Anonymous, 1848). A number of writers tried to pen a New World Iliad or Aeneid. Cornelius Matthews (1839) wrote *Behemoth: A Legend of the Mound Builders*, and a decade later William Pidgeon (1858) authorized *Traditions of De-Coo-Dah*.

The people that promoted the myth of the mound builders were not like Jefferson and his East Coast ilk. They were by and large frontiersmen, who were active in the removal of Indian people and who stood to profit from the economic growth of the region. Among them were such men as presidents Andrew Jackson and William Henry Harrison; Secretary of War Lewis Cass; the postmaster of Circleville, Ohio, Caleb Atwater; Ohio doctor E. H. Davis; and Ohio newspaperman E. G. Squier (Silverberg, 1968).

During and after the Mexican-American War, United States army columns crisscrossed lands that would become the states of Arizona and New Mexico. Here they found huge stone ruins. The officers of these units described these great stone piles, and in the pages of their journals, they composed a Southwestern version of the myth of the mound builders. They argued that the ruins were the abodes of a lost race. Some later speculations in the popular press attributed the ruins to Europeans, but most of the early observers were inspired by Prescott's (1843) *The Conquest of Mexico* and the legend of a Aztec origin in the north. They gave the ruins names like Aztec and Montezuma's Castle, because they believed they had found the ancestral home of the Aztec (Brandes 1960).

This tale rent the Pueblo people from their past. The Pueblos were an anomaly for United States Indian policy. They looked civilized, with solid stone homes, fields, and livestock, and the treaty in which Mexico ceded the Southwest to the United States required that the United States respect their rights and extend them citizenship. The Anglos who flocked to New Mexico coveted Pueblo fields, range lands, and water. They used the myth to argue that the things that gave the Pueblo people the guise of civilization were nothing more than a thin veneer taken from the Spanish (G. E. Hall, 1984:118). The Pueblo people were only latter-day imitators of the lost race that had left the great ruins. This idea legitimated the taking of Pueblo assets and the denial of their civil rights (Lekson, 1988).

In the face of these attacks on the Indian past, the dual image of the Indian both as the noble savage and as the first American survived and grew among East Coast artists, scholars, and intellectuals. Noble savages thrived in paintings, poems, and novels from 1830 to 1860. They showed up on the canvases of Bodmer, Kane, and Bierstadt (Goetzmann and Goetzmann, 1986:36–57, 145), in Henry Wadsworth Longfellow's poem "Hiawatha" and in the "leatherstocking" tales by James Fenimore Cooper (Mitchell, 1981). Liberal scholars contested the theory of a lost mound-builder race; among them were Jefferson's Secretary of the Treasury Albert Gallatin, Samuel F. Haven (1856), and Henry Roe Schoolcraft (1857:135–136). Schoolcraft dug at the Grave Creek Mound in Ohio to try to prove that Indian people had built the mounds (Silverberg, 1968:107–108).

Both the notion of the Indian as a fallen noble savage and the mound-builder myth used the Indian past to legitimate the white nation. All during the nineteenth century, the clash of these two positions was the major focus for anthropological and archaeological debate. The conservative position denied the humanity of Indian people and gave them no place in the nation. The liberal position upheld the humanity of Indian people but allowed them a place in the nation only if they gave up their Indianness. Few people saw the need to ask Indian people how they felt about their past or the whites' uses of it.

The Indian in Victorian America

By the late 1870s the United States army had herded all the tribes into small, isolated areas or forced them into the less desirable corners of the West (Hagan, 1979:112–119). Indian people had been driven from the land. This reduction of the tribes to reservations opened up the West for white settlement, and it also eliminated Indians from the day-to-day experience of most whites in the West, as well as the East (Dippie, 1982:162). The Indian people on the reservations, contrary to earlier predictions, did not vanish as a race but lived on as *fallen noble savages;* the notion of the vanishing Indian endured because Indian people could survive as human beings only if they were lifted from their debased condition. They could not return to nature, so they had to assimilate and put aside their Indianness to escape a debased life (Dippie, 1982:162–164). Policymakers did not envision a romantic death for the Indian, but rather a less dramatic cultural extinction as Indians cast off their primitiveness to join the melting pot of U.S. society.

The scientific world met the movement of Indian policy to assimilation with a theory of cultural evolution. Some used the theory to argue that Indian people could not be raised from their savagery because such progress took thousands of years and could not be hastened or guided. Others used it to hold out the hope that whites could teach Indian people to be like them (Dippie, 1982:106). In 1879 John Wesley Powell founded the Bureau of American Ethnology (BAE) and began social research based on evolutionary ideas. His goals were much like those of Indian scholars of a generation before: to record the vanishing culture of the American Indian and to advise the government on Indian policy (Dippie, 1982:167–169, Berkhofer, 1978:54).

The Indian was still a part of nature. Powell, along with many of the other late nineteenth-century ethnologists, among them McGee, Morgan, and Mc-Clintock, made their study of the Indian part of a larger study of natural history (Dippie, 1982:223–228; Fowler and Fowler, 1991). These scholars dealt with Indians as objects of nature, their remains to be collected the same as those of fossils, plants, and animals. By 1870 this view was firmly institutionalized and taken for granted. This was true in the BAE, and in the major natural history museums, the National Museum, the Peabody, the Field Museum, and the American Museum of Natural History, all begun in the mid-to-late 1800s (Willey and Sabloff, 1980:41–45). In the great expositions and world fairs of the late nineteenth century and early twentieth century, Indian people were displayed as objects of curiosity along with the flora and fauna of the nation (Fowler and Fowler, 1991).

In the later half of the 1800s archaeology became a professional career, and bit by bit, people with special technical training and academic credentials took over the practice of archaeology (Willey and Sabloff, 1980:34). Archaeologists started to argue that they should control Indian sites because only they had the special skills and know-how to study them.

Archaeology in the United States began as a subfield of anthropology, a part of a holistic study of the disappearing American Indian, and was housed in the museums of natural history. The new professionals did more than dig sites; they also studied language, myth, custom, and crafts. They were, by and large, from the East Coast, and an East Coast establishment paid for their work (Patterson, 1986). They tended to take the liberal view of the Indian past, and to reject the lost-race theory (Silverberg, 1968:174–221).

A former entomologist, Cyrus Thomas, was hired by the BAE to establish a Division of Mound Excavations and investigate the origins of the mounds and the people that built them. He finally put the mound-builder controversy to rest in 1894 (Thomas, 1894). Indian people had built the mounds. Just 4 years before, on December 29, 1890, the seventh calvary slaughtered over 250 men, women, and children at Wounded Knee, South Dakota, bringing the Indian Wars in the West to a bloody conclusion (Hagan, 1979:133). The Dawes Act of 1886 sought to break the reservations up into small parcels for individuals to farm and own. Whites rushed in to take what was left over. This last great land-grab cost Indian people two thirds of their remaining land by 1934 (Hagan, 1979:147). Thomas was not the first to say that Indians built the mounds, and most of the data he used in his proof had been available many years before. In 1894 few people felt the need to justify the taking of Indian land and the breaking of tribal military power. The deed was done. The data could now carry the field in the debate over the past.

At about the same time, the Aztec theory was set aside in the Southwest. An 1876 Supreme Court decision, U.S. vs Joseph, had ruled that Pueblo lands were not reservation lands and so, they could be bought and sold. This ruling sanctioned a rush for Pueblo lands. Anglos used the Aztec theory to argue that the

Pueblo's claim to their lands lacked time depth. The first archaeological technicians to work in the region, Adolph Bandelier (1884), Frank Cushing (1886),
Jessie Fewkes (1896), and Cosmo Mindeleff (1891) rebuffed the Aztec theory for
the Indian past, and argued that the Pueblo people had built the great stone
ruins. They dug in the ruins to verify Pueblo origin tales. By the late 1890s they
had proven that Pueblo people built the ruins.

These and other analyses that asserted the humanity of Indian people and
their place in an American heritage were an antidote to ideas and policies that
would have been genocidal for Indian people. They did not, however, allow
Indian people self-determination in their lives and cultures; they framed the
pasts of Native Americans in terms of white interests, debates, and agendas.
Even among liberal scholars, the potential of Indian people continued to be
denied. In the 1800s the theory of cultural evolution guided both archaeology
and cultural anthropology. As Trigger (1980a) points out, these early archaeologists consistently would not admit Indian progress along the unilineal evolutionary ladder. They saw the Indian as the prime models of only two stages of
evolution, savagery and barbarism (Patterson, 1988). They gave little time depth
to the most elaborate archaeological sites. They dated the construction of both
the mounds in the East and the stone walled ruins in the Southwest to, at most, a
few hundred years before European contact and conquest.

The Early Twentieth Century

All during the first third of the twentieth century, both the public and the
scholarly communities accepted the idea that the demise of the first American
was both inevitable and imminent (Dippie, 1982:273). Franz Boas wrenched
United States anthropology away from an evolutionary theory but, like several
generations of researchers before him, he and his students took to the field to
record what they could of fading Indian cultures (Berkhofer, 1978:61–69). In
archaeology, Boasians such as A. V. Kidder, Nels Nelson, and Manuel Gamio
shifted the aims of archaeology away from the study of myth and evolution to
the building of chronologies and the tracing of cultural boundaries (Willey and
Sabloff, 1980:83). Archaeology became more specialized, and more limited to
the study of the past. Interest in Indian ethnology on the part of most archaeologists declined, so that only a few gained any appreciation for the views of
Indian people about the past (Trigger, 1980a:667). In the West, mainly in California and in the Southwest, the holistic study of Indian people went on, but
more and more people only did archaeology. In the East most archaeologists
had little or no contact with Indian people at all. The model of diffusion and
migration, which ruled in archaeology until the 1960s, allowed for little innovation in the Indian past and reinforced popular ideas that the tribes had never
been stable and were always moving.

With the turn of the century came a widespread fear that the natural wonders of the United States were in danger, and a nation-wide conservationist movement developed to save them (Mitchell, 1981). This movement linked the protection of Indian sites with the defense of nature (Dippie, 1982:222–236). The U.S. Congress passed the Antiquities Act of 1906 to protect Indian sites on federal land and to allow for the establishment of national monuments to save both the sites and the wonders of nature. Laws passed in the 1930s, 1960s, and 1970s carried on this precedent of defining Indian sites as archaeological resources and reserving the study of them for archaeologists (King *et al.*, 1977). The kingpin of modern United States environmental law, the National Environmental Policy Act of 1969, listed Indian sites as environmental resources.

The first serious and widely accepted challenge to the notion that the Indian was the vanishing American came out of New Mexico in the 1920s (Dippie, 1982:274–279). In 1922 H. O. Bursum introduced a bill in the United States Congress that would settle the land claims of whites on Pueblo lands. The bill would have ransacked the Pueblo land base. White groups, led by the artists' colony in Santa Fe, fought the bill. Edgar L. Hewitt and Charles F. Lummis used archaeology to portray the Pueblos as an ancient people, as peaceful farmers, one with the land, and as an enduring race that would not fade away (Lekson, 1988). In 1923 the bill went down in defeat.

By the 1920s the Indian people of the Southwest had taken on a new role in white society – they had become a tourist attraction (McLuhan, 1985). In the late 1800s Wild West shows had taken the now exotic redman to the East and to Europe. The Santa Fe railroad did one better; it brought tourists to see live Indian people in the exotic locale of the Southwest (McLuhan, 1985). Tourism made the primitive otherness of Indian people into a commodity that whites could sell in tours, shops, and hotels.

The tourists wanted mementos of their trips so they bought the pottery made by Pueblo women. As tastes changed with the new century, the Spanish-influenced baroque styles of the late nineteenth-century Pueblo design fell into disfavor, and the demand for such pottery ebbed (Tanner, 1968). In 1890 Jessie Fewkes dug at the site of Sikyatki, and the Hopi potter Nampayo copied designs from the sherds he found to revive the ancient, purely Indian, style of that site on her pots (Brew, 1979:517). In 1911 Edgar L. Hewitt and Kenneth Chapman encouraged Maria Martinez at San Ildefonso to revive the black-on-white style they found in sites of the area. Maria experimented with ceramic production and painting to invent the black-on-black style of modern San Ildefonso pottery (Simmons, 1979:219). These changes breathed new life into the pueblo pottery market and into the selling of Indianness.

The idea that the Indian people of the Southwest would endure was not accepted by all archaeologists. Many voiced honest concern for Indian people, but in their popular presentations, they still spoke of a race that would soon fade away, a race that had left its past for their study.

Twelve-year-old Deric Nusbaum (1926), the stepson of Jessie Nusbaum, then superior of Mesa Verde National Park, wrote a book for boys called *Deric in Mesa Verde*. The book presumes that Indian people had given up the cliff ruins and that these ruins now were the heritage of the whites. Deric makes a comic figure of an old Hopi man who comes to lay claim to his past. The story the old man tells is treated as a myth, in contrast to the true story told by the science of the archaeologist. In two dream sequences Deric goes back in time, and the ancient people of the cliffs take him in as one of their own.

Ann Axtell Morris (1933), the wife of archaeologist Earl Morris, wrote one of the most popular books about Southwestern archaeology for the period, *Digging in the Southwest*. In it she soundly rejects the Aztec theory and links the Anasazi and the Pueblo. She, however, speaks of the modern Pueblo people as if they were an anachronism. She says "they are archaeology still alive" and that their time is almost done (Morris, 1933:74).

> *Their course is about run. They are swamped on all sides, and although some friends at court are laboring to procure them freedom from molestation, the deadly absorptive White American culture is creeping into their lives, with its inevitable tendency to level and destroy whatever of the primitive it touches.*

Like Jefferson over 100 years before, she valued the noble savage but lamented that he must perish with the onrush of white civilization.

For 5 consecutive years from 1926 to 1930, local Anglos used mound B at Casa Grande National Monument as a stage for a public pageant about the ruins. Byron Cummings (1930a,b), the founder of both the Arizona State Museum and the Department of Anthropology at the University of Arizona wrote the script and helped direct the 1930 pageant. His goals were admirable:

> *In this series of pictures that we shall try to present to you in this pageant we want you to appreciate better the struggles of the early inhabitants of Arizona, live again their terrors and their joys, and learn that their descendants, the native tribes of our state, are human, that they know injustice and appreciate our honorable sympathetic interest in their welfare. They do not ask us to patronize them; they ask us to treat them as men and women. (Cummings, 1930a:16)*

The pageant told of the demise of the people of Casa Grande and of the Pima who came after them. In the first part the people are weakened by gambling, internal strife, and a wily stranger that steals their princess "the bride of the sun." Then the Pima descend on them and raze their town. In the second part the Apache steal a Pima woman. The Pima pursue the raiders and recover the woman. The pageant uses stock stereotypical images of the Indian princess, the abduction of women, war, and gambling to show Indian culture as unstable (Stedman, 1982), and it denies a link between the ruin and the local Pima.

In 1938 John Collier, then director of the Bureau of Indian Affairs, announced that the Indian was no longer vanishing. In a major policy reversal, the federal government moved to save the tribes with the Indian Reorganization Act of 1934, an Indian New Deal (Taylor, 1980; Deloria and Lytle, 1984). The tribes that reorganized along the lines set out by the act got federal aid, but traditionalists on the reservations fiercely opposed the new European governmental forms imposed by the act.

From Termination to Self-Determination

In the mid- to late 1940s United States Indian policy reverted to its old course. If Indian people would not vanish, then the Congress would terminate them. Two programs strove toward this goal. Relocation moved thousands of Indian people to the cities, while at the same time, termination dissolved tribal governments and passed out tribal land and assets to tribal members (Deloria and Lytle, 1984; Fixico, 1986). The tribes fought the new policy, but the specter of termination would haunt them until the late 1960s.

In 1946 Congress set up the Indian Claims Commission to settle all treaty-based land claims with Indian tribes, and the commission met until 1978 (U.S. Indian Claims Commission, 1978). The commission was to aid the policy of termination by cleaning the slate of all governmental obligations to the Indian tribes (Fixico, 1986:28; Deloria and Lytle, 1984:191). Many archaeologists and anthropologists helped the tribes by doing both research and testifying before the commission. It soon became clear to Indian people that the commission gave little weight to the traditional knowledge of their culture or of their past and that it favored the testimony of white experts. Many archaeologists point with pride to the discipline's involvement in these cases as evidence of how archaeology has helped Indian people (Ford, 1973). There is cause for this pride, but most archaeologists are seemingly unaware that many Indian people hold much more ambiguous feelings about this testimony. They appreciate the monetary returns that resulted from settlements but, as Deloria and Lytle (1984:191) discuss, fear that far more was lost than gained in the process. The commission existed as part of a general strategy to destroy their existence as a people. In the minds of many Indian people, the white experts that testified were tainted by their association with the process. The commission followed a white agenda, used white rules of evidence, and discredited traditional knowledge, giving power to the white expert instead of traditional Native American leaders.

The thrust of anthropological research on Indians shifted in the 1930s to study cultural change, and then in the late 1960s, to a glorification of the survival of Indian tribes and groups. These shifts had only a small impact on archaeology. The emphasis on scientific method and the discovery of universal laws of cultural change that began in the early 1960s only increased the alienation of archaeologists from Indian peoples' interests in their own past (Trigger 1980a:672).

Indian people won their battle against termination in the late 1960s. Since the early 1970s the official Indian policy of the United States has been self-determination, that Indian people should decide their own fate and control their own reservations. At least that is the theory. Three laws, the Indian Self-Determination Act of 1973, the Indian Education Act of 1973, and the Indian Religious Freedom Act of 1978, codify this policy, and it is also embodied in the recent reburial and repatriation legislation. In the Reagan years, self-determination was often used as an excuse to cut off government aid to Indian people (Deloria and Lytle, 1984).

Archaeologists have viewed the trends of the last 20 years, the growing expression of Indian self-awareness and the increased control of tribal lands by Indian people, with some alarm. Most U.S. archaeologists were genuinely shocked and confused in the early 1970s when Indian activists obstructed digs and seized collections. On most reservations the tribe has taken over the permitting of archaeological excavations from the Bureau of Indian Affairs (BIA), and many tribes do not allow excavation except when historic or environmental protection law requires it (for example, see Gila River Indian Community, 1982; Salt River Indian Community, 1986). Some tribes have also taken over the contract archaeology on their reservations and started their own tribal museums. The Zuni, Hopi, and Navajo nations now have their own archaeology programs. The provisions of the Indian Religious Freedom Act of 1978 for the first time gave Indian people a legal right to burials and sacred sites. They seem to be at odds with the provisions of historic preservation laws that treat these things only as objects of scientific inquiry (Echo-Hawk, 1986; Moore, 1989). Many Indian people are today openly challenging the privilege of archaeology that has been built up over the last 200 years (Hill, 1977; Hammil and Zimmerman, 1983; Talbot, 1984; Quick, 1985; NCAI, 1986; Antone, 1986; Hammil and Cruz, 1989).

The Vanishing American in the Southwest

The general public has been slow to discard the notion of the vanishing Indian. Very few Americans have regular contact with Indian people, and the vast majority derive what they do know about Indians from the media and their public school educations. During the early 1970s Indians became something of a cause célèbre in the media, and several major magazines proclaimed that the Indian was no longer vanishing (Dippie, 1982:xi). Despite this flash of attention, the popular media and many public school texts still tend to stereotype Indians as a foreign and vanishing race different and removed from the rest of us (Hirschfelder, 1982; Stedman, 1982; Hoxie, 1985; Wilson, 1986).

Archaeologists still reinforce this popular image of a vanished Indian race in their public programs and statements, even when such a view is directly contrary to what archaeologists know about prehistory. Often the myth is an unintended consequence of some other explicit moral about ecology or pot-hunting. Other times the archaeologist is made the hero of the story for solving the riddle created by the disappearance of the people in the past. They speak as if the sites were abandoned only to await white discovery. The Southwest is the region of the country where Indian people have most plainly not faded away, so it is somewhat surprising that the myth of the vanishing American shows up regularly in popular books, films, and articles about the archaeology of the region. All such accounts do not succumb to the myth, but it is amazing how many do. Archaeologists have not challenged strongly enough the use of vanishing imagery in these works,[10] and they have encouraged the homage paid to themselves as the heroes of these stories.

A few examples that talk about Anasazi archaeology make the point. Let me note that the Anasazi are known to be the ancestors of the modern pueblo peoples of New Mexico and Arizona (Woodbury, 1979:27). There is debate about the exact link between prehistoric sites and specific modern pueblos or language groups, but no serious archaeologist would debate the broad ancestral connection. Many of the works contradict themselves saying early on that the Anasazi people had vanished and then later noting that their descendants live in the modern pueblos. A Bureau of Land Management anti-pot hunting film called "Antiquities" uses film of cliff dwellings in southeast Utah. It ends with the assertion that the Anasazi simply vanished. An article on Chaco Canyon in the February 9, 1987 *U.S. News and World Report* notes that the Anasazi mysteriously disappeared. It quotes paleoecologist Julio Betancourt as saying "The needles and twigs disappeared from the pack-rat heaps almost exactly when the Anasazi vanished — AD 1200." The overt point of the article was a warning about mismanaging the environment. A travel article on the Southwest is titled "The Mystery of the Ancient Ones" (Keith, 1987). The author writes that the Anasazi left "few clues as to why, they gradually disappeared." A coffee-table book, *Anasazi, Ancient People of the Rock* overtly uses all of the stock images (Pike, 1974). The lead chapter to the book is "The People Who Have Vanished." The dust jacket states:

> *The cities they [the Anasazi] built have loomed like giant questions marks, beckoning scientists and intriguing travelers ever since white men discovered the first site.*

The book begins with a device that is standard in popular works and common even in scholarly ones, a device I have used myself (McGuire and Schiffer, 1982). It starts by describing the finding of the ruin by a European.

Two articles on Anasazi ruins in the 1982 *National Geographic* follow part of the pattern but also break from it in a useful way. The lead article "Riddles in the Ruins" begins with William Henry Jackson's 1877 visit to Chago Canyon and glorifies the archaeologist as the solver if the riddle (Canby, 1982). It does, however, draw a very strong link between the ruins and modern Pueblo people, and it leads into an article by Jake Page (1982), which talks about the meaning of these ruins and the past to the Hopi. These two articles strike some balance between the views of archaeologists and Indian people.

The notion of the vanishing American affects the way we do archaeology today. The image allows archaeologists to glorify their object, the Indian past, and yet detach it from the descendants of this past, living Indian people. The heros of the prehistoric tale become the archaeologists that have been able to interpret this past and not the Indian people whose lives flow from it.

Indian Pasts and Indian Activism

Many archaeologists have rightly wondered why reburial, repatriation, and control of Indian pasts became such a key issue in the 1980s. It is not a coincidence, and it relates to how Indian activists have harnessed the politics of nationalism to assert the right of Indian peoples to exist as nations within the United States. Archaeologists would, however, be making a fundamental mistake to assume that reburial, repatriation, and control of Indian pasts are simply political issues of the moment. They reflect long and deeply held concerns of many, if not most, Indian people, that became important in the political arena of the 1980s because they legitimated Indian peoples as nations entitled to govern their own destiny.

Indian people have long objected to the disturbance of their graves and to what we archaeologists do. In 1655 a delegation of Narragansett sachems confronted Roger Williams at Warwick Rhode Island, to demand satisfaction for the robbing of a Narragansett grave by a Dutchman. Williams described the act as a "gastly and stincking vilanie agst them" (LaFantasie, 1988:425). In the 1840s Indians in Minnesota asked William Pidgeon to stop digging in the burial mounds of their ancestors (Silverberg, 1968:139). In the late 1960s and early 1970s American Indian Movement activists confronted archaeologists and museums over burials and excavations (Deloria, 1973; Sprague, 1974).

Traditionalists within Indian groups have always put heritage and culture at the core of the confrontation with white society (Deloria and Lytle, 1984:233–234). Their orientation has been to their own tribe and family, and they are the ones who most tenaciously maintained the tribal culture, religion, customs, and past. They did not hold a linear view of past leading to present. Their past is manifest in the present and is known through spiritual sources, ritual, and oral tradition. It does not need to be discovered (Zimmerman, 1989). These traditionalists were by and large bypassed when tribal governments were formed under the Indian New Deal in the 1930s, and their voices were rarely heard outside the reservations (Taylor, 1980:39–62; Haudenosaunee, 1986).

Indian activism began in the 1960s among children of the families relocated to the cities in the 1950s (Deloria and Lytle, 1984:198–200). In the urban Indian ghettos, a pan-Indianism grew, and in 1968 the American Indian Movement was organized along lines that paralleled other minority action groups. Indians in the cities and on the reservations gained access to antipoverty programs equating them to other minority groups, part of a multicultural American heritage. The traditionalists reacted negatively to all this (Deloria and Lytle,

1984:263). They were Dine, O'odham, or Lakota, and pan-Indianism was yet another attack on their culture. They were not the same as other minority groups; they were members of separate nations that the United States was bound by treaty to recognize and deal with accordingly. Finally, they did not agree with the confrontational tactics of the radicals.

Starting in the 1970s with the 1972 Indian march on Washington, an alliance grew between the traditionalists and the activists. In 1974 this alliance led to the formation of the International Treaty Council and greater recognition of the traditionalists concerns by the National Congress of American Indians. The emphasis of the Indians' struggle shifted from a pan-Indianism to an effort to assert the sovereignty of Indian tribes as internal dependent nations. This shift has made issues of identity, heritage, and culture the keys to the current, ongoing struggle for Indian rights (Deloria and Lytle, 1984:245; Talbot, 1984; NARF, 1985; Wilson, 1986:22; Haudenosaunee, 1986). Indian peoples are not vanishing from the face of the earth nor are they slipping into a hyphenated pan-Indian Americanism.

CONCLUSION

The time has came for archaeologists to reunite their object of study, the Indian past, with its descendants and to ask about the needs of Indian people and address those needs (Trigger, 1980a; Sprague, 1974; Anyon, 1991a). This is not just a problem of public relations or education. It requires more than just a compromise or an accommodation between disciplinary interests and the interests of Indian people. It requires that archaeologists initiate a process of dialogue with Indian peoples that will fundamentally alter the practice of archaeology in the United States. This dialogue will alter our perceptions of the past, how we deal with living Native Americans, how we train students, and how we present our results to each other and the general public.

We do have some cases and examples to build on. Florence Hawley Ellis has devoted her life to the study of the Rio Grande Pueblos as a people with a past and a present, and she insisted that her archaeology students had to know the Pueblos as people, not just potsherds (Cordell, 1986:26). Larry Zimmerman has worked with the Cheyenne and Sioux on the northern plains to use archaeology to resist the white view of western history (McDonald *et al.*, 1991). Richard Effland has built a successful private contract business and involved O'odham and Maricopa people from southern Arizona in his research (Effland, 1987). In the northeast William Robinson and Patricia Rubertone have worked with the Narragansett of Rhode Island (Rubertone, 1989; Robinson, 1990). In the northwest Roderick Sprague and Richard Holmer have collaborated with the Nez Perce and the Shoshone-Bannock of Idaho since 1967 (Sprague, 1974). Tribal archaeology programs at Zuni and the Navajo Nation have been very successful in unifying the interests of archaeologists and Indian people. Archaeologists associated with those programs including T. J. Ferguson (1984, 1991), Roger Anyon (1991b), Joe Zuni, Kieth Kintigh (1991), Barbara Mills (1991), Robert Leonard (1991), Allen Downer, and Anthony L. Klesert have done impressive research and still addressed Native American interests and concerns. A similar case can be made for Charles Adams' decade-long association with the Hopi and their past (Adams, 1984). None of these archaeologists has given up scholarly goals, and all would argue that cooperation with Indian people has enriched their research.[11] These examples clearly show that addressing the concerns of Indian people does not automatically, or necessarily, destroy research or scholarship. It does, however, require that archaeologists integrate that scholarship into a diversity of interests.

Archaeologists should first ask what is it that their enterprise has to offer a diversity of interests. I would answer that it is archaeology's craft – the skill of using material remains to interpret past experiences and situations. This skill is the basis of the archaeologists' authority, for not everyone has mastered the craft of dealing with the past archaeologically. This is scholarship. The problem is that many Indian people do not recognize the value of archaeological knowledge or even share the scholarly notion of what the past is (Hammil and Zimmerman, 1983; Talbot, 1984; Quick, 1985; Antone, 1986; Hammil and Cruz, 1989; Turner, 1989; Haudenosaunee, 1986; Zimmerman, 1989; Anyon, 1991a). Public relations or education programs, in which archaeologists attempt to instruct others without submitting their own practice to scrutiny and change, will inevitably fail (Zimmerman, 1989; Goldstein and Kintigh, 1990).

The cases of successful collaboration suggest that it would be well to look to the practical applications of archaeology's craft and to build trust and dialogue from these applications. Such practical applications as building testimony in a lands claims case or providing compliance with historic preservation laws for a construction project may be useful in this regard. Indian people call on archaeologists for these reasons. Most of the long-term collaborations that exist between archaeologists and Indian peoples had their beginnings in such practical applications. They, however, went beyond the outcomes of these applications to build trust. Often this trust started with a common interest in preserving archaeological sites. This process entailed a long-term commitment by the archaeologist to the Indian people involved. It required lots of time and a respect by the archaeologist for the concerns and interests of those people. With this trust came dialogue, and in each of the cases I have cited above, this dialogue altered the practice and research of the archaeologist involved even as it raised the Indian communities' interest in, and valuation of, archaeological knowledge. Such a practice can only be worked out in specific cases, addressing specific interests and needs, and involving specific personalities and politics. It, however, implies a global change in how archaeologists do business.

This change can occur only if we see our discipline as a study of people, not just as things, as a study of a people with a present and a future as well as a past. It challenges many of the taken-for-granted practices of our discipline. Most simply, we can no longer practice archaeology without consulting and involving Indian people, even if the descendants of the people we study now live on the other side of the country. Long-term relations and trust cannot be established in hit-and-run contract archaeology where firms move where the money is instead of establishing long-term relations with specific groups of Indian people. We need to rethink how archaeology students are trained, and train them more as anthropologists who can engage in archaeology as a human endeavor and not simply the study of material culture. Our publication and dissemination of results needs to consider the sensitivities and concerns of Indian people. Finally, it challenges the notion that archaeology should have a sole or primary goal and suggests instead that a diversity of archaeologies should arise from our relationships with different communities, both Native American and scholarly.

The change that I am suggesting will not be easy. It raises a host of problems archaeologists are poorly prepared to handle. Substantial mistrust exists between many Indian communities and archaeology; it will be hard to overcome. Indeed, archaeologists may never overcome it as a group, only as individual researchers working with specific communities.[12] Archaeologists will find themselves involved in the politics of these communities, politics that can be a morass for any outsider. Such outside scholars will have to make long-term research commitments to Indian peoples, part of long-term commitments to archaeology in a region. It does not require that archaeology give up its scientific and scholarly interests, but that archaeologists recognize that those interests are not the only legitimate ones at stake, and that a process of dialogue should be initiated that will modify our scholarship within a diversity of interests.

The United States should protect the heritages of all of the people that live within it. Archaeology as part of building national heritage needs to be transformed into the writing of specific peoples' histories as a validation of their heritage, an activity that requires an active collaboration between us and the people that we study.[13] This "righting" of history is part of a global process in which cultural heritage is being reasserted and is replacing the Enlightenment view of human nature as progressively rational.

ENDNOTES

1. Patterson (1986, 1988) identifies these two factions of the U.S. ruling class as the East Coast and Midwestern establishments. He provides a fascinating discussion of how the development of U.S. archaeology was shaped by conflicts between these two class factions.

2. I have developed the substantive ideas presented in this chapter in two

earlier papers (McGuire, 1989b, n.d.b). At the same time as I was completing this chapter, I was also finishing an article using some of this same material for *American Anthropologist* (McGuire, 1992). Each of these represents a different stage or moment in the development of my ideas about the nature of relations between Native Americans and archaeologists. They both substantially overlap in content and differ in sophistication and eloquence.

3. My personal commitment to archaeology springs from a profound fascination with Indian cultures. Parts of my childhood were spent in Oklahoma and Montana where I had first-hand contact with Indian people. I did not see the noble savage. I saw clusters of white crosses on the road to Browning, Montana, each marking where a Blackfoot person, usually drunk, died on the highway. A few days before Thanksgiving one year in elementary school, my father and I drove up to an Indian community on hill 47 near the edge of Great Falls, Montana, to deliver food baskets. I had never before seen people living in tarpaper shacks; it was cold, even in the big warm car. There was a sign in a shop window on the main street, "No dogs or Indians allowed." As a teenager and college student in Austin, Texas, I slipped away to Fort Worth and to Oklahoma to attend powwows and visit Indian friends. My friends taught me many things, but always they admonished that the knowledge was for me, and I was not to write it down or gossip about it like a cultural anthropologist. So I did not become a cultural anthropologist, but I did become an archaeologist. I never told my friends; I knew they would not approve. The more time I spent on archaeology, the less time I had for them; we drifted apart. In the spring of 1972 AIM activists walked into the physical anthropology lab at Colorado State University and demanded the return of a burial I had excavated in a field school the summer before. For a decade I ignored what I knew to be true: that what we did as archaeologists caused many Indian people great emotional distress. In the 1980s Indian people once again made the past a site of struggle (Hill, 1977; Hammil and Zimmerman, 1983; Talbot, 1984; Quick, 1985; NCAI, 1986; Antone, 1986; Hammil and Cruz, 1989), and I knew I had to examine my place in that struggle.

4. Archaeologists, anthropologists, and historians often testify before federal and state courts and commissions considering claims by Native American nations, groups, and individuals for land, water, and restitutions. The largest series of such claims as considered by the United States Indian Claims Commission between 1946 and 1978. The organization, rules of evidence, and precedents established by this commission are the primary models for such cases in the United States today (U.S. Indian Claims Commission, 1978). The commission based the substance of its decisions primarily on the testimony of expert witnesses, archaeologists, anthropologists, and historians, and the final report of the commission makes no mention of testimony by Native American elders (U.S. Indian Claims Commission, 1978). The "experts" had access to documentary evidence, whereas the pasts of the Native Americans was an oral past.

White society holds a written past to be more legitimate than an oral one. The commission clearly placed a higher value on white understandings and perspectives on Native American pasts than the understandings and perspectives of Indian people.

5. I should note that in a recent editorial in *Antiquity* magazine Brian Fagan (1991) called for a dialogue with Native Americans. His proposal is in the spirit of and compatible with the suggestions made in this chapter.

6. I must thank Jonathan Hill for his earlier comments on a draft of this article. I have liberally borrowed from these comments to write this paragraph.

7. For a discussion of these views in terms of Native American — white relations in the United States, see Every (1966), Horsman (1967), Berkhofer (1978), Dippie (1982), Fixico (1986), and McLoughlin (1986).

8. It would, perhaps, be more accurate to ask why we were the stewards of Indian pasts, since federal legislation of the last 2 years forces us to share that stewardship.

9. This historical summary is taken from Dippie (1982) and Hagan (1979).

10. The failure of archaeologists to challenge this vanishing imagery reflects a broader failure of anthropologists to effectively articulate with the mass media. Many times archaeologists have allowed or tolerated such imagery simply because they were unaware of the damaging role of this image in the history of white–Native American relations.

11. This list does not cover every example of cooperative programs with archaeologists and Indians, but such efforts remain the exception and not the rule.

12. I have, on numerous occasions, been present when Indian people have derided archaeology and archaeologists, only to qualify their remarks by stating that so-and-so is an exception and an OK person.

13. This chapter has focused on relations between archaeologists and Native Americans. The general point of a need for cooperation between archaeologists and the descendents of the people we study, however, applies equally well to the Afro-American, Chinese, and Hispanic peoples that are so often the objects of historical archaeology.

CHAPTER 9

The Praxis of Archaeology

Almost every statement in prehistory should be qualified by the phrase: "On the evidence available today the balance of probability favors the view that." The reader is hereby requested to insert this or some similar reservation in most of my statements.

(*Childe, 1951a:xxii*)

For nearly three decades the leading theorists of our discipline have repeatedly told us that if archaeologists could just develop the right theory, philosophy, methodology, or technique, we would then be able to know what happened in the past and answer the questions that vex us. More recently, archaeologists have been warned that they can never truly know the past, and that our interpretations of the past can never be more than distorted visions from our present. The first of these positions sees our endeavor as a journey toward a destination that we can reach if only we wear the right shoes, carry the right gear, and follow the right bearing. The second argues that archaeologists do not travel down a path but rather only look back down the road through a kaleidoscope that is constantly turning. This volume has taken neither of these positions. Knowledge of the past does not lie at the end of the road nor do the lenses through which we see the world make such knowledge simply unattainable. Our knowledge of the past will always be tentative and shifting; we gain it in the journey and not at a destination that we can never reach. As we travel our point of view changes, and as our line of sight shifts, so too does our vision of the world. It is a vision complexly created by where we stand on the journey, the lenses through which we gaze, and the reality that is out there to see.

Archaeologists need not await new developments in theory or the latest pronouncement of the philosophers in order to do good archaeology. We can do it now and have been doing it for many years. Archaeologists have built up a credible knowledge of the past through an active engagement in a dialogue between ourselves and the material culture we study (Kohl, 1985; Trigger, 1989a). We will never obtain perfect knowledge, but we have developed sound understandings of the past through a never-ending series of successive, tentative approximations. My most fundamental point in this book is not that archae-ology *should* be dialectical but that we have *always been engaged* in a dialectic between past and present, consciousness and reality, and theory and practice. This book is a moment in that dialectic, and as such, is neither an end nor a beginning in our journey.

Good archaeology is not, however, done by standing still. After a time there is nothing new to see from one viewpoint, and increasingly what is seen challenges the theory that led to that point. Good archaeology requires a constant dynamic of theoretical debate that identifies multiple directions to move and rigorous observation of the world that constrains our choice of directions. The marxist perspective taken here challenges the dominant scientific model of Anglo-American archaeology and suggests changes in the practice of archaeology that will move us on our journey. At least three major aspects of the perspective have important implications for the practice of archaeology: (1) the substitution of a dialectical view of the human condition for a systemic view; (2) an emphasis on understanding the lived experience of people (everyday life) as opposed to a search for abstract models, laws, or theories of cultural change; and (3) a self-reflexive awareness of archaeology's place in the modern world. Each of these aspects has implications for the practice of archaeology both in how we collect data (make observations of reality), and how we communicate our interpreta-tions of the world.

A SUMMARY OF A MARXIST PERSPECTIVE[1]

Marxism is a rich intellectual tradition that originated with the ideas of Karl Marx and has matured, developed, and grown for more than 100 years. Like other grand theories of humankind and society, it has come to include a great variety of different perspectives, drawn insights from other theories, and served as a source of inspiration for persons outside of the tradition. Also, like other grand theories, it has been bent and hammered into an instrument for per-nicious purposes. For social science in general, and archaeology in particular, this tradition is a rich source of insights, theories, concepts, and ideas about the nature of cultural change. More specifically, a dialectical marxist perspective, derived from a view of marxism as a theory of internal relations, offers us a way to escape the irresolvable oppositions of science and humanism, evolution and history, materialism and mentalism, and determinism and relativism, that be-devil archaeological theory today (Ollman, 1976; Sayer, 1987).

The Dialectic

One of the most widely accepted principles imparted by the New Archaeology is the notion that culture is a system that serves to integrate a society with the environment and other societies. Such systems are made up of interconnected parts that form a whole so that change in one of the parts or subsystems of the whole affects changes in the other parts. Because such a system is functionally integrated, the parts and subsystems that make up the whole must be compatible; that is, they must fit comfortably together.

This notion of a system shares with the dialectic, the idea that society is an interconnected whole but differs in a fundamental way. In a systemic approach, social entities (the parts) exist before and apart from their interconnection with other social entities. A systemic view atomizes the whole into its parts and sees changes in the parts (variables) as the source of change in the whole. Since parts can exist separate from their linkages, we can speak of some parts as being causal to others, and we can speak of some aspects, subsystems, variables, or levels of the system as determining other aspects, subsystems, variables, or levels. The dialectic, on the other hand, views the social whole as a complex web of internal relations within which the relation of any given entity to others governs what that entity will be. You cannot have teachers without students; each social entity exists because of the relationship that creates them both, and if that relation is broken, the entities dissolve away, or more properly, are transformed into something else. By this same token, causes do not exist free of their effects, and no variable is ever independent. This social world has an intrinsic dynamic because change in any part of the world alters the whole of the relations, sustaining all elements forever in flux.

In a dialectic the entities that make up the social whole are not expected to fit comfortably together; they may, but the dynamics of change are not to be found in these functional relations. Rather, they lie in relational contradictions that spring from the fact that social categories are defined by and require the existence of their opposite. Thus, a single underlying relationship of slavery defines both the master and the slave. For one to exist so too must the other, yet they are opposites and, as such, potentially in conflict. Each has contrary interests and a different lived experience in the context of a shared history. Change in these relations is never simply quantitative or qualitative. Quantitative change can lead to qualitative change, and qualitative change necessarily implies a quantitative change. Conflicts that result from relational contradictions may result in quantitative changes in those relations that build to a qualitative change. Rebellion by slaves may lead the masters to enforce stricter and stricter discipline, thereby heightening slave resistance until the relation of slavery is overthrown. The social relations that result from such a qualitative change are a mix of the old and the new; the old social form is remade, not replaced.

Understanding the Lived Experience of People

People make history. They do not, however, make it as individuals free to act as they please. They make it as members of social groups whose common consciousness derives from the shared social relations, lived experiences, cultures, and ideologies that link them to each other and oppose them to other social groups in the world around them. Their actions are constrained by material conditions and social structures inherited from their past, the products of past human action. These constraints never determine in any direct or simple way what history will be because these constrains, whether they be in nature, the economy, social structure, or culture are, at the same time, limiting and enabling. That is, even as they inhibit some forms of action, they must be present to empower other forms of action. Contradictions arise from this ambiguity of limiting and enabling, and it is in those contradictions that we will find the dynamics of history. We gain access to this dynamic by looking at the nature of power (the universal ability of all humans to act) in real societies, and how it works in the production and reproduction of everyday life.

A dialectical archaeology should start and end with the real, lived experience of people and seek an understanding of how that experience changed over time. Much current theory in archaeology transforms real human experience such as the San family or the Inka state into abstract categories, the "family" or the "state," and treats these abstractions as what should be explained; what is a household mode of production, or what caused the rise of the state? In the dialectic a cover term, such as the family, refers to things and their interrelations and as such, these terms acquire a substantive meaning only from the particular context in which they are applied. To call a variety of real social forms, families – the San family, the Hopi family, the American family, etc. – does imply certain commonalities of scale and form between these concrete social realities. Such similarities of form frequently, however, spring from radically different underlying social relations. The San family is nuclear, with a man, a woman, and their children, and so too is the ideal modern U.S. family, yet the underlying social relations that link these individuals and the larger sets of social relations that the families are embedded in are radically different. The contradictions that drive social change will lie in these relations and not in the social forms. The abstract notion of the family may assist us to define a scale of analysis in the study of a concrete case, or it may help us to compare historical processes of change between cases, but it cannot be the object of explanation. Thus in the dialectic, abstractions are tools for understanding the production and reproduction of real social forms, not the end of our analyses.

The goal of our analyses is to understand history as a material social process. This process involves both changes in the relations between social groups and transformations of whole social orders. To study this kind of history we ask about the commonalities and differences between social groups and the larger historical and environmental context in which these commonalities and differences emerged. We also need to look for unevenness in historical developments. Uneven development begets social groups that have different interests within a social order, and as they try to act to meet those interests, they create conflicts that drive social change. Such a history should be multiscalar. As we change our scale of analysis, we frame a different set of relations; the unevenness in these relations will disappear at a new scale as a fresh pattern of unevenness appears. Social groups also live and act in a world of varying scales, and their relations change as their scale of reference changes.

Historical process is both contingent and unpredictable. The prior conditions of a historical sequence, material relations, social structures, culture, and ideology define a range of possible actions that people can both conceive of and perform. Which of this possible range of actions people will undertake, however, is not determined but contingent. The conditions that structure human action leave broad channels and lots of room for actions and consequences that cannot be known in advance. Small changes in events or circumstances, actions taken or not taken, can, over time, have dramatic and unforeseeable consequences for the course of history.

A Self-Reflexive Archaeology

Just as it is people who make history, it is also people who write history, who do archaeology. As scholars we are also social beings who live and work in a social context. Our social, cultural, and political point of view affects how we will see the world, what questions we will ask, what assumptions we will make, what observations we will value, and what answers we will accept. Our understandings of the past must always fit the knowledge we have of past events and practices, but many explanations will always fit such descriptions. A dialectical point of view urges us to accept that there was a real past but that our knowledge of that past must be made in the present. As a result, such knowledge is never a simple product of either past or present but a complex mix of both. Our assessments cannot be complete unless we also ask why we, as socially situated scholars, might favor one possible explanation over another.

In answer to this question, we must study archaeology's social history as a material social process. Our own history bequeaths beliefs and social relations to us as social beings and scholars. This inheritance conditions our scholarship, setting up paths of least resistance that we may travel without realizing why they exist or what the repercussions of our journey may be, for ourselves or others. A self-critical historical analysis reveals alternative paths and asks why the paths we are following were laid out, why we should follow them, to what ends they take us, and whose interests they serve. With such knowledge we hope we can more wisely navigate our journey.

Recognizing that archaeology is a social product and process, and that multiple stories, addressing different interests in the present will always be possible, raises questions of what interests archaeology should serve and how these interests are best served. Archaeology legitimately serves a variety of interests or communities, including the academy, the people who pay for our work, the museum-going public, Native American Nations, etc. The interests of these various communities may be in harmony, irrelevant to each other, or in conflict.

Archaeologists have not given enough attention to identifying these interests or to building dialogues between those interests and ourselves.

THE PRACTICE OF ARCHAEOLOGY

We have been led to believe that the practice of archaeology should be divided up into bits that can be hierarchically arranged from high-order theories, to methodology, to techniques, and finally to data (Schiffer, 1988). Several authors have defined the key problem of archaeology as the development of a middle-range theory that links higher-order theory and empirical observations (Binford, 1983; Watson, 1986; Salmon, 1982). The processual view of archaeology, like the processual view of culture, is atomistic and systemic. It divides archaeology up into entities and organizes these in subsystems. It then gives some of these subsystems (the theoretical) a privileged position of determining the action of the other subsystems.

Since researchers tend to focus their efforts in a limited number of these subsystems, this ranking also becomes a hierarchy of practice within the discipline. In this scheme the higher levels of analysis each appropriate the products of the lower in their practice, so that the theorist is accorded greater reknown than the prehistorian; the field director, a higher position than the laboratory director; and the synthesizer, more attention than the faunal analyst. Archaeologists have divided our field into some of us that synthesize, generalize, and theorize as opposed to others of us that sort, dig, and identify. As Gero (1991) points out, this hierarchy does more than just rank activities; it has a more profound social dimension. Embedded in this hierarchy of practice is a gender division of labor that relegates women's knowledge production to the lower rungs of the hierarchy of practice and depreciates them as knowers. This hierarchy is also a class hierarchy that elevates the theoretician above the dirt archaeologist and the academic above the contract archaeologist. Even in fieldwork, the labor of archaeology has been divided into specialized tasks and routinized so that managers think about what is to be done, and the field workers do it (Paynter 1983).

The practice of archaeology today is an alienated practice; the intellectual activity of thinking about archaeology has been separated from the labor of doing archaeology. This alienation extends from the separation of theory and data to the social organization of archaeology. Humans must think to act, and human labor invokes thought. The alienation of theory from practice, reason from action, and thought from labor, breaks apart those things that are naturally joined in human action. These things are reunited in praxis, the uniquely human ability to knowingly make and change both the world around us and ourselves. A praxis of archaeology is dialectical, constantly moving between theory and practice, reason and action, and thought and labor. In a praxis of archaeology, thinking about archaeology, doing archaeology, and the sociopolitics of archaeology are part of a single whole, so that our practice in each of these realms affects and reflects our practice in the others.

Making Observations of the World

Archaeology is at once a natural and a social science. Most of the traditional field and laboratory research of archaeology studies the physical world; it makes observations about natural phenomena such as radioactive decay rates in ^{14}C dating, asks about the distribution of artifacts and features in the archaeological record, and seeks to identify events and practices in the past. As a social science, archaeology seeks to understand process of cultural change and the long-term history of humankind. The methods of natural science can give us a description of the physical world, but when we try to make sense of it, to explain, and to give meaning to this world and how it changes, we enter a web of dialectical relations.

Archaeologists should strive to make our descriptions of the world as rigorous as possible. We should be able to empirically answer questions, such as "Did sheep in a given site have horns?" "When did humans first cross the Bering land bridge?" "Did the Aztec eat sacrificial victims?" and "What were Clovis points used for?" Some form of the hypodeductive method may work well for answering such questions and was used in archaeology for this purpose long before the New Archaeology (for example, see Haury, 1962). Sloppy technique, careless excavation, or slipshod measurement obscures such descriptions and deceives us. Our skill and mastery of the archaeological craft has always been essential to a sound understanding of the past.[2] In this regard statistics are a valuable tool for rigorous description because descriptive questions are often best asked in quantitative terms, "Did a majority of sheep in the site have horns?" "What was the rate of human movement over the Bering land bridge?" and "How many sacrificial victims did the Aztec eat in a year?" To answer these questions we need to quantify our observations and look to the adequacy of our samples for that purpose.[3]

The descriptions that we make of the world, the artifact distributions, ^{14}C dates, faunal lists, pollen counts, features measurements, etc., do not speak for themselves; archaeologists have to give them meaning (Leone, 1982). Moreover, the physical world does not exist apart from the social world either in the pasts that we study or in our studies. Once we have made an observation about the world, we usually then seek to assign it meaning in relational terms. For example, André Leroi-Gourhan (1982) found that horse and bison composed 60–70% of the animal images on Paleolithic caves in southern Europe, and that other animals occurred in groups of lesser frequencies. He used this distribution as well as other observations on the placement of these images in these caves to reconstruct a Paleolithic mythogram, a structure that guided the painting of the caves (Conkey, 1989). The images either appear in the proportions or positions that Leroi-Gourhan identified or they do not, but the mythogram that he constructs is a complex mix of the patterns he found and interests, beliefs, assumptions, and social relations in the present. Furthermore, the animals portrayed on the walls of the cave are of nature, but once humans hunt them and invest them with meaning on the walls of the cave, they enter into one social relation or another; they exist in both natural and social worlds.

Our theories of the past must fit the observations we can make of the physical world, but these theories will also structure how we observe that world. They nudge us toward certain types of questions, limit the range of observations we will make, and structure how we will make observations. Nowhere it this more clear than in the issue of how we choose the sites, areas, or artifacts that we will study.

The so-called *Normative Archaeology* used a Boasian notion of culture as a shared set of rules or norms for behavior. These norms could not be directly observed but manifest themselves in behavioral, ideological, and material traits that could be observed. These archaeologists observed cultural change by changes in the distribution of material traits due to processes of invention, diffusion, and migration (Haury, 1952:19–20). Given this theory, the most appropriate contexts to study were those that would produce the most traits, resulting in an emphasis on digging burials and the centers of major sites. Since only the shared traits were of interest, there was no reason, given the theory, that smaller, and/or more impoverished locales should be investigated.

In a processual archaeology, culture was the human's extrasomatic system of adaptation (Binford, 1962). The emphasis was on how the parts and subsystems of the system functioned together in human adaptation. This led to the idea that a sample must represent the whole of the system, a search for patterning in the archaeological record that reflected the system of culture. The focus on parts or variables was compatible with a notion of random sampling of those parts to gain a representative sample of the parts that made up the whole. The notion that the system was functionally integrated also supported the strategy of studying one subsystem to understand some aspect of the whole. Because culture is a system, each material culture category should reflect the evolutionary stage or level of cultural complexity of its culture. This strategy is most clearly seen in the study of mortuary remains to reconstruct social organization (see Chapter 7 of this volume).

In the dialectic we define societies as dynamic webs of social relations that define (create) social entities (social groups, roles, organization, etc.) that stand in contradictory relationships to each other. Like a processual archaeology, the emphasis here is on patterns, but instead of the units that exist in the pattern being the objects of interest, the relations between units are the focus of study. This is a contextual approach that examines how different aspects of a case are related. In a processual archaeology, contradictions between different artifact classes, such as egalitarian architecture existing with marked inequalities between burials in Colonial and Sedentary Period Hohokam villages, are anomalies that do not fit the assumption of culture as an integrated system. In a dialectical contextual analysis, such anomalies between classes of artifacts and different social contexts, the mundane and the ritual, become the keys to understanding the internal dynamics of society. This form of analysis does not reduce the richness of past social life to abstract categories, but rather attempts to reveal the complex interplay of the real relations of production and reproduction.

A dialectical contextual analysis jettisons the use of random sampling for the study of spatial relationships.[4] A random sample, or one of the many variations on the notion of random sampling, selects sample units out of their spatial context (Nance, 1983; Redman, 1987). The units are usually classified in functional categories, such as storage rooms, grinding rooms, and habitation rooms in Southwestern pueblos, and generalizations are made about the characteristics of these categories. What is lost in this process is the spatial relationships between these units. These relationships may be the most important informative aspect of the underlying pattern we are seeking to expose. These problems are magnified when the sample units are not the behavioral units of interest but instead recovery spaces, test pits, grids, trenches, or transects (Reid et al., 1975). This type of cluster sampling is very inefficient when the real units of interest have a patterned distribution (Nance, 1983:297). Numerous empirical studies have shown that random cluster sampling is not a very effective technique for pattern discovery and that a systematic sample gives a better picture of underlying patterns (Judge et al., 1975; Asch, 1975; Cowgill, 1975b). From a dialectical point of view, a random sample selects units and often obscures the relations between units, the spatial structures, that are our primary interest.[5]

If archaeologists wish to examine the relations in spatial patterns then they need to employ a full-area coverage. Such an approach has been advocated by non-marxist archaeologists who recognize its superiority for pattern definition and identification (see the papers in Fish and Kowalewski, 1990). Full-area coverage is "the systematic examination of contiguous blocks of terrain at a uniform level of intensity" (Fish and Kowalewski, 1990:2). Such coverage is never truly 100%. The intensity may vary and is almost infinitely refinable, with more and more complexities of the underlying pattern being revealed by greater and greater levels of intensity (Fish et al., 1990:189). Full-area coverage allows for the systematic definition of pattern boundaries, feature complexes, and the recognition of rare and singular-occurring distributions.

A dialectical archaeology defines the study of the reproduction and production of everyday life as the focal point of our research. This is not necessarily a new idea in archaeology. It appears in Willey's (1965) classic study of Mayan house mounds at Barton Ramie, if not before. It is in part an interest that grew out of Steward's cultural ecology with its emphasis on reconstructing diet, adaptive activities, and social organization (*vis à vis* settlement pattern studies). This interest in environmental adaptation has been a part of archaeology for almost 50 years (since just after World War II), and a host of techniques, among them faunal analysis, lithic edge-wear analysis, palynology, phytolyth analysis, and floatation, have been developed for reconstructing such mundane matters. These techniques and the information they supply remain an important aspect of any study of lived experience. In a dialectical archaeology researchers would add a stress on the social and ideological aspects of everyday life with an emphasis on contradictions that may exist between these different aspects of everyday life.

To add these components, archaeologists need to ask how the people of the past would have experienced life. This is a difficult question to ask, and we have not spent 50 years developing techniques to answer it. The key lies in the aforementioned notions of context and contradiction. In my example of Hohokam burials at the site of La Ciudad, I attempted such an analysis by asking what the context of mortuary ritual was, public or private, and by examining how individuals would have experienced the built environment they lived in. I found that in the Sedentary period, cremation and burial were public events with marked inequalities in scale and elaboration between different events. In contrast, the built environment exhibited differential labor investment primarily in public structures, ball courts, and platform mounds, and little differentiation in domestic architecture. In the subsequent Classic period, these relations reversed. Burial rites became private, status was marked more by location than goods; and very obvious differences existed in domestic architecture, with elite residences on mounds, and others living in compounds or scattered pithouses. These differences in the mundane built environment created a situation whereby the day-to-day lived experience of people living in each of these housing types would have been plainly dissimilar.

Everyday life is technically, methodologically, and practically much easier to study than hypercoherence, heterogeneity, cultural complexity, scalar stress, or any of the other dozens of abstractions that processual archaeologists have charged us to study. They have asked us to recast our observations of the concrete as measures of these abstractions. People do not experience these abstractions in their day-to-day lives; they experience pain, death, birth, passion, joy, hunger, envy, and a host of other things that archaeologists rarely talk about. These real-life experiences motivate human action. In a dialectical archaeology we look at the concrete as evidence of the production and reproduction of everyday life.

A dialectical archaeology also charges archaeologists to be self-reflexive about our data collection and to examine the sociopolitical context of that practice. What effects do our data collection have on the present-day lived experience of peoples? Who owns the past? What are the sociopolitics of our own discipline, both at home and abroad?

In the United States most archaeologists are white, and the pasts that they study are the pasts of Native American peoples. Chapter 8 explored the history of that relationship and discussed how archaeologists might change it. New federal legislation forces us to consider the interests of these people in our data collection. In the near future, reburial and repatriation will be key issues that all archaeologists will have to deal with because our practice affects the lives of living people. Archaeologists can no longer practice as if the only community they needed to address were the discipline of archaeology; a variety of interests need to be served. More fundamentally, archaeologists must now reconstruct our discipline as a study of people and not just of things.

Archaeologists also need to take a hard look at the human relations within our discipline (Gero *et al.*, 1983). Feminist authors have initiated this process by asking why it is that women do different labor in archaeology than men, and why the products of female labor are valued less than what men do (Gero, 1983, 1985, 1991; Conkey and Gero, 1991). Little has been done to examine the class relations within archaeology. Paynter (1983) has shown how the alienation of thinking about archaeology and doing archaeology has created a proletariate of field workers in contract archaeology. Ortiz-Aguilu (1986) discusses how contract archaeology has become an aspect of colonialism in Puerto Rico, where U.S. firms get the lion's share of the contracts because of technological advantages and because, as English-speaking Americans, they have an advantage in dealing with the federal agencies in Washington, D.C., that award most of the big contracts on the island. Finally, we need to look to the relations of power within the archaeological academy, a process well under way in England (see the papers in Baker *et al.*, 1990; Tilley, 1990) but barely begun in the United States (Wobst and Keene, 1983; Wobst, 1989).

Communicating Archaeology

The problem of communicating the results of archaeology is most often framed in terms of an opposition between conveying findings within the discipline and reporting results to a general public. Most discussions of this issue assume that we are reasonably skilled at the former but hopelessly inept at the latter (Fagan, 1991). The last 10 years has seen an increased emphasis in U.S. archaeology on "making archaeology meaningful to the public" (Judge, 1989:4). This has resulted in innumerable public programs, pamphlets, interpretation centers, and dig tours. Nearly every issue of the *Bulletin of the Society for American Archaeology* contains a discussion of the overall issue or an announcement of another public program, radio show, PBS special, or brochure. At every Society for American Archaeology meeting of the last 5 years I have picked up a slick poster or two admonishing the public to "Save our past for the future" or warning them of "A thief of time: He's stealing from you," and each time, I have viewed a new antilooting video. Despite what is now a major and growing effort, the general perception in the field seems to be that we are not getting through. A common rationale for public programs rests on the notion that through public programs, archaeologists can stop or retard the looting of archaeological sites (Judge, 1989). Yet, the consensus seems to be that looting is getting worse instead of better (Knudson, 1989; Cheek, 1990; Keel et al., 1990).

A consumerist model lies at the heart of most of our efforts to communicate with the public. "If there is one single message which emerges from the Taos conference it is that the archaeological profession must become more responsible to the public, the ultimate consumer of our efforts and the ultimate provider of support for our research" (Judge, 1989:4).[6] In this model the archaeologist produces a product, usually a watered-down version of the academic product, that is then packaged, and sold to the general public (DeCicco, 1988). The usually implicit assumption is that archaeologists have the authority, the knowledge, the skill, and the right to determine how the past should be interpreted and what that interpretation should be. The problem then becomes one of how to communicate, or make relevant, that interpretation to a general public; how do we educate them to see things our way (Lynott, 1990)?

An alternative approach to the consumerist model can be found in the work of Parker Potter (1989, 1990, 1991). He suggests that archaeologists could communicate with the public better if we tried to develop an ethnographic understanding of what people in local communities need from studies of the past. For Potter this ethnography involves immersion by the archaeologist in the local community and an interpretation of the texts, cultural performances, and speech acts about the past that the archaeologists finds there. In terms of looting, Potter (1989:36–42) urges archaeologists to ask why individuals engage in this activity and what needs of theirs it fulfills? He argues that such an understanding will allow us to more effectively address the issue of looting than will an approach of righteous indignation.

A dialectical perspective on society suggests that society is made up of varied social groups with distinct and often conflicting interests and that an undifferentiated general public is a myth. In this context we should ask what interests archaeology serves. Such a question leads us not only to examine archaeology's position in a social order but also to develop understandings that allow us to more effectively address our own interests in that social order.

A number of marxist archaeologists have argued that modern archaeology is primarily a middle-class pursuit and that it most often expresses the ideology of that class[7] (Kristiansen, 1981; Patterson, 1986; Trigger, 1989a:15). A large number of systematic and detailed studies have not been done in the United States or Great Britain to establish the socioeconomic make-up of the public audience for archaeology. A handful of existing studies and some anecdotal evidence suggest that this audience is a middle-class audience. Trotter (1989:2), in a study of visitors to Wupatki National Monument in Arizona, found that they were predominantly well-educated, middle-class Anglos and that "black,

Native American, and Hispanic visitors are the exception." A similar conclusion can be drawn at Historic Annapolis where Afro-Americans made up a far lower proportion of local visitors than their representation in the local population (Potter, personnel communication, 1991). Merriman's study of archaeological museum visitors and nonvisitors in England came to a similar conclusion. The museum visitors were predominantly well-educated, middle-class individuals. The readership of *Archaeology Magazine* is decidedly middle and upper class, with 64% college graduates and 83% professionals, administrators, or managers (*Archaeology*, 1989).

Participants in field programs set up by professional archaeologists for the public are also predominantly middle class. In the United States archaeology is rarely taught in high schools, and when it is, it tends to be in suburban predominantly middle-class schools, so that most people can obtain formal instruction in archaeology only if they attend college. The current emphasis on public education has led to a series of field programs in eastern Canada and the northeastern United States that seek to involve members of the general public in an archaeological experience outside of the university campus. Reports on such programs in Ontario (Knight, 1991; Smardz, 1991) Rhode Island (Leveille, 1991), Massachusetts (Krass, 1991), and New Hampshire (Hume and Boisvert, 1991) suggest that the vast majority of participants in these programs were professionals, administrators, and managers, with little or no participation by working-class individuals and people of color.[8] More than 94% of the participants in Earth Watch's expeditionary programs are in, or retired from, middle-class occupations (students, professionals, managers, or administrators).[9] Merriman's (1987) survey of participants in archaeological field projects in Great Britain suggests the same conclusions.

There is nothing necessarily wrong with archaeology's addressing a middle-class audience. These people are often politically active and capable of lending support and legitimacy to archaeology's legal and political agendas. Indeed, the success of archaeology in reaching this audience may account for our success in getting archaeological preservation and antilooting legislation passed on the local, state, and national level. Seeing this audience as the *general public*, however, may interfere with our attempts to combat looting and blind us to other legitimate interests in the past, different from our own.

Limited data suggest that the public audience for archaeology in the United States and Great Britain is middle class, but other, equally limited, evidence suggests that the looters we fear come from working-class backgrounds. Merrimam's (1987) study showed that metal-detector users who looted archaeological sites were largely working-class individuals with slightly above average incomes. In a similar vein, Gero's (1989) discussion of Celtic constructions in New England notes the existence of a middle-class scholarly community that rejects the authenticity of Celtic claims and a working-class community of advocates who avidly embrace the Celtic origin of these edifices.[10] In my own visits to artifact fairs in upstate New York, I have observed styles of dress, cars, and patterns of speech that suggest a different class background than what I see when I wander around the Cooperstown Farmer's Museum.

It is clear that the people who loot archaeological sites and promote cult archaeologies have a different concept of the past and its value than we do as archaeologists. We might do well to consider that these differences are not necessarily the result of ignorance or greed. They may reflect that social groups in our society have different interests in the past. Archaeology may lack meaning for much of the public not because we have been inept at communicating to them, but instead, because our interests in the past may not reflect or may even be contrary to theirs. The programs that have been advanced to educate the public on archaeology – exhibits, site tours, participation in field projects, brochures, newspaper articles, and pamphlets – appeal to middle-class individuals who look to books and authorities for knowledge, but do not necessarily appeal to working-class people. Both Merrimam's (1987) study and Gero's (1989) suggest that these individuals have a profound interest in the past, but they also have been alienated from the discourse of archaeologists, which they regard as elitist. We do not make our discourse less elitist in their minds by simply watering down or simplifying what we have to say. As Potter has suggested, we need to understand what their needs for the past are and address those needs.

My comments on the class structure of looting and archaeology are quite speculative because I have very little empirical evidence to back up my hunches about what is going on.[11] I make them here to challenge archaeologists to ask about the class relations involved in academic archaeology, avocational archaeology, cult archaeology, and looting today, and to suggest that the knowledge gained from such studies may help us to better preserve the archaeological record for the future. More fundamentally, I would also question the consumerist model that drives our public programs and the practice of archaeology itself. An archaeology built solely, or primarily, on middle-class interests is not only ineffective in dissuading looters but also hides other legitimate interests in the past.

At the 1988 American Anthropological Association meetings in Phoenix, Arizona, Vernon Masayesva, then vice-chair of the Hopi tribe, spoke to one of the symposia. In an eloquent and moving speech he discussed how publication of an article in a Phoenix paper, *The Arizona Republic*, had upset and caused great emotional harm among Hopi people. The article had reported on archaeological evidence for cannibalism in a mass grave of Hopi individuals dating to the late seventeenth century. The archaeological analysis that the newspaper report was based on had been published in *American Antiquity* (Turner and Morris, 1970) nearly 20 years before, but was given to the paper that year as a press release by a physical anthropologist at Arizona State University. Mr. Masayesva allowed that archaeologists should publish and discuss such things in our professional publications but asked that we use more care in what we released to the press. He noted that the paper had sensationalized the report, and that this sensationalism had caused distress for many Hopi people. He asked that we recognize and serve two interests in our study of Arizona's past – our scholarly interests and the interests of the Hopi people. The conflict that he brought to us in Phoenix that day is not one that will be resolved through education programs that attempt to instruct people without submitting our own practice to scrutiny and change.

The alternative to the consumerist model is to recognize that there are many different legitimate interests in the past. Archaeology can offer these interests our craft, the ability to use material culture to make observations about the events and practices of the past, and to weave these into reconstructions of life in the past. The craft of archaeology may serve many different communities: the academy, a municipality, a social class, an ethnic group, a Native American nation, etc. This is an application of interests, in every sense of the word. Different interests may involve different archaeological products. In most cases the archaeologist should serve more than one community, and a single project may entail or require multiple products. Such an interchange between archaeologist and client community is not one way. Archaeologist should not simply accept the terms and interests of the client. A good work of craft enhances, alters, and creates new possibilities of experience, however modestly. It involves a dialogue that changes and shapes all who participate in it.

This dialogue brings us full circle and unites all of our activities as praxis. For if such a dialogue is successful, it will lead us to ask different questions of the past. The answers to these questions will in turn alter our interpretations of the past that we bring to the dialogue. Thus, archaeology undertakes a never-ending journey through which our knowledge of the past becomes sounder and more diverse.

CONCLUSION

It is an exciting time to be an archaeologist, with a host of competing theories vying in the field. It is also an unsettling time. It is difficult to know how to practice archaeology or what to make of the *sturm und drang* of the theoretical debate. The unsettled nature of archaeology today is in fact good, because it forces us constantly and critically to examine all that we do and why we do it. With no chance of complacency, archaeologists must always confront the deficiencies in what they do and the questions that they ask. This gives rise to a powerful dynamic that drives our research in the field. We do not, however, need to await a resolution of these theoretical debates to do good archaeology. We already know how to do good archaeology, and we do it through a dialectic between past and present, consciousness and reality, and theory and practice. This dialectic impels us to constantly refine and rethink our understandings of the past; through this process, we lop off our ignorance one cubic millimeter at a time.

I do not wish everyone who reads this book to become a marxist archaeologist and accept the program of research contained within the book, for were they to do so, then the journey that we are on would grind to a halt. The goal of my arguments is not to win coverts, but rather to argue that there should be a theoretical space in Anglo-American archaeology for marxism, and to try to convey some understanding of a dialectical theory that should occupy some of that space. Marxism as a theory of internal relations dissolves away many of the oppositions that have vexed us as archaeologists by encouraging us to accept their ambiguities and look to these ambiguities as driving forces of cultural change. It exploits the ambiguities by asking us to account for the past in terms of the real, lived experience of people, in the reproduction and production of everyday life, rather than in terms of the abstract poles of the oppositions. This viewpoint is a useful and valuable one that will aid us in coming to understandings of the past.

> *But of course one never knows. There are lots of things we don't know yet, Giuseppe. We're really just at the beginning.* (Life of Galileo, *scene 15; Brecht, 1987:113*).

ENDNOTES

1. In an effort to produce a clear, readable, and easily intelligible summary I have used references sparingly and eliminated most qualification and finer nuances of arguments. These things are more fully developed in the chapters that are summarized.

2. It is perhaps paradoxical that in the early days of the New Archaeology, great emphasis was placed on conceptual rigor, but technical rigor was ignored or even denigrated. This lack of technical rigor is readily apparent in the excavation photographs from the Vernon field school that are published in various volumes of the *Fieldiana: Anthropology* series from the Field Museum of Chicago.

3. Explanatory statistics, however, have little or no use in a dialectical approach because they manipulate variables and not relations, often seeking explanation in prediction or the influence of independent variables on dependent variables.

4. Emil Haury once commented to me that he did not believe in random sampling, because human behavior was not random. It took me nearly a decade to realize that this was a comment of great insight and not of great innocence.

5. This discussion should not be interpreted to indicate that random sampling has no place in a dialectical approach. It has no use as a discovery technique or as way to studying patterning, but it remains a valuable aid to research when an archaeologist needs to select a subset of like units, for example, 200 vessels out of a group of 1000, for analysis.

6. The Taos Fort Burgwin Conference was held at the Fort Burgwin Research Center in Taos, New Mexico. The conference was sponsored by the Society for American Archaeology to discuss what archaeologists could do to stem the looting of archaeological sites.

7. I note again here as I have earlier that the marxist notion of a middle class should not be confused with the common U.S. equation of middle class with middle income. A class is middle in a marxist sense when it stands between other classes or mediates between classes in a structure of relations. In capitalism the middle class are the managers, administrators, professionals, and small-business owners who do not control the means of production, but tend to have significant control over their own labor, and direct the labor of the working class.

8. The Massachusetts program (Krass, 1991) was set up for and targeted at public school teachers with an overt intention of reaching a broader class, racial, and ethnic audience through the teachers.

9. According to the 1990 annual report of The Center for Field Research, 85% of the participants in Earth Watch programs had college degrees, and more than 50% had advanced degrees. Only 4% of the participants had no schooling beyond high school, and an unknown number of these were recent high school graduates who had not yet started college. The breakdown of participants by occupation was 8% students, 23% professionals, 12% administrators, 14% in science and engineering, 19% in education, 18% retired, and 6% other. Archaeology expeditions made up 28% of the Earth Watch programs in 1990.

10. My own roots lie in the rural working class of northern Colorado that my father attempted to escape by joining the military. Whenever I return home, my uncle, who worked on my grandparent's ranch and in a cement plant all his life, takes me out onto the plains or up into the mountains and shows me cracks and stains on the bedrock that he is convinced are Celtic ruins. In every case I have been able to convince him that the specific marks were natural phenomena, but his faith in an ancient Celtic past in northern Colorado remains unshaken.

11. In formulating a class-based study of these relations, we should also consider the collectors who drive the antiquities market through their demand for artifacts. On one level, many of these are the same people who are the looters, but the international fine arts market is composed of wealthy, upper-class individuals.

REFERENCES

Abercombie, Nicholas, Stephen Hill, and Bryan S. Turner
    1980   *The Dominant Ideology Thesis.* Allen and Unwin, London, England.
Ackerly, Neal W., Jerry B. Howard, and Randall H. McGuire
    1987   La Ciudad Canals: A Study of Hohokam Irrigation Systems at the Community Level.
           Anthropological Field Studies 17. Arizona State University, Tempe, Arizona.
Adams, E. Charles
    1984   Archaeology and the Native American: A Case at Hopi, *In Ethics and Values in Archae-*
           ology. ed. by E. L. Green, pp. 236–242. Free Press, New York.
Adams, Robert McC.
    1965   *The Land Behind Baghdad.* University of Chicago Press, Chicago, Illinois.
    1966   *The Evolution of Urban Society.* Aldine, Chicago, Illinois.
Adorno, Theodor
    1950   *The Authoritarian Personality.* Harper & Row, New York.
    1973a   *Philosophy of Modern Music.* Seabury, New York.
    1973b   *Negative Dialectics.* Seabury, New York.
Aggar, Ben
    1979   *Western Marxism: An Introduction.* Goodyear Publishing Co., Santa Monica, California.
Allen, Garland
    1980   Dialectical Materialism in Biology. *Science and Nature* **3**:43–57.
Allen, Jim
    1985   Comments on Complexity and Trade: A View From Melanesia. *Archaeology in Oceania*
           20:49–57.
Althusser, Louis
    1969   *For Marx.* Pantheon, New York.
    1971   *Lenin and Philosophy.* Monthly Review Press, New York.
Althusser, Louis and Etienne Balibar
    1970   *Reading Capital.* Pantheon Books, New York.
American Anthropological Association
    1983   Professional Ethics. American Anthropological Association, Washington, D.C.
Ammerman, Albert J. and William Andrefsky, Jr.
    1982   Reduction Sequences and the Exchange of Obsidian in Neolithic Calabria. *In Contexts*
           for Prehistoric Exchange, ed. by J. E. Ericson and T. K. Earle, pp. 149–172. Academic
           Press, New York.
Amin, Samir
    1974   *Accumulation on a World Scale.* Monthly Review Press, New York.
Anderson, Benedict
    1983   *Imagined Communities: Reflections on the Origin and Spread of Nationalism.* Verso, Lon-
           don, England.
Anderson, Keith M.
    1986   Hohokam Cemeteries as Elements of Settlement Structure and Change. In Anthro-
           pology of the Desert West, ed. by C. J. Condie and D. D. Fowler, pp. 180–201.
           University of Utah Anthropological Papers 110. Provo, Utah.

Anderson, Perry
1976   *Considerations on Western Marxism.* NLB, London, England.
1977   The Antinomies of Antonio Gramsci. *New Left Review* **100**:5–78.
1980   *Arguements within English Marxism.* Verso Editions, London, England.
1983   *In the Tracks of Historical Materialism.* Verso Editions, London, England.
Andreson, John M.
1983   Hohokam Murals at the Clan House, Casa Grande Ruins National Monument, *The Kiva* **48**:267–278.
Anonymous
1848   The Western Mound Builders. *Literary World* **5**:134–136.
Antieau, John M.
1981   The Palo Verde Archaeological Investigations Hohokam Settlement at the Confluence: Excavations along the Palo Verde Pipeline. *MNA Research Paper 20.* Flagstaff, Arizona.
Antone, Cecil F.
1986   Reburial: A Native American Point of View. Paper presented at the World Archaeological Congress, Southampton, England.
Anyon, Roger
1991a   Protecting the Past, Protecting the Present: Cultural Resources and American Indians. *In Protecting the Past: Readings in Archaeological Resource Protection,* ed. by G. S. Smith and J. E. Ehrenhard. The Telford Press, Caldwell, New Jersey.
1991b   Historic and Cultural Resource Preservation: The Zuni Archaeology Program. *Zuni History* **2**:23-24.
Archaeology
1989   Archaeology Magazine: A Subscriber Profile. *Archaeology Magazine,* New York.
Archer, Margaret Scotford
1988   *Culture and Agency: The Place of Culture in Social Theory.* Cambridge University Press, Cambridge, Massachusetts.
Arnold, Bettina
1990   The Past as Propaganda: Totalitarian Archaeology in Nazi Germany. *Antiquity* **64**:464–478.
. Arthur, Christopher John
1986   *Marx and His Relation to Hegel.* Basil Blackwell, Oxford, England.
Asch, David L.
1975   On Sample Size Problems and the Uses of Nonprobabilistic Sampling. *In Sampling in Archaeology,* ed. by J. W. Mueller, pp. 170–191. University of Arizona Press, Tucson, Arizona.
Ashmore, Wendy, and Richard Wilk
1988   House and Household in the Mesoamerican Past: an Introduction. *In Household and Community in the Mesoamerican Past,* ed. by R. Wilk and W. Ashmore, pp. 1–28. University of New Mexico Press, Albuquerque, New Mexico.
Avineri, S.
1968   *The Social and Political Thought of Karl Marx.* Cambridge University Press, Cambridge, Massachusetts.
Bahn, Paul G.
1984   Do Not Disturb? Archaeology and the Rights of the Dead. *Oxford Journal of Archaeology* **3**(1):127–139.
1986   Skeletons in the Cupboard. *New Scientist* **13**, November:58.
Baker, Frederick
1988   Archaeology and the Heritage Industry. *Archaeological Review from Cambridge* **7**(2):141–145.

Baker, Frederick and Julian Thomas
1990   *Writing the Past in the Present.* Saint David's University College, Lampeter, Wales.

Baker, Frederick, Sarah Taylor, and Julian Thomas
1990   Writing the Past in the Present: An Introductory Dialogue. *In Writing the Past in the Present,* ed. by F. Baker and J. Thomas, pp. 1–11. Saint David's University College, Lampeter, Wales.

Bandelier, Adolph F.
1884   Reports by A. F. Bandelier on His Investigations in New Mexico During the Years 1883–1884. *In Archaeological Institute of America, Fifth Annual Report of the Executive Committee,* pp. 88–98. John Wilson & Sons, Cambridge, Massachusetts.

Bapty, Ian and Timothy Yates (editors)
1990   *Archaeology After Structuralism.* Routledge & Kegan Paul, London, England.

Barnes, H. E.
1960   Foreward. *Essays in the Science of Culture.* ed. by G. Dole and R. Carneiro, pp. xi–xlvi. Thomas Y. Cromwell, New York.

Bartel, Brad
1982   A Historical Review of Ethnological and Archaeological Analyses of Mortuary Practices. *Journal of Anthropological Archaeology* 1(1):32–58.

Bate, Luis Felipe
1978   *Sociedad, Formación Económico Social y Cultura.* Ediciones Cultura Popular, México.
1984   *Cultura, Clases y Cuestión étnico-nacional.* Juan Pablos, México.

Beaudry, Mary C.
1980   "Or What Else You Please to Call It": Folk Semantic Domains in Early Virginia Probate Inventories. Ph.D. dissertation, Department of Anthropology, Brown University, Providence, Rhode Island.

Beaudry, M. C., L. J. Cook, and S. J. Mrozowski
1991   Artifacts and Active Voices: Material Culture as Social Discourse. *In The Archaeology of Inequality,* ed. by R. H. McGuire and R. Paynter, pp. 125–150. Basil Blackwell, Oxford, England.

Beauregard, Alan B.
1989   Relations of Production and Exchange in 17th Century New England: Interpretive Contexts for the Archaeology of Culture Contact. *In Conflicts in the Archaeology of Living Traditions,* ed. by R. Layton, pp. 22–31. Unwin and Hyman, London, England.

Belovsky, Gary E.
1988   An Optimal Foraging-Based Model of Hunter-Gatherer Population Dynamics. *Journal of Anthropological Archaeology* 7(4):329–372.

Bender, Barbara
1981   Gatherer-hunter Intensification. *In Economics Archaeology,* ed. by A. Sheridan and B. Bailey, pp. 149–57. British Archaeological Reports, Oxford, England.
1985a   Emergent Tribal Formations in the American Midcontinent. *American Antiquity* 50(1):52–62.
1985b   Prehistoric Developments in the American Midcontinent and in Brittany, Northwest France. *In Prehistoric Hunter-Gatherers,* ed. by T. D. Price and J. A. Brown, pp. 21–57. Academic Press, Orlando, Florida.
1989   The Roots of Inequality. *In Domination and Resistance,* ed. by D. Miller, M. Rowlands, and C. Tilley, pp. 83–95. Unwin and Hyman, London, England.
1990   The Dynamics of Nonhierarchical Societies. *In The Evolution of Political Systems: Socio-Politics in Small Scale Sedentary Societies.* ed. by Steadman Upham, pp. 247–263. Cambridge University Press, Cambridge, Massachusetts.

Benjamin, Walter
1979   *One Way Street and Other Writings.* New Left Books, London, England.

Berkhofer, R. F., Jr.
    1978   *The White Man's Indian.* Alfred A. Knopf, New York.
Bernal, Ignacio
    1980   *A History of Mexican Archaeology.* Thames and Hudson, London, England.
Bernstein, Edward
    1909   *Evolutionary Socialism.* Huebsch, New York.
Bettelheim, Charles
    1976   *Class Struggles in the USSR.* Monthly Review Press, New York.
Bhaskar, Roy
    1983   Dialectics. *In A Dictionary of Marxist Thought.* ed, by Tom Bottomore, pp. 122–129.
            Harvard University Press, Cambridge, Massachusetts.
    1986   *Scientific Realism and Human Emancipation.* Verso, London.
Binford, Lewis R.
    1962   Archaeology as Anthropology. *American Antiquity* **28:**217–25.
    1971   Mortuary Practices: Their Study and Their Potential. *Society for American Archaeology
            Memoirs* **25:**6–29.
    1972   *An Archaeological Perspective.* Academic Press, New York.
    1981   *Bones: Ancient Men and Modern Myths.* Academic Press, New York.
    1983   *Working at Archaeology.* Academic Press, New York.
    1986   In Pursuit of the Future. *In American Archaeology Past and Future.* ed. by D. J. Meltzer,
            D. D. Fowler, and J. A. Sabloff, pp. 459–479. Smithsonian Institution Press, Wash-
            ington, D.C.
    1987   Data Relativism, and Archaeological Science. *Man* **22:**391–404.
    1989   The "New Archaeology" Then and Now. *In Archaeological Thought in America.* ed. by
            C. C. Lamberg-Karlovsky, pp. 50–62. Cambridge University Press, Cambridge, Mas-
            sachusetts.
Binford, Lewis R. and Jeremy A. Sabloff
    1983   Paradigms, Systematics, and Archaeology. *In Working at Archaeology,* by L. R. Binford,
            pp. 395–410. Academic Press, New York.
Bintliff, John
    1988   A Review of Contemporary Perspectives on the "Meaning" of the Past. *In Extracting
            Meaning from the Past.* ed. by John Bintliff, pp. 2–36. Oxbow Books, Oxford, England.
Blanton, R. E. and Gary Feinman
    1984   The Mesoamerican World System. *American Anthropologist* **86:**673–682.
Blanton, R. E., S. A. Kowalewski, G. Feinman, and J. Appel
    1981   *Ancient Mesoamerica.* Cambridge University Press, Cambridge, Massachusetts.
Bloch, Maruice
    1985   *Marxism and Anthropology.* Oxford University Press, Oxford, England.
    1986   *From Blessing to Violence.* University of Cambridge Press, Cambridge, Massachusetts.
Bocock, Robert
    1986   *Hegemony.* Ellis Horwood Ltd., Chichester, England.
Bottomore, Tom (editor)
    1983   *A Dictionary of Marxist Thought.* Basil Blackwell, Oxford, England.
Bourdieu, Pierre
    1977   *An Outline of a Theory of Practice.* Cambridge University Press, Cambridge, Mas-
            sachusetts.
Braidwood, Robert J.
    1989   Robert J. Braidwood. *The Pastmasters: Eleven Modern Pioneers of Archaeology.* ed. by G.
            Daniel and C. Chippendale, pp. 83–98. Thames and Hudson, London, England.
Brandes, Ray
    1960   Archaeological Awareness of the Southwest as Illustrated in Literature to 1890. *Arizona
            and the West* **1:**6–25.

Braudel, Fernand
  1979   *Civilisation Materielle, Economie et Capitalisme, XV–XVIII Siecle.* Armand Colin,
          Paris.
  1980   *On History.* University of Chicago Press, Chicago, Illinois.
Braun, Claude and Lester Talkington
  1989   On Trends in the Status of Dialectical Logic: A Brief Study of Lefebure, Ilyenkov, and
          Wald. *Science and Nature* **9** & **10:**2–12.
Braun, David P.
  1990   Selection and Evolution in Nonhierarchical Organization. *In The Evolution of Political
          Systems: Socio-Politics in Small Scale Sedentary Societies.* ed. by Steadman Upham, pp. 61–
          86. Cambridge University Press, Cambridge, Massachusetts.
Brecht, Bertolt
  1987   *Bertolt Brecht Plays: Three.* Methuen, London, England.
Brew, J. O.
  1979   Hopi Prehistory and History to 1850. *In Handbook of North American Indians: Vol. 9
          Southwest,* ed. by Alfonso Ortiz, pp. 206–223. Smithsonian Institution Press, Wash-
          ington, D.C.
Brewster-Wray, Michael
  1988   Kinship and Labor in the Structure of the Inca Empire. Ph.D. dissertation, Depart-
          ment of Anthropology, State University of New York at Binghamton, Binghamton,
          New York.
Bromlei, I. V. and A. I. Pershits
  1985   Friederich Engels and Contemporary Problems Concerning the History of Primitive
          Society. *Soviet Anthropology and Archaeology* **23**(4):68–93.
Brown, Claude and Lester Talkington
  1989   On Trends in the Status of Dialecticallogic: A Brief Study of Lefebure, Ilyenkov, and
          Wald. *Science and Nature* **9:**2–12.
Brumfiel, Elizabeth M.
  1980   Specialization, Market Exchange, and the Aztec State: A View from Huexotla. *Current
          Anthropology.* **21:**459–78.
  1983   Aztec State Making: Ecology, Structure, and the Origin of the State. *American An-
          thropologist* **85:**261–284.
  1988   Fractions, Class, and Inter-Ethnic Alliance at Late Postclassic Xaltocan. Paper pre-
          sented at the 46th International Congress of Americanists, Amsterdam, The
          Netherlands.
  1989   Factional Competition in Complex Society. *In Domination and Resistance,* ed. by D.
          Miller, M. Rowlands, and C. Tilley, pp. 127–139. Unwin and Hyman, London, En-
          gland.
  1991   Weaving and Cooking: Women's Production in Aztec Mexico. *In Engendering Archae-
          ology.* ed. by J. Gero and M. Conkey, pp. 224–254. Basil Blackwell, Oxford, England.
Brunson, Judy
  1985   Cushing's Los Muertos: The Dead Will Rise Again. Paper presented at the annual
          meeting of the Society for American Archaeology, May 1–5, Denver, Colorado.
  1989   The Social Organization of the Los Muertos Hohokam: A Reanalysis of Cushing's
          Hemenway Expedition Data. Ph.D. dissertation, Arizona State University, Tempe,
          Arizona.
Bukharin, Nikolai Ivanovich
  1969   *Historical Materialism.* University of Michigan Press, Ann Arbor, Michigan.
Bulkin, V. A., L. S. Klejn, and G. S. Lebedev
  1982   Attainments and Problems of Soviet Archaeology. *World Archaeology* **13:**272–295.
Canby, Thomas Y.
  1982   The Anasazi: Riddles in the Ruins. *National Geographic* **162**(5):562–592.

Carlson, R. L.
 1982   The Mimbres Katchina Cult. *In Mogollon Archaeology: Proceedings of the 1980 Mogollon Conference.* ed. by P. H. Beckett, 147–156. Acoma Books, Ramona, California.
Carneiro, Robert
 1970   A Theory of Origin of the State. *Science* **169**:733–738.
Cassell, Mark S.
 1988   "Farmers of the Northern Ice": Relations of Production in the Traditional North Alaskan Inupiat Whale Hunt. *Research in Economic Anthropology* **10**:89–116.
Castetter, Edward F. and Willis H. Bell
 1951   *Yuman Indian Agriculture: Primitive Subsistence on the Lower Colorado and Gila Rivers.* University of New Mexico Press, Albuquerque, New Mexico.
Catlin, George
 1841   *North American Indians, Being Letters and Notes on Their Manners, Customs, Written During Eight Years of Travel Amongst the Wildest Tribes of Indians in America.* 3 vols. John Grant, Edinburgh, Scotland.
Chabot, Nancy Jo
 1988   The Women of Yorvik. *Archaeological Review from Cambridge* **7**(1):67–76.
 1990   A Man Called Lucy: Self-Reflections in a Museum Display. *In Writing the Past in the Present.* ed. by F. Baker and J. Thomas, pp. 18–23. Saint David's University College, Lampeter, Wales.
Chang, Kwang-Chih
 1967   *Rethinking Archaeology.* Random House, New York.
Chard, Chester S.
 1969   *Man in Prehistory.* McGraw-Hill, New York.
Chase, A. K.
 1989   Perceptions of the past among North Queensland aboriginal people: The Intrusion of Europeans and consequent social change. *In Who Needs the Past?* ed. by Robert Layton, pp. 95–104. Unwin Hyman, London, England.
Chase-Dunn, Christopher
 1989   *Global Formation: Structures of the World Economy.* Basil Blackwell, Oxford, England.
Cheek, Annetta L.
 1990   Saving the past for the future: Implications for the profession. *SAA Bulletin* **8**(4):8–9.
Chernykh, E. N.
 Ancient Metallurgy in the USSR, in press. University of Cambridge Press, Cambridge, Massachusetts.
Childe, V. Gordon
 1944   *Progress and Archaeology.* Cobbett, London, England.
 1946a   *What Happened in History.* Penguin Books, New York.
 1946b   *Scotland before the Scots.* Methuen, London, England.
 1947   *History.* Cobbett, London, England.
 1950   The urban revolution. *Town Planning Review* **21**(1):3–17.
 1951a   *Man Makes Himself.* New American Library, New York.
 1951b   *Social Evolution.* Schuman, New York.
 1956   *Society and Knowledge: The Growth of Human Traditions.* Harper, New York.
 1958   *The Prehistory of European Society.* Penguin, Harmondsworth, England.
 1989   Retrospect. *The Pastmasters: Eleven Modern Pioneers of Archaeology.* ed. by G. Daniel and C. Chippendale, pp. 10–19. Thames and Hudson, London, England.
Chippindale, Christopher
 1985   Time for a Stonehenge celebration. *Current Archaeology* **98**:84–85.
Choy, Emilio
 1960   La Revolución Neolítica en los Orígenes de la Civilización Americana. *In Antiguo Peru,* ed. by Ramiro Matos, pp. 149–198. Libreria Editorial Juan Mejia Baca, Lima, Peru.

Claassen, Cheryl P.
    1991   Gender, shellfishing, and the shell mound archaic. *In Engendering Archaeology.* ed. by J.
            Gero and M. Conkey, pp. 255–275. Basil Blackwell, Oxford, England.
Claassen, Henri J. M.
    1984   The internal dynamics of the early state. *Current Anthropology.* **25**(4):365–379.
Clark, J. G. D.
    1939   *Archaeology and Society.* Methuen, London, England.
    1952   *Prehistoric Europe: The Economic Base.* Methuen, London, England.
    1970   *Aspects of Prehistory.* University of California Press, Berkeley, California.
    1976   Prehistory before Childe. *Bulletin of the Institute of Archaeology, University of London*
            13:1–21.
Clark, Lynn
    1987   Gravestones: Reflectors of ethnicity or class? *In Consumer Choice in Historical Archae-
            ology.* ed. by S. M. Spencer-Wood, pp. 383–396. Plenum Press, New York.
Clarke, David L.
    1968   *Analytical Archaeology.* Columbia University Press, New York.
Cleere, Henry
    1988   Whose archaeology is it anyway? *In Extracting Meaning From the Past.* ed. by John
            Bintliff, pp. 2–36. Oxbow Books, Oxford, England.
Cohen, G. A.
    1978   *Karl Marx's Theory of History: A Defense.* Oxford University Press, Oxford, England.
Cohen, Lizabeth
    1980   Embellishing a life of labor: An interpretation of the material culture of American
            working-class homes, 1885–1915. *Journal of American Culture* **3**(4):752–775.
Cohen, Ronald and Elman R. Service
    1978   *Origins of the State: The Anthropology of Political Evolution.* Institute for the Study of
            Human Issues, Philadelphia, Pennsylvania.
Collins, Jane
    1990   Unwaged labor in comparative perspective. *In Work Without Wages,* ed. by J. Collins
            and M. Gimenez, pp. 3–24. SUNY Press, Albany, New York.
Collins, Jane, and Martha Gimenez (eds)
    1990   *Work without Wages.* SUNY Press, Albany, New York.
Commager, Henry Steele
    1975   *Jefferson, Nationalism and the Enlightenment.* George Braziller, New York.
Condori, Carlos Mamami
    1989   History and prehistory in Bolivia: What about the Indians? *In Conflicts in the Archae-
            ology of Living Traditions.* ed. by Robert Layton, pp. 46–59. Unwin Hyman, London,
            England.
Conkey, Margaret
    1978   An Analysis of Design Structure Variability among Magdalenian Engraved Bones from
            Northcoastal Spain. Ph.D. dissertation, Department of Anthropology, University of
            Chicago, Chicago, Illinois.
    1989   The structural analysis of Paleolithic art. *In Archaeological Thought in America.* ed. by C.
            C. Lamberg-Karlovsky, pp. 135–154. Cambridge University Press, Cambridge, Mas-
            sachusetts.
    1991   Contests of action, contexts for power: Material culture and gender in the Magdale-
            nian. *In Engendering Archaeology.* ed. by J. Gero and M. Conkey, pp. 57–92. Basil
            Blackwell, Oxford, England.
Conkey, Margaret W., and Janet Spector
    1984   Archaeology and the study of gender. *Advances in Archaeological Method and Theory* **7**:1–29.
Conkey, Margaret, and Joan Gero
    1991   Tensions, pluralities, and engendering archaeology: An introduction to women and

prehistory. *In Engendering Archaeology.* ed. by J. Gero and M. Conkey, pp. 3–30. Basil Blackwell, Oxford, England.

Cordell, Linda S.
  1979   *Cultural Resources Overview: Middle Rio Grande Valley, New Mexico.* USDA Forest Service, Albuquerque, New Mexico.
  1984   *Prehistory of the Southwest.* Academic Press, New York.
  1986   Women Archaeologists in the Southwest. Paper presented at the Wenner-Gren Conference, Daughters of the Desert, March 12–23, Tucson, Arizona.

Cordell, Linda S., and F. Plog
  1979   Escaping the Confines of Normative Thought: A Reevaluation of Puebloan Prehistory. *American Antiquity* **44**, 405–429.

Cowgill, George L.
  1975a   Population Pressure as a Non-Explanation. *American Antiquity* **40**(2):127–131.
  1975b   A Selection of Samplers: Comments on Archaeo-statistics. *In Sampling in Archaeology,* ed. by J. W. Mueller, pp. 258–276. University of Arizona Press, Tucson, Arizona.

Crosby, Constance
  1988   From Myth to History. or Why King Philip's Ghost Walks Abroad. *In The Recovery of Meaning: Historical Archaeology in the Eastern United States,* ed. by M. P. Leone and P. B. Potter, Jr., pp. 183–211. Smithsonian Institution Press, Washington, D.C.

Crown, Patricia L.
  1990   The Hohokam of the American Southwest. *Journal of World Prehistory* **4**(2):223–255.
  1991   The Role of Exchange and Interaction in Salt-Gila Basin Hohokam Prehistory. *In Exploring the Hohokam: Prehistoric Desert Peoples of the American Southwest,* ed. by G. J. Gumerman, pp. 383–416. University of New Mexico Press, Albuquerque, New Mexico.

Crumley, Carol L. and William Marquart
  1987   *Regional Dynamics: Burgundian Landscapes in Historical Perspective.* Academic Press, Orlando, Florida.

Cummings, Byron
  1930a   An Outline of the Casa Grande Ruins Pagaent. *Progressive Arizona and the Great Southwest* **10**(3):16–18.
  1930b   Casa Grande Pageant: The People of the Casa Grande Valley, M.S. on file, Casa Grande National Park, Arizona.

Cushing, Frank Hamilton
  1886   A Study of Pueblo Pottery as Illustrative of Zuni Cultural Growth. *Fourth Annual Report of the Bureau of American Ethnology,* pp. 467–521. Washington, D.C.

Dahlberg, Frances
  1981   *Women the Gatherer.* Yale University Press, New Haven, Connecticut.

Dahlgren, Barbra
  1979   *Mesoamérica: Homenaje al Doctor Paul Kirchoff.* Instituto Nacional de Antropoloía e Historia, México.

Dalton, G.
  1961   Economic Theory and Primitive Society. *American Anthropologist* **63**:1–25.

D'Altroy, Terence N. and Timmothy Earle
  1982   Staple Finance, Wealth Finance, and Storage in the Inka Political Economy. *In Current Anthropology* **26**(2):187–206.

Daniels, Glyn
  1981   *A Short History of Archaeology.* Thames and Hudson, London, England.
  1983   Foreward. to *Man Makes Himself.* by V. Gordon Childe, New American Library, New York.

Davis, Hester
  1990   Public Archaeology Forum. *Journal of Field Archaeology* **17**(2):211–216.

de. Ste. Croix, G. E. M.
   1982   *The Class Struggle in the Ancient Greek World.* Duckworth, London, England.
DeCicco, Gabriel
   1988   A Public Relations Primer. *American Antiquity* **53**(4):840–856.
Deetz, James D.
   1977   *In Small Things Forgotten.* Anchor Press, Garden City, New York.
Deloria, Vine, Jr.
   1968   *Custer Died For Your Sins.* The Macmillan Co., London, England.
   1973   *God is Red.* Grosset and Dunlap, New York.
Deloria, Vine Jr. and Clifford Lytle
   1984   *The Nations Within: The Past and Future of American Indian Sovereignty.* Pantheon
           Books, New York.
Derrida, J.
   1978   *Writing and Difference.* Routledge & Kegan Paul, London, England.
Diamond, Stanley
   1974   *In Search of the Primitive: A Critique of Civilization.* Transaction Books, New Brunswick,
           New Jersey.
Dincauze, Dena F. and Robert J. Hasenstab
   1989   Explaining the Iroquois: Tribalization on a Prehistoric Periphery. *In Centre and Periph-
           ery.* ed. by T. Champion, pp. 67–87. Unwin and Hyman, London, England.
Di Peso, Charles C.
   1956   The Upper Pima Indians of San Cayetano del Tumacacori. *Amerind Foundation Publica-
           tion 7.* Amerind Foundation, Dragoon, Arizona.
Di Peso, Charles C.
   1979   Prehistory: Southern Periphery. In Southwest, edited by Alfonso Ortiz, pp. 152–161.
           Handbook of North American Indians 9, William C. Sturtevant, general editor. Smithso-
           nian Institution, Washington, D.C.
Dippie, Brian W.
   1982   *The Vanishing American White Attitudes and U.S. Indian Policy.* Wesleyan University
           Press, Middletown, Connecticut.
Dobe, Maurice
   1946   *Studies in the Development of Capitalism.* International Publishers, New York.
Dobres, Marcia Ann
   1988   Feminist Archaeology and Inquiries into Gender Relations: Some Thoughts on Uni-
           versals, Origins Stories, and Alternating Paradigms. *Archaeological Review from Cam-
           bridge* **7**(1):30–34.
Doelle, William H., Frederick W. Huntington, and Henry D. Wallace
   1986   Rincon Phase Community Reorganization in the Tucson Basin. *In The Hohokam Vil-
           lage.* edited by D. Doyel. American Association for the Advancement of Sciences,
           Symposium Proceedings.
Dolitsky, Alexander
   1989   Glasnost Digs Out From the Past: A Personal View. *SAA Bulletin* **8**(4):7.
Dommasnes, Liv Helga
   1982   Late Iron Age in Western Norway. Female Roles and Ranks as Deduced From an
           Analysis of Burial Customs. *Norwegian Archaeological Review* **1**:70–84.
   1990   Feminist Archaeology: Critique or Theory Building? *In Writing the Past in the Present.*
           ed. by F. Baker and J. Thomas, pp. 24–31. St. Davids University College, Lampeter,
           Wales.
Doyel, David
   1974   Excavations in the Escalante Ruin Group, Southern Arizona. *Arizona State Museum
           Archaeological Series 37.* Tucson, Arizona.
   1980   Hohokam Social Organization and the Sedentary to Classic Transition. In Current

Issues in Hohokam Prehistory. ed. by David Doyel and Fred Plog, pp. 23–40. *Arizona State University Anthropological Research Paper 23.* Tempe, Arizona.

Drennan, Robert and Carlos Uribe (editors)

1987 *Chiefdoms in the Americas.* University Presses of America, Boston, Massachusetts.

Dunnell, Robert C.

1980 Evolutionary Theory and Archaeology. *In Advances in Archaeological Method and Theory, vol. 3.* ed. by Michael B. Schiffer, pp. 35–99. Academic Press, New York.

1986 Five Decades of American Archaeology. *In American Archaeology Past and Future.* ed. by D. J. Meltzer, D. D. Fowler and J. A. Sabloff, pp. 23–52. Smithsonian Institution Press, Washington, D.C.

1989 Aspects of the Application of Evolutionary Theory in Archaeology. *In Archaeological Thought in America.* ed. by C. C. Lamberg-Karlovsky, pp. 35–49. Cambridge University Press, Cambridge, Massachusetts.

Earle, Timothy K.

1987 Specialization and the Production of Wealth: Hawaiian Chiefdoms and the Inka Empire. *In Specialization, Exchange, and Complex Societies,* ed. by E. M. Brumfiel and T. K. Earle, pp. 64–75. Cambridge University Press, Cambridge, Massachusetts.

Earle, Timothy K. and Robert W. Preucel

1987 Processual Archaeology and the Radical Critique. *Current Anthropology* **28**:501–538.

Echo-Hawk, Walter R.

1986 Museum Rights vs. Indian Rights: Guidelines for Assessing Competing Legal Interests in Native Cultural Resources. *New York University Review of Law* **14**(2):437–53.

Eddy, Frank W.

1984 *Archaeology: A Cultural-Evolutionary Approach.* Prentice-Hall, Englewood Cliffs, New Jersey.

Edwards, Philip C.

1989 Revising the Broad Spectrum Revolution. *Antiquity* **63**(239):225–246.

Effland, Richard W., Jr.

1987 Emotions, Learning, and Understanding: Critical Concepts for Arizona's Native American and Archaeological Communities. Paper presented at the symposium Indians and Archaeologists, Arizona State University, January 13 and 14, Tempe, Arizona.

Eggan, Fred

1983 Comparative Social Organization. *Handbook of North American Indians, Southwest* 10, ed. by Alfonso Ortiz, pp. 723–742. Smithsonian Institution, Washington, D.C.

Ehrenberg, Margaret

1989 *Women in Prehistory.* University of Oklahoma Press, Norman, Oklahoma.

Eighmy, Jeffrey and Randall H. McGuire

1988 Archaeomagnetic Dates and the Hohokam Phase Sequence. *Colorado State University Archaeomagnetic Lab Technical Series 3.* Fort Collins, Colorado.

Ekholm, K. and J. Friedman

1982 "Capital", Imperialism and Exploitation in Ancient World Systems. *Review* **4**:87–109.

Emerson, E. W. & W. E. Forbes (editors)

1914 *Journals of Ralph Waldo Emerson.* 10 Vols. Houghton Mifflin, Boston, Massachusetts.

Emerson, Thomas E. and Paula G. Cross

1990 The Sociopolitics of the Living and the Dead: The Treatment of Historic and Prehistoric Remains in Contemporary Midwest America. *Death Studies* **14**:555–576.

Engels, Fredrick

1888 Annotations for *The Communist Manifesto.* Appleton-Century-Crofts, New York.

1895 The Part Played by Labour in the Transition from Ape to Man. *Dir Neue Zeit* **14**:23–38.

1927 *The Dialectics of Nature.* Foreign Language Publishers, Moscow.

1954 *Anti-Dühring.* Foreign Language Publishers, Moscow.

1972   *The Origins of the Family Private Property and the State.* International Publishers, New York.

Ericson, Jonathon E., and Timothy K. Earle
1982   *Contexts for Prehistoric Exchange.* Academic Press, New York.

Every, Dale Van
1966   *Disinherited.* Avon, New York.

Fabian, Johannes
1983   *Time and the Other: How Anthropology Makes Its Object.* Columbia University Press, New York.

Fagan, Brian M.
1985   *In the Beginning: An Introduction to Archaeology.* 5th Ed. Little, Brown, Boston, Massachusetts.

1991   Editorial. *Antiquity* **65**:183–191.

Fedigan, Linda Marie
1986   The Changing Role of Women in Models of Human Evolution. *Annual Review of Anthropology* **15**:25–66.

Feher, Frank Heller and G. Markus
1983   *Dictatorship Over Needs.* Basil Blackwell, Oxford, England.

Feinman, Gary and Jill Neitzel
1984   Too Many Types: An Overview of Prestate Sedentary Societies in the Americas. *Advances in Archaeological Method and Theory* **7**:39–102.

Ferguson, T. J.
1984   Archaeological Ethics and Values in a Tribal Cultural Resource Management Program at the Pueblo of Zuni. *In Ethics and Values in Archaeology.* ed. by E. L. Green, pp. 224–236. Free Press, New York.

1991   Zuni Archaeology and Culture History. *Zuni History* **1**:3–4.

Fetscher, Iring
1970   *Karl Marx and Marxism.* Herder, New York.

Fewkes, Jesse W.
1896   The Prehistoric Culture of Tusayan. *American Anthropologist* **9**:151–174.

Fish, Suzanne K., Fish Paul R., and John H. Madsen
1990   Analyzing Regional Agriculture: A Hohokam Example *In The Archaeology of Regions: A Case for Full-Coverage Survey.* ed. by S. K. Fish and S. A. Kowalewski, pp. 189–218. Smithsonian Institution Press, Washington, D.C.

Fish, Suzanne K. and Stephen A. Kowalewski (editors)
1990   *The Archaeology of Regions: A Case for Full-Coverage Survey.* Smithsonian Institution Press, Washington, D.C.

Fixico, Donald L.
1986   *Termination and Relocation: Federal Indian Policy 1945–1960.* University of New Mexico Press, Albuquerque, New Mexico.

Flannery, Kent V.
1968   The Olmecs and the Valley of Oaxaca: A Model for Interaction in Formative Times. *Dumbarton Oaks Conference on the Olmec.* 79–110. Washington, D.C.

1972   The Cultural Evolution of Civilizations. *Annual Review of Ecology and Systematics* **3**:399–426.

1982   The Golden Marshalltown: A Parable for the Archaeology of the 1980s. *American Anthropologist* **2**:265–278.

Flannery, Kent V. and Joyce Marcus
1983   *The Cloud People.* Academic Press, New York.

Fleming, Andrew and Matthew Johnson
1990   The Theoretical Archaeology Group (TAG): Origins, Retrospect, Prospect. *Antiquity* **64**:303–306.

Folbre, Nancy
    1985   Cleaning House: New Perspectives on Households and Economic Development. Paper presented at the U.N. University's Conference on New Directions in Development Theory, Boston, Massachusetts.
Ford, James A.
    1962   A Quantitative Method for Deriving Cultural Chronology. *Pan-American Union, Technical Manual 1*, Washington, D.C.
Ford, Richard I.
    1973   Archaeology Serving Humanity. *In Research and Theory Current Archaeology.* ed. by Charles Redman, pp. 83–93. John Wiley, New York.
Ford, R. I., A. H. Schroeder and S. L. Peckham
    1972   Three Perspectives on Pueblo Prehistory. *In New Perspectives on the Pueblos.* ed. by Alfonso Ortiz, pp. 19–39. University of New Mexico Press, Albuquerque, New Mexico.
Forde, C. Daryll
    1931   Ethnography of the Yuma Indians. *University of California Publications in American Archaeology and Ethnology 28.* Berkeley, California.
Foucault, Michel
    1974   *The Order of Things.* Tavistock, London, England.
    1979   *Discipline and Punish: The Birth of the Prison.* Vintage, New York.
    1984   *The Foucault Reader.* Pantheon, New York.
Fowler, Don D.
    1986   Conserving American Archaeological Resources. *In American Archaeology Past and Future.* ed. by D. J. Meltzer, D. D. Fowler and J. A. Sabloff, pp. 135–162. Smithsonian Institution Press, Washington, D.C.
    1987   Uses of the Past: Archaeology in the Service of the State. *American Antiquity* 52(2):229–248.
Fowler, Don D. and Catherine S. Fowler
    1991   The Use of Natural Man in Natural History. *In Columbian Consequences 3: The Spanish Borderlands in Pan-American Perspective,* ed. by D. H. Thomas, pp. 37–71. Smithsonian Institution Press, Washington, D.C.
Francis, Julie E.
    1991   Gender Studies in Plains Anthropology: A Commentary to the 1987 Symposium. *Plains Anthropologist* **36**:77–84.
Frank, Andrew Gunder
    1967   *Capitalism and Underdevelopment in Latin America.* Monthly Review Press, New York.
Frankenstein, Susan and Michael J. Rowland
    1978   The Internal Structure and Regional Context of Early Iron Age Society in South-Western Germany. *London University Institute of Archaeology Bulletin* **15**, 73–112.
Fried, Morton H.
    1967   *The Evolution of Political Society.* Random House, New York.
    1968   On the Concept of the "Tribe" and "Tribal Society." *In Essays on the Problems of Tribe.* ed. by June Helm, pp. 3–24. American Ethnological Society, University of Washington Press, Seattle, Washington.
Friedman, Jonathan
    1974   Marxism, Structuralism and Vulgar Materialism. *Man* 9:444–469.
    1979   *System, Structure and Contradiction.* The National Museum of Denmark, Copenhagen, Denmark.
    1989   Culture, Identity and World Process. *In Domination and Resistance.* ed. by D. Miller, C. Tilley, and M. Rowlands, pp. 246–260. Unwin and Hyman, London, England.
Friedman, Jonathan and Michael Rowlands (editors)
    1978   *The Evolution of Social Systems.* Duckworth, London, England.

Frisby, David and Derek Sayer
    1986.   *Society*. Ellis Horwood Ltd., London, England.
Fritz, John M. and Fred Plog
    1970   The Nature of Archaeological Explanation. *American Antiquity* **35**(4):405–412.
Fromm, Eric
    1942   *Fear of Freedom*. Routledge & Kegan Paul, London.
    1961   *Marx's Concept of Man*. Fredrick Ungar, New York.
Gailey, Christine Ward
    1985   The State of the State in Anthropology. *Dialectical Anthropology* **9**(1–4):65–91.
    1987   Culture Wars: Resistance to State Formation. *In Power Relations State Formation*. ed. by
             T. C. Patterson and C. W. Gailey, pp. 35–56. American Anthropological Association,
             Washington, D.C.
Gailey, Christine W., and Thomas C. Patterson
    1987   Power Relations and State Formation. *In Power Relations and State Formation*. ed. by C.
             W. Gailey and T. C. Patterson, pp. 1–26. American Anthropological Association,
             Washington, D.C.
Gandara, Manuel
    1981   La Vieja "Nueva Arqueología." *Boletín de Antropología Americana* **3**:7–70.
Gasser, Robert
    1976   Hohokam Subsistence: A 2000-Year Continuum in the Indigenous Exploitation of the
             Lower Sonoran Desert. *USDA Forest Service Southwestern Region Archaeological Report
             11*. Albuquerque, New Mexico.
Gathercole, Peter
    1989   Childe's Early Marxism. *In Critical Traditions in Contemporary Archaeology*. ed. by A.
             Wylie and V. Pinsky, pp. 68–79. Cambridge University Press, Cambridge, Mas-
             sachusetts.
Geertz, Clifford
    1980   *Negara: The Theater State in Nineteenth-Century Bali*. Princeton University Press,
             Princeton, New Jersey.
Geras, Norman
    1988   Ex-Marxism Without Substance: Being a Reply to Laclau and Mouffe. *New Left Review*
             169:34–62.
Gerbi, Antonello
    1973   *The Dispute Over the New World: The History of a Polemic, 1750–1900*. University of
             Pittsburgh Press, Pittsburgh, Pennsylvania.
Gero, Joan M.
    1983   Gender Bias in Archaeology: A Cross-cultural Perspective. *In* The Socio-Politics of
             Archaeology. *University of Massachusetts, Department of Anthropology Research Report 23*.
             ed. by J. M. Gero, pp. 51–57. Amherst, Massachusetts.
    1985   Socio-politics and the Women-at-home Ideology. *American Antiquity* **50**:342–
             350.
    1989   Producing Prehistory, Controlling the Past: The Case of New England Beehives. *In
             Critical Traditions in Contemporary Archaeology*. ed. by A. Wylie and V. Pinsky, pp. 96–
             103. Cambridge University Press, Cambridge, Massachusetts.
    1990   Review of *Women in Prehistory*. *American Anthropologist* **92**(4):1033.
    1991   Genderlithics: Women's Role in Stone Tool Production. *In Engendering Archaeology*.
             ed. by J. Gero and M. Conkey, pp. 163–193. Basil Blackwell, Oxford, England.
Gero, Joan, David M. Lacy, and Michael L. Blakey
    1983   The Socio-Politics of Archaeology. *Research Report 23, Department of Anthropology,
             University of Massachusetts*, Amherst, Massachusetts.
Gero, Joan M. and Margaret W. Conkey (editors)
    1991   *Engendering Archaeology: Women and Prehistory*. Basil Blackwell, Oxford, England.

Geuss, Raymond
    1981   *The Idea of Critical Theory: Habermas and the Frankfurt School.* Cambridge University
            Press, Cambridge, Massachusetts.
Giddens, Anthony
    1984   *The Constitution of Society.* Polity Press, Cambridge, Massachusetts.
Gila River Indian Community
    1982   Archaeological Licenses Ordinance No. GR-01-82.
Gilchrist, Ruberta
    1988   The Spatial Archaeology of Gender Domains: A Case Study of Medieval English
            Nunneries. *Archaeological Review from Cambridge* 7(1):21–29.
Gilman, Antonio
    1981   The Development of Social Stratification in Bronze Age Europe. *Current Anthropology*
            22(1):1–24.
    1984   Explaining the Upper Paleolithic Revolution. *In Marxist Perspectives in Archaeology.* ed.
            by Matthew Spriggs, pp. 115–126. Cambridge University Press, Cambridge, Mas-
            sachusetts.
    1989   Marxism in American Archaeology. *In Archaeological Thought in America,* ed. by C. C.
            Lamberg-Karlovsky, pp. 63–73. Cambridge University Press, Cambridge, Mas-
            sachusetts.
Gjessing, Gutorm
    1963   Archaeology, Nationalism, and Society. *American Anthropological Association Memoir*
            94:261–267.
Glassie, Henry
    1975   *Folk Housing in Middle Virginia.* University of Tennessee Press, Knoxville, Tennessee.
Gledhill, John
    1988   Introduction: The Comparative Analysis of Social and Political Transitions. *In State
            and Society.* ed. by J. Gledhill, B. Bender, and M. T. Larsen, pp. 3–21. Unwin and
            Hyman, London, England.
Godelier, Maurice
    1977   *Perspectives in Marxist Archaeology.* Cambridge University Press, Cambridge, Mas-
            sachusetts.
    1980   Processes of the Formation, Diversity and Bases of the State. *International Social Science
            Journal* **32**(4):610–623.
    1982   The Ideal in the Real. *In Culture Ideology and Politics,* ed. by R. Samuel and G. S. Jones,
            pp. 12–38. Routledge & Kegan Paul, London, England.
    1986   *The Mental and the Material: Thought, Economy, and Society.* Verso, London, England.
Goetzmann, W. H. and W. N. Goetzmann
    1986   *The West of the Imagination.* W. W. Norton, New York.
Goldstein, Lynne and Keith Kintigh
    1990   Ethics and the Reburial Controversy. *American Antiquity* **55**(3):585–591.
Golson, Jack
    1989   The Origins and Development of New Guinea Agriculture. *In Foraging and Farming,*
            ed. by Dr. Harris and G. C. Hillman, pp. 678–687. Unwin Hyman, London, England.
Goode, Patrick
    1979   *Karl Korsch.* MacMillan, London, England.
González Marcén, P. and Robert Risch
    1990   Archaeology and Historical Materialism: Outsiders' Reflections on Theoretical Dis-
            cussions in British Archaeology. *In Writing the Past in the Present,* ed. by T. Baker and J.
            Thomas, pp. 95–104. Saint David's University College, Lampeter, Wales.
Gorman, Robert A.
    1982   *Neo-Marxism: The Meaning of Modern Radicalism.* Greenwood Press, Westport, Con-
            necticut.

Gould, Stephen Jay
    1989   *Wonderful Life: The Burgess Shale and the Nature of History.* W. W. Norton and Co., New York.

Gowlett, John
    1984   *Ascent to Civilization: The Archaeology of Early Man.* Alfred Knopf, New York.

Grady, Mark A.
    1976   *Aboriginal Agrarian Adaptation to the Sonoran Desert: A Regional Synthesis and Research Design.* Ph.D. dissertation, Department of Anthropology, University of Arizona, Tucson, Arizona.

Gramsci, Antonio
    1971   *Selections from the Prison Notebooks.* International Publishers, New York.

Green, S.
    1981   *Prehistorian: A Biography of V. Gordon Childe.* Moonraker Press, Bradford-on-Avon, England.

Green, Stanton W. and Stephen Perlman (editors)
    1985   *Archaeology of Frontiers and Boundaries.* Academic Press, New York.

Groube, Les
    1985   The Ownership of Diversity: The Problem of Establishing a National History in a Land of Nine Hundred Ethnic Groups. *In Who Owns the Past?* ed. by Isabel McBryde, pp. 49–74. Oxford University Press, Oxford, England.
    1989   The Taming of the Rain Forests: A Model for Late Pleistocene Forest Exploitation in New Guinea. *In Foraging and Farming.* ed. by D. R. Harris and G. C. Hillman, pp. 688–695. Unwin and Hyman, London, England.

Guenther, Todd R.
    1991   The Horse Creek Site: Some Evidence for Gender Roles in a Transitional Early to Middle Plains Archaic Base Camp. *Plains Anthropologist* **36**:9–25.

Gumerman, George J. (editor)
    1991   *Exploring the Hohokam.* University of New Mexico Press, Albuquerque, New Mexico.

Gumerman, George J. and David A. Philips Jr.
    1978   Archaeology beyond Anthropology. *American Antiquity* **43**:184–191.

Haas, Jonathan
    1982   *The Evolution of the Prehistoric State.* University of Columbia Press, New York.

Habicht-Mauche, Michael Geselowitz, and John Hoopes
    1987   Where's the Chief?: The Archaeology of Complex Tribes. Paper presented at the annual meetings of the Society for American Archaeology, Toronto, Ontario, Canada.

Habermas, Jürgen
    1971   *Knowledge and Human Interests.* Beacon Press, Boston, Massachusetts.
    1974   *Theory and Practice.* Heinemann, London, England.
    1976   *Legitimation Crisis.* Heinemann, London, England.
    1984   *Theory of Communicative Action I.* Heinemann, London, England.

Hack, J. T.
    1942   The Changing Physical Environment of the Hopi Indians of Arizona. *Papers of the Peabody Museum of American Archaeology and Ethnology* **35**:1–85.

Hagan, William T.
    1979   *American Indians.* University of Chicago Press, Chicago, Illinois.

Hall, G. Emlen
    1984   *Four Leagues of Pecos.* University of New Mexico Press, Albuquerque, New Mexico.

Hall, Martin
    1984   The Burden of Tribalism: The Social Context of Southern African Iron-Age Studies. *American Antiquity* **49**(3):455–467.
    1987   *The Changing Past: Farmers, Kings, and Traders in Southern Africa 200–1860.* David Phillip, Capetown, South Africa.

Hall, Robert L.
    1977   An Anthropocentric Perspective for Eastern United States Prehistory. *American Antiquity* **42**(4):499–518.

Hall, Thomas D.
    1989   *Social Changes in the Southwest 1350–1800*. University Press of Kansas, Lawrence, Kansas.

Hammack, Laurens. C., and Alan P. Sullivan (editors)
    1981   The 1968 Excavations at Mound 8 Las Colinas Ruins Group Phoenix, Arizona. *Arizona State Museum Archaeological Series 154*. Tucson, Arizona.

Hammil, Jan and Robert Cruz
    1989   Statement of American Indians against Desecration before The World Archaeological Congress. *In Conflicts in the Archaeology of Living Traditions*. ed. by Robert Layton, pp. 46–59. Unwin Hyman, London, England.

Hammil, Jan and Larry J. Zimmerman
    1983   *Reburial of Human Skeletal Remains: Perspectives From Lakota Spiritual Men and Elders*. University of South Dakota Archaeology Laboratory, Vermillion, South Dakota.

Handsman, Russell G.
    1980   The Domains of Kinship Settlement in Historic Goshen: Signs of a Past Cultural Order. *Artifacts* **9**(1):4–7.
    1981   Early Capitalism and the Center Village of Canaan, Connecticut: A Study of Transformations and Separations. *Artifacts* **9**:1–21.
    1983a   Historical Archaeology and Capitalism, Subscriptions and Separations: The Production of Individualism. *North American Archaeologist* **4**(1):63–79.
    1983b   Towards Archaeological Histories of Robbins Swamp. *Artifacts* **11**(3):1–20.
    1991   Whose Art Was Found at Lepenski Vir? Gender Relations and Power in Archaeology. *In Engendering Archaeology*. ed. by J. Gero and M. Conkey, pp. 329–365. Basil Blackwell, Oxford, England.

Handsman, Russell G. and Mark P. Leone
    1989   Living History and Critical Archaeology in the Reconstruction of the Past. *In Critical Traditions in Contemporary Archaeology* ed. by Valerie Pinsky and Alison Wylie, pp. 117–135, Cambridge University Press, Cambridge, Massachusetts.

Hanson, N. R.
    1969   *Patterns of Discovery*. Cambridge University Press, Cambridge, Massachusetts.

Haraway, Donna J.
    1989   *Primate Visions: Gender, Race, and Nature in the World of Modern Science*. Routledge, New York.
    1991   *Simians, Cyborgs, and Women: The Reinvention of Nature*. Routledge, New York.

Harding, Sandra
    1986   *The Science Question of Feminism*. Cornell University Press, Ithaca, New York.

Hareven, Tamara
    1984   Themes in the Historical Development of the Family. *Review of Child Development Research* **7**:137–178.

Harner, Michael
    1970   Population Pressure and the Social Evolution of Agriculture. *Southwestern Journal of Anthropology* **26**(1):67–86.

Harris, Marvin
    1968   *The Rise of Anthropological Theory*. Crowell, New York.
    1977   *Cannibals and Kings*. Random House, New York.
    1979   *Cultural Materialism: The Struggle for a Science of Culture*. Vintage Books, New York.

Hart, Keith
    1983   The Contribution of Marxism to Economic Anthropology. *In Economic Anthropology*;

Topics and Theories. ed by Sutti Ortiz, pp. 105–146. University Press of America, Lanham, Maryland.

Hartman, Hedi
1981   The Unhappy Marriage of Marxism and Feminism: Towards a More Progressive Union. *In Women and Revolution.* ed. by L. Sargent, pp. 1–41. South End Press, Boston, Massachusetts.

Haselgrove, C.
1982   Wealth, Prestige, and Power: the Dynamics of Late Iron Age Political Centralization in South-east England. *In Ranking, Resource, and Exchange.* ed. by C. Renfrew and S. Shennan, pp. 102–124. Cambridge University Press, Cambridge, Massachusetts.

Hassan, Fekri A.
1981   *Demographic Archaeology.* Academic Press, New York.

Hastorf, Christine A.
1990   One Path to the Heights: Negotiating Political Inequality in the Sausa of Peru. *In The Evolution of Political Systems: Socio-Politics in Small Scale Sedentary Societies.* ed. by Steadman Upham, pp. 146–176. Cambridge University Press, Cambridge, Massachusetts.
1991   Gender, Space, and Food in Prehistory. *In Engendering Archaeology.* ed. by J. Gero and M. Conkey, pp. 132–162. Basil Blackwell, Oxford, England.

Hatton, Alf
1988   Museums and Heritage: Is There Really Any Conflict? *Archaeological Review From Cambridge* 7(2):157–169.

Haudenosaunee Grand Council of Chiefs
1986   Communique regarding the Cultural Patrimony and National Cultural Treasures of the Haudenosaunee. Onondaga Nation, February 2, 1986.

Haury, Emil
1945   The Excavations of Los Muertos and Neighboring Ruins in the Salt River Valley, Southern Arizona. *Peabody Museum Papers, Vol. 24, No. 1.* Harvard University, Cambridge, Massachusetts.
1952   Exploring the Corridors of Time. *The Kiva* 17(3–4):1–24, Arizona Archaeological and Historical Society, Tucson, Arizona.
1962   HH-39: Recollections of a Dramatic Moment in Southwestern Archaeology. *Tree-Ring Bulletin* 24(3–4).
1976   *The Hohokam: Desert Farmers and Craftsmen.* University of Arizona Press, Tucson, Arizona.

Haven, Samuel F.
1856   The Archaeology of the United States. *In Smithsonian Contributions to Knowledge* 8. Washington, D.C.

Haviland, William A. and Marjory W. Power
1981   *The Original Vermonters: Native Inhabitants, Past, and Present.* University of Vermont Press, Hanover, Vermont.

Hawkes, Kristen, K. Hill, and John F. O'Connell
1982   Why Hunters Gather: Optimal Foraging and Atche of Eastern Paraguay. *American Ethnologist* 9:379–398.

Headland, Thomas N. and Lawrence A. Reid
1989   Hunter-Gatherers and Their Neighbors from Prehistory to the Present. *Current Anthropology* 3(1):43–66.

Heckewelder, John
1876 [original 1818].   *History, Manners, and Customs of the Indian Nations Who Once Inhabited Pennsylvania and the Neighboring States.* Arno Press, Philadelphia, Pennsylvania.

Heilbroner, Robert L.

  1980   *Marxism: For and Against.* W. W. Norton and Co., New York.

Held, David

  1980   *Introduction to Critical Theory: Horkheimer to Habermas.* University of California Press, Berkeley, California.

Heller, Agnes (editor)

  1983   *Lukács Revalued.* Basil Blackwell, Oxford, England.

Hemple, Carl G.

  1966   *Philosophy of the Natural Sciences.* Prentice-Hall, Englewood Cliffs, New Jersey.

Henderson, T. Kathleen

  1987   Structure and Organization at La Ciudad. *Anthropological Field Studies 18.* Arizona State University, Tempe, Arizona.

Henry, Donald O.

  1989   *From Foraging to Agriculture: The Levant at the End of the Ice Age.* University of Pennsylvania Press, Philadelphia, Pennsylvania.

Hesse, Mary

  1980   *Revolutions and Reconstructions in the Philosophy of Science.* Indiana University Press, Bloomington, Indiana.

Hewett, Edgar L.

  1930   *Ancient Life in the American Southwest.* Bobbs-Merrill Co., New York.

Hewison, Robert

  1987   *The Heritage Industry: Britain in a Climate of Decline.* Methuen, London, England.

Hill, Christopher

  1975   *The World Turned Upside Down: Radical Ideas during the English Revolution.* Penguin Books, New York.

  1982   *The Century of Revolution, 1603–1714.* Norton and Co., New York.

Hill, James N. (editor)

  1977   *The Explanation of Prehistoric Change.* University of New Mexico Press, Albuquerque, New Mexico.

Hill, Richard

  1977   Reclaiming Cultural Artifacts. *Museum News* **May/June:**43–46.

Hilton, Rodney

  1976   *The Transition from Feudalism to Capitalism.* New Left Books, London, England.

Hindess, B. and P. Q. Hirst

  1975   *Precapitalist Modes of Production.* Routledge & Kegan Paul, London, England.

  1978   *Mode of Production and Social Formation: An Autocritique.* Humanities Press, Atlantic Highlands, New Jersey.

Hirschfelder, A. B. (ed.)

  1982   *American Indian Stereotypes in the World of Children: A Reader and Bibliography.* The Scarecrow Press, Metuchen, New Jersey.

Hoare, Quintin and Geoffrey N. Smith

  1971   General Introduction. *In Selections from the Prison Notebooks,* by Antonio Gramsci, International Publishers, New York.

Hobsbawm, Eric. J.

  1964   Introduction to *Pre-Capitalist Economic Formations,* by Karl Marx, pp. 1–67. International Publishers, New York.

  1967   *Labouring Men: Studies in the History of Labour.* Anchor Books, New York.

  1975   *The Age of Capital 1848–1875.* Scribners, New York.

  1978–82 *The History of Marxism.* Harvester Press, Brighton, England.

  1983   Mass-Producing Traditions: Europe, 1870–1914. *In The Invention of Tradition,* ed. by E. Hobsbawm and T. Ranger, pp. 263–308, Cambridge University Press, Cambridge, Massachusetts.

Hobsbawm, Eric and Terence Ranger (editors)
   1983   *The Invention of Tradition.* Cambridge University Press, Cambridge, Massachusetts.
Hodder, Ian
   1982a   Theoretical Archaeology: A Reactionary View: *In Symbolic and Structural Archaeology.* ed. by Ian Hodder, pp. 1–16. Cambridge University Press, Cambridge, Massachusetts.
   1982b   *Symbols in Action.* Cambridge University Press, Cambridge, Massachusetts.
   1984   Archaeology in 1984. *Antiquity* **58**:25–32.
   1986   *Reading the Past: Current Approaches to Interpretation in Archaeology.* Cambridge University Press, Cambridge, Massachusetts.
   1989   Comments on Archaeology into the 1990s. *Norwegian Archaeological Review* **22**(1):15–18.
   1990   *The Domestication of Europe.* Basil Blackwell, London, England.
Hole, Frank, Kent V. Flannery, and James A. Neely
   1971   Prehistory and Human Ecology of the Deh Luran Plain. *In Prehistoric Agriculture.* ed. by Stuart Struever, pp. 252–312. The Natural History Press, Garden City, New York.
Hole, Frank and Robert F. Heizer
   1973   *An Introduction to Prehistoric Archaeology (3rd Ed.).* Holt, Rinehart & Winston, New York.
Hood, J. Edward
   1985   Hohokam Burial Practices: A Contextual Approach. BA honors thesis, Department of Anthropology, State University of New York at Binghamton, New York.
Hoopes, John
   1988   The Complex Tribe in Prehistory: Sociopolitical Organization in the Archaeological Record. Paper presented at the annual meeting of the Society for American Archaeology, Phoenix, Arizona.
Horkeimer, Max
   1947   *Eclipse of Reason.* Oxford University Press, Oxford, England.
   1974   *Critique of Instrumental Reason.* Seabury, New York.
Horkeimer, Max and Theodor Adorno
   1972   *Dialectic of Enlightenment.* Herder, New York.
Horsman, Reginald
   1967   *Expansion and American Indian Policy.* Michigan State University Press, East Lansing, Michigan.
Howard, Jerry B.
   1985   Courtyard Groups and Domestic Cycling: A Hypothetical Model of Growth. *In* Proceedings of the 1983 Hohokam Symposium 1, ed. by Alfred Dittert Jr. and Donald Dove, pp. 311–326. *Arizona Archaeological Society,* Occasional Paper 2, Phoenix, Arizona.
Hoxie, Frederick E.
   1985   The Indians versus the Textbooks: Is There a Way Out? *Perspectives* **23**:5–17.
Hoy, David Couzens
   1986   Power, Repression, Progress: Foucault, Lukes, and the Frankfurt School. *In Foucault: A Critical Reader,* ed. by David Couzens Hoy, pp. 123–147. Basil Blackwell, New York.
Hrdy, Sarah Blaffer
   1981   *The Woman That Never Evolved.* Harvard University Press, Cambridge, Massachusetts.
Hubert, Jane
   1989   A Proper Place For the Dead. *In Conflicts in the Archaeology of Living Tradition.* ed. by Robert Layton, pp. 46–59. Unwin Hyman, London, England.
Hughes, Robert
   1981   *The Shock of the New.* Alfred Knopf, New York.
Hughes, Susan S.
   1991   Division of Labor at a Besant Hunting Camp in Eastern Montana. *Plains Anthropologist* **36**:25–50.

Hume, Gary W. and Richard A. Boisvert
    1991   New Hampshire SCRAP: An Adult Education Program. Paper presented at the an-
            nual meeting of the Northeastern Anthropological Association, Waterloo, Ontario,
            Canada.
Huntington, Richard, and Peter Metcalf
    1979   *Celebrations of Death: The Anthropology of Mortuary Ritual.* Cambridge University Press,
            Cambridge, Massachusetts.
Isbell, William H. and Katharina J. Schreiber
    1978   Was Huari a State? *American Antiquity.* **43**:372–389.
Isaac, Glynn L.
    1978   The Food-Sharing Behavior of Protohuman Hominids. *Scientific American* pp. 160–
            176. April.
    1984   The Archaeology of Human Origins: Studies of the Lower Pleistocene in East Africa.
            Advances in World Archaeology **3**:1–87.
James, Susan
    1984   *The Content of Social Explanation.* Cambridge University Press, Cambridge, Mas-
            sachusetts.
Jay, Martin
    1973   *The Dialectical Imagination.* Little, Brown, Boston, Massachusetts.
Jefferson, Thomas
    1964 [original 1785].   *Notes on the State of Virginia.* Torchbooks, New York.
Jessop, Bob
    1982   *The Capitalist State.* New York University Press, New York.
Johnson, Allen W. and Timothy Earle
    1987   *The Evolution of Human Society.* Stanford University Press, Stanford, California.
Johnson, Gregory
    1975   Locational Analysis and the Investigation of Uruk Local Exchange Systems. *In Ancient
            Civilization and Trade.* ed. by J. A. Sabloff and C. C. Lamberg-Karlovsky, pp. 285–340.
            University of New Mexico Press, Albuquerque, New Mexico.
    1982   Organizational Structure and Scalar Stress. *In Theory and Explanation in Archaeology.*
            ed. by C. Renfrew, M. J. Rowlands, and B. A. Seagraves, pp. 389–421. Academic Press,
            New York.
Johnson, Matthew H.
    1989   Conceptions of Agency in Archaeological Interpretation. *Journal of Anthropological
            Archaeology* **8**(2):189–211.
Judge, W. J.
    1989   The View from Taos. *Bulletin of the Society for American Archaeology* **7**(5):4.
Judge, W. J., James I. Ebert, and Robert K. Hitchcock
    1975   Sampling in Regional Archaeological Survey. *In Sampling in Archaeology.* ed. by J. W.
            Mueller, pp. 82–123. University of Arizona Press, Tucson, Arizona.
Kahn, Joel S. and Josep R. LLobera (editor)
    1981   *The Anthropology of Pre-Capitalist Societies.* Humanities Press, Atlantic Highlands, New
            Jersey.
Kamenka, Eugene
    1969   *Marxism and Ethics.* St. Martins, New York.
Kautsky, Karl
    1908   *Foundations of Christianity: A Study in Christian Origins.* International Publishers, New
            York.
    1909   *The Road to Power.* S. A. Bloch, Chicago, Illinois.
Keat, Russell and John Urry
    1982   *Social Theory as Science.* Second Ed. Routledge & Kegan Paul, London, England.

Keel, Bernie C., Francis P. McManamon, and George S. Smith
  1990   Looting, Vandalism and Law Enforcement: The Federal Perspective. *SAA Bulletin*
          8(4):10–11.
Keeley, Lawrence H.
  1988   Hunter-Gatherer Economic Complexity and "Population Pressure": A Cross-Cultural
          Analysis. *Journal of Anthropological Archaeology* **7**(4):373–411.
Keen, Benjamin
  1988   *A History of Latin America.* Houghton Mifflin, Boston, Massachusetts.
Keene, Arthur S.
  1983   Biology, Behavior, and Borrowing: A Critical Examination of Optimal Foraging The-
          ory in Archaeology. *In Anthropological Hammers and Theories.* ed. by J. A. Moore and A.
          S. Keene, pp. 137–155. Academic Press, New York.
Keesing, Roger M.
  1987   Anthropology as Interpretive Quest. *Current Anthropology.* **28**(2):161–176.
Keith, Sandra L.
  1987   The Mystery of the Ancient Ones. *Friendly Exchange* **7**(3):10–15.
Kelley, Jane H. and Marsha P. Hanen
  1988   *Archaeology and the Methodology of Science.* University of New Mexico Press, Albuquer-
          que, New Mexico.
Kelley, William H.
  1977   Cocopa Ethnography. *Anthropological Papers of the University of Arizona* 29, Tucson,
          Arizona.
King, Thomas, Patrician Parker Hickman, and Gary Berg
  1977   *Anthropology in Historic Preservation: Caring for Culture's Clutter.* Academic Press, New
          York.
Kintigh, Keith W.
  1991   Archaeological Work at Heshot Ula. *Zuni History* 2:26.
Kipp, Rita Smith and Edward M. Schortmann
  1989   The Political Impact of Trade in Chiefdoms. *American Anthropologist* **91**(2):370–
          385.
Kirch, Patrick Vinton
  1980   The Archaeological Study of Adaptation: Theoretical and Methodological Issues. *In*
          Advances in Archaeological Method and Theory, vol. 3. ed. by Michael B. Schiffer, pp. 101–
          156. Academic Press, New York.
  1984   *The Evolution of Polynesian Chiefdoms.* Cambridge University Press, Cambridge, Mas-
          sachusetts.
Kirchoff, Richard
  1959   The Principle of Clanship in Human Society. *In Readings in Anthropology,* Vol 2, ed. by
          M. H. Fried, pp. 259–70. Crowell, New York.
Kisselburg, Joanne
  1987   The Economy of Community Systems at La Ciudad. *In The Hohokam Community of La*
          Ciudad. ed. by Glen Rice, pp. 173–184. Office of Cultural Resource Management
          Report 67, Department of Anthropology, Arizona State University, Tempe, Arizona.
Klejn, L. S.
  1977   A Panorama of Theoretical Archaeology. *Current Anthropology* **18**:1–42.
Kluckhohn, Clyde and Dorothea Leighton
  1946   *The Navajo.* Harvard University Press, Cambridge, Massachusetts.
Knight, Dean H.
  1991   The Ball Site: A 16-Year Perspective on Archaeological Field Schools. Paper presented
          at the annual meeting of the Northeastern Anthropological Association, Waterloo,
          Ontario, Canada.

Knudson, Ruthann
  1986   Contemporary Cultural Resource Management. *In American Archaeology Past and Future.* ed. by D. J. Meltzer, D. D. Fowler and J. A. Sabloff, pp. 135–162. Smithsonian Institution Press, Washington, D.C.
  1989   North America's Threatened Heritage. *Archaeology* 42(1):71–73, 106.
Kohl, Philip L.
  1979   The "World Economy" of West Asia in the Third Millenium B.C. *In South Asian Archaeology 1977.* ed. by M. Taddei, pp. 55–85. Instituto Universitario Orientale, Naples, Italy.
  1981   Materialist Approaches to Prehistory. *Annual Review of Anthropology* 10:89–118.
  1983   Archaeology and Prehistory. *In Dictionary of Marxist Thought.* ed. by T. Bottomore, L. Harris, V. G. Kiernan, and R. Miliband, pp. 25–28. Harvard University Press, Cambridge, Massachusetts.
  1984   Force, History, and the Evolutionist Paradigm. *In Marxist Perspectives in Archaeology.* ed by M. Spriggs, pp. 127–134. Cambridge University Press, Cambridge, Massachusetts.
  1985   Symbolic, Cognitive Archaeology: A New Loss of Innocence. *Dialectical Anthropology.* 9:105–117.
  1986   The Regional Tradition of Soviet Archaeology: Its Complementary Strengths and Weaknesses. Paper presented at the annual meeting of the Society for American Archaeology, New Orleans, Louisiana.
  1987a   State Formation: Useful Concept or Idée Fixe? *In Power Relations and State Formation.* ed. by T. C. Patterson and C. W. Gailey, pp. 27–34. American Anthropological Association, Washington, D.C.
  1987b   The Use and Abuse of World Systems Theory. *Advances in Archaeological Method and Theory* 11:1–35.
  1988   Limits to a Post-Processual Archaeology. Paper presented at the annual meeting of the Society for American Archaeology, Phoenix, Arizona.
  1989   The Use and Abuse of World Systems Theory: The Case of the "Pristine" West Asian State. *In Archaeological Thought in America.* ed. by C. C. Lamberg-Karlovsky, pp. 218–222. Cambridge University Press, Cambridge, Massachusetts.
Kohl, Philip L. and Rita P. Wright
  1977   Stateless Cities: The Differentiation of Society in the Near Eastern Neolithic. *Dialectical Anthropology.* 2:271–283.
Kolakowski, Leszek
  1978   *Main Currents of Marxism.* Oxford University Press, Oxford, England.
Kornfeld, Marcel
  1991   Approaches to Gender Studies in Plains Anthropology: An Introduction. *Plains Anthropologist* 36:1–8.
Korsch, Karl
  1970a   *Marxism and Philosophy.* New Left Books, New York.
  1970b   *Three Essays on Marxism.* Pluto, London, England.
Kosík, Karel
  1976   *Dialectics of the Concrete: A Study on Problems of Man and World.* D. Reidel Publishing Co., Dordrecht, The Netherlands.
Kottak, Conrad Philip
  1979   *Cultural Anthropology.* Second Ed. Random House, New York.
Krader, Lawrence, (editor)
  1971   *The Ethnological Notebooks of Karl Marx.* Van Gorcum, Assen. The Netherlands.
Kramer, Carol and Miriam Stark
  1988   The Status of Women in Archaeology. *Anthropology Newsletter* 29(9):1, 11–12.
Krass, Dorthy
  1991   Reaching Teachers: Understanding the Native American Experience in Southern New

England. Paper presented at the annual meeting of the Northeastern Anthropological Association, Waterloo, Ontario, Canada.

Kristiansen, Kristian
1981   A Social History of Danish Archaeology. *In Towards a Native of Archaeology*, ed. by Glyn Daniel, pp. 20–44. Thames and Hudson, London, England.
1982   The Formation of Tribal Systems in Later European Prehistory: Northern Europe, 4000–5000 B.C. *In Theory and Explanation in Archaeology*, ed. by Colin Renfrew, M. J. Rowlands and B. A. Segraves, pp. 5–24. Academic Press, New York.
1984   Ideology and Material Culture: An Archaeological Perspective. *In Marxist Perspectives in Archaeology.* ed. by Matthew Spriggs, pp. 72–100. Cambridge University Press, Cambridge, Massachusetts.
1988   The Black and The Red: Shanks and Tilley's Programme for a Radical Archaeology. *Antiquity* **62**(236):473–482.
1989   Paper presented at the Wenner-Gren Conference Critical Approaches in Archaeology: Material Life, Meaning, and Power in Cascais, Portugal.

Kroeber, Alfred L.
1925   Handbook of the Indians of California. *Bureau of American Ethnology Bulletin* 78, Washington, D.C.

Kus, Susan
1982   Matters Materials and Ideal. *In Symbolic and Structural Archaeology.* ed. by Ian Hodder. pp. 47–62. Cambridge University Press, Cambridge, Massachusetts.
1984   The spirit and Its Burden: Archaeology and Symbolic Activity. *In Marxist Perspectives in Archaeology.* ed. by M. Spriggs, pp. 101–107. Cambridge University Press, Cambridge, Massachusetts.
1989a   Sensuous Human Activity and the State: Towards an Archaeology of Bread and Circuses. *In Domination and Resistance.* ed. by D. Miller, C. Tilley, and M. Rowlands, pp. 140–154. Unwin and Hyman, London, England.
1989b   Time is On My Side. Paper presented at the Wenner-Gren Conference Critical Approaches in Archaeology: Material Life, Meaning, and Power, in Cascais, Portugal.

Laclau, Ernesto
1977   *Politics and Ideology in Marxist Theory.* NLB, London, England.

Laclau, Ernst and Chantal Mouffe
1985   *Hegemony and Socialist Strategy, Towards a Radical Democratic Politics.* Verso Press, London, England.

Lafargue, Paul
1910   *The Evolution of Property from Savagery to Civilization.* Charles H. Kerr, Chicago, Illinois.

LaFantasie, Glenn W.
1988   *The Correspondence of Roger Williams.* Brown University Press, Hanover, Rhode Island.

Lamphere, Louise
1986   From Working Daughters to Working Mothers: Production and Reproduction in an Industrial Community. *American Ethnologist* **13**:118–130.

Landau, Miscia
1984   Human Evolution as Narrative. *American Scientist* **72**:262–268.

Larrain, Jorge
1983   *Marxism and Ideology.* Macmillan, London, England.

Larsen, Mogens Trolle
1989   Orientalism and Near Eastern Archaeology. *In Domination and Resistence,* ed. by D. Miller, M. Rowlands, and C. Tilley, pp. 229–239. Unwin and Hyman, London, England.

Layton, Robert (editor)
1989a   *Conflicts in the Archaeology of Living Traditions.* Unwin and Hyman, London, England.

1989b   *Who Needs the Past?* Unwin and Hyman, London, England.
Leacock, Eleanor B.
1972   *Introduction to Origins of the Family, Private Property and the State.* ed. by F. Engels, pp. 7–68. New World Paperbacks, New York.
1981   *Myths of Male Dominance.* Monthly Review Press, New York.
1983   Interpreting the Origins of Gender Inequality: Conceptual and Historical Problems. *Dialectical Anthropology* **7**(4):263–285.
Leaf, Murray J.
1979   *Man, Mind, and Science: A History of Anthropology.* Columbia University Press, New York.
Lee, Richard B.
1990   Primitive Communism and the Origin of Social Inequality. *In The Evolution of Political Systems: Socio-Politics in Small Scale Sedentary Societies.* ed. by Steadman Upham, pp. 225–246. Cambridge University Press, Cambridge, Massachusetts.
Legge, James (translator)
1962   *The Sacred Books of China: The Texts of Taosim.* Dover Publications, New York.
Lekson, Stephen H.
1988   The Idea of the Kiva in Anasazi Archaeology. *The Kiva* **53**(3):213–234.
Lenin, V. I.
1908   *Materialism and Empirio-Criticism.* International Publications, New York.
1918   *The State and Revolution.* 2nd Ed. Foreign Languages Publishing House, Moscow.
1972   *Philosophical Notebooks.* Foreign Language Press, Peking.
Leonard, Robert D.
1989   Resource Specialization, Population Growth, and Agricultural Production in the American Southwest. *American Antiquity* **54**:491–503.
1991   The Change from Small Village to Large Pueblos after A.D. 1275. *Zuni History* **2**:26.
Leone, Mark P.
1972   Archaeology as the Science of Technology: Mormon Townplans and Fences. *In Research and Theory in Current Archaeology.* ed. by C. L. Redman. Wiley and Sons, New York.
1977   The New Mormon Temple in Washington, D.C. *In Historical Archaeology and the Importance of Material Things.* ed. by Leland Ferguson, pp. 43–61. Society for Historical Archaeology. Washington, D.C.
1981   The Relationship between Artifacts and the Public in Outdoor History Museums. *Annuals of the New York Academy Sciences* **376**:301–314.
1982   Some Opinions about Recovering Mind. *American Antiquity* **47**:742–760.
1986   Symbolic, Structural, and Critical Archaeology. *In American Archaeology Past and Future.* ed. by D. J. Meltzer, D. D. Fowler, and J. A. Sabloff, pp. 415–38. Smithsonian Institution Press, Washington, D.C.
1988   The Georgian Order as the Order of Merchant Capitalism in Annapolis, Maryland. *In The Recovery of Meaning: Historical Archaeology in the Eastern United States,* ed. by M. P. Leone and P. B. Potter, Jr., pp. 263–292. Smithsonian Institution Press, Washington, D.C.
Leone, Mark P. and Parker B. Potter, Jr.
1984   *Archaeological Annapolis.* Archaeology in Annapolis, Annapolis, Maryland.
Leone, Mark P., Parker B., Potter, Jr., and Paul A. Shackel
1987   Toward a Critical Archaeology. *Current Anthropology.* **28**:283–302.
Leroi-Gourhan, André
1982   *The Dawn of European Art.* Cambridge University Press, Cambridge, Massachusetts.
Leveillee, Alan
1991   Cultural Resource Management, Educational Programs, and Public Outreach: Syn-

ergistic Experiments in Southeastern New England. Paper presented at the annual meeting of the Northeastern Anthropological Association, Waterloo, Ontario, Canada.

Levins, Richard and Richard Lewontin
   1985   *The Dialectical Biologist.* Harvard University Press, Cambridge, Massachusetts.

Lewis, Kenneth E.
   1984   *The American Frontier.* Academic Press, Orlando, Florida.

Lilley, Ian
   1985   Chiefs without Chiefdoms. Comments on Prehistoric Sociopolitical Organization in Western Melanesia. *Archaeology in Oceania* **20**:60–66.

Linton, Ralph
   1936   *The Study of Man.* Appleton-Century-Crofts, New York.

Little, Barbara, J.
   1988   Craft and Culture Change in the 18th-Century Chesapeake. *In The Recovery of Meaning: Historical Archaeology in the Eastern United States,* ed. by M. P. Leone and P. B. Potter, Jr., pp. 263–292. Smithsonian Institution Press, Washington, D.C.

Little, Barbara J. and Paul A. Shackel
   1989   Archaeology of Colonial Anglo-America. *Antiquity* **63**(240):495–409.

Lorenzo, José L.
   1976   La Arqueolgía Mexicana y los Arqueólogos Norteamericanos. Departmento de Prehistoria INAH, *Cuadernos de Trabajo 14.* Mexico City, Mexico.
   1982   Archaeology South of the Rio Grande. *World Archaeology* **13**(2):190–208.

Lorenzo, José L., Antonio Pérez Lias, and Joaquín García-Bárcena
   1976   *Hacia una Arqueología Social: Reunión de Teotihuacan.* INAH, Mexico City, Mexico.

Lowenthal, David
   1985   *The Past is a Foreign Country.* University of Cambridge Press, Cambridge, Massachusetts.

Lowie, Robert
   1937   *The History of Ethnological Theory.* Holt, Rinehart & Winston, New York.

Lubbock, John
   1869   *Prehistoric Times.* 2nd ed. William and Northgate, London, England.

Lukács, George
   1950   *Studies in European Realism.* Hillway, London, England.
   1954   *Die Zerstörung der Vernumft.* Aufbau, Berlin, Germany.
   1971   *History and Class Consciousness.* MIT Press, Cambridge, Massachusetts.

Lumbreras, Luis G.
   1974   *La Arquealogía como Ciencia Social.* Ediciones Hista, Lima, Peru.

Luxemburg, Rosa
   1913   *The Accumulation of Capital.* Yale University Press, New Haven, Connecticut.
   1961   *The Russian Revolution.* University of Michigan Press, Ann Arbor, Michigan.

Lynott, Mark J.
   1990   Archaeology and Public Relations. *Bulletin of the Society for American Archaeology* **8**(3):2.

MacKenzie, David
   1984   Marx and the Machine. *Technology and Culture* **25**:473–502.

MacKinnon, Catharine A.
   1982   Feminism, Marxism, Method, and the State: An Agenda for Theory: *In Feminist Theory: A Critique of Ideology,* ed. by N. O. Keohane, M. Z. Rosaldo, and B. C. Gelpi, pp. 1–30. University of Chicago Press, Chicago, Illinois.

Males, Antonio
   1989   Past and Present of Andean Indian Society: The Otavalos. *In Who Needs the Past?* ed. by Robert Layton, pp. 95–104. Unwin and Hyman, London, England.

Mandel, Ernest
   1978   *Late Capitalism.* Verso, London.
Mangi, Jo
   1989   The Role of Archaeology in Nation Building. *In Conflicts in the Archaeology of Living Traditions*, ed. by Robert Layton, pp. 217–227. Unwin and Hyman, London, England.
Marcus, George E. and Michael M. J. Fischer
   1986   *Anthropology as Cultural Critique.* University of Chicago Press, Chicago, Illinois.
Marcuse, Herbert
   1955   *Eros and Civilization.* Beacon Press, Boston, Massachusetts.
   1964   *One Dimensional Man.* Beacon Press, Boston, Massachusetts.
   1979   *The Aesthetic Dimension.* Macmillan, London, Massachusetts.
Mariátegui, José Carlos
   1943   *Siete Ensayos de Interpretación de la Realidad Peruana.* Editorial Amauta, Lima, Peru.
Marquardt, William H.
   1988   Politics and Production among the Calusa of South Florida. *In Hunters and Gatherers 1: History, Evolution, and Social Change.* ed. by Tim Ingold, David Riches, and James Woodburn, pp. 161–188. BERG, Oxford, England.
   1989   Agency, Structure, and Power: Operationalizing a Dialectical Anthropological Archaeology. Paper prepared for Symposium no. 108, "Critical Approaches in Archaeology: Material Life, Meaning, and Power," Wenner-Gren Foundation for Anthropological Research, an International symposium, Cascais, Portugal, March 1989.
   n.d.   Dialectical Archaeology. *Archaeological Method and Theory.* (in press)
Marquardt, William and Carole L. Crumley
   1987   Theoretical Issues in the Analysis of Spatial Patterning. *In Regional Dynamics: Burgundian Landscapes in Historical Perspective.* ed. by C. L. Crumley and W. H. Marquardt, pp. 1–18. Academic Press, Orlando, Florida.
Marx, Karl
   1847   Wage Labour and Capital. *In Karl Marx and Friederick Engels Collected Works*, vol 9, Progress Press, Moscow.
   1906   *Capital: A Critique of Political Economy.* The Modern Library, New York.
   1959   *Economic and Philosophic Manuscripts of 1844.* Progress Publishers, Moscow.
   1964   *Pre-Capitalist Economic Formations.* ed. by E. J. Hobsbawn, translated by J. Cohen, International Publishers, New York.
   1967   *Capital.* vol. 3, translated by S. Moore and E. Aveling. International Publishers, New York.
   1968   Preface to a Contribution to the Critique of Political Economy. *In Selected Works.* by K. Marx and F. Engels, translated by S. W. Ryazanskaya, pp. 123–132. Lawrence and Wishart, London, England.
   1970   *A Contribution to the Critique of Political Economy.* Progress Publishers, Moscow.
   1971   *The Poverty of Philosophy.* International Publishers, New York.
   1973   *Grundrisse: Foundations of the Critique of Political Economy.* Allen Lane, London, England.
   1978   *The Eighteenth Brumaire of Louis Bonaparte.* Foreign Language Press, Peking.
Marx, Karl and Frederick Engels
   1848   *The Communist Manifesto.* The Communist League, London, England.
   1970   *The German Ideology.* International Publishers, New York.
   1977   *Selected Letters.* Foreign Language Press, Peking.
Mathews, Cornelius
   1839   *Behemoth: A Legend of the Mound-Builders.* Weeks and Jordon Co., Boston, Massachusetts.

McAllister, Martin
  1976 Hohokam Social Organization: A Reconstruction. M.A. thesis, Department of An-
        thropology, San Diego State University, San Diego, California.
McBryde, Isabel (editor)
  1985 *Who Owns the Past?* University of Oxford Press, Oxford.
McCafferty, S. D. and McCafferty, G. G.
  1988 Powerful Women and the Myth of Male Dominance in Aztec Society. *Archaeological
        Review from Cambridge* 7(1):45–59.
  n.d. Mexican Spinning and Weaving as Female Gender Identity. *In Textile Traditions of
        Mesoamerica and the Andes: An Anthology.* ed. by M. S. Schevill, J. C. Berlo, and N.
        Dwyer. Garland Press, New York. (in press).
McConnell, Brian E.
  1989 Mediterranean Archaeology and Modern Nationalism. Paper presented at the Joint
        Archaeological Congress, Baltimore, Maryland.
McDonald, J. Douglas, Larry J. Zimmerman, A. L. McDonald, William Tall Bull and Ted
  Rising Sun
  1991 The Northern Cheyenne Outbreak of 1879: Using Oral History and Archaeology as
        Tools of Resistance. *In The Archaeology of Inequality*, ed. by R. H. McGuire and R.
        Paynter, pp. 125–150. Basil Blackwell, Oxford, England.
McGimsey, Charles R., III
  1972 *Public Archaeology.* Seminar Press, New York.
McGovern, Thomas H.
  1980 Cows, Harp Seals, and Churchbells: Adaptation and Extinction in Greenland. *Human
        Ecology* 8:245–75.
McGuire, Randall H.
  1983a Breaking Down Cultural Complexity: Inequality and Heterogeneity. *Advances in Ar-
        chaeological Method and Theory* 6:91–142.
  1983b The Role of Shell Trade in the Explanation of Hohokam Prehistory. Paper presented
        at the 1983 Hohokam Conference, Tempe, Arizona.
  1986 Economies and Modes of Production in the Prehistoric Southwestern Periphery. *In
        Ripples in the Chichimec Sea: New Considerations of Southwestern-Mesoamerican Interac-
        tions.* ed. F. J. Mathien and R. H. McGuire, pp. 243–269. Southern Illinois University
        Press, Carbondale, Illinois.
  1987 Death, Society, and Ideology in a Hohokam Community: Colonial and Sedentary
        Period Burials from La Ciudad. *OCRM Report* 68, Arizona State University, Tempe,
        Arizona.
  1988 Dialogues With The Dead: Ideology and the Cemetery. *In The Recovery of Meaning*, ed.
        by M. P. Leone and P. B. Potter, pp. 435–480. Smithsonian Institution Press, Wash-
        ington, D.C.
  1989a The Mexican-American West as a Periphery of Mesoamerica. *In Centre and Periphery.*
        ed. by T. C. Champion, pp. 40–66. Unwin and Hyman, London, England.
  1989b The Sanctity of the Grave: White Concepts and American Indian Burials. *In Conflicts
        in the Archaeology of Living Traditions.* ed. by Robert Layton, pp. 167–184. Unwin and
        Hyman, London, England.
  1991 From the Outside Looking In: The Concept of Periphery in Hohokam Archaeology.
        In Exploring the Hohokam: Prehistoric Desert Dwellers of the Southwest. ed. by G. J.
        Gumerman, University of New Mexico Press, Albuquerque, New Mexico.
  1992 Archaeology and the Vanishing American. *American Anthropologist* **94.**
  n.d.a *Death, Society, and Ideology in the Hohokam Community of La Ciudad*, AD 800 to 1100.
        Westview Press, Boulder, Colorado.

n.d.b   Why Do Archaeologists Think That the Real Indians Are Dead and What Should We Do About It? *In Indians and Anthropologists Since Custer*, ed. by Tom Biolsi and Larry Zimmerman. University of Oklahoma Press, Norman, Oklahoma.

McGuire, Randall H. and Ann Valdo Howard
1987   The Structure and Organization of Hohokam Shell Trade. *The Kiva* **52**(2):113–146.

McGuire, Randall H. and Michael Schiffer
1982   On the Threshold of Civilization: The Hohokam of Arizona. *Archaeology* **Sept/Oct**:22–29.

McGuire, Randall H., Joan Smith, and William G. Martin
1986   Patterns of Household Structures and the World Economy. *Review* **10**(1):75–98.

McGuire, Randall H. and Cynthia Woodsong
1990   Making Ends Meet: Unwaged Work and Domestic Inequality in Broome County, New York, 1930–1980. *In Work Without Wages: Comparative Studies of Domestic Labor and Self-Employment*. ed. by J. L. Collins and Martha Gimenez, pp. 168–192. State University of New York Press, Albany, New York.

McLellan, David
1979   *Marxism after Marx*. The MacMillan Press, London, England.

McLoughlin, William G.
1986   *Cherokee Renascence in the New Republic*. Princeton University Press, Princeton, New Jersey.

McLuhan, T. C.
1985   *Dream Tracks: The Railroad and the American Indian 1890–1930*. Harry N. Abrams, New York.

Meggers, Betty J.
1960   The Law of Cultural Evolution as a Practical Research Tool. *In Essays in the Science of Culture*, ed. by G. E. Dole and R. L. Carniero, pp. 302–315. Crowell, New York.

Meggers, Betty J. and Clifford Evans
1957   Archaeological Investigations at the Mouth of the Amazon. *BAE Bulletin 167*. Washington, D.C.

Mehring, Franz
1962   *Karl Marx*. University of Michigan Press, Ann Arbor, Michigan.

Meighan, Clement W.
1985   Archaeology and Anthropological Ethics. *Anthropology Newsletter* **26**(9):20.

Meillassoux, Claude
1981   *Maidens, Meal, and Money*. Cambridge University Press, London, England.

Mepham, John
1979   The Theory of Ideology in Capital. *In Issue in Marxist Philosophy III* ed. by John Mepham and D. H. Ruben, pp. 141–174. Humanities Press, Atlantic Highlands, New Jersey.

Merleau-Ponty, Maurice
1947   *Humanism and Terror*. Beacon Press, Boston, Massachusetts.
1955   *Adventures of the Dialectic*. Heinemann, London, England.

Merquior, J. G.
1986   *Western Marxism*. Paladin, London, England.

Merriman, Nick
1987   Museums and Archaeology: The Public Point of View. Paper presented at the annual conference of the Society of Museum Archaeologists, Lincoln, Nebraska.
1988   The Heritage Industry Reconsidered. *Archaeological Review from Cambridge* 7(2):146–156.

Miller, Daniel
1982   Structures and Strategies: An Aspect of the Relationship between Social Hierarchy and

Cultural Change. *In Symbolic and Structural Archaeology.* ed. by Ian Hodder, pp. 89–98. Cambridge University Press, Cambridge.

1987 *Material Culture and Mass Consumption.* Basil Blackwell, Oxford.

Miller, Daniel and Christopher Tilley (eds)
1984 *Ideology, Power, and History.* Cambridge University Press, Cambridge.

Miller, M. O.
1956 *Archaeology in the USSR.* Atlantic Press, London.

Mills, Barbara J.
1991 Zuni Ceramic Production and Distribution during the 15th through 17th Centuries. *Zuni History* **2**:27.

Mindeleff, Victor
1891 A Study of Pueblo Architecture. *Eighth Annual Report of the Bureau of Ethnology.* Washington, D.C.

Mintz, Sidney
1974 *Worker in the Cane.* 2nd Ed. Norton, New York.
1985 *Sweetness and Power — the Place of Sugar in Modern History.* Viking, New York.

Mitchell, Douglas R.
1991a An Investigation of Two Classic Period Hohokam Cemeteries. *North American Archaeologist* **12**(2):109–127.
1991b Burials and Households: A Preliminary Spatial Analysis of a Large Hohokam Cemetery. Paper presented at the annual meeting of the Society for American Archaeology, New Orleans, Louisiana.

Mitchell, Lee Clark
1981 *Witness to a Vanishing America.* Princeton University Press, Princeton, New Jersey.

Montena, Julio
1980 *Marxismo y Arqueología.* Ediciones de Cultura Popular, Mexico City, Mexico.

Moore, Henretta L.
1988 *Feminism and Anthropology.* University of Minnesota Press, Minneapolis, Minnesota.

Moore, James A.
1983 The Trouble with Know-it-alls: Information as a Social and Ecological Resource. *In Anthropological Hammers and Theories.* ed. by J. A. Moore and A. S. Keene, pp. 173–191. Academic Press, New York.

Moore, Stephen
1989 Federal Indian Burial Policy: Historical Anachronism or Contemporary Reality? *In Conflicts in the Archaeology of Living Traditions.* ed. by Robert Layton, pp. 46–59. Unwin and Hyman, London.

Morris, Ann Axtell
1933 *Digging in the Southwest.* Doubleday, Garden City, New Jersey.

Mouffe, Chantal (editor)
1979 *Gramsci and Marxist Theory.* Routledge & Kegan Paul, London, England.

Mouzelis, Nicos
1988 Marxism or Post-Marxism? *New Left Review* **167**:107–123.

Mukhopadhyay, Carol C. and Patricia J. Higgins
1988 Anthropological Studies of Women's Status Revisited: 1977–1987. *Annual Review of Anthropology* **17**:461–475.

Muller, Viana
1985 Origins of Class and Gender Hierarchy in Northwest Europe. *Dialectical Anthropology* **10**(1 + 2):93–106.
1987 Kin Reproduction and Elite Accumulation in the Archaic States of Northwest Europe. *In Power Relations and State Formation.* ed. by T. C. Patterson and C. W. Gailey, pp. 81–97. American Anthropological Association, Washington, D.C.

Mulvaney, John
    1985   A Question of Values: Museums and Cultural Property. *In Who Owns the Past?* ed. by
            Isabel McBryde, pp. 86–98. Oxford University Press, Oxford, England.
Murphy, Robert F.
    1971   *The Dialectics of Social Life.* George Allen and Unwin, London, England.
Murra, John
    1984   An Interview. *Hispanic American Historical Review* **64**(4):633–654.
NARF
    1985   Annual Report 1985, Native American Rights Fund, Boulder, Colorado.
Nance, Jack D.
    1983   Regional Sampling in Archaeological Survey: The Statistical Perspective. *Advances in
            Archaeological Method and Theory* **6**:289–356.
Nash, June
    1979   *We Eat the Mines and the Mines Eat Us.* Columbia University Press, New York.
    1980   Aztec Women: The Transition from Status to Class in Empire and Colony. *In Women
            and Colonization,* ed. by Mona Etienne and Eleanor Leacock, pp. 134–148. Praeger,
            New York.
    1981   Ethnographic Aspects of the World Capitalist System. *Annual Review of Anthropology*
            10:393–423.
NCAI
    1986   Resolution Passed by the National Congress of American Indians, P-86-57-CC, Phoe-
            nix, Arizona, October 1986.
Nelson, Richard S.
    1981   The Role of a Puchteca System in Hohokam Exchange. Ph.D. dissertation, Depart-
            ment of Anthropology, New York University, New York.
Netting, Robert McC.
    1971   The Ecological Approach in Cultural Study. *In A McCaleb Module in Anthropology,*
            Module 6:1–30. Addison-Wesley Modular Publications, Cummings Publishing, Men-
            lo Park, California.
    1990   Population, Permanent Agriculture, and Polities: Unpacking the Evolutionary Port-
            manteau. *In The Evolution of Political Systems: Socio-Politics in Small Scale Sedentary
            Societies.* ed. by Steadman Upham, pp. 21–61. Cambridge University Press, Cam-
            bridge, Massachusetts.
Netting, Robert, Richard R. Wilk, and Eric J. Arnold
    1984   Introduction. *In Households: Comparative and Historical Studies of the Domestic Group.* ed.
            by R. Netting, R. R. Wilk and E. J. Arnold, pp. xiii–xxxviii. University of California
            Press, Berkeley, California.
Nials, Fred L., David Gregory, and Donald Graybill
    1989   Salt River Streamflow and Hohokam Irrigation Systems. *In* The 1982–1984 Excava-
            tions at Las Colinas: Environment and Subsistence. pp. 145–169. *Arizona State Muse-
            um Archaeological Series* 162(5), Tucson, Arizona.
Nocete, Francisco and Arturo Ruiz
    1990   The Dialectic of the Present and the Past in the Construction of a Scientific Archae-
            ology. *In Writing the Past in the Present,* ed. by F. Baker and J. Thomas, pp. 105–112.
            Saint David's University College, Lampeter, Wales.
Noel Hume, Ivor
    1982   *Martins Hundred.* Knopf, New York.
Nordbadh, Jarl
    1989   Comments on Archaeology into the 1990s. *Norwegian Archaeological Review* **22**(1):24–28.
Norman, Richard and Sean Sayers
    1980   *Hegel, Marx and Dialectic: A Debate.* The Harvester Press, Sussex, England.

Nusbaum, Deric
 1926   *Deric in Mesa Verde.* Putnam, New York.
O'Brien, Patricia J.
 1991   Evidence for the Antiquity of Women's Roles in Pawnee Society. *Plains Anthropologist*
     36:51–64.
Ollman, Bertell
 1976   *Alienation.* 2nd Ed. Cambridge University Press, Cambridge, Massachusetts.
Olsen, Bjørnar
 1989   Comments on Archaeology into the 1990s. *Norwegian Archaeological Review* **22**(1):18–21.
Opler, Morris E.
 1961   Cultural Evolution, Southern Athapaskans, and Chronology in Theory. *Southwestern*
     Journal of Anthropology **17**:1–20.
Orser, Charles E. Jr.
 1988   The Archaeological Analysis of Plantation Society: Replacing Studies and Caste with
     Economy and Power. *American Antiquity* **53**(4):735–751.
Ortiz-Aguilu, Juan Jose
 1986   Have Trowel Will Travel: The Socio-Political Impact of Comercial Archaeology in
     Puerto Rico. Paper presented at the World Archaeology Congress, Southampton,
     England.
Orwell, George
 1949   *1984.* Harcourt Brace Jovanovich, New York.
O'Shea, John M.
 1984   *Mortuary Variability: An Archaeological Investigation.* Academic Press, Orlando, Florida.
Page, Jake
 1982   Inside the Sacred Hopi Homeland. *National Geographic* **162**(5):607–629.
Palerm, Ángel
 1980   *Antropología y Marxismo.* Editorial Nueva Imagen, México.
Palerm, Angel and Eric R. Wolf
 1957   Ecological Potential and Cultural Development in Mesoamerica. *In Studies in Human*
     Ecology. pp. 1–37. Anthropological Society of Washington, D.C.
Panameno, R. and E. Nalda
 1978   Arqueologia, Para Quien? *Nueva Antropología* **12**:111–124.
Patterson, Thomas C.
 1973   *America's Past: A New World Archaeology.* Scott, Foresman, London.
 1986   The Last Sixty Years: Towards a Social History of Americanist Archaeology in the
     United States. *American Anthropologist* **88**(1):7–26.
 1987   Tribes, Chiefdoms, and Kingdoms in the Inca Empire. *In Power Relations and State*
     Formation. ed. by T. C. Patterson and C. W. Gailey, pp. 117–127. American An-
     thropological Association, Washington, D.C.
 1988   Savages, Barbarians and Civilized Peoples: The Construction of Americanist Archae-
     ologists in the United States. Paper presented at the Graduate Center, City University
     of New York, October 20.
 1989a History and the Post-Processual Archaeologies. *Man.* **24**(3):555–566.
 1989b Political Economy and a Discourse Called "Peruvian Archaeology." *Culture and His-*
     tory **4**:35–64.
 1990   Some Theoretical Tensions within and between the Processual and Postprocessual
     Archaeologies. *Journal of Anthropological Archaeology* **9**:189–200.
Paynter, Robert
 1981   Social Complexity in Peripheries: Problems and Models. *In Archaeological Approaches to*
     the Study of Complexity, ed. by S. E. van der Leeuw, Universiteit van Amsterdam,
     Amsterdam, The Netherlands.

1983   Field or Factory? Concerning the Degradation of Archaeological Labor. *In The Socio-Politics of Archaeology*, ed. by J. M. Gero, D. M. Lacy and M. L. Blakey, Department of Anthropology, University of Massachusetts, Amherst, Massachusetts.

1985   Surplus Flow between Frontiers and Homelands. *In Archaeology of Frontiers and Boundaries*. ed. by S. W. Green and Stephen Perlman, pp. 125–137. Academic Press, Orlando, Florida.

1989   The Archaeology of Inequality. *Annual Review of Anthropology* **18**:369–99.

Paynter, Robert and Randall H. McGuire

1991   The Archaeology of Inequality: An Introduction. *In The Archaeology of Inequality*. ed. by R. H. McGuire and R. Paynter, pp. 1–11. Basil Blackwell, Oxford, England.

Paz, Octavio

1972   *The Other Mexico: Critique of the Pyramid.* Grove Press, New York.

Pearce, Roy H.

1965   *Savagism and Civilization: A Study of the Indian and the American Mind.* Johns Hopkins University Press, Baltimore, Maryland.

Pearson, Michael Parker

1982   Mortuary Practices, Society and Ideology: An Ethnoarchaeological Study. *In Symbolic and Structural Archaeology.* ed. by Ian Hodder, pp. 99–114. Cambridge University Press, Cambridge, Massachusetts.

1984   Social Change, Ideology, and the Archaeological Record. *In Marxist Perspectives in Archaeology*, ed. by M. Spriggs, pp. 59–70. University of Cambridge Press, Cambridge, Massachusetts.

Peebles, Christopher and Susan M. Kus

1977   Some Archaeological Correlates of Ranked Societies. *American Antiquity* **42**:421–448.

Pepper, George H.

1920   *Pueblo Bonito.* Anthropological Papers of the American Museum of Natural History No. 27, New York.

Piaget, Jean

1954   *The Construction of Reality in the Child.* Basic Books, New York.

Pidgeon, William

1858   *Traditions of De-Coo-Dah.* Horace Thayer, New York.

Pike, Donald G.

1974   *Anasazi: Ancient People of the Rock.* American West Publishing Co., Palo Alto, California.

Pinsky, Valerie and Alison Wylie (editors)

1989   *Critical Traditions in Contemporary Archaeology.* Cambridge University Press, Cambridge, Massachusetts.

Pinsky, Valerie

1989   Introduction: Historical Foundations. *In Critical Traditions in Contemporary Archaeology.* ed. by A. Wylie and V. Pinsky, pp. 51–54. Cambridge University Press, Cambridge, Massachusetts.

Plekhanov, G. V.

1961   *Selected Philosophical Works.* 5 vols. Lawrence and Wishart, London, England.

Plog, Fred

1983   Political and Economic Alliances on the Colorado Plateaus A.D. 400 to 1450. *Advances in World Archaeology* **2**:289–330.

Plog, Fred, Steadman Upham and Phil C. Weigand

1982   A Perspective on Mogollon–Mesoamerican Interaction. *In Mogollon Archaeology: Proceedings of the 1980 Conference.* ed. P. H. Beckett, pp. 227–238. Acoma Books, Ramona, California.

Plog, Stephen
    1990   Agriculture, Sedentarism, and Environment in the Evolution of Political Systems. *In The Evolution of Political Systems: Socio-Politics in Small Scale Sedentary Societies.* ed. by Steadman Upham, pp. 177–202. Cambridge University Press, Cambridge, Massachusetts.
Polanyi, Karl
    1944   *The Great Transformation.* Holt, Rinehart & Winston, New York.
Pollack, Susan
    1991   Women in a Man's World: Images of Sumerian Women. *In Engendering Archaeology.* ed. by J. Gero and M. Conkey, pp. 366–387. Basil Blackwell, Oxford, England.
Poster, Mark
    1984   *Foucault, Marxism and History.* Polity Press, Oxford.
Potter, Parker B., Jr.
    1989   Archaeology in Public in Annapolis: An Experiment in the Application of Critical Theory to Historical Archaeology. Ph.D. dissertation, Department of Anthropology, Brown University, Providence, Rhode Island.
    1990   The "What" and "Why" of Public Relations for Archaeology: A Postscript to DeCicco's Public Relations Primer. *American Antiquity* 55(3):608–613.
    1991   Where do Our Questions Come from, and Where do the Answers Go? Paper presented at the annual meeting of the Society for American Archaeology, New Orleans, Louisiana.
Potts, Richard
    1988   *Early Hominid Activities at Olduvai.* Aldine de Gruyter, New York.
Powell, J. M.
    1982   Plant Resources and Palaeobotanical Evidence for Plant Use in the Papua New Guinea Highlands. *Archaeology in Oceania* 17:28–37.
Powers, R. P., W. B. Gillespie and S. H. Lekson
    1983   *The Outlier Survey.* Reports of the Chaco Center No. 3. National Park Service, Albuquerque, New Mexico.
Prescott, William H.
    1843   *History of the Conquest of Mexico.* J. B. Lippincott Co., Philadelphia, Pennsylvania.
Price, Barbara J.
    1982   Cultural Materialism: A Theoretical Review. *American Antiquity* 47:709–741.
Quick, Polly McW. (editor)
    1985   *Proceedings, Conference on Reburial Issues.* Society for American Archaeology, Washington, D.C.
Quimby, George I.
    1960   Habitat, Culture, and Archaeology. *In Essays in the Science of Culture*, ed. by G. E. Dole and R. L. Carneiro, pp. 380–89. Random House, New York.
Rapp, Rayna
    1978   Gender and Class: An Archaeology of Knowledge concerning the Origin of the State. *Dialectical Anthropology* 2(4):309–314.
    1982   Family and Class in Contemporary America: Notes towards an Understanding of Ideology. *In Rethinking the Family: Some Feminist Questions.* ed. by Barrie Thorne and Marilyn Yalom, pp. 168–187. Longman, New York.
Rathje, William
    1971   The Origin and Development of Lowland Classic Maya Civilization. *American Antiquity.* 36:275–285.
Rathje, William L. and Randall H. McGuire
    1982   Rich Men . . . Poor Men. *American Behavioral Scientist* 25(6):705–716.

Rathje, William L. and Michael B. Schiffer
    1982   *Archaeology.* Harcourt Brace Jovanovich, New York.
Ray, Krishnendu and Ravi Sundaram
    1990   Socialism at the End of the Century: Reflections on an Epoch Passed. *Economic and Political Weekly* **July 21**:1595–1606.
Redman, Charles L.
    1987   Surface Collection, Sampling, and Research Design: A Retrospective. *American Antiquity* **52**(2):249–265.
    1991   In Defense of the Seventies. *American Anthropologist* **93**(2):295–307.
Reid, J. Jefferson, Michael B. Schiffer, and Jeffrey M. Neff
    1975   Archaeological Considerations of Intrasite Sampling. *In Sampling in Archaeology*, ed. by J. W. Mueller, pp. 209–226. University of Arizona Press, Tucson, Arizona.
Renfrew, Colin
    1972   *The Emergence of Civilization: The Cyclades and the Aegean in the Third Millennium* BC. Methuen, London.
    1975   Trade as Action at a Distance: Questions of Integration and Communication. *In Ancient Civilization and Trade*, eds. J. Sabloff and C. C. Lamberg-Karlovsky, pp. 3–59. University of New Mexico Press, Albuquerque, New Mexico.
    1982   Explanation Revisited. *In Theory and Explanation in Archaeology.* ed. by Colin Renfrew, M. J. Rowlands and B. A. Segraves, pp. 5–24. Academic Press, New York.
    1986   Introduction: Peer Polity Interaction and Socio-political Change. In *Peer Polity Interaction and Socio-political Change*, ed. by Colin Renfrew and J. F. Cherry, pp. 1–18. Cambridge University Press, Cambridge, Massachusetts.
    1989   Comments on Archaeology into the 1990s. *Norwegian Archaeological Review* **22**:33–41.
Resnick, S. and R. Wolff
    1987   Classes in Marxian Theory. *Review of Radical Political Economics* **13**:1–18.
Rice, Glen E.
    1987   *A Spatial Analysis of the Hohokam Community of La Ciudad.* with contributions by T. Kathleen Henderson. Anthropological Field Studies 16. Arizona State University, Tempe, Arizona.
Rindos, David
    1985   Darwinian Selection, Symbolic Variation, and the Evolution of Culture. *Current Anthropology* **26**(1):65–88.
Robinson, Paul A.
    1990   The Struggle Within: The Indian Debate in Seventeenth Century Narragansett Country. Ph.D. dissertation, SUNY, Binghamton, New York.
Rohn, A. H.
    1971   *Mug House, Mesa Verde National Park, Colorado.* National Park Service Publications in Archaeology No. 7D. Washington, D.C.
Roseberry, William
    1978   Historical Materialism and *The People of Puerto Rico. Revista/Review Interamerican* **8**(1):26–36.
    1988   Political Economy. *Annual Review of Anthropology* **17**:161–85.
    1989   *Anthropologies and Histories.* Rutgers University Press, New Brunswick, New Jersey.
Ross, Anne
    1985   Archaeological Evidence for Population Change in the Middle to Late Holocene in Southeastern Australia. *Archaeology in Oceania* **20**:81–89.
Ross, Margaret Clunies
    1989   Holding on to Emblems: Australian Aboriginal Performances and the Transmission of Oral Traditions. *In Who Needs the Past?* ed. by Robert Layton, pp. 162–168. Unwin Hyman, London, England.

Rowlands, Michael
  1982   Processual Archaeology as Historical Science. *In Theory and Explanation in Archaeology*,
          ed. by Colin Renfrew, M. J. Rowlands, and B. A. Segraves, pp. 155–174. Academic
          Press, New York.
  1984a   CA Comment on The Internal Dynamics of Early States by H. J. M. Claessen. *Current
          Anthropology* **25**(4):374.
  1984b   Objectivity and Subjectivity in Archaeology. *In Marxist Perspectives in Archaeology*, ed.
          by Matthew Spriggs, pp. 108–114. Cambridge University Press, Cambridge, Mas-
          sachusetts.
  1987   Power and Moral Order in Pre-Colonial West-Central Africa. *In Specialization, Ex-
          change, and Complex Societies*, ed. by E. Brumfiel and T. Earle, Cambridge University
          Press, Cambridge, Massachusetts.
  1989   A Question of Complexity. *In Domination and Resistance*. ed. by D. Miller, M.
          Rowlands, and C. Tilley, pp. 29–40. Unwin and Hyman, London, England.
Rowlands, M. J., M. T. Larsen, and Kristian Kristiansen
  1987   *Core and Periphery Relations in the Ancient World*. Cambridge University Press, Cam-
          bridge, Massachusetts.
Rubertone, Patricia
  1989   Archaeology, Colonialism and 17th-Century Native America: Towards an Alternative
          Interpretation. *In Conflicts in the Archaeology of Living Traditions*. ed. by Robert Layton,
          pp. 32–45. Unwin and Hyman, London, England.
Russell, Frank
  1975   *The Pima Indians*. The University of Arizona Press, Tucson, Arizona.
Sacks, Karen
  1976   State Bias and Women's Status. *American Anthropologist*. **78**:565–569.
Sahlins, Marshall D.
  1972   *Stone Age Economics*. Aldine-Atherton, Chicago, Illinois.
  1985   *Islands of History*. University of Chicago Press, Chicago, Illinois.
Sahlins, Marshall David and Elman R. Service (editors)
  1960   *Evolution and Culture*. University of Michigan Press, Ann Arbor, Michigan.
Said, E. W.
  1978   *Orientalism*. Vintage Books, New York.
Saitta, Dean
  1984   The Archaeology of Households: Alternative Approaches. *Man in the Northeast* **28**:1–
          10.
  1987   Economic Integration and Social Development in Zuni Prehistory. Ph.D. dissertation,
          University of Massachusetts, Amherst, Massachusetts.
  1988   Marxism, Prehistory, and Primitive Communism. *Rethinking Marxism* **1**(4):146–168.
  1989   Dialectics, Critical Inquiry, and Archaeology. *In Critical Traditions in Contemporary
          Archaeology*. ed. by A. Wylie and V. Pinsky, pp. 38–43. Cambridge University Press,
          Cambridge, Massachusetts.
Saitta, Dean J. and Arthur S. Keene
  1990   Politics and Surplus Flow in Prehistoric Communal Societies. *In The Evolution of
          Political Systems: Socio-Politics in Small Scale Sedentary Societies*. ed. by Steadman Upham,
          pp. 203–224. Cambridge University Press, Cambridge, Massachusetts.
Salmon, Merrilee H.
  1982   *Philosophy and Archaeology*. Academic Press, New York.
Salomon, Roger B.
  1961   *Twain and the Image of History*. Yale University Press, New Haven, Connecticut.
Salt River Indian Community
  1986   Antiquities Ordinance, SRO-102-86.

Sanders, William T., and Deborah L. Nichols
    1988   Ecological Theory and Cultural Evolution in the Valley of Oaxaca. *Current Anthropology* **29**(1):33–80.

Sanders, William and Barbara Price
    1968   *Mesoamerica: The Evolution of a Civilization.* Random House, New York.

Sanders, William T. and David Webster
    1978   Unilinealism, Multilinealism, and the Evolution of Complex Societies. *In Social Archaeology: Beyond Subsistence and Dating,* ed. by Charles Redman, pp. 249–302. Academic Press, New York.

Sanoja, Mario and Iraida Vargas
    1978   *Antiguas Formaciones y Modos de Producción Venezolanos.* Monte Avila Editores, Caracas, Venezuela.

Sapir, Edward
    1958   Culture, Genuine and Spurious. *In Selected Writings of Edward Sapir in Language, Culture, and Personality,* ed. by D. G. Mandelbaum, pp. 308–331. University of California Press, Berkeley, California.

Sargent, Lydia
    1981   *Women and Revolution.* South End Press, Boston, Massachusetts.

Sartre, Jean-Paul
    1936   *The Transcendence of the Ego.*
    1960   *Critique of Dialectical Reason.* New Left Books, London, England.
    1972   *Between Existentialism and Marxism.* New Left Books, London, England.

Satz, Ronald N.
    1975   *American Indian Policy in the Jackson Era.* University of Nebraska Press, Lincoln, Nebraska.

Saunders, Tom
    1990   Prestige and Exchange: Althusser and Structural Marxist Archaeology. *In Writing the Past in the Present.* ed. by F. Baker and J. Thomas, pp. 69–78, St. Davids University College, Lampeter, Wales.
    1991   Marxism and Archaeology: The Origins of Feudalism in Early Medieval England. Ph.D. dissertation, Department of Archaeology, University of York, York, England.
    n.d.   The Feudal Construction of Space: Power and Domination in the Nucleated Village. *In The Social Archaeology of Houses,* ed. by Ross Samson, Edinburgh University Press, Edinburgh, Scotland. (in press)

Saxe, Alfred A.
    1970   Social Dimensions of Mortuary Practices. Ph.D. dissertation, University of Michigan, Ann Arbor, Michigan.

Sayer, Derek
    1979   *Marx's Method: Ideology, Science and Critique in Capital.* The Harvester Press, Sussex, England.
    1987   *The Violence of Abstraction: The Analytical Foundations of Historical Materialism.* Basil Blackwell, Oxford, England.

Sayers, Sean
    1980a   On the Marxist Dialectic. *In Hegel, Marx and Dialectic: A Debate.* ed. by Richard Norman and Sean Sayers, pp. 1–25. Humanities Press, Atlantic Highlands, New Jersey.
    1980b   Dualism, Materialism, and Dialectics. *In Hegel, Marx and Dialectic: A Debate,* ed. by Richard Norman and Sean Sayers, pp. 67–143. Humanities Press, Atlantic Highlands, New Jersey.

Schiffer, Michael B.
    1976   *Behavioral Archaeology.* Academic Press, New York.

1987   *Formation Processes of the Archaeological Record.* University of New Mexico Press, Albuquerque, New Mexico.

1988   The structure of Archaeological Theory. *American Antiquity* **53**(3):461–486.

Schneider, Jane

1977   Was There a Pre-Capitalist World System? *Peasant Studies* **6**(1):20–29.

Scholte, Bob

1972   Toward a Reflexive and Critial Anthropology. *In Reinventing Anthropology.* ed. by Dell Hymes, pp. 430–458. Random House, New York.

Schoolcraft, Henry R.

1857   *Information Respecting the History, Condition, and Prospects of the Indian Tribes of the United States.* 6 Vols, Philadelphia, Pennsylvania.

Schrire, Carmel

1980   An Enquiry into the Evolutionary Status and Apparent Identity of San Hunter-Gatherers. *Human Ecology* **8**:9–32.

Schroeder, Albert H.

1957   The Hakataya Cultural Tradition. *American Antiquity* **23**:176–78.

1979   Prehistory: Hakataya. *In Southwest,* ed. by Alfonso Ortiz, pp. 100–107. *Handbook of North American Indians 9,* William C. Sturtevant, general editor. Smithsonian Institution, Washington, D.C.

Seddon, David (ed.)

1974   *Relations of Production: Marxist Approaches to the Study of Economic Anthropology.* Frank Cass, London, England.

Sellers, Charles Coleman

1980   *Mr. Peale's Museum.* W. W. Norton, New York.

Semenov, S. A.

1964   *Prehistoric Technology.* Barnes and Noble, New York.

Semenov, V. A.

1985   The Ancient History of Mankind. *Soviet Anthropology and Archaeology* **23**(4):68–93.

Service, Elman R.

1962   *Primitive Social Organization.* Random House, New York.

1975   *Origins of the State and Civilization: The Process of Cultural Evolution.* W. W. Norton, New York.

Seymour, Deni J.

1988   An Alternative View of Sedentary Period Hohokam Shell Ornament Production. *American Antiquity* **53**(4):812–828.

Shanks, Michael and Randall H. McGuire

1991   The Craft of Archaeology. Paper presented at the annual meeting of the Society for American Archaeology, New Orleans, Louisiana.

Shanks, Michael and Christopher Tilley

1982   Ideology, Symbolic Power, and Ritual Communication: A Reinterpretation of Neolithic Mortuary Practices. *In Symbolic and Structural Archaeology.* ed. by Ian Hodder, pp. 129–54. Cambridge University Press, Cambridge, Massachusetts.

1987a   *Reconstructing Archaeology.* Cambridge University Press, Cambridge, Massachusetts.

1987b   *Social Theory and Archaeology.* Polity Press, Cambridge, Massachusetts.

1989   Archaeology into the 1990s. *Norwegian Archaeological Review* **22**(1):1–12, 42–54.

Shapiro, Jonathan

1982   *A History of the Communist Academy, 1918–1936.* University Microfilms, Ann Arbor, Michigan.

Sharer, Robert J. and Wendy Ashmore

1987   *Archaeology Discovering Our Past.* Mayfield Publishing Co., Palo Alto, California.

Shipman, Pat
  1986   Scavaging or Hunting in Early Hominids: Theoretical Frameworks and Tests. *American Anthropologist* **88**:27–43.
Silberman, Neal A.
  1982   *Digging For God and Country.* Alfred A. Knopf, New York.
Silverberg, Robert
  1968   *Mound Builders of Ancient America.* New York Graphic Society, Greenwich, Connecticut.
Silverblatt, Irene
  1980   "The Universe Has Turned Inside Out. . . There is No Justice for Us Here:" Andean Women Under Spanish Rule. *In Women and Colonization,* ed. by Mona Etienne and Elanor Leacock, pp. 149–185. Praeger Publishing Co., New York.
  1987   *Moon, Sun, and Witches: Gender Ideologies and Class in Inca and Colonial Peru.* Princeton University Press, Princeton, New Jersey.
  1988   Women in States. *Annual Review of Anthropology* **17**:427–460.
Simmons, Marc
  1979   History of the Pueblos Since 1821. *In Handbook of North American Indians: Vol. 9 Southwest,* ed. by Alfonso Ortiz, pp. 206–223. Smithsonian Institution Press, Washington, D.C.
Sires, Earl W., Jr.
  1983   Archaeological Investigations at Los Fosas (AZ:U:15:19). *In Hohokam Archaeology Along the Salt-Gila Aqueduct, Central Arizona Project, VI: Habitation Sites on the Gila River,* ed. by L. S. Teague and P. L. Crown, part 5, *Arizona State Museum Archaeological Series 150,* Tucson, Arizona.
Slocum, Sally
  1975   Women the Gatherer: Male Bias in Anthropology. *In Toward and Anthropology of Women.* ed. by Rayna Rapp, pp. 36–50. Monthly Review Press, New York.
Smardz, Carolyn E.
  1991   Little Hands on the Past: The Archaeological Resource Centre of the Toronto Board of Education. Paper presented at the annual meeting of the Northeastern Anthropological Association, Waterloo, Ontario, Canada.
Smith, Bruce D. (editor)
  1978   *Mississippian Settlement Patterns.* Academic Press, New York.
Soffer, Olga
  1983   Politics of the Paleolithic in the USSR: A Case of Paradigms Lost. *In* The Socio-Politics of Archaeology. *Research Report 23,* Department of Anthropology, University of Massachusetts, Amherst, Massachusetts.
  1985   *The Upper Paleolithic of the Central Russian Plain.* Academic Press, New York.
  1990   Storage, Sedentism, and the Paleolithic. *Antiquity* **63**:719–732.
Solway, Jacqueline S. and Richard B. Lee
  1990   Foragers, Genuine or Spurious? Situating the Kalahari San in History. *Current Anthropology* **31**(2):109–146.
Sorensen, M. L. S.
  1988   Is There a Feminist Contribution to Archaeology? *Archaeological Review from Cambridge* **7**(1):9–20.
South, Stanely
  1977   *Method and Theory in Historical Archaeology.* Academic Press, New York.
Spaulding, Albert C.
  1988   Archaeology and Anthropology. *American Anthropologist* **90**:263–271.
Spector, Janet D.
  1991   What This Awl Means: Toward a Feminist Archaeology. *In Engendering Archaeology.* ed. by J. Gero and M. Conkey, pp. 388–406. Basil Blackwell, Oxford, England.

Spencer, Chalres S.
  1990   On the Tempo and Mode of State Formation: Neoevolutionaism Reconsidered. *Journal of Anthropological Archaeology* **9**(1):1–30.

Spencer-Wood, Suzanne
  1991   Toward an Historical Archaeology of Materialistic Domestic Reform. In *The Archaeology of Inequality*, ed. by R. H. McGuire and R. Paynter, pp. 125–150. Basil Blackwell, Oxford, England.

Spier, Leslie
  1970   *Yuman Tribes of the Gila River.* Cooper Square Publishers, New York.

Sprague, Roderick
  1974   American Indians and American Archaeology. *American Archaeology* **39**(1):1–2.

Spriggs, Matthew
  1984   Another Way of Telling: Marxist Perspectives in Archaeology. In *Marxist Perspectives in Archaeology*, ed. by Matthew Spriggs, pp. 1–9. Cambridge University Press, Cambridge, Massachusetts.

Stalin, Joseph V.
  1938   *Dialectical and Historical Materialism.* International Publishers, New York.

Stanish, Charles
  1989   Household Archaeology. *American Anthropologist* **91**(1):7–24.

Stedman, Raymond William
  1982   *Shadows of the Indian.* University of Oklahoma Press, Norman, Oklahoma.

Stein, Jess (editor)
  1984   *The Random House College Dictionary.* Random House, New York.

Steward, Julian
  1937   Ecological Aspects of Southwestern Society. *Anthropos* **32**:87–104.
  1955   *Theory of Culture Change: The Methodology of Multilinear Evolution.* University of Illinois Press, Urbana, Illinois.

Steward, Julian and Frank M. Setzler
  1938   Function and Configuration in Archaeology. *American Antiquity* **4**:4–10.

Stewart, Donald Ogden
  1923   *Aunt Polly's Story of Mankind.* George H. Doran Company, New York.

Stilgoe, John R.
  1982   *Common Landscapes of America 1580–1845.* Yale University Press, New Haven, Connecticut.

Stocking, G. W., Jr.
  1982   *Race, Culture, and Evolution: Essays in the History of Anthropology.* 2nd Ed. University of Chicago Press, Chicago, Illinois.
  1987   *Victorian Anthropology.* Free Press, New York.

Strathern, Marilyn
  1987   An Awkward Relationship: The Case of Feminism and Anthropology. *Signs: Journal of Women in Culture and Society* **12**(2):276–292.

Strong, William Duncan
  1936   Anthropological Theory and Archaeological Fact. In *Essays in Honor of A. L. Kroeber*, ed. by R. H. Lowie. University of California Press, Berkeley, California.

Sullivan, Sharon
  1985   The Custodianship of Aboriginal Sites in South-Eastern Australia. In *Who Owns The Past?* ed. by Isabel McBryde, pp. 139–156. Oxford University Press, Oxford, England.

Sweezy, Paul
  1950   A Critique. *Science and Society* **Spring**, 33–54.

Tábio, Ernesto and Estrella Rey
  1966   *Prehistoria de Cuba.* Departmento de Antropología, Academia de Ciencias, La Habana, Cuba.

Tainter, Joseph A. and David A. Gillio
    1978   Mortuary Practice and the Study of Prehistoric Social Systems. *Advances in Archae-ological Method and Theory* **1**:106–43.
    1980   *Cultural Resources Overview: Mt. Taylor Area, New Mexico.* USDA Forest Service, Albu-querque, New Mexico.
Talbot, Steve
    1984   Desecration and American Indian Religious Freedom. *Akwesasne Notes* **16**(4):20–21.
Tanner, Clara Lee
    1968   *Southwest Indian Craft Arts.* University of Arizona, Tucson, Arizona.
Tanner, Nancy M.
    1981   *On Becoming Human.* Cambridge University Press, Cambridge, Massachusetts.
Taylor, Graham D.
    1980   *The New Deal and American Indian Tribalism.* University of Nebraska Press, Lincoln, Nebraska.
Taylor, Sarah
    1990   "Brothers" in Arms? Feminism, Post-Structuralism, and the Rise of "Civilization". *In Writing the Past in the Present.* ed. by F. Baker and J. Thomas, pp. 32–41. St. Davids University College, Lampeter, Wales.
Teague, Lynn S.
    1984   Role and Ritual in Hohokam Society. *In* Hohokam Archaeology along the Salt Gila Aqueduct Central Arizona Project IX: Synthesis and Conclusions, ed. by L. S. Teague and P. L. Crown, pp. 155–185. *Arizona State Museum Archaeological Series 150.* Tucson, Arizona.
    1989   The Postclassic and the Fate of the Hohokam. *In* The 1982–1984 Excavations at Las Colinas: Summary and Conclusions. ed. by Lynn S. Teague and W. L. Deaver, pp. 145–169. *Arizona State Museum Archaeological Series* 162(6), Tucson, Arizona.
Terray, Emmanuel
    1974   Long-Distance Exchange and the Formation of the State: The Case of the Abron Kingdom of Gyaman. *Economy and Society* **3**:315–345.
Therkorn, Linda
    1987   The Interrelationships of Materials and Meanings: Some Suggestions on Housing Concerns within Iron Age Noord-Holland. *In The Archaeology of Contextual Meanings,* ed. by I. Hodder, pp. 102–110. University of Cambridge Press, Cambridge, Mas-sachusetts.
Thomas, Cyrus
    1894   Report on the Mound Excavations of the Bureau of Ethnology. *Bureau of American Ethnology Twelfth Annual Report* 3–730.
Thomas, Julian
    1987   Relations of Production and Social Change in the Neolithic of North West Europe. *Man* **22**:405–430.
    1989   Technologies of the Self and the Constitution of the Subject. *Archaeological Review from Cambridge* 8(1):101–107.
    1990a   Same, Other, Analogue: Writing the Past. *In Writing the Past in the Present,* ed. by F. Baker and J. Thomas, pp. 18–23. Saint David's University College, Lampeter, Wales.
    1990b   Archaeology and the Notion of Ideology. *In Writing the Past in the Present,* ed. by F. Baker and J. Thomas, pp. 63–68. Saint David's University College, Lampeter, Wales.
Thomas, Nicholas
    1989   *Out of Time: History and Evolution in Anthropological Discourse.* Cambridge University Press, Cambridge, Massachusetts.
Thompson, E. P.
    1963   *The Making of the English Working Class.* Pantheon, New York.

1978   *The Poverty of Theory.* Merlin, London, England.
Thorne, Barrie and Marilyn Yalom (eds)
1982   *Rethinking the Family: Some Feminist Questions.* Longman, New York.
Thurnwald, Richard C.
1932   *Economics in Primitive Communities.* University of Oxford Press, Oxford, England.
Tilley, Christopher
1989   Interpreting Material Culture. *In The Meaning of Things: Material Culture and Symbolic Expression.* ed. by Ian Hodder, pp. 185–194. Unwin and Hyman, London, England.
1990   *Reading Material Culture.* Basil Blackwell, Oxford, England.
Tobias, Philip V.
1961   *The Meaning of Race.* South African Institute of Race Relations, Johannesburg, South Africa.
Tosi, Maurizio
1984   The Notion of Craft Specialization and Its Representation in the Archaeological Record of Early States in the Turanian Basin. *In Marxist Perspectives in Archaeology,* ed. by Matthew Spriggs, pp. 22–52. University of Cambridge Press, Cambridge, Massachusetts.
Trigger, Bruce
1978   *Time and Traditions: Essays in Archaeological Interpretation.* Columbia University Press. New York.
1980a   Archaeology and the Image of the American Indian. *American Antiquity* **45**:662–676.
1980b   *Gordon Childe: Revolutions in Archaeology.* Thames and Hudson, London, England.
1984   Alternative Archaeologies: Nationalist, Colonialist, and Imperialist. *Man* **19**:355–370.
1985a   Marxism in Archaeology: Real or Spurious? *Reviews in Anthropology* **12**:114–123.
1985b   The Past as Power: Anthropology and the North American Indian. *In Who Owns the Past?* ed. by Isabel McBryde, pp. 49–74. Oxford University Press, Oxford, England.
1986   Prehistoric Archaeology and American Society. *In American Archaeology Past and Future.* ed. by D. J. Meltzer, D. D. Fowler and J. A. Sabloff, pp. 135–162. Smithsonian Institution Press, Washington, D.C.
1989a   *A History of Archaeological Thought.* University of Cambridge Press, Cambridge, Massachusetts.
1989b   Comments on Archaeology into the 1990s. *Norwegian Archaeological Review* **22**(1):15–18.
1990   Maintaining Economic Equality in Opposition to Complexity: An Iroquoian Case Study. *In The Evolution of Political Systems: Socio-Politics in Small-Scale Sedentary Societies.* ed. by Steadman Upham, pp. 119–145. Cambridge University Press, Cambridge, Massachusetts.
Tringham, Ruth E.
1971   Hunters, Fishers and Farmers of Eastern Europe, 6000–3000 B.C. Hutchinson, London, England.
1983   V. Gordon Childe 25 Years After: His Relevance for the Archaeology of the Eighties. *Journal of Field Archaeology* **10**:85–100.
1991   Household With Faces: The Challenge of Gender in Prehistoric Architectural Remains. *In Engendering Archaeology.* ed. by J. Gero and M. Conkey, pp. 93–131. Basil Blackwell, Oxford, England.
Trotsky, Leon D.
1962   *The Permanent Revolution and Results and Prospects.* Pioneer, New York.
Trotter, Robert T.
1989   Summary: Results of Wupatki National Monument Summer Ethnographic Field School. Ms. on file, Wupatki National Monument, Flagstaff, Arizona.

Turnbull, Colin M.
   1967   *The Forest People.* Simon and Schuster, New York.
Turner, Christy G.
   1986   What is Lost With Skeletal Reburial? *Quarterly Review of Archaeology* 7(1):1.
Turner, Christy G. and Donald H. Morris
   1970   A Massacre at Hopi. *American Antiquity* 35(3):320–331.
Turner, Ernest
   1989   The Soul of My Dead Brothers? in *Conflicts in the Archaeology of Living Traditions,* ed. by Robert Layton, pp. 46–59. Unwin and Hyman, London, England.
Turney, Omar A.
   1929   Prehistoric Irrigations. *Arizona Historical Review* 2(2):11–52.
Ucko, Peter J.
   1983   Australian Academic Archaeology, Aboriginal Transformation of Its Aims and Practices. *Australian Archaeology* 16:11–26.
Underhill, Ruth
   1939   Social Organization of the Papago Indians. *Columbia University Contributions to Anthropology* 30, Columbia University, New York.
United States Indian Claims Commission
   1978   *Final Report.* U.S. Government Printing Office, Washington, D.C.
Upham, Steadman
   1982   *Politics and Power.* Academic Press, New York.
Upham, Steadman (editor)
   1990   *The Evolution of Political Systems: Socio-Politics in Small Scale Sedentary Societies.* Cambridge University Press, Cambridge, Massachusetts.
Upham, Steadman, and Glen Rice
   1980   Up the Canal Without a Pattern: Modeling Hohokam Interaction and Exchange. *In* Current Issues in Hohokam Prehistory, ed. by David Doyel and Fred Plog, pp. 78–105. *Arizona State University Anthropological Research Papers 23.* Tempe, Arizona.
Vayada, Andrew P. and Roy A. Rappaport
   1968   Ecology, Cultural, and Noncultural. *In Introduction to Cultural Anthropology,* ed. by J. A. Clifton, pp. 477–497. Boston, Massachusetts.
Wallace, Michael
   1981   Visiting the Past: History Museums in the United States. *Radical History* 25:63–100.
Wallerstein, Immanuel
   1974   *The Modern World System I.* Academic Press, New York.
   1978   Civilization and Modes of Production. *Theory and Society* 5:1–10.
   1980a   *The Modern World System II.* Academic Press, New York.
   1980b   The States in the Institutional Vortex of the Capitalist World-Economy. *International Social Science Journal* 32(4):743–751.
   1984   Household Structures and Labor-Force Formation in the Capitalist World-Economy. *In Households and the World-Economy.* ed. by J. Smith, I. Wallerstein, & H. Evers, pp. 17–22. Sage, Beverly Hills, California.
Wallerstein, Immanuel and Joan Smith (editors)
   n.d.   *Creating and Transforming Households.* Cambridge University Press, Cambridge, Massachusetts. (in press)
Washburn, Sherwood, L. and C. S. Lancaster
   1968   The Evolution of Hunting. *In Man the Hunter.* ed. by R. B. Lee and I. DeVore, pp. 292–303. Aldine, Chicago, Illinois.
Wasley, William W., and David E. Doyel
   1980   Classic Period Hohokam. *The Kiva* 45:337–352.

Wasley, William W., and Alfred E. Johnson
    1965   Salvage Archaeology in the Painted Rocks Reservoir Western Arizona. *Anthropological Papers of the University of Arizona 9*. Tucson, Arizona.

Watson, Patty Jo
    1986   Archaeological Interpretation 1985. *In American Archaeology Past and Future*. ed. by D. J. Meltzer, D. D. Fowler, and J. A. Sabloff, pp. 439–457. Smithsonian Institution Press, Washington, D.C.

Watson, Patty Jo, and Mary C. Kennedy
    1991   The Development of Horticulture in the Eastern Woodlands of North America: Women's Role. *In Engendering Archaeology*. ed. by J. Gero and M. Conkey, pp. 255–275. Basil Blackwell, Oxford, England.

Watson, Patty Jo, Steven A. LeBlanc, and Charles L. Redman
    1971   *Explanation in Archaeology: An Explicitly Scientific Approach*. Columbia University Press, New York.
    1984   *Archaeological Explanation: The Scientific Method in Archaeology*. Columbia University Press, New York.

Webb, Malcolm D.
    1975   The Flag Follows Trade: An Essay on the Necessary Interaction of Military and Commercial Factors in State Formation. *In Ancient Civilization and Trade*. ed. by J. A. Sabloff and C. C. Lamberg-Karlovsky, pp. 155–210. University of New Mexico Press, Albuquerque, New Mexico.

Weber, Max
    1978   *Economy and Society*. University of California Press, Berkeley, California.

Webster, Gary S.
    1990   Labor Control and Emergent stratification in Prehistoric Europe. *Current Anthropology* **31**(4):337–366.

Wenke, Robert J.
    1981   Explaining the Evolution of Cultural Complexity: A Review. *Advances in Archaeological Method and Theory* **4**:79–128.
    1984   *Patterns in Prehistory*. Oxford University Press, Oxford, England.

White, Leslie
    1949   *The Science of Culture: A Study of Man and Civilization*. Farrar, Straus and Giroux, New York.
    1959   *The Evolution of Culture*. McGraw-Hill, New York.

White, J. Peter and James F. O'Connell
    1982   *A Prehistory of Australia, New Guinea, and Sahul*. Academic Press, Sydney, Australia.

Whitecotten, Joseph W. and Richard A. Pailes
    1986   New World Precolumbian World Systems. *In Ripples in the Chichimec Sea: New Considerations of Southwestern-Mesoamerican Interactions*. ed. by F. J. Mathien and R. H. McGuire, pp. 183–204. Southern Illinois University Press, Carbondale, Illinois.

Wilcox, David R.
    1987   Frank Midvale's Investigation of the Site of La Ciudad. *Arizona State University, Office of Cultural Resource Management, Anthropological Field Studies* 19, Tempe, Arizona.
    1989   Hohokam Social Complexity. Paper presented at the Advanced Seminar Cultural Complexity in the Arid Southwest: The Hohokam and Chacoan Regional Systems. School of American Research, Santa Fe, New Mexico.

Wilcox, David R., and Thomas R. McGuire and Charles Sternberg
    1981   Snaketown Revisited. *Arizona State Museum Archaeological Series 155*. Tucson, Arizona.

Wilcox, David R., and Lynette O. Shenk
    1977   The Architecture of the Casa Grande and Its Interpretation. *Arizona State Museum Archaeological Series 115*, Tucson, Arizona.

Wilcox, David R. and Robert Sternberg
    1983   Hohokam Ballcourts and Their Interpretation. *Arizona State Museum Archaeological Series 160.* Tucson, Arizona.
Wilk, Richard R.
    1983   Little House in the Jungle: The Causes of Variation in House Size among the Modern Kekchi Maya. *Journal of Anthropological Archaeology* 2(2):99–116.
    1985   The Ancient Maya and the Political Present. *Journal of Anthropological Research* 41(3):307–326.
Wilk, Richard R. and Wendy Ashmore (editors)
    1988   *Household and Community in the Mesoamerican Past.* University of New Mexico Press, Albuquerque, New Mexico.
Wilk, Richard R. and William L. Rathje (editors)
    1982   Archaeology of the Household. *American Behavioral Scientist* 26(6):611–728.
Willey, Gordon R.
    1953   Prehistoric Settlement Patterns in the Viru Valley Peru. *Bureau of American Ethnology, Bulletin* 155, Washington, D.C.
    1965   Prehistoric Maya Settlements in the Belize Valley. *Papers of the Peabody Museum* 54, Peabody Museum Harvard, Cambridge, Massachusetts.
Willey, Gordon R. and Philip Phillips
    1958   *Method and Theory in American Archaeology.* University of Chicago Press, Chicago.
Willey, Gordon R. and Jeremy A. Sabloff
    1980   *A History of American Archaeology* (2nd Ed.) Thames and Hudson, London, England.
Williams, Raymond
    1973   *The Country and the City.* University of Oxford Press, Oxford, England.
    1990   *The People of the Black Mountain.* University of Oxford Press, Oxford, England.
Williams, Elizabeth
    1985   Estimations of Prehistoric Populations of Archaeological Sites in Southwestern Victoria: Some Problems. *Archaeology in Oceania* 20:73–80.
Williamson, Tom
    1990   Garden, Class, and Social Identity in Eighteenth-Century England. Paper presented at the annual meeting of the Theoretical Archaeology Group, Lampeter, Wales.
Williamson, Tom and Liz Bellamy
    1987   *Property and Landscape: A Social History of Land Ownership and the English Countryside.* G. Philips, London, England.
Wilmsen, Edward
    1989   *Land Filled With Flies: A Political Economy of the Kalahari.* University of Chicago Press, Chicago, Illinois.
Wilson, James
    1986   *The Original Americans: U.S. Indians.* The Minority Rights Group, London, England.
Winter, Marcus C.
    1976   The Archaeological Household Cluster in the Valley of Oaxaca. *In the Mesoamerican Village.* ed. by Kent V. Flannery, pp. 25–30. Academic Press, New York.
Winterhalder, Bruce, William Baillargeon, Francesca Cappelletto, I. Randolph Daniel, Jr., and Chris Prescott
    1988   The Population Ecology of Hunter-Gatherers and Their Prey. *Journal of Anthropological Archaeology* 7(4):289–328.
Wittfogel, Karl A.
    1957   *Oriental Despotism: A Comparative Study of Total Power.* Yale University Press, New Haven, Connecticut.
Wobst, H. Martin
    1989   A Socio-politics of Socio-politics in Archaeology. *In Critical Traditions in Contemporary*

Archaeology. ed. by A. Wylie and V. Pinsky, pp. 136–140. Cambridge University Press, Cambridge, Massachusetts.

Wobst, H. Martin and Arthur S. Keene
1983   Archaeological Explanation as Political Economy. *In* The Socio-Politics of Archaeology. ed. by J. M. Gero, D. M. Lacy and M. L. Blakey, pp. 79–90. *Research Report 23, Department of Anthropology, University of Massachusetts,* Amherst, Massachusetts.

Wolf, Eric. R.
1959   *Sons of the Shaking Earth.* University of Chicago Press, Chicago, Illinois.
1969   *Peasant Wars of the Twentieth Century.* Harper & Row, New York.
1976   Introduction. *In The Valley of Mexico: Studies in Pre-Hispanic Ecology and Society.* ed. by E. R. Wolf, pp. 1–10. University of New Mexico Press, Albuquerque, New Mexico.
1982   *Europe and the People without History.* University of California Press, Berkeley, California.
1984   Culture: Panacea or Problem? *American Antiquity* 49(2):393–400.
1987   An Interview with Eric Wolf. *Current Anthropology.* 28(1):107–117.

Wolpe, Harold
1980   Introduction. *In The Articulation of Modes of Production.* ed. by Harold Wolpe, pp. 1–43. Routledge & Kegan Paul, London, England.

Wood, J. Scott, and Martin McAllister
1980   Foundation and Empire: The Colonization of the Northeastern Hohokam Periphery. *In* Current Issues in Hohokam Prehistory, ed. by David Doyel and Fred Plog, pp. 180–200. *Arizona State University Anthropological Research Papers 23,* Tempe, Arizona.

Woodbury, Richard B.
1979   Prehistory: Introduction. *In Handbook of North American Indians: Vol. 9 Southwest,* ed. by Alfonso Ortiz, pp. 22–30. Smithsonian Institution Press, Washington, D.C.

Wright, Henry T.
1977   Recent Research on the Origin of the State. *Annual Review of Anthropology* 6:379–397.
1984   Prestate Political Formations. *In On the Evolution of Complex Societies: Essays in Honor of Harry Hoijer 1982.* ed. by T. Earle, pp. 41–77. Undena Publications, Malibu, California.
1986   The Evolution of Civilizations. *In American Archaeology Past and Future.* ed. by D. J. Meltzer, D. D. Fowler, and J. A. Sabloff, pp. 323–369. Smithsonian Institution Press, Washington, D.C.

Wright, Henry and Gregory Johnson
1975   Population, Exchange and Early State Formation in Southwestern Iran. *American Anthropologist* 77:267–76.

Wright, Rita P.
1991   Women's Labor and Pottery Production in Prehistory. *In Engendering Archaeology.* ed. by J. Gero and M. Conkey, pp. 194–223. Basil Blackwell, Oxford, England.

Wurst, LouAnn
1991   "Employees Must Be of Moral and Temperate Habits", Rural and Urban Elite Ideologies. *In The Archaeology of Inequality,* ed. by R. H. McGuire and R. Paynter, pp. 125–150. Basil Blackwell, Oxford, England.

Wylie, Allison
1981   Positivism and the New Archaeology. Ph.D. dissertation, Department of Philosophy, State University of New York at Binghamton, Binghamton, New York.
1985a   The Reaction against Analogy. *Advances in Archaeological Method and Theory* 8:63–112.
1985b   Putting Shakertown Back Together: Critical Theory in Archaeology. *Journal of Anthropological Archaeology* 4(2):133–147.
1987   The Philosophy of Ambivalence: Sandra Harding on the Science Question in Feminism. *Canadian Journal of Philosophy* 13:59–73.

1989   Feminist Analyses of Social Power: Substantive and Epistemological Issues. Paper presented at the Wenner-Gren Conference, Critical Approaches in Archaeology: Material Life, Meaning, and Power, in Cascais, Portugal.

1991   Gender Theory and the Archaeological Record: Why is There No Archaeology of Gender? *In Engendering Archaeology.* ed. by J. Gero and M. Conkey, pp. 31–56. Basil Blackwell, Oxford, England.

Yen, D. E.

1989   The Domestication of the Environment. *In Foraging and Farming.* ed. by D. R. Harris and G. C. Hillman, pp. 55–78. Unwin and Hyman, London, England.

Yentsch, Anne

1975   Understanding Seventeenth and Eighteenth-Century Families: An Experiment in Historical Ethnography. M.S. thesis, Department of Anthropology, Brown University, Providence, Rhode Island.

1991   The Symbolic Divisions of Pottery: Sex-Related Attributes of English and Anglo-American Household Pots. *In The Archaeology of Inequality,* ed. by R. H. McGuire and R. Paynter, pp. 125–150. Basil Blackwell, Oxford, England.

Yoffee, Norman

1979   The Decline and Rise of Mesopotamian Civilization: An Ethnoarchaeological Perspective on the Evolution of Social Complexity. *American Antiquity* **44:**5–34.

1985   Perspectives on "Trends Towards Social Complexity in Prehistoric Australia and Papua New Guinea." *Archaeology in Oceania* **20:**40–49.

n.d.   Too Many Chiefs? or Safe Texts for the 90s. *In Archaeological Theory Who Sets the Agenda?* ed. by Andrew Sherratt and Norman Yoffee. Cambridge University Press, Cambridge, Massachusetts (in press).

Yoffee, Norman and George Cowgill (editors)

1988   *The Collapse of Ancient States and Civilizations.* University of Arizona Press, Tucson, Arizona.

Young, Robert M.

1983   Nature. *In A Dictionary of Marxist Thought.* ed. by Tom Bottomore, pp. 351–355. Harvard University Press, Cambridge, Massachusetts.

Zagarell, Allen

1986   Trade, Women, Class, and Society in Ancient Western Asia. *Current Anthropology* 27(5):415–431.

Zihlman, Adrienne L. and Tanner, Nancy M.

1978   Gathering and Hominid Adaptation. *In Female Hierarchies.* ed. by L. Tiger and H. Fowler. Beresford Books, Chicago, Illinois.

Zimmerman, Larry J.

1987   The Impact of the Concept of Time and Past on the Concept of Archaeology: Some Lessons From the Reburial Issue. *Archaeological Review From Cambridge* 6(1):42–50.

1989   Human Bones as Symbols of Power: Aboriginal American Belief Systems towards Bones and the "Grave-Robbing" Archaeologist. *In Conflicts in the Archaeology of Living Traditions.* ed. by Robert Layton, pp. 46–59. Unwin Hyman, London, England.

INDEX

1968, 40
1984, 216
A History of American Archaeology, 53–54, 87
A History of Archaeological Thought, 79
A History of Latin America, 87
Abercombie, Nicholas, 141
Abron Kingdom, west Africa, 166
Abstract and concrete, 5–9, 13–14, 44, 47, 74, 80–81, 146–150, 155, 159–158, 164–165, 170–171, 172–173, 176, 256
Accuracy in Academics, 45
Acheulean hand axe, 110
Adams, Charles, 242
Adams, Robert McComack, 73, 74, 173, 175
Adams, Samuel, 229
Adaptation, 123, 131, 174, *see also* Culture, as adaptation
Adorno, Theodore, 51
Afro-American, 114, 245, 258–259
Agency, 9, 15, 28–29, 33–35, 37–39, 41–43, 44, 48–51, 79, 84, 96, 102–103, 118–119, 122, 131, 133–134, 136, 142–144, 151–152, 163–164, 171, 176, 185, 187, 210
Alabama, 114
Alienation, 34, 49, 55, 87, 106, 252–253, 257, 260
Alienation, 93
Allende, Salvadore, 40, 65
Alternative archaeologies, *see* Archaeology, alternative
Althusser, Louis, 8, 41–43, 65, 66, 75, 77, 79, 92, 125, 134–135, 140
Ambiguity, 1, 13, 93, 118, 129, 143–144, 169
American Anthropological Association, 75, 88, 221, 260
American Anthropologist, 244
American Antiquarian Society, 230
American Antiquity, 260
American Indian Movement (AIM), 240–241, 244
American Museum of Natural History, 233
American Philosophical Society, 230

American studies, 4
Analogy
   archaeology as a journey, 247
   archaeology as a kaleidoscope, 247
   cultural evolution to a string of beads, 155, 176
   ethnographic, *see* ethnographic analogy
   history as a crossroads, 171
   history to a tapestry, 176
   states to fruits, 149
   theory to mixing paint, 9
Anarchy, philosophy of, 19, 45, 63, 115
Anasazi, 105, 236, 239–240
Anasazi, Ancient People of the Rock, 239
Anderson, Kieth, 197
Anderson, Perry, 46–47
Androcentrism, *see* Gender, bias
Anglo-American archaeology, 12, 15, 16, 22, 53, 55, 66, 68–83, 150
Anthropology, 4
   archaeology in, 4, 233
   biological, 4
   cultural, 3, 109
   marxism in, 46
   Mexican, 31
   political economy, 80–81, 86
Anthrogeography, 28
Antiguas Formaciones Modos de Producción en Venezuela, 66
Antiquities, 239
Antiquities Act of 1906, 219, 225, 235
Antiquity, 71, 107, 245
Anyon, Roger, 242
Apache, Indians, 236
Archaeological Review from Cambridge, 88
"Archaeology as Anthropology", 88
Archaeology,
   alternative, 2–3, 75–83, 84–86
   Anglo-American, *see* Anglo-American archaeology
   as craft, 4–5, 242, 261
   as middle class pursuit, 55, 214, 258–261